MISDEMEANORLAND

Misdemeanorland

Criminal Courts and Social Control in an Age of Broken Windows Policing

Issa Kohler-Hausmann

PRINCETON UNIVERSITY PRESS

PRINCETON AND OXFORD

Requests for permission to reproduce material from this work
should be sent to Permissions, Princeton University Press

Published by Princeton University Press,
41 William Street, Princeton, New Jersey 08540

In the United Kingdom: Princeton University Press,
6 Oxford Street, Woodstock, Oxfordshire OX20 1TR

press.princeton.edu

Jacket design by Faceout Studio, Spencer Fuller

Page 25: Excerpt from *Police Strategy No. 5*, 1994,
published in the National Criminal Justice Service
Reference and used with permission.

Page 99: Excerpt from Norbert Elias, *The Civilizing
Process*, vol. 2, *State Formation and Civilization* (1939;
Oxford: Basil Blackwell, 2000), 366. With permission
by John Wiley & Sons.

Pages 143, 183, and 221: Excerpts from *The Trial* by
Franz Kafka, translated by Willa Muir and Edwin Muir,
translation copyright © 1937, 1956, renewed 1965, 1984
by Penguin Random House LLC. Used by permission
of Schocken Books, an imprint of the Knopf Doubleday
Publishing Group, a division of Penguin Random House
LLC. All rights reserved.

Parts of text appearing in chapters 4, 5, and 6 have
been previously published in the *American Journal of
Sociology*. Parts of text appearing in chapters 1 and 2
have been previously published in the *Stanford Law
Review*.

ISBN 978-0-691-17430-3
Library of Congress Control Number: 2017959806

British Library Cataloging-in-Publication Data is available

This book has been composed in Adobe Text Pro and Gotham

Printed on acid-free paper. ∞

Printed in the United States of America

10 9 8 7 6 5 4 3 2 1

CONTENTS

ACKNOWLEDGMENTS

This project was made possible through interactions with people who work in or pass through misdemeanorland—some by choice, some by force. I am thankful to all of them—defendants, attorneys, judges, court personnel, and others—who took time to share their thoughts and experiences. It is no small thing to ask people who were just released from police custody or experienced an arrest to talk to a random lady in the hallway of the one place from which they are dying to escape and to which they hope never to return. And yet, that so many men and women did so is a testament to the fact that there are a lot of people who desperately want to share their thoughts on how the institutions that touch their lives and shape their communities ought to be run. Countless lawyers and court professionals extensively discussed their experiences and insights about New York City's lower criminal courts. Not all will agree with all of my analysis and conclusions in this book; I can only hope that it will nonetheless instigate a meaningful conversation about how state power is used in this space.

Nor would this project have been possible without the support and guidance of the committee of scholars who were willing to take me on as a student during my years in graduate school at New York University. Jeff Manza has shaped and guided most of my adult academic life; he has been a patient and generous teacher, friend, and mentor. His encyclopedic knowledge of the field of sociology and sharp analytic mind pushed me to expand the ambitions of the project and refine the delivery of my work. He believed in me, encouraged me, and saw me through a lot. Graduate school involves a lot of ups and downs. I can only assume that even well-adjusted people are battered by the challenges of learning a discipline; trying to master methods, fieldwork, and writing; experiencing the inevitable sting of failures and rejections from grant applications and article submissions and resubmissions; entering the job market, and so forth. I certainly would have dropped out of graduate school many times over without his encouragement, and for better or for worse, he kept me in the game.

In the study of oft-neglected lower courts, Malcolm Feeley's work on misdemeanor courts is the giant upon whose shoulders I could only dream of hoisting my own work. I was not sure if I could succeed in reaching those shoulders, but his careful readings and incisive feedback on this project gave me the confidence to try to do so. My entire orientation to the fields of penal theory and history was shaped by being a student of David Garland, and his ideas have been formative in my approach to research since its inception. His ability to analyze broad themes and place my data in larger theoretical frameworks during our discussions has always been both exhilarating and intimidating. Lynne Haney showed much munificence and faith in taking me on as a student with my vague research plan and minimal experience as a qualitative researcher. I could not have done this project without her expert instruction in qualitative methods and patient coaching about how to move from micro observations to social theory. David Greenberg was an exceedingly generous teacher and promoter, sharing his understanding of the criminal justice world and research methodologies.

Beyond my committee, so many people at NYU's department of sociology were supportive and generous with time and feedback throughout my graduate school years. I can't list them all, but I want to extend special gratitude to Gabi Abend, Jen Jennings, Colin Jerolmack, Eric Klinenberg, Pat Sharkey, and Florencia Torche. Beyond NYU, Mitch Dunnier took me on as surrogate student, and his insights provided invaluable guidance. I also want to thank influential professors from law school, both from my first year at Northwestern and from two years at Yale, including Brett Dignam, Michael Gratz, Andrew Koppelman, Janice Nadler, Robert Post, and Dorothy Roberts. One person who might never know how important his interpersonal kindness and intellectual encouragement was to me at an incredibly sad and difficult time is Larry Marshall: you were always a model for the type of human and scholar I wanted to become. Al Klevoric was also an unbelievably influential mentor to me, encouraging and kind as a professor, patient at a collaborator, and now—luckily for me—wonderful as a colleague.

NYU was a special place not just for the amazing professors, but also for the community of graduate students that fostered a lively and fun academic community (and the best parties at ASA). At the risk of leaving some people out, I want to acknowledge the many formative friendships and intellectual connections from this world, including my first officemates, Amy LeClair, Caitlin Petre, and Adaner Usmani, who were so supportive and hilarious in that tiny windowless room—and when we hustled our way into a windowed office, Jen Herwig and Ruthie Brownstein as well. I could not have survived those final years without those ladies. Max Besbris, Brian McCabe, Alison McKim, Mike McHulky (aka DS2/Mike Effx), Poulami Roychowdhury, Chris Seeds, and many other NYU graduate students: we all read each other's work and bought each other drinks to numb failures or celebrate successes. I could not have asked for a better group of people to be young and broke with in New York City. I feel fortunate to also have had an extended community of scholars and friends, or scholar friends, in sociology and beyond whose work, support, or feedback have been formative, including Preeti Chauhan, Matt Desmond, Phil Goodwin, Jeff Lane, Josh Page, Michelle Phelps, Jeremy Travis, Nicole Van Cleve, Bruce Western, and others. I want to give a special thank you to those who read and commented on early versions of articles or chapters from this book. Megan Comfort has been an unbelievably inspiring force, as an intellectual model, political change agent, and wonderful friend. Armando Lara-Millán read and provided extensive comments on chapter 6, and his feedback and ideas were invaluable to my own thinking. To Sarah Brayne and Forrest Stuart: What do I say? You both read versions of this work when it was total garbage juice and helped me develop my own analysis and writing. My work has been deeply shaped by your research and writing, and I am beyond fortunate to have dear friends who are both really brilliant and really fun.

Ilissa Brownstein took me in as a green attorney in 2009, and with her I learned criminal court from the ground up. She was understanding and giving in my long learning process, and I am eternally grateful that she gave me the opportunity to practice with her. During the final five years of this project, I began representing clients who were facing an indeterminate life sentence for crimes committed as juveniles. Through this work I met a number of men and woman who dedicated their entire adult lives to reconciling their capacity to do great damage to other human beings with their capacity to fundamentally transform themselves and to seek atonement without ever losing sight of the traces of pain and loss that they had left in the world. To all of you, particularly Dempsey Hawkins: I have learned so much from your dedication to redemption through an honest encounter with the past, an encounter that holds out the possibility of grace. I also want to extend profound gratitude to Randall Eiger, who has tried to help me extend my belief in redemption and grace to myself over the past seven years.

This project was developed from a dissertation into a book during my first three years at Yale Law School, which is an opportunity to be part of the type of supportive and thrilling intellectual environment I only imagined existed. I cannot name everyone, but I am eternally grateful that, like ABBA, they took a chance on me and have continued to support both my research and my pro bono practice during my years as a junior professor. Although I truly am grateful to all of my colleagues, I would like to extend special gratitude to Monica Bell, Amy Chua, Fiona Doherty, Heather Gerken, Miriam Gohara, Amy Kapczynski, Douglas Kysar, Yair Listokin, Daniel Markovits, Marisol Orihuela, Robert Post, Judith Resnik, Jed Rubenfeld, David Schleicher, Scott Shapiro and Alison MacKeen, Reva Siegel, Mike Wishnie, and John Witt, who responded to my work and otherwise helped me adjust to junior professor life; Nick Parrillo and Jim Whitman, who read and provided deep commentary on drafts of work that evolved into chapter 3; Tracey Mears, whose fierce support and guidance has been central to my academic and personal growth at Yale; and of course Gideon Yaffee, who has been a constant intellectual support and, along with Sue and Oona, welcomed me into their lovely family.

The second round of quantitative data collection was supported by the Oscar M. Ruebhausen Fund at Yale Law School, and the analysis could not have been done without the assistance of the most amazing research assistants of all time: Natalia Nazarewicz and Angela Zorro Medina, who are both meticulous and brilliant. It was an honor to work with you, and I hope we can continue to work together. I can't wait to see what remarkable things you will do in the world. I would like to also thank all of the staff at New York State Office of Court Administration, New York City Criminal Court, and especially New York State's Department of Criminal Justice Services, who provided data in a responsive and timely fashion. Not all state agencies work that way, and they are an exemplar of what we can learn when state agencies are committed to transparency and professionalism regarding public data. I also owe special gratitude to Debbie Ivens Lewites, who painstakingly transcribed hours upon hours of interviews, often with very distracting ambient background noise! This manuscript was greatly improved by the developmental editing of Beth Gianfagna, who somehow managed to cut over twenty thousand words, despite my deep anxieties about losing content, and the graphic work of Emma Burns. I also want to thank the two anonymous reviewers for Princeton University Press for providing careful comments and insightful feedback on the manuscript.

This book would not have been possible without the faith and perseverance of the folks at Princeton University Press, including Samantha Nader, Natalie Baan, and especially my editor, Meagan Levinson, who provided invaluable substantive editing, development feedback, and emotional support. Thank you.

I have been blessed, truly blessed, to have a community of friends and family that anchors me through thick and thin, including my aunts and uncles on both sides of my family and my beloved cousin clan, including Aunt Marie, Uncle Brian, Aunt Helen, cousins Will, Jennie, Catherine and Mark, and Marie and Steve, and Annie and Ormond and their lovely children. Kate Shaw and Chris Hayes have adopted me into their world since we met in 2003, and I love you guys and your growing family so much. I am constantly in awe of your energy and capacity for love. Cassie Fennel is an academic inspiration and personal one too; I have learned so much from our friendship and your academic brilliance. There are so many other beautiful friends who made this project possible, including Emma Andersson, Ian Bassin, Zach Bendiner, Talleah Bridges, Merlin Camozzi, Avery Gilbert, Sigun Kahl, Marie Ledger, John Mangin, Jessie Pavone-Baker, Emilie Prattico, Meg Rooney, and Lauren Silvers.

The nine years of this project almost perfectly tracked my time with Martin LaFalce. It is hard to know how to acknowledge all of the countless ways he shaped this project, from directly assisting me in every stage from conception to execution, serving as an in-house expert on my research, picking me up from my failures, holding me up to my successes, and brainstorming ideas, to reading and commenting on drafts. He humbled and inspired me by being a brilliant, selfless, and passionate attorney, the type that every person facing criminal charges deserves but so rarely gets. And he transformed my life by being a deeply loving and fiercely dedicated partner. I never promised you normal, and on that at least I delivered, but I hope you know that I am who I am and this work is what it is because of what we were together.

My family made me who I am, and they continue to help me to be the person I strive to be. My mother, Julilly Kohler, has insatiable intellectual curiosity and wide-ranging interests that inspire my intellectual pursuits. She helped me move from and into countless apartments and helped me move through countless heartbreaks and setbacks, all the time offering the deep wisdom and tender compassion that one can only expect from a mother. My father, Charles Hausmann, modeled outside-the-box creativity and hustle combined with resilience in the face of adversity. He has showed me how to practice law and advocate in an area where being right and smart more often meets with losses than wins, and how to pick yourself up and get back in the game when those inevitable losses come. I am also deeply grateful to my stepmother, Jean Hausmann, for centered spirituality and thoughtfulness. I have been lucky to have three wonderful stepsisters and their families—Bridget Madigan Sharp and her husband Greg Sharp, Kate Madigan, and Kelly Reese and her husband Adam Reese—for loving support and grounding humor; and my brother-in-law, Victor Pickard, for being a patient presence in a large family of intense women and a wonderful husband to my sister and father to Lilia and Zaden.

I dedicate this book to my sister, Julilly Kohler-Hausmann, not just because I would not have survived this life without her but also because she is the type of person who makes this world a better place. She is a brilliant academic and a loving soul; a giving mother, partner, daughter, sister, and participant in the world; all the while producing powerful scholarship that comes from a place of deep personal commitment to social justice. To me, she is the rock that kept my head above water in many storms.

MISDEMEANORLAND

INTRODUCTION

In the 1970s, the United States embarked on a political and social project that has, decades later, come to be known as mass incarceration.[1] Once discussed only in academic and activist circles, the volume of humans held in our nation's prisons and jails has become a mobilizing issue in public forums, new social movements, and local and national elections. Against the backdrop of mass incarceration, low-level encounters with the criminal justice system that do not result in prison time might look trivial. Many of these encounters involve mundane infractions of law such as driving without a license, stealing a candy bar, urinating in public, or smoking marijuana.

Yet, these comparatively trivial infractions entangle people in the tentacles of the criminal justice system, impose burdens to comply with judicial processes, require time away from work and children, entail fees and fines, and generate records that can be accessed by potential employers, landlords, or other important decision makers. Many people will have a single encounter with law enforcement for a low-level offense at some point in their lives. But in some spaces, namely, low-income minority neighborhoods, many people have frequent encounters with law enforcement for low-level offenses that result in tickets, summonses, or arrests.[2]

Minor crimes have always been more common than major crimes.[3] But over the past few decades, popular new (or revived) schools of policing have called for the intentional expansion of enforcement against such of-fenses. Flying under the banner of Broken Windows, order maintenance, or quality-of-life policing, these theories posit low-level enforcement as the key to urban crime control strategies, and accordingly, police forces in many of the nation's largest cities have vastly expanded arrests and citations for subfelony crimes. In many municipalities, both small and large, there is a tragically perverse incentive to expand tickets, citations, or arrests for traffic infractions or misdemeanor crimes, as the resulting fines and fees help to fund local court systems or generate general revenue.[4] The seemingly inconsequential world of minor crime enforcement and lower criminal courts has become an urgent political and moral issue in the United States.

It is probably impossible to reliably estimate the number of arrests for subfelony offenses such as misdemeanors, violations, or infractions, much less the volume of citations or tickets issued, across the thousands of law enforcement entities in the United States. But we do know that in most jurisdictions with publicly available data, misdemeanor arrests significantly outpace felony arrests.[5] And we also know that low-level arrests have become an increasingly important element of local law enforcement as a result of both popular theories of policing and the role of court fines and fees in municipal finances. But what is interesting about this world of subfelony enforcement is that a substantial number—perhaps even the majority—of actions terminate in a disposition that involves no jail time, and, quite often, not even a criminal conviction.[6] Therefore, exclusively focusing on the historically and internationally unprecedented numbers of people the United States puts into prison and jails cells *understates* the reach of the criminal justice system and, in some sense, *misrepresents* the modal criminal justice encounter. If we want to understand the full implications of our distended criminal justice apparatus, we need to look at all levels of its operations. And if we want to understand the precise ways the criminal justice system functions as a form of social control, we need to look beyond custodial sentences and even criminal convictions.

This book is about misdemeanor justice in one jurisdiction: New York City, which pioneered the intentional expansion of low-level enforcement as part of a new policing strategy. Beginning in the 1990s, the New York City Police Department (NYPD) adopted a series of tactical and organizational reforms that have—perhaps somewhat misleadingly—been classified under the unifying rubric of "Broken Windows," order maintenance, or quality-of-life policing.[7] Various key elements of the New York model have disseminated to other cities as former NYPD brass offered training sessions or took up positions in local police departments elsewhere. This policing model, in its various incarnations, has been the subject of a number of excellent studies addressing its efficacy as a law enforcement tactic or its effects on the communities targeted. I address a different question: What happens to all of those arrests when they arrive in the courts?

Misdemeanorland

After a person is arrested as part of New York City's famed Broken Windows enforcement, that person has to go somewhere. And where that person goes is misdemeanorland. "Misdemeanorland" is a colloquialism used by people who work in the courts that receive the large volume of cases generated by the city's signature policing tactics. The term designates a jurisdictional and physical space where these cases are processed. In some boroughs, there is a separate building for Criminal Court—the court that has jurisdiction over misdemeanors and petty offenses (and unindicted felonies)—and in other boroughs, there are designated Criminal Court "parts" (the word used in New York City for courtrooms) that process only subfelony cases.[8] But the expression "misdemeanorland" also signifies the widely shared notion that there is something unique about the operations of justice in the subfelony world. The following chapters unpack what that is and why we should care about it.

Many social science and media accounts of the US criminal justice system tend to address either the back or front end of the system. In the age of mass incarceration, much public and scholarly focus has been directed at the back end, at what many of us assume to be the end point of most arrests: prison or jail. The advent of Broken Windows policing and the frequency with which tragic deaths at the hands of police are being captured on video have also brought a renewed interest in the front end: policing and law enforcement tactics, especially in low-income and minority neighborhoods. But between police and jails stands an institution assigned the role of deciding which people identified by police will end up in jail, prison, or elsewhere: criminal court.

According to popular accounts—indeed, according to most academic accounts—the criminal court is the institution that determines who ought to be punished for breaking the law and how. Substantive criminal law (called the penal law) lays out a list of proscribed acts. The role of criminal courts is to use the methods authorized by the rules of criminal procedure to see if an accused has, in fact, done something on this list. Courts may perform this function badly, unjustly, or in a manner divergent from the official plan of formal adversarial adjudication. But it is the apparent province of criminal courts to determine the legal—and therefore social—status of the alleged offender by adjudicating the facts of the case. The court sends off those found guilty to some other site to mete out punishment. The forms of punishment that have received the most attention are custodial sentences (jail or prison) or noncustodial sentences (such as probation or alternative programs) that threaten custody if certain conditions are not met.

Misdemeanorland defies this model. The New York City experiment in Broken Windows policing embarrasses our traditional understanding of how an expansion of criminal enforcement should work: as misdemeanor arrests climbed dramatically as part of an intentional law enforcement strategy, the rate of criminal conviction fell sharply. This result is particularly surprising because one of the most common allegations levied at lower criminal courts by higher courts, academics, and the media over the past century has been that of "assembly-line justice": mechanically and automatically convicting defendants and imposing one-size-fits-all punishments. But if lower criminal courts were not systematically convicting and locking up people identified as potential lawbreakers through these policing tactics, then what role were they playing in this coordinated, intentional law enforcement effort?

Drawing on mixed qualitative and quantitative research, I advance two interrelated arguments about New York's well-publicized, yet not well-understood, experiment in mass misdemeanor arrests. First, criminal law can operate as a form of social control without doing the things it is formally set up to do. Among my empirical findings are that misdemeanorland is a place that produces very few criminal convictions and even fewer jail sentences relative to the volume of cases processed there, and it is a site where legal actors do very little adjudication. Are frontline criminal justice actors intentionally thwarting the policing experiment by refusing to convict and punish the people arrested from Broken Windows policing, unintentionally undercutting its potential efficacy by simply failing to adjudicate cases because of system overload, or perhaps using the doctrines of criminal law and processes of criminal procedure to accurately sort the factually guilty from the innocent in an expanding pool of people accused by virtue of sloppy police work? None of these accounts quite fits the story of what happened in the city that pioneered Broken Windows policing.

I argue that lower criminal courts in New York City's age of mass misdemeanors have largely abandoned what I call the *adjudicative* model of criminal law administration—concerned with deciding guilt and punishment in specific cases—and instead operate under what I call the *managerial* model—concerned with managing people through engagement with the criminal justice system over time. Under this model, criminal court actors are still doing what we can think of as social control work, but they are not doing it by performing the traditional role of criminal courts, which is to select the right people for punishment through adjudication and then to send them off to jail or to some alternative site with the threat of jail hanging over their heads. Instead, court actors are using the assorted tools of criminal law and procedure to sort, test, and monitor people over time.

Second, these criminal courts are using tools for social control work that differ from those with which we are familiar in the age of mass incarceration. In place of conviction and carceral sentences, social control in misdemeanorland is primarily sought through three primary techniques that I call "marking," "procedural hassle," and "performance." Marking involves the generation, maintenance, and regular use of official records about a person's criminal justice contacts and behavior for making critical decisions about his or her fate. Procedural hassle entails all of the burdens and opportunity costs attendant on complying with the demands of legal proceedings. Performance means the evaluation of an executed accomplishment, whether it was demanded formally by the court *ex ante* or offered as evidence of responsibility or rehabilitation *ex post*. Thus, instead of seeking social control by judging if the accused in fact committed a proscribed act in the past and then inflicting punishment, managerial misdemeanor courts seek social control by sorting and testing defendants into the future by building records on their law enforcement contacts, evaluating their rule-abiding propensities through measured compliance with a series of procedural requirements, and gradually ratcheting up the punitive response with each successive encounter or failure to live up to the court's demands.

Criminal Justice and Social Control

Sociology has long regarded criminal law as a key mechanism of social control. Before I proceed to use the term, a bit of conceptual brush clearing is in order. Social control is a capacious concept that references the mechanisms of maintaining social order, facilitating coordination, and reinforcing shared norms and communal cohesion.[9] Because conceptual clarity of such a wide-ranging idea is difficult to achieve with abstract definitions, it is useful to explore precisely how sociologists have theorized that penal institutions—from police, to courts, to jails and prisons—produce or seek social control. This overview is not meant to be a comprehensive theoretical treatment of the field, but rather a way to give some precision to the term by looking at examples of penal mechanisms of social control, which, in turn, reveals what is interesting about the study of misdemeanorland.

By most accounts, criminal law functions as social control by establishing a list of forbidden acts in the penal law (or what I will sometimes call the substantive criminal law) that a particular political community has deemed contrary to its shared moral codes or sense of proper order. The police enforce the proscriptions by looking for people who have violated the penal law or by deterring people from violating it by their mere presence and threat of arrest and apprehension. The role of criminal courts is to determine if the people identified by the police as possible lawbreakers have, in fact, committed an act on the proscribed list. They are authorized to deploy the processes for investigation and fact-finding laid out in the rules of criminal procedure to adjudicate the defendant's guilt and level of blameworthiness. Courts then impose some measure of punishment on those judged guilty. Punishment is not just any unpleasant experience received at the hands of an authority; it is the intentional imposition of harsh treatment that embodies a social condemnation of the offender's act.[10] In this model, criminal law functions as a form of social control by controlling criminal acts.

Seminal sociological theorists have long explored how punishment functions as an instrument of social control beyond being a deterrent, incapacitation, or retribution to the person found guilty of an offense. For example, Émile Durkheim, writing at the end of the nineteenth century, argued that punishment is a social enterprise that expresses a group's foundational, shared moral order and sustains it by enacting rituals that communally reject threats to the collective moral conscience.[11] By this account, punishment functions as social control less by controlling the deviant acts of criminals than through collective acts that meaningfully demonstrate commitment to the values making common life possible. For Max Weber, the manner by which modern punishment is decided and administered explains how it can be a mode of social control beyond its effects on the offender. Weber argued that modern states maintain social order through a distinctive form of authority, what he called rational authority. Rational authority is based on recognition of the legality of commands and procedures, and it differs from traditional authority, based on recognition of the sanctity of traditions, or charismatic authority, based on devotion to an exceptional leader. The modern state claims monopoly over the use of force by making its exercise legitimate on legal grounds (as opposed to passion, custom, or vengeance), which means limiting the exercise of coercive control and violence to the precise modes and methods authorized by law.[12] Thus, modern punishment can achieve social control not just by punishing the offender, but by securing voluntary compliance with the state's directives by engendering a sense of legitimacy in its commands and sanctions. This is achieved by rationalizing the determination of punishment with predetermined procedures for fact-finding and adjudication, and by confining the imposition of punishment to bureaucracies with professional staff governed by clear rules and boundaries. Although Karl Marx, another seminal theorist of sociology, did not write extensively about punishment, a Marxian approach understands punishment as social control by being an instrument of class control. The mechanisms include creating cultural orientations that lead to the acceptance of an exploitative system by promoting a false faith in the class neutrality of the legal system or physically incapacitating labor excess to the needs of capitalist production that might pose a potential threat to political and economic stability.[13] By this account, the forms of punishment in our society are determined by the needs of the ruling class to control the laboring classes.

From these very broad strokes of classic sociology of punishment, we can discern a rough picture of what might be distinctive about how the criminal law of lesser crimes seeks social control. The following chapters show that most of the accusations addressed in lower criminal courts do not look like conduct that violates foundational moral values making collective life possible or conduct that elicits a ritualistic expiation to restore social solidarity. The allegations may involve conduct that people find problematic, perhaps even wrongful, but I try to delineate the precise social meaning of the type of crimes addressed in misdemeanorland and the relevance of the qualitative distinction between these crimes and how we have traditionally thought about penal law. I also show that the manner in which the great majority of these lesser offenses are processed involves very few formal procedures to investigate facts or adjudicate guilt. In fact, court actors routinely engage in behaviors that forcefully discourage such activities, and therefore the legal apparatus cannot be fairly seen as trying to secure legitimacy by acting according to authorized means. And the most common forms of punishment imposed in misdemeanorland do not look like those that could neutralize class conflict.

In fact, we will see that the composition of sentences imposed from misdemeanor arrests raises another interesting set of questions about how precisely the criminal law seeks social control through punishment. One specific form of punishment occupies a preeminent place in current sociological thinking about modern penal power and social control: the prison. Many social scientists view the emergence of the "carceral state" and mass incarceration as one of the most significant developments in recent American political history.[14] Incarceration is cited in both popular and academic literature as one of the primary means of governing marginal populations.[15] And yet, in New York City, for the largest class of criminal law enforcement actions—subfelonies—a jail sentence is an infrequent outcome. In order to appreciate the differences and similarities between the ways lower courts might operate as a form of social control, it is helpful to review precisely *how* social scientists have understood the social role of modern punishment.

Michel Foucault, one of the best-known recent theorists of punishment, presented the prison as the paragon of what he called disciplinary power, the mode of domination and control characteristic of modern states and institutions. In contrast to ancient forms of punishment that targeted the bodies of offenders in striking spectacles of violence and subjugation, disciplinary power targets what Foucault calls the "souls" of offenders by seeking to modify their inner dispositions and thoughts, train their habits and routines, and mold their minds and capacities for action.[16] The prison exemplifies modern disciplinary power because it confines people in a totalizing environment where their movements are constantly observed and corrected; its physical layout is designed to compel subjects to internalize norms and behaviors valued by those exercising power.[17]

In the age of mass incarceration, some scholars argue that prison plays a new role in the exercise of social control. Instead of reform through disciplinary practices, its role is that of "warehouse," "punitive segregation," and social "exile." Others have suggested that in a post-Fordist, neoliberal, capitalist order—in which entire populations are superfluous to the productive needs of the economy—the prison is not directed at training and deploying bodies for a capitalist system in need of docile labor. Instead, it aims at identifying and segregating the dangerous from laborious classes.[18] Thus, the mechanism of removal and physical segregation is another means by which we conceptualize the social control capacity of modern punishment.

The threat of prison is another means of social control. Probation and parole populations have grown even faster than prison populations during the past thirty years.[19] As Michelle Phelps and others have pointed out, the majority of people under formal criminal justice supervision have been sentenced to serve their punishment in the community under probationary supervision, constituting an ever-growing pool of potential prisoners, often for technical violations or new minor arrests.[20] This group is legally constrained and routinely inspected for fitness to maintain their limited liberty. For example, Alice Goffman's ethnography of one neighborhood in Philadelphia captured the effects of intensive policing on a group of young men with outstanding links to the criminal justice system through probation, parole, or court warrants. Her study found that the form of power operative in the ghetto was incomplete and sporadic, leading her to conclude that the residents were less like captives in a Foucauldian panoptic power regime and more like fugitives within porous social and physical spaces, seeking to evade detection, since they were already "candidates" for removal to prison.[21]

The mark of prison time or, more broadly, of a felony conviction is another social control mechanism that social scientists have studied in the era of mass incarceration. A substantial literature shows how a felony conviction curtails labor market prospects[22] and imposes a host of civil disabilities, often extending beyond the legal offender.[23] A felony conviction often restructures democratic access[24] and shapes how individuals conceive of their citizenship status and relationship to the government.[25] It is almost always a permanent mark (absent the rare possibility of expungement in some states) and has such wide-reaching implications in so many venues that theorists have analyzed the social standing of felons in conceptual terms such as caste, class, and status group.[26]

We cannot talk about prison as social control in the United States without discussing its role as a system of racial and ethnic domination. Mass incarceration is highly concentrated by race, ethnicity, class, and space.[27] An astonishing 35 percent of black men aged twenty to thirty-four without high school diplomas were estimated to be imprisoned in 2008 compared with approximately 10 percent of similarly educated and aged white men. Imprisonment is now a "modal event" in the life course of black men without high school diplomas: the cumulative risk of incarceration for this group in the birth cohort of 1975–79 is 68 percent, whereas for similar white men in the cohort, it is 28 percent.[28] Racial disparities in incarceration have deep historic roots, and prison has been an active tool not just in the physical subjugation and segregation of black Americans, but also in the very production and maintenance of racial categories in the United States. Some argue that there is a direct continuity—in terms of function and effects—between earlier systems of racialized social control, such as slavery and Jim Crow, and mass incarceration.[29]

The Possibilities of Social Control in Misdemeanor Justice

Misdemeanor justice does not involve the large-scale removal of bodies into total institutions where they will be warehoused or subject to disciplinary retraining. Nor does it regularly produce the permanent mark of a serious criminal record that denotes a lifetime status of denigrated citizenship and civil rights. And misdemeanor justice does not necessarily even hold out the threat of long-term custodial sanctions or criminal conviction. If it does not generate the types of punishments we have come to understand as constitutive of modern penal regimes and their social control methods, then what does it do? Does it operate as a mode of social control? If so, how?

This book seeks to answer these questions with an in-depth study of misdemeanor justice in New York City. It takes a sociological approach to these questions by conceptualizing the lower criminal courts as an organizational field embedded in larger institutions. I draw on organizational sociology, ethnography, and socio-legal studies to document how the concrete, practical circumstances of doing legal work in misdemeanorland shape the ways in which ground-level legal actors make sense of and deploy legal rules and, consequently, the social control tools they use and the logic of action by which those tools are deployed.

I organize the analysis of the qualitative and quantitative data I collected into two sets of arguments that can be summarized fairly succinctly. Part 1 is dedicated to developing the claim that the city's misdemeanor courts have largely abandoned the adjudicative model of criminal law administration and instead operate under the managerial model, concerned with managing people over time through engagement with the criminal justice system.[30] I proffer a series of explanations to account for why this model of criminal law administration is currently flourishing in misdemeanorland and to explain its persistence.

Part 2 explicates the techniques through which misdemeanor criminal court actors extend social control over the populations they encounter—techniques that differ markedly from the forms familiar to the study of mass incarceration and felony courts. The most common penal outcomes experienced by misdemeanor defendants are not removal to total institutions or the burden of a permanently spoiled identity. Rather, they involve a set of ongoing entanglements with and obligations to various organs of the criminal justice system—from police to courts to private social service providers—and result in people cycling in and out of various legal statuses over time, often based on how they perform under these obligations. In misdemeanorland, penal power operates primarily through the techniques of *marking* through criminal justice record keeping, the *procedural hassle* of case processing, and mandated *performance* evaluated by court actors. Part 2 unpacks this tripartite conceptual schema and uses it to explain how the operations of misdemeanor justice are used to further social control ends, often without securing conviction or formal punishment. I conclude by arguing that the study of justice in lower courts in New York City illuminates a set of urgent moral and political questions about the criminal justice system as an instrument of social control and its role in reproducing class and racial inequality in the United States.

I do not focus extensively on the aspect of criminal justice encounters that has received most media and academic attention: jail. Despite the unprecedented surge in incarceration, it is the noncarceral penal operations—covering probation, parole, alternative programs, and sentences such as conditional discharge, fines, community service, and of course nonconviction—that continue to constitute the largest component of our criminal justice system's operations. Jail is certainly a pressing policy issue in New York City because of the long-standing and well-documented violence and human rights violations at Rikers Island, the city's largest jail complex, which houses both pretrial defendants and those serving city time.[31] And misdemeanor arrests do sometimes result in jail sentences; it just is less common than I suspect most people would guess. I have therefore chosen to focus on penal techniques at the lower reaches of the pyramid that have received less attention and that, at least in New York City, are much more frequently encountered. Understanding such noncarceral social control tools is vital to a building a more complete theoretical picture of our criminal justice system's social control role.

The study of misdemeanorland reveals that criminal courts can operate as a form of social control while doing little of what they are formally designed to do, which is adjudicate guilt and impose formal punishments. In that sense, the story here reveals some similarities with accounts that trace how institutions produce social control functions with means quite different from their official design. One notable historical example is Douglas Hay's account of eighteenth-century England, during which Parliament massively expanded the list of capital statutes but, contrary to its bloody rhetoric, did not carry out a proportionate increase in executions.[32] Hay argues that the state nonetheless consolidated its social control power via criminal law during this period. This was accomplished not by executing more death sentences, but by enhancing the criminal law's status as a class-neutral institution through rigid enactments of legal formalism, which displayed the law as a constraining force on class power. Furthermore, as the opportunities for imposing death expanded, so did the opportunities for nobles and members of the gentry to show mercy through a pardon or commutation, which had the effect of cementing the interpersonal allegiance of the ruled to the rulers.

Or consider an example from the turn of the most recent century in Forrest Stuart's study of an intensive policing initiative launched in Los Angeles's Skid Row that saturated the area with patrol officers directed to enforce a version of zero tolerance or quality-of-life policing.[33] Stuart notes that such a broad mandate in an area of dense poverty and homelessness means that the police essentially faced ubiquitous targets of enforcement, well beyond their functional capacity even at the heightened levels of patrol strength authorized by the program. In this initiative, the police did not simply maximize punitive enforcement, but rather established a symbiotic relationship with the only other major institutions in Skid Row, the collection of private social service organizations and "mega-shelters" that populate the area. The significant numbers of arrests and summonses must be understood in light of the massive number that *could* have been issued but were not because the police regularly presented potential arrestees with a choice: arrest or enrollment in a private rehabilitative "program." Stuart also demonstrates with ethnographic detail how the police routinely used arrests and citations not with the end of securing legally authorized punishments, but to wear down Skid Row residents who resisted entering the restrictive mega-shelters. Therefore, the police were not using their designated power to identify the maximum number of lawbreakers to the end of getting courts to impose formal punishment or even to deter them from public disorder. Rather, they were seeking maximum street-level leverage over the population, which required Skid Row residents to actually be in violation of one of the countless municipal ordinances or penal law offenses in order to coerce them into other systems of social control such as shelters or "rehabilitative programs," which the police and politically influential stakeholders deemed more effective than criminal sanctions.

While this book is dedicated to making sense of criminal law practices in the subfelony world, this approach is important to the study of criminal law more broadly. William Stuntz once described the content of criminal law not as "rules in the shadow of which litigants must bargain," but rather as "items on a menu from which the prosecutor may order as she wishes."[34] A similar thing can be said of the rules of criminal procedure: they are not a recipe directing legal actors how to achieve a clearly defined goal, but rather ingredients that court actors can combine in different ways to produce assorted penal experiences. Put differently, statutorily authorized punishments and legal rules offer little guidance to the empirical regularities of existing criminal courts and criminal punishment. But those empirical regularities are not random. To understand the activity of criminal courts, we must ask what it is about the material and social contexts in which legal actors operate that leads them to systematically order from the menu or combine ingredients as they do.

That fundamental question—how legal actors use the law and what shapes that practice—motivates the two theoretical contributions I develop in this book. The first is to propose that in the study of legal organizations we move away from conceptualizing procedural or substantive law as providing clear directives for action or supplying a well-defined set of values or goals.[35] I suggest instead that we move toward conceptualizing them as tools or plans that must always be implemented and interpreted in concrete action settings. As a conceptual matter, this means starting from the premise that legal actors always need to make a practical determination about what the law means in the first instance in constrained situations of choice. As a methodological matter, it means taking an internal and inductive approach to the study of legal organizations. It means studying law from the ground up by carefully examining the practical circumstances of daily activities to ask how those circumstances shape the very purposes that legal actors come to embrace—the ends that they think the legal rules ought to be *used for* in their ongoing activities.

The second theoretical thread unwinds from the first. How the law ends up being used in misdemeanorland is neither random nor perfectly determined. With careful study, we can apprehend a logic of action—a discernable patterned use that can be interpreted as aiming toward social control but not necessarily achieving it.[36] The defining logic of legal activity in lower criminal courts is not something that actors—including those at the top of various constitutive organizational hierarchies—necessarily intend, plan, or even consciously embrace. Although many actors might affirm the logic of action both as an accurate description of their activities and a desirable one (if offered the opportunity to reflect), I believe it is a mistake to think of the actor's evaluation as the cause of these patterns. Rather, the defining logic of social control and the modal techniques of penal power in misdemeanorland emerge as legal actors routinize a set of solutions to recurrent problem situations in which they and defendants find themselves. For this reason, I propose studying lower criminal courts as a legal field, one where various actors—both individuals, such as defendants, and organizations, such as prosecutors' offices and public defender organizations—come together in a physical and legal space structured by legal rules as well as certain defining resource limitations. The logic of social control observed in this field is the product of a series of interdependent and strategic decisions made under conditions of constraint and uncertainty.

These theoretical moves have implications for what sorts of claims we find satisfying by way of *explanation*—that is, what renders misdemeanorland more intelligible and comprehensible. If we are interested in understanding the patterned ways in which legal actors use legal rules and the recurrent ways in which people are affected by them, then the most illuminating accounts will be detailed analyses of the multiple overlapping constraints and layers of uncertainty under which people act. It will be less illuminating to operationalize vectors of misdemeanorland as discrete variables in order to assert that a change in magnitude of one variable caused (in the counterfactual sense) a change in magnitude of another variable measuring some other aspect of the system. Without getting too deep into the weeds of philosophy of science, I confess adherence to a particular vision of the explanatory ambitions of social science, one that is not reducible to the issuance of strong counterfactual causal claims or the subsumption of a phenomenon under a general covering law.

Because such claims are the dominant mode of explanation currently practiced by many social scientists in the United States, I want to be upfront about what will be on offer in this book. The mode of explanation engaged here does not consist of isolating facets of the object of study in order to determine how a change in one component of it might have propelled a change in another component. Instead, I discuss how the defining features of misdemeanorland combine to present themselves as a cohesive action dilemma to the actors operating in that field. I approach the study of law in existing legal institutions as proceeding from the premise that legal actors make grounded determinations about how to use law in an ongoing course of activity. I take what Matt Desmond calls a relational approach to a field, in which the objects of study are "*processes* involving configurations of relations among different actors or institutions."[37] I describe the repeated problem situations legal actors encounter, analyze how obstacles challenge certain established organizational interests or habits, and rationally reconstruct an account of why some means are selected over others in the actors' daily activities. These factors work together to produce a set of outcomes that are surprising, given the received wisdom about criminal law in general, and lower courts in specific. I undertake this explanatory approach because outcomes in misdemeanorland (as in many fields) are produced by interdependent activity and strategic interactions in the field. Therefore, to understand the pattern of outcomes, we should analyze how the combined elements mutually constrain each other.

I turn away from strong causal claims of the counterfactual variety not merely because, as some social scientists have suggested, the enterprise of "reverse causal inference"—identifying the causes of observed effects—is "fraught with insurmountable conceptual challenges."[38] Certainly it is. Nevertheless, some of the most alluring objects of research are precisely those that are, for both methodological and conceptual reasons, the least susceptible to explanations of the counterfactual causal variety. We are often drawn to research sites or topics that exemplify the qualities of an alluring high school crush: singular, extreme, anomalous, jarring, experimental, pioneering, original, tattooed. We are drawn to those objects of research that most confound counterfactual causal inference by virtue of their complexity, distinctiveness, or rarity for the same reasons the outsider high school crushes were alluring—they are interesting!

The mode of explanation in this book could be captured in the terms that Abend, Petre, and Sauder use to describe the explanatory practices of sociology south of the Rio Grande: to "tell a persuasive story about, give a good account of, or shed light upon [an] empirical problem."[39] I propose to do so by giving a careful account of the machinery of lower criminal courts, analyzing the role and relationships between actors there, and building a conceptual schema with the purpose of suggesting "how best to view, interpret, or understand what is going on" in misdemeanorland in terms that are "novel, illuminating, instructive, insightful, helpful, or edifying."[40]

Does that mean the information and claims made about New York City's misdemeanor justice are not generalizable to other lower criminal courts? Perhaps. Free from the intellectually normalizing strictures of journal review, a book is a good place to be epistemologically honest. I suspect it is more conceivable than many sociologists like to admit that the particulars that make an object or site of study *interesting*—meaning, something people are excited and curious to know about—are precisely the factors that make it challenging to know if the understandings achieved about the object are applicable to another site.

New York City's misdemeanor courts are characterized by qualities that make them simultaneously interesting and atypical. New York is not a representative American city in most respects. It is the biggest city in the nation, uncharacteristically spatially dense, and has a large police force practicing—probably in the most intense fashion of any municipal police force—the quality-of-life policing model. But the city's law enforcement experiment is also widely looked to as a national model for crime control. Other large urban centers, such as Los Angeles and Chicago, have adopted major elements of New York's policing model, flooding local courts with subfelony cases.[41] Across the country, it appears that misdemeanor filings outnumber felony filings by a factor of at least two-to-one.[42] To state the obvious, every local criminal court is characterized by a particular political culture; policies and practices indigenous to the local prosecutor's office, defense bar, and judiciary; a defining arrangement of legal and organizational relations among those actors; and a particular assortment of legal tools defined by the state's substantive and procedural criminal law. It would be foolish to assume that the host of factors that make each jurisdiction unique would not affect, for example, how caseload pressures translate into disposition patterns.

That does not mean the insights from the study of New York City's misdemeanorland are not valuable to the study of other sites, even if they are not directly generalizable. Findings from one place can alert us to phenomena at a different one, such as noncarceral penal power that operates by virtue of record keeping, iterative encounters with courts, or the evaluation of actions during those encounters. Or it could model a method of explanation useful in another site, such as looking at the constraints and conditions under which legal actors operate to account for a pattern of outcomes or analyzing how the unintended upshots of case processing are appropriated to new uses—uses for which they were not intended but that nonetheless serve functions the actors value.

Studying Misdemeanor Justice in New York City

The conceptual apparatus and explanatory tools developed here are based on data from mixed-method, multiyear research in New York City. I draw on quantitative data about misdemeanor arrests and dispositions; legal research about criminal procedure, sealing laws, and court administrative practices; extensive qualitative data gathered over more than three years of fieldwork, including ethnographic observation and interviews; and more than three years of personal experience working as a criminal defense attorney in New York. Each source adds an essential component to our understanding of misdemeanorland because each provides different types of insights.

For about three years, from 2009 to 2011, I worked part-time as a criminal defense attorney for a solo practitioner in one of New York City's boroughs. When I began my fieldwork in April 2010, I selected a borough different from where I worked as the site of my study so as to minimize perceived or true biases, preconceptions, or limits on access stemming from my professional position in an adversarial system. I spoke to people occupying various positions within the criminal justice system (judges, defense attorneys, prosecutors, court personnel), up and down the organizational hierarchy (new attorneys and judges along with supervisors and long-serving judges) and horizontally spanning those with reputations as stern and lenient, traditional and progressive.[43] To minimize data collection bias from my professional experience, I tried, as much as possible, to select an "inconvenient sample" by *not* relying on professional connections for entrée, not mentioning my own work to gain rapport, and using blind approaches, e-mails, or calls to initiate conversations and interviews.[44] Although I do not use any current or former client as a research subject, I draw on my own experience and understandings from my professional experience to make sense of things I heard or observed.

The majority of my qualitative data comes from more than three years of fieldwork in one of New York City's busiest Criminal Courts. I did intensive fieldwork from 2010 to 2013 in one borough, identified as Borough A to maintain confidentiality as requested by many participants, and all names have been disguised to preserve anonymity. I did additional sporadic fieldwork and interviews in 2014 through 2016 in what I call Borough B. All told, fieldwork included extensive ethnographic observation in courtrooms and interviews with judges, defense attorneys, prosecutors, defendants, and various court personnel. I spent between one and three full days per week sitting and observing various misdemeanor courtrooms that process all phases of subfelony cases. During my observational visits, I sat in almost every one of Borough A's fourteen active misdemeanor parts (as courtrooms are called in New York City), including all of the arraignment parts, the all-purpose parts where cases are sent after arraignment, the bench and jury trial parts, the compliance part, and the specialized court parts. I took extensive notes on courtroom proceedings and case dispositions that I witnessed, asking questions in person and following up with phone calls and short interviews where possible. I conducted semi-structured interviews with assistant district attorneys (ADAs), defense attorneys, judges, and court personnel. In addition, I conducted in-depth interviews with defendants—where possible, following their cases throughout the adjudication process—and I tried to reconstruct their case histories through interviews with their defense attorneys, publicly available court records, and discussions with the defendants themselves.

Much of what we can know about the criminal justice trajectories of those arrested for misdemeanor crimes comes from analyzing official administrative state data, the collection and organization of which is directed by state law, local court rules, and local organizational practices. Therefore, I also present some information about the legal rules and administrative practices governing data keeping in New York City, not merely because such information is salacious and thrilling, but also because these facts shape the outcomes of misdemeanor justice and are essential for understanding how penal techniques produce effects. Furthermore, official record keeping itself tells us about the priorities of states and about how states keep tabs on their subjects.

I also present quantitative data in various forms supplied by state and local government agencies or organizations affiliated with the courts. Much of this information is presented in aggregate form, meaning the unit of analysis is some jurisdictional or spatial aggregation such as a police precinct, a particular borough's Criminal Courts, or all of New York City's Criminal Courts. Sometimes social scientists use the phrase "mere description" in a dismissive way or pass over descriptive tables in quantitative projects as an obligatory but unexciting prelude to regression analysis, where the real explanatory action presumably takes place.

I emphasize these aggregate descriptive tables and charts for several reasons. First, we have heretofore very little sense of what happens in the lower criminal courts of a major urban jurisdiction that has undertaken a radical law enforcement experiment aimed at subfelony crimes. Second, we have little precedent for what *ought* to happen once these arrests arrive at a criminal court charged with determining an appropriate punishment. Little ink has been spilled by philosophers or legal scholars arguing over the just deserts for public urination, turnstile jumping, petit larceny, or even assault where (by definition) the victim incurred no serious physical harm. Much of the academic and public commentary that argued for Broken Windows policing was focused on what police ought to do with low-level offenses, not how courts ought to process these cases.

These descriptive tables therefore provide a valuable picture of large-scale changes in the inputs, processes, and outcomes in the city's lower criminal courts over more than two decades of Broken Windows policing. I also engage this aggregate data alternatively, as something to be explained—that is, why would this law enforcement experiment yield a decrease in criminal convictions when the entire thrust was to get tough with low-level offending—and as a source of explanation—that is, suggesting that we have to understand what courts are doing in reference to the volume of cases or the composition of cases and defendants. Additionally, the aggregate picture provides an interpretive backdrop to the qualitative data I present throughout the book, such as what proportion of arrests or dispositions a particular illustrative case might be representative of in the universe of misdemeanor justice.

Most quantitative data comes from the New York State Department of Criminal Justice Services (DCJS), the agency charged with collecting and maintaining records from local courts and producing rap sheets.[45] Other figures might come from the Chief Clerk's office of New York City's Criminal Courts, the New York City Criminal Justice Agency, or the New York City Police Department, because these agencies keep different sorts of records that are essential to our story, such as metrics of local court functioning, bail practices and trends, or arrests and complaints in the city's precincts.[46]

In addition to aggregate data, I also analyze unique micro-level data obtained from the New York DCJS. This data set was designed to study the arrest and disposition trajectories of persons entering New York City's misdemeanor justice system at different time periods. One can only reliably track the later criminal justice encounters of a new entrant to misdemeanor justice after he or she experiences a disposition from an arrest that authorizes the DCJS to maintain a person's fingerprints, which are then linked to a stable New York State Identification (NYSID)—the number that connects arrest events to a unique person. Therefore, the selection criteria I adopted identifies two groups of entrants to misdemeanorland without prior criminal convictions who experienced a disposition that allows me to reliably document their later criminal justice encounters: those whose misdemeanor arrest terminated in a special type of conditional dismissal for marijuana cases called a marijuana adjournment in contemplation of dismissal (MJACD) and those whose misdemeanor arrest terminated in a first-time criminal conviction.[47] I selected year-pairs at five-year intervals starting with the earliest year reliable data were available and ending with the last date that would give me three years of post-arrest observations: 1980–81, 1985–86, 1990–91, 1995–96, 2000–2001, 2005–6, and 2010–11. The *MJACD group* tracks the population of misdemeanor arrestees without prior criminal convictions arrested in any of my seven cohort year-pairs whose cases terminated in an adjournment in contemplation of dismissal specific to marijuana offenses. The *first-time misdemeanor conviction group* tracks the population of misdemeanor arrestees in any of my seven cohort year-pairs without prior criminal convictions at the time of the arrest whose cases terminated in a first-time misdemeanor conviction. This data is described in detail in the statistical appendix linked to on the book's Princeton University Press website, http://press.princeton.edu/titles/11264.html.

No single type of data conclusively proves the various claims I advance about misdemeanorland. However, I often try to triangulate my claims by presenting evidence from various sources and of different types—quantitative, legal, ethnographic—that each illuminates a different angle of the issue under discussion. I offer my analysis of these data to advance the study of this massive, yet unduly neglected, component of the criminal justice system in the way social science often advances knowledge—not by establishing a narrow claim with ironclad methods beyond refute, but by engaging a large and complicated question whose explanation lies in not just documenting proximate causes of events, but also in describing the social meaning and logic by which events operate.

Overview

The first part of this book covers the *what* and the *why*. Chapter 1 sets up the empirical puzzle by explaining the revolution in the intensity and form of policing pioneered by the NYPD in the early 1990s that placed subfelony enforcement at the center of its urban crime-control strategy and generated an influx of court cases into misdemeanorland.

Chapter 2 starts by reviewing what we might expect to happen in response to this flood of cases. Given the received wisdom that lower criminal courts deliver "assembly-line justice," it would be logical to assume that the increase of misdemeanor cases would result in lots of convictions and jail sentences. This chapter presents descriptive data that show what happened instead: a decline in the rate of criminal conviction and an increase in the rate of dismissal. I propose that a good way to make sense of the disposition trends of the past twenty-five years is to understand that misdemeanor justice in New York City has largely abandoned the adjudicative model of criminal law administration and instead hews more closely to what I call the managerial model, where the criminal process is deployed to figure out the rule-abiding propensities of people and to calibrate formal regulation accordingly.

Chapter 3 explores why criminal court actors turn to using the tools of criminal procedure and criminal law to sort, regulate, test, and manage the populations that flow through misdemeanorland instead of adjudicating individual guilt and innocence. Drawing on organizational and field theory, I examine those features of misdemeanor justice that allow for the flourishing of a managerial as opposed to adjudicative modality of criminal law administration. The analytic of the field is helpful because it allows us to understand how a pattern of activity and logic of action emerge not just from the formal goals of organizations, but from the structure of constraints actors face in a particular setting and from the precise ways individual and collective actors interact in their daily affairs. The disposition patterns and reliance on marking, procedural hassle, and performance as penal techniques can be understood as a result of creative problem solving in the face of the specific dilemmas and practical circumstances of doing legal work in misdemeanorland in the era of Broken Windows policing.

Part 2 turns to the how. If criminal court actors are sorting, testing, and managing defendants over time, then *how* do they do so? Chapter 4 discusses the technique of marking—the generation, maintenance, and regular use of official records for critical decisions about a person's criminal justice contacts and status determinations about the individual. This chapter explains precisely how marks are created and stored in misdemeanorland and discusses how the practices there differ from those in felonyland. It also presents quantitative evidence about the import of marks in misdemeanor case processing.

Chapter 5 is dedicated to procedural hassle—the degradation of arrest and police custody, the stress and frequency of court appearances, and the opportunity costs incurred in order to make court appearances or to comply with court orders. I show that these experiences are something more than a set of inconvenient burdens that dissuade defendants from pushing adjudication or even a collection of informal means by which judges and prosecutors punish defendants. They can be also a set of active, productive tools in the ongoing relationship of social control that lower courts have with defendant populations.

Chapter 6 analyzes the technique of performance—that set of activities the defendant is instructed by the court or prosecution to undertake and later to present as a successful achievement demonstrating responsibility and governability. I explore a wide range of such tasks—from in-patient drug treatment to community service—and show how these duties are assigned and evaluated as performances revealing the defendant's character or capacity to be directed by official rules. The unifying logic behind disparate performance activities is evaluating *how* a defendant has executed the act. The technique of performance seeks normalization but does not involve constant engagement and supervision: it entails a command and a sanction-backed compliance check.

The final chapter revisits the various types of insights that the study of justice in misdemeanorland offers to our sociological understanding about legal organizations. It also address how meso- and macro-level trends are produced from micro-level conditions. I conclude by arguing that the study of mass misdemeanors—like that of mass incarceration—ultimately points out larger political questions about what role we, as a democratic society, will countenance for criminal justice in establishing social order.

PART I

The Logic of Lower Courts

1

The Rise of Mass Misdemeanors

New Yorkers have for years felt that the quality of life in their city has
been in decline, that their city is moving away from, rather than toward
the reality of a decent society. The overall growth of violent crime
during the past several decades has enlarged this perception. But so has
an increase in the signs of disorder in the public spaces of the city.
—*POLICE STRATEGY NO. 5*, 1994

For most of the peak crime years in New York City—about 1988 to 1991—
felony arrests outpaced misdemeanor arrests. In 1993 that changed. Rudolph
Giuliani was elected mayor, and he appointed William Bratton police commissioner. In 1994, they introduced a series of tactical and organizational
reforms to the NYPD that have—perhaps somewhat misleadingly—been
collectively classified under the unifying rubric of Broken Windows or
quality-of-life policing. In policy documents and speeches, the NYPD and
mayor aligned themselves with the central claims made by criminologist
George L. Kelling and political scientist James Q. Wilson in their 1982
seminal article "Broken Windows." The article maintained that the police
ought to refocus on maintaining order in urban spaces and reducing fear
of generally disorderly conditions.[1] Embracing these arguments, the NYPD
announced in a 1994 policy document titled *Police Strategy No. 5: Reclaiming
the Public Spaces of New York*, a new policing regime.

This chapter briefly recounts the origins of the policing experiment
of the early 1990s that flew under the Broken Windows banner and

explores how that experiment has become an institutionalized feature of New York City's law enforcement since then. The history is tailored to highlight those changes in enforcement that most affected the flow and composition of cases into the lower criminal courts and how the justifications for this policing model demanded bureaucratic practices that in turn shaped how these low-level cases came to be processed by criminal justice actors. Specifically, I emphasize the new record-keeping and record-sharing practices that the police and courts innovated in this period in an effort to mark suspected persons for later encounters and to check up on prior records to identify and target persistent or serious offenders.

Lower criminal courts are not islands of judicial activity; they are part of a larger field of criminal justice in a particular space and time. The law enforcement practices and political understandings that generated the flow of misdemeanor arrests are essential context for understanding the logic by which lower courts currently process those arrests. Therefore, this chapter also touches on the sociological and political understandings that underpin the Broken Windows policing model to foreshadow how those understandings inflected the entire field of misdemeanor justice. I then present data from a number of sources to profile what these changes in policing tactics meant for the types of cases and defendants that were fed into misdemeanorland.

The Plan: *Police Strategy No. 5* and the Broken Windows Theory

The document that established New York's Broken Windows regime made two claims that have endured as guiding principles of the city's policing. First, *Police Strategy No. 5* identified low-level offenses as an intrinsically important enforcement priority. It listed a series of quality-of-life conditions the police would target—noise complaints such as loud music, motorcycles, and car alarms; illegal double parking; blocking traffic; prostitution; aggressive panhandling; squeegee cleaners; graffiti; illegal peddling and vending; aggressive bicyclists; loud clubs and discos; and public drunkenness. The mayor and police department proclaimed their intent to take these issues seriously in an effort to restore New York to a "society of civility."[2] As Bill Bratton explained in a 2013 interview, "[Q]uality of life crimes actually didn't victimize a person, but what they were victimizing was the city psyche about itself. . . . [They] contributed to the decaying of neighborhoods. The victim was the neighborhood. The victim was the borough. The victim was the city. And this malaise was spreading because it looked like government and the police—as the agents of the government—weren't addressing what was creating fear and unease in people as they watched their neighborhoods deteriorate."[3]

Second, the strategy document endorsed another central claim from Kelling and Wilson's article, which was that "disorder and crime are usually inextricably linked, in a kind of developmental sequence."[4] Although the paper was released after the city hit its peak of violent crime, it was not obvious at the time that the trend would continue in the downward direction, much less that crime would decrease at the magnitude it eventually did. Announcing their new plan, the NYPD and the mayor declared, "*Police Strategy No. 5: Reclaiming the Public Spaces of New York* will emerge as the linchpin of efforts now being undertaken by the New York Police Department to reduce crime and fear in the city."[5] They repeated such claims in various other pronouncements during this period, arguing that a renewed focus on low-level crime was instrumental in reducing serious violent and property street crime through various mechanisms.[6]

Much of the theory and practice of New York's signature policing model laid out in the early 1990s has endured over changes in the city's political and police leadership. More than two decades after authoring *Police Strategy No. 5* under Republican Mayor Rudy Giuliani, Bratton returned to take up the position of NYPD commissioner under a progressive Democratic mayor, Bill de Blasio.[7] Both the mayor and the commissioner reaffirmed their broad support for the model and tactics of Broken Windows policing, albeit with some stated modifications. Bratton repeatedly reiterated the intertwined theoretical claims presented in early iterations of Broken Windows, namely, that disorderly conditions license serious offending, that violent criminals are also committing minor crimes, and that minor criminals will grow up into major criminals if not interdicted early in their offending arc. He also reaffirmed his faith in the efficacy of tactics that he gathered under the rubric of Broken Windows policing.[8] In a 2015 NYPD publication titled *Broken Windows and Quality-of-Life Policing in New York City*, Bratton explains that his reasons for initially embracing Broken Windows policing were verified by his experience in the early 1990s:

We wouldn't ignore the little things. Fare evasion and graffiti would no longer be considered too petty to address. In fact, we'd focus on them as vigorously as on serious crimes like robberies, if not more so. Why? Because serious crime was more likely to occur in a lawless environment—and ubiquitous low-level disorder signaled lawlessness even more than serious crime, which was less common. We also quickly learned that the serious criminals committed petty crimes, too. When they weren't committing robberies or assaults, they were hopping turnstiles, unlawfully moving between cars, and generally diminishing the quality of life that should have been enjoyed by other, fare-paying riders. A subway criminal arrested for a misdemeanor rather than a felony wouldn't be going to prison, but he wouldn't be victimizing anyone for a while, either.[9]

This same document went on to insist that the Broken Windows policing model was not only responsible for the major crime decline in New York City, but also for New York State's significant incarceration decline. "Arresting someone for a misdemeanor frequently prevents him from graduating to committing felonies, for which severe sanctions like prison may result. That's why index-crime arrests are down 36% from 1994 . . . [and] from 1990 to 2012, New York City has sent 69% fewer people to state prisons."[10]

Both early and current proponents of Broken Windows policing have put forward various mechanisms whereby enforcement against low-level offenses would cause a reduction in serious street crime. The most familiar of these is what Bernard Harcourt calls the "social meaning" thesis, which holds that disorderly conditions send a signal to potential lawbreakers that there is no collective enforcement of norms or law.[11] As Kelling and Wilson put it in their seminal article, "Window-breaking does not necessarily occur on a large scale because some areas are inhabited by determined window-breakers whereas others are populated by window-lovers; rather, one unrepaired broken window is a signal that no one cares, and so breaking more windows costs nothing."[12]

Another mechanism whereby intense low-level enforcement activity might reduce violent street crime is by offering frequent possibilities for information collection and surveillance. When police stop, summon, or arrest people, they have the opportunity to question them about unsolved crimes, check for outstanding warrants, and initiate records collection on the people encountered. Bratton's memoir *The Turnaround* illustrates how the police understood the value of quality-of-life policing as an information source about serious crime and its perpetrators. In it, he recounts a meeting from the 1990s in New York at which Jack Maple, Bratton's deputy commissioner, urges a precinct commander reporting a series of shootings in public housing to engage the pretextual intelligence-gathering uses of quality-of-life enforcement: "How are we doing with the buy-and-busts? Are we debriefing prisoners? When you have CIs [confidential informants], are you bringing them in to look at photos so they can give you the organizational structure of the criminal element in and about the housing project? . . . Are we doing any quality-of-life enforcement? Are we doing warrant checks? Have you done the overlays from the computer with the people with active bench warrants and parole warrants and systematically gone through them, arrested them for warrants, and debriefed them to find out who was engaged in this activity?"[13]

In this and other arguments for the assorted tactics under the Broken Windows rubric, he highlighted how low-level enforcement had tactical value beyond signaling a norm of order maintenance. He noted that these tactics would identify scofflaws, those with the potential to commit violent crimes, and those who had outstanding warrants for serious charges. Intensive, low-level arrests were of value to the overall crime-fighting mission by bringing the serious offenders back to court to be adjudicated and keeping tabs on marginal offenders. But in order to do so, the NYPD had to transform how patrol cops approached their beat, because they had long thought of low-level enforcement as piddly police work. Bratton explained:

So it was a matter of changing the attitude of the cops; that these crimes were important to address. And one of the ways that cops began to understand the linkage between quality-of-life, minor crime and more serious crime was as they began to encounter these people they found that many of them were wanted on warrants for other offenses that they hadn't bothered to show up in the courts for. Why? Because the department didn't go out and arrest them when they didn't show up because they were minor offenses. But many of these people were wanted for very serious offenses. . . . So by going after quality of life we were also having an impact on more serious crime, because we were finding people who had failed to show up in court. We were finding people who were carrying weapons into the [subway] system—many who were carrying them into the system to use them.[14]

So the police came to understand that in order to use these tactics as a means of stopping the underlying conduct that constituted quality-of-life offending or as a means of deterring and incapacitating people who were on their way to commit serious crimes, they had to engage mechanisms to identify and sort *who was who* in high-crime or ostensibly disorderly spaces. They had to implement enforcement in a way that would allow them to figure out who was committing the serious crimes; who was an occasional troublemaker, one-time errant citizen, or incorrigible misdemeanant; who had disregarded the obligation to show up at court; who had information on other serious street crime; and who might be on his way to becoming a persistent low-level offender or serious criminal.[15] Formal enforcement against low-level offenses with summonses or arrests—instead of informal admonishments—offered the opportunity to do this by generating records about people and engaging them in the demands of the court system.[16]

WHAT CHANGED UNDER BROKEN WINDOWS POLICING? FREQUENCY AND FORMALITY

In order to effectively sort people living in high-crime or ostensibly disorderly spaces, the police needed *both* more low-level contacts and new tools in these contacts. They needed more uniformed bodies on the street observing and intercepting low-level offending, and they needed mechanisms for recording encounters so they could reliably trace people through space and time. Luckily for Bratton, the new tactical changes he proposed were implemented in an era of rapidly increasing police staffing. Starting in 1990 under Mayor David Dinkins and Police Commissioner Lee Brown, the city added thousands of new uniformed officers to the ranks of the NYPD. Figure 1.1 shows that, relative to a 1990 baseline, the NYPD expanded its total uniformed officers by 30 percent by 1995 and by 42 percent by 2000 (excluding the ranks of Housing Authority Police and Transit Police, which were formally incorporated into the NYPD in 1995).[17] The figure also shows that the largest increase in staffing levels during the mid-to-late 1990s was in patrol and narcotics officers.

With increased capacity, especially in patrol and narcotics units, the police were able to engage in more street-level enforcement activities. The absolute staffing levels began to fall in the early 2000s, but relative to index crime, NYPD staffing is much higher today than it was in the 1990s. During

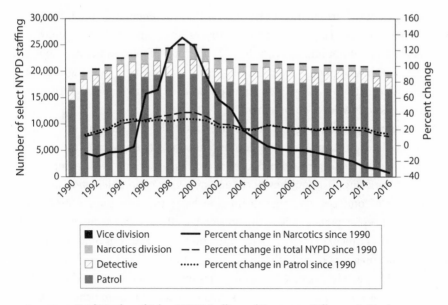

FIGURE 1.1. Total Number of Select NYPD Staffing and Percentage Difference in Total Uniformed Officers Relative to 1990, Excluding Transit Police and Housing Authority Police
Note: Data from NYPD.

the past ten years, the overall ranks of the NYPD have fluctuated between 12 and 25 percent *above* 1990 levels, with both index violent crime and index property crime between 73 and 79 percent *below* the 1990 levels.[18] Therefore, the NYPD has a much larger force of police officers, especially in basic patrol units, out on the streets and trained to detect and enforce low-level crimes. The department used that enhanced capacity not only to increase the *frequency* of low-level enforcement, but the *formality* of the enforcement actions.

The police have long had a range of different tools to deal with low-level crimes.[19] They can choose to disregard certain low-level offenses or informally address the conduct (by telling the person to desist or "move along"), or to formally engage the conduct (by issuing a summons or making an arrest).[20] Police can also, in many instances, choose what level of offense to charge for a given conduct.[21] They have engaged dramatically different strategies and tactics in reaction to perceived disorder or low-level offending over different historical periods.[22]

During most of the peak crime years of the 1980s until 1993, the police either paid less attention to low-level offenses or dealt with the conduct informally. When they did formally engage, the record keeping and organizational arrangements were such that the encounter often lacked, as one interviewee put it, "teeth."[23] That is, the response lacked punitive effect and did not link up with the larger record-keeping systems enabling the tracking of people over time and space.[24] The new policing regime introduced in the early 1990s entailed both qualitative and quantitative changes to low-level enforcement.

Fully understanding the changes that took place in policing under the umbrella of Broken Windows requires a measure of engagement with the gritty detail about arrest procedures and official state record-keeping law. New York law distinguishes between "non-fingerprintable" and "finger-printable" offenses, and that distinction has implications for a range of record-keeping practices. Non-fingerprintable offenses are classified as violations (not crimes) in the penal law, infractions under various other statutes, or misdemeanors outside the penal law.[25] "Fingerprintable" offenses are, by and large, felonies or Class A or B misdemeanors for which the police are authorized to take the arrestee's fingerprints and transmit them to the Division of Criminal Justice Services (DCJS),[26] the state agency responsible for maintaining criminal records and producing and transmitting criminal history reports (aka rap sheets).[27]

For many low-level offenses, the same conduct could be charged as a violation or misdemeanor offense, and which level offense is charged has important implications for potential sentences and record keeping.[28] A person arrested for an A misdemeanor faces higher potential sanctions than, say, a person arrested for a violation, because the penal law authorizes up to one year in jail for an A misdemeanor but only fifteen days for a violation.[29] But it also determines what type of records the police can retrieve on the person at the time of arrest, what records the court will see at the time of disposition, what criminal records systems the encounter will be entered into, and what records of the encounter will be accessible at a later time. Rap sheets are generated and matched to the criminal court files only for fingerprintable offense arrests.[30] As will be explained in more detail below, this means that *most* non-fingerprintable offenses are adjudicated without legal actors accessing a record of the person's prior encounters and prior adjudications.

Most, but not all, non-fingerprintable violations and infractions are addressed by police with what is called a summons.[31] The summons is an "accusatory instrument"; it must include the code or penal law provision the recipient is accused of violating and when and where to appear to answer the summons.[32] Although the police have the legal authority to make a custodial arrest for most non-fingerprintable offenses (if the officer observes it firsthand), it is both official policy and standard practice to issue a summons for violations and infractions in most circumstances.[33]

New York also authorizes different types of arrest procedures.[34] The most common is called an "online" arrest.[35] The name comes from the NYPD's Online Booking System, which indicates that the person is booked into that system at the time of arrest. The arrestee is detained at a local precinct for arrest photos, fingerprinting, and completion of the online booking paperwork.[36] The person is then transferred to Central Booking, where more paperwork is generated and the arrestee is held in detention cells until seen by a judge for arraignment. The typical arrest-to-arraignment time is twenty-four hours for an online arrest.

The other type of arrest is called a desk appearance ticket (DAT).[37] The police still execute an arrest on the street: the person is handcuffed and transported back to the precinct in custody. He or she is then photographed and fingerprinted at the precinct as discussed above. But instead of being transferred to Central Booking to await arraignment, the defendant is released from the precinct with an appearance ticket indicating a date to appear in court for arraignment. The law limits the offenses eligible for DATs to essentially less serious offenses, but that still leaves wide discretion for patrol officers (subject to approval by the desk officer), because eligible offenses cover the majority of arrests made.[38] Since 2013, the NYPD has significantly increased the proportion of misdemeanor enforcement actions given DATs, but online arrests are still far more common.[39] Figure 1.2 presents a simplified summary of the information above.

The import of the changes launched by *Police Strategy No. 5* is only apparent if we understand what distinguishes different types of low-level enforcement options. Bill Bratton explained that, prior to his tenure, inadequate capacity to trace people summoned for low-level offenses was a major law enforcement concern. "There was nobody showing up. Until we basically got into place our warrant units—and we had six hundred officers going out every day serving the warrants. . . . It quickly became understood if you didn't show up in court with your DAT [desk appearance ticket], we were going to send officers to arrest you in your home. . . . And so the idea was: ensure compliance with the law. If you were going to compound your initial offense by breaking the law by not showing up in court—we needed to close all those loopholes, if you will, where people were dropping through the net and dropping out of the system."[40] *Police Strategy No. 5* declared that "permissive and poorly

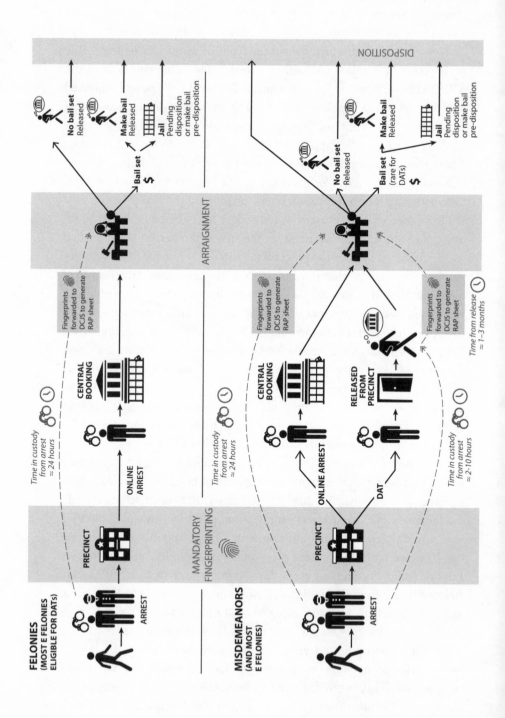

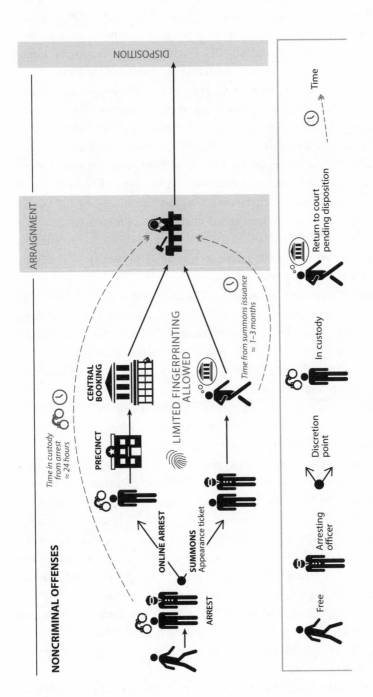

FIGURE 1.2. Enforcement Actions by Offense Type and Records Generated

Note: Only E felonies are eligible for DATs, except the following: PL § 130.25 (rape in the third degree), 130.40 (criminal sexual act in the third degree), 205.10 (escape in the second degree), 205.17 (absconding from temporary release in the first degree), 205.19 (absconding from a community treatment facility), and 215.56 (bail jumping in the second degree). NY CPL § 150.20 (1).

monitored policies regarding issuance of summonses and Desk Appearance Tickets have enabled many offenders to flaunt the criminal justice system, thereby undermining the authority of police officers who respond to these conditions."[41] In response, new policies would be implemented: "tighter eligibility requirements, higher identification standards, and supervisory screening of release decisions," with respect to both the issuance of desk appearance tickets (or, as the police called them prior to 1994, "desk *disappearance* tickets") and summonses.[42] The preference would now be for full online arrests. Individuals without government identification would be ineligible for desk appearance tickets or summonses so as to prevent the use of false addresses and increase the burdens of the encounter. All these enforcement mechanisms would now be docketed and backed by warrant.[43] Taken together, these changes in enforcement practices allowed the police to both generate new records about the people they targeted and also to use the encounter as an opportunity to check the records of the person's prior encounters.

Various other policy innovations demonstrated that the NYPD brass were increasingly concerned not only with generating and maintaining records for their own law enforcement uses, but also with transmitting those records about street encounters to courts for their use in case processing. For example, *Police Strategy No. 5* cites lack of adequate record keeping and communication as an impediment to an effective policy dealing with "dangerous mentally ill street people," saying "there is no capability within the Police Department to keep a history record of contacts with a chronically mentally ill person to assist the medical professional or the criminal justice system in making informed judgments."[44] Around this same time, the NYPD implemented the use of the "Domestic Incident Report" (DIR), a form that "police officers will be required to prepare . . . after responding to incident between family/ household . . . to alleviate the Department's reliance on Complaint Report and On-Line Booking arrest reports as sole sources for compiling information concerning domestic incidents."[45] The police also developed a DIR database, "keeping current data on victims' status, contact, OOPs [orders of protection], and arrest history"; this information was used to "monitor and identify locations requiring special attention" through "home visits, telephone calls, letters to victims and interviews at the precinct station house."[46]

The Domestic Incident Report is a perfect example of how police record-keeping innovations had significant implications for both enforcement and courtroom practices. The police consult the database to determine if a crime has occurred when they respond to a domestic service call—that is, to see if there is a current order of protection in place forbidding contact between the parties. It is also used to calibrate the police response, because the NYPD Patrol Guide mandates arrest if officers find on file prior DIRs between parties involved in the current call for service.[47] The DIR database currently also plays a central role in judicial and prosecutorial decision making on bail, plea offers, sentencing, and other legal determinations in any arrest classified as a domestic violence (DV) case. Judges, for example, regularly ask if there were "prior DIRs" between the parties when setting bail on such cases, and prosecutors regularly reference the same in determining offer policies or recommendations regarding orders of protection.

In sum, the new policing tactics rolled out in the early 1990s under the Broken Windows banner called for not only more frequent enforcement actions against low-level offenses, but also more formal and intense police responses. They emphasized strategies to increase overall collection of information about people encountered on the street in order to ensure the maintenance of records and to secure transmission of those records to institutions down the line—namely, prosecutors and criminal courts—so that court actors would know about the frequency and nature of a person's law enforcement contacts and prior performance with the courts.

The concern with record generation and maintenance has persisted over the past two decades of Broken Windows policing. The NYPD has often actively lobbied to maintain the maximum discretion possible in low-level encounters, pushed to retain the legal option to make fingerprintable arrests in the largest number of offenses, and to maintain as many records as possible of all street encounters.[48] For example, even after Mayor de Blasio swept into office on a platform to reform low-level police encounters, the NYPD successfully defeated a package of reforms that would disallow custodial arrests for municipal noncriminal violations and infractions. The measures that did eventually pass merely added the discretion to issue civil summonses for certain city code violations, which would not be subject to warrants if the person to whom it was issued failed to appear, as opposed to removing the authority to arrest. As Bratton explained, "The new legislation will allow the NYPD to use the full range of enforcement tools we currently have to address these offenses, while still providing us with the additional option to issue a civil summons instead of a criminal summons or arrest in appropriate circumstances."[49] To further illustrate the importance of record collection and maintenance to the NYPD's low-end enforcement practices, the Patrol Guide was amended after passage of the legislation to designate certain "recidivists"—namely, anyone who had two or more prior felony arrests in the past two years, was currently on parole or probation, or had three or more unanswered civil summonses in the past eight years—ineligible for a civil summons.[50]

Not every aspect of current subfelony enforcement practice is the result of calculated, deliberate design. Many of the practices initiated by *Police Strategy Number 5* were intentional strategies aimed at achieving a set of clearly identified goals, such as reducing serious street crime and eliminating certain designated affronts to quality of life in the city. But, as so often happens when large and complex organizations initiate significant reforms, many of the current practices have emerged as the "unanticipated consequences of purposive action."[51]

COMPSTAT AND SOME UNINTENDED CONSEQUENCES OF THE PLAN

The changes instituted by the NYPD in the mid-1990s were not just external, having to do with how officers interacted with the city they policed. They were also internal, affecting how the police functioned as an organization. These tactical, managerial, and organizational changes had significant impacts on the number and nature of low-level enforcement actions. In fact, the internal changes may be the most important factors driving the number and nature of encounters for low-level offenses in the recent decade of stable low property and violent crime.

The NYPD extensively reformed its organizational and management structure starting in 1994. The most famous of these reforms, which has since proliferated to police organizations around the country, is what has come to be called CompStat. There is some debate as to whether the name comes from a shortening of "compare statistics" or "computer statistics," but in any case, the term has come to encompass a range of practices relating to the collection and analysis of real-time crime data and its consistent use in both tactical and management decisions.

By most accounts, Jack Maple was largely responsible for innovating the practices that grew into CompStat.[52] Maple was a former transit cop who came into Bratton's inner circle in the early 1990s when Bratton was chief of the New York City Transit Police. He eventually became Bratton's second-in-command (deputy commissioner) when Bratton was named chief of the entire NYPD, and together they innovated the practices that grew into what is now collectively called CompStat.[53] As a lieutenant in the Transit Police, Maple famously kept colored maps of the type and location of crimes on the subway system, called "charts of the future," in order to direct enforcement efforts to locations where there had been a concentration of recent robberies.[54] When Bratton named Maple to detective lieutenant, and eventually special assistant to the chief during his tenure as chief of Transit, they worked together to collect and analyze statistics about transit crime incidents and enforcement.[55]

After Bratton took over as commissioner of the entire NYPD in 1994, one of the primary reforms he instituted with Maple and the rest of his team was the collection of up-to-date crime complaint and enforcement activity data. As taken for granted as the practice is now, it was novel in 1994. Central Command often had to wait three to six months to receive aggregate crime and arrest reports from precincts or other command posts.[56] Bratton and Maple began extracting aggregate arrest data from the Online Booking System, which was at that time the relatively new computerized arrest system. They used that information, in conjunction with data about the number and type of crime complaints filed in precincts, to evaluate commanders and their enforcement efforts.[57] These numbers quickly became integral to the NYPD top command's management strategy over precinct and squad commanders as a concrete accountability metric.

The rise of CompStat was deeply intertwined with a series of organizational and management changes allocating enforcement capacity—and accountability—to precinct commanders and away from citywide commands such as detectives or specialized enforcement units.[58] The precinct commanders and patrol borough commanders were expected to prove efficacy over their spatial jurisdiction by demonstrating aggressive administration. Bratton explained that up-to-date data on crime complaints and enforcement activity was essential to this reorganization: "Having given the precinct commanders increased power, I had to make sure they were handling it properly through accountability and relentless assessment."[59]

This usually took the form of weekly CompStat meetings at which commanders were grilled on local crime conditions and asked to account for their proactive enforcement efforts in response to changes in crime rates. Unsurprisingly, these same metrics shaped relationships all the way down the organizational hierarchy, with middle management relying on the numbers to gauge successful performance of patrol officers.[60] Because the model underpinning the new policing tactics posited the targeting of low-level offenses as a key mechanism of crime reduction, misdemeanor and summonses numbers emerged as an important metric of effort for area commanders.[61] As Bratton and Kelling explained in another 2015 defense of Broken Windows policing, low-level enforcement actions were measured because the top of the hierarchy strongly believed that intensive low-level enforcement was the very means by which serious street crime would be reduced: "To counter the violence, the NYPD undertook a concerted effort, beginning in 1994, to regain control of street corners and commercial strips, using quality-of-life policing as an essential tool."[62] The organizational currency was showing a reduction in major crime incidents and demonstrating proactive enforcement activity. This same currency was used to demonstrate the NYPD's success to the public and to the executive and legislative branches.[63]

In a 2015 document, Bratton explained that CompStat functioned on the same logic as Broken Windows policing, only applied internally to the police organization. He argued that top police brass can rationally allocate resources and effectively develop strategies to prevent crime only if they track low-level enforcement activity at the local level. "Using crime mapping and organizational accountability practices, CompStat recreated, at the executive command level, the Broken Windows philosophy of sweating the small stuff before it became the big stuff. The advent of quality-of-life policing for the cops and management accountability for the commanders amounted to a public safety revolution that was about more than fighting crime—it was about preventing crime."[64]

CompStat both reflected and induced a shift in the organization's orientation toward its task. Means can easily transform into ends in themselves, especially as organizations formalize measurement of the efforts ground-level actors take to advance organizational goals.[65] Serious violent and property crime actually peaked a few years before misdemeanor arrests and summonses were ramped up aggressively under Bratton's first command of NYPD, as shown in figure 1.3. Many people, both inside and outside of the NYPD, have asserted that showing increases or at least steady levels of low-level enforcement activity has become an internal imperative up and down the organizational hierarchy.[66] Some have maintained that the NYPD commanders explicitly set enforcement quotas. In 2010, NYPD officer Adrian Schoolcraft released a series of secretly recorded conversations with commanders clearly making two sets of demands on beat cops: show more "activity," meaning misdemeanor arrests, stops, and summonses, but write up fewer violent crime complaints.[67]

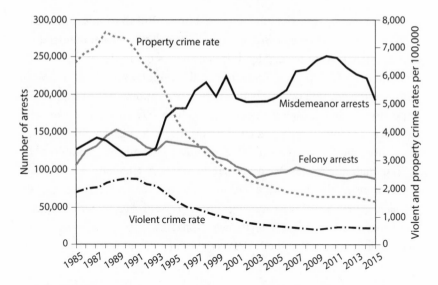

FIGURE 1.3. Violent and Property Crime Rates vs. Misdemeanor and Felony Arrests, New York City, 1985–2015

Notes: Violent and property crime rates from 1985 to 2012 from the US Department of Justice Uniform Crime Reporting (UCR) database, http://www.ucrdatatool.gov/Search /Crime/Local/LocalCrimeLarge.cfm. Violent and property crime rates from 2013 to 2015 from the New York State Division of Criminal Justice Services, http://www.criminaljustice .ny.gov/crimnet/ojsa/countycrimestats.htm. Numbers of misdemeanor and felony arrests from DCJS.

The state legislature passed a bill in 2010 making it illegal to enforce arrest or ticket quotas.[68] But even in subsequent years, significant evidence has emerged that both precinct-level commanders and beat cops continue to feel pressure to "make numbers" and that promotions and evaluations are largely influenced by these numbers.[69] The NYPD has repeatedly stated there are no formal or informal arrest or summons quotas, both before and after the bill banning quotas passed.[70] Nonetheless, a number of lawsuits filed by police officers or civil rights groups allege explicit violations of the anti-quota bill or implicit violation in the form of informal policies demanding a quantity of enforcement actions or pressures to make stops, issue summonses, or make arrests with less than reasonable suspicion or probable cause.[71] Commissioner Bratton issued many public statements after retaking command in 2014 disavowing the use of enforcement activity to gauge performance, arguing that "results matter, not numbers," and called allegations in a federal lawsuit that patrol officers face informal quotas "bullshit."[72]

Nonetheless, high levels of misdemeanor arrest and summons activity have persisted in the city over the past decade of record-low violent crime.

An NYPD document from 2015 authored under Bill Bratton's supervision proclaiming the success of Broken Windows policing also announced the disbursement of a "peace dividend" in the form of reduced numbers of stop, question, frisk (SQF) encounters, criminal summonses, and misdemeanor arrests in recognition of the changed crime conditions in the city. A close inspection of that "peace dividend" shows it mainly consists of a massive reduction of stops largely achieved before Bratton took command and a much more modest decrease in "C-summonses" and misdemeanor arrests.[73]

Thus, although there have been reductions in subfelony enforcement in recent years, the intensity of enforcement persists well above the levels prevalent during New York City's high crime years. Broken Windows policing and management practices seem to have locked in a certain level of subfelony enforcement actions that the NYPD is either unable or unwilling to reduce.

The Yield from the Plan: Offenses, People, and Places

The plans detailed in the prior section were explicitly formulated to change how police conducted low-level enforcement. But much less deliberation and planning addressed what legal actors ought to do with these cases when they arrived at the courthouse. Here I present extensive descriptive data for the same reason that I presented detailed information about record-keeping practices. The records legal actors have available to them to make decisions and the valence this information was given in the larger criminal justice field in which they operate, which includes the NYPD's embrace of tenets of the Broken Windows model, is essential context for understanding the pattern of action that emerged in misdemeanorland. So too are the social meaning of the offenses, defendants, and spaces from which defendants were arrested, because those social meanings shape precisely what legal actors find acceptable to do with these cases.

OFFENSES

As New York City's policing reforms of the 1990s were explicitly formulated to increase low-level enforcement, it is certainly not surprising that they succeeded in doing so. However, the sheer volume of this expansion, and its persistence even in the past decade of low violent crimes, is striking. The total number of misdemeanor arrests expanded almost fourfold, from about 65,000 arrests in 1980 to a high of about 251,000 in 2010.[74] As figure 1.3 shows, even as serious violent and property crime fell to historically low levels, misdemeanor arrests rose in the first decade of the 2000s. The

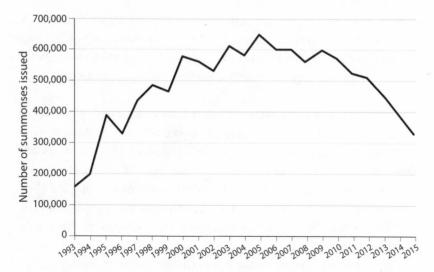

FIGURE 1.4. Summonses Issued, New York City, 1993–2015
Notes: Data from *Police Strategy No. 5* for 1993; Criminal Court of the City of New York, Chief Clerk's Office for 1994 through 2000; the Criminal Court of the City of New York annual reports from 2000 through 2015, https://www.nycourts.gov/COURTS/nyc/criminal /annual-reports.shtml. Filings are reported by NYPD and other agencies issuing summonses and are recorded before defect review.

policing tactics introduced in the early 1990s held steady and even expanded in this later period of stable low violent crime.[75]

Misdemeanor arrests in New York City began to decrease at a modest rate after 2010. By 2015, the annual misdemeanor arrest volume was about 23 percent lower than it was at its height in 2010. Most of the recent decrease in total misdemeanor arrests has been driven by a change in two penal law arrest categories, marijuana and trespass. Marijuana arrests are down by about 64 percent from the highest point of 60,662 in 2000 and by about 43 percent from the most recent second-highest point of 57,549 in 2010 to 21,614 in 2015. Misdemeanor arrests under New York Penal Law (NY PL) § 140, which are almost exclusively for criminal trespass in the second or third degree, have gone down by about 52 percent from the highest point in 2009.[76] The decrease in marijuana arrests was the result of a policy announced by Mayor Bill de Blasio and the NYPD in November 2014, and the decrease in trespass arrests was the result of organizing, media, and litigation pressure against the NYPD's "vertical sweep" program in public housing and low-income private apartment buildings.[77]

According to *Police Strategy No. 5*, about 160,000 summonses were issued annually in the period preceding the quality-of-life initiative.[78] Figure 1.4 displays the summons numbers from 1994 to 2015, showing a steep, threefold increase in yearly summonses between 1994 and the high point of 2005. Over the past five years, summonses have gone down substantially, with 327,306 issued in 2015, which is still a number 105 percent larger than the annual summonses reported in 1993, the year before *Police Strategy No. 5* was issued.

We can never directly interpret arrest rates as an index of underlying criminal behavior because reporting and police practices mediate criminal events and arrests. This is especially true of misdemeanors. In a city like New York, the police can find as many instances of marijuana or drug possession, petit larceny, unlicensed vending, misdemeanor physical altercations, public alcohol consumption, turnstile jumping, prostitution, and disorderly conduct as they devote time and resources to finding. Therefore, recent changes in misdemeanor arrest numbers are largely an artifact of changes in policing practices rather than changes in the frequency of low-level deviance.[79] Figure 1.5 shows trends in the top ten misdemeanor arrest categories from 1990 to 2014. It reveals that misdemeanor arrests cover a wide range of conduct, yet the greatest number of arrests are for offenses where a surge in underlying behavior is an unlikely (or at least difficult to prove) explanation.

Marijuana was by far the largest arrest category for most of the Broken Windows policing era. Concealed possession of less than twenty-five grams of marijuana is classified as a noncriminal violation, which means police have the discretion to make an arrest but typically issue a summons. Marijuana possession is a misdemeanor only if the possessed weight is greater than twenty-five grams or the drug is "open to public view."[80] During the period when marijuana arrests were the largest arrest category in the city, the most common accounts of these encounters involved either a street stop during which the officer would direct the person to remove all items from his or her pockets and then, if marijuana was revealed, make an arrest for misdemeanor marijuana possession because the drug was then "open to public view," or alternatively, merely commence a search of pockets or personal effects (often, according to those stopped, without any legal basis for such a search) and, when marijuana was retrieved, make an arrest for misdemeanor marijuana open to public view.[81] The police narrative sometimes alleged that the arresting officer observed the marijuana open to public view at some point prior to the arrestee putting it back in his pockets, thus giving the officer probable cause to make the arrest and search the arrestee's pockets.[82] The police version of these arrests was rarely tested in court because few of these arrests ever proceed to an

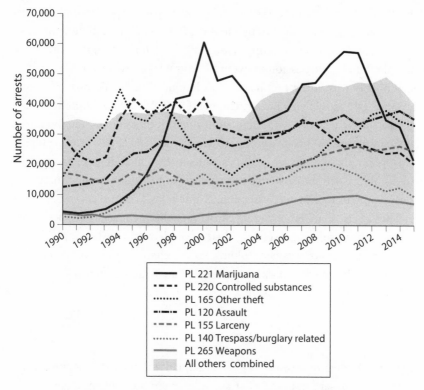

FIGURE 1.5. Top Misdemeanor Arrests by Penal Law, New York City, 1990–2015
Notes: Data from DCJS. Arrests are limited to adult arrests (persons aged sixteen and older, and juvenile offenders prosecuted in the adult courts) for fingerprintable offenses. "Other theft" primarily consists of theft of services, aka turnstile jumping. "All others combined" includes, but is not limited to, public order offenses, prostitution, gambling, driving while impaired, and other vehicle and traffic offenses.

evidentiary hearing much less a trial; almost every arrest terminated in a plea or dismissal.[83]

In response to these accounts, media coverage of the arrests, public organizing, protest, and litigation, there was an attempt in 2012 to amend the penal law directed at the New York Legislature that would have redefined "public view" only as smoking marijuana in public.[84] The effort was somewhat puzzlingly publicly supported by the very people who engineered and carried out the arrest and prosecution policy, such as Mayor Bloomberg, Police Commissioner Kelly, and the elected district attorneys of the five boroughs.[85] Nonetheless, the push was unsuccessful, largely blocked by upstate Republicans.[86]

The misdemeanor marijuana arrests continued for ten months into newly elected Mayor de Blasio's and newly (re)appointed police Commissioner

Bratton's tenure, but in November 2014, the mayor and police commissioner did what they could have done all along.[87] They issued a policy directive instructing beat cops to stop making misdemeanor marijuana arrests of people found in possession of twenty-five grams or less and treat it as what it probably was in the first place: a violation.[88] The breakdown of misdemeanor arrests by penal law article therefore looked very different in 2015 than in prior years. For the first time since the rise of Broken Windows policing almost twenty-five years ago, the city's single largest arrest category was a complainant-driven arrest, assault in the third degree, as opposed to an officer-driven, proactive arrest, such as turnstile jumping, narcotics possession, or marijuana possession. Nonetheless, the top seven penal law articles of arrest are largely officer-driven, including marijuana possession, controlled substance possession, theft of services (turnstile jumping), and weapons possession (usually folding knives charged as "gravity knives"), which together vastly outnumber those that are largely complainant-driven, such as petit larceny and assault.[89]

PEOPLE

Mass misdemeanor arrests—as Loïc Wacquant has pointed out about mass incarceration—are not "mass" at all, as they are not a phenomena widely shared over populations and spaces.[90] They are highly concentrated by race, ethnicity, gender, age, space, and class. Certain characteristics of misdemeanor arrestees did not change significantly over the period of Broken Windows policing, and others did. For example, the gender composition of misdemeanor arrestees has changed very little. In 1990, about 77 percent of misdemeanor arrests were of men, and that figure has never exceeded 82 percent over the past twenty-five years.[91] Figure 1.6 shows that over the past twenty-five years, somewhere between 60 and 70 percent of misdemeanor arrests were of people aged between sixteen and thirty-five. But arrests of older people make up a larger share of misdemeanor arrests in the Broken Windows era. In 1990, about 3 percent of the misdemeanor arrests were of people aged fifty or older, representing about 4,000 arrests that year; by 2015, almost 13 percent of these arrests were of people aged fifty or older, representing about 28,500 arrests.

One of the justifications offered for intensive low-level enforcement was to identify people with serious, violent criminal pasts who were also committing minor offenses and to arrest persistent misdemeanants. To state the obvious, counts of misdemeanor arrests reflect arrests where

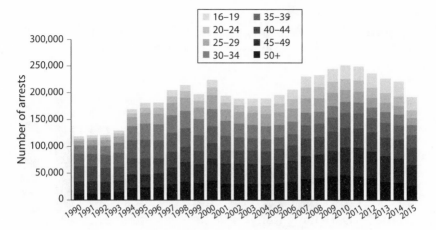

FIGURE 1.6. Misdemeanor Arrests by Age of Arrestee, New York City, 1990–2015
Notes: Data from DCJS. Arrests are limited to adult arrests (persons aged sixteen and older, and juvenile offenders prosecuted in the adult courts) for fingerprintable offenses.

the most serious arrest charge was a misdemeanor, not a felony. But to what extent are the *people* arrested for misdemeanors the same people who had prior felony or prior misdemeanor convictions? Because of New York's laws governing sealing of nonconviction criminal records, measures of prior arrests are unreliable and meaningless at best and misleading at worst, because individuals are not traceable over time until they have a disposition that allows the state to permanently maintain fingerprints (see fig. 1.2).[92] Figure 1.7 therefore shows the number of unique misdemeanor arrestees by top prior conviction status for select years from 1980 to 2015.[93]

This figure shows that these tactics swept significant numbers of people into misdemeanorland each year. According to DCJS estimates, there were a total of 49,091 unique individuals arrested for misdemeanor crimes in 1980; at the height of misdemeanor arrests, that number had risen to 191,185, an increase of 289 percent, before dropping to 145,448 in 2015. Figure 1.7 also shows that most of the increase in misdemeanor arrestees over the past three decades was driven by arrests of persons *without* prior criminal convictions at the time of their misdemeanor arrest. The percentage of misdemeanor arrestees with prior felony convictions has remained strikingly constant over the past twenty-five years, hovering between 23 percent at its height in 2005 and a low of 19 percent during the years 2012–15. The proportion of misdemeanor arrestees who have only prior misdemeanor convictions has gone down over the past three decades, from a high of 26 percent in 1980 to about 12 percent in recent years.

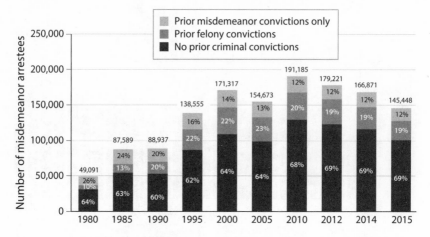

FIGURE 1.7. Prior Criminal Conviction History among New York City Misdemeanor Arrestees, 1980–2015

Notes: Arrestee counts of persons without prior criminal convictions are based on DCJS's best estimate, using NYSID, of unique persons, and therefore might overcount (insofar as persons without prior criminal convictions who are rearrested multiple times within a year are issued new NYSIDs) or undercount (insofar as non–penal law misdemeanor arrests are not fingerprintable). Prior to 1978, DCJS disposition data was incomplete, and therefore the prior convictions of the 1980 defendants might be undercounted.

Do those misdemeanor arrestees without prior convictions grow up to become felony offenders? The next set of figures show *later* felony arrest and conviction trajectories of those individuals represented in MJACD and first-time misdemeanor conviction cohort data.

Figures 1.8 and 1.9 show the percentage of the MJACD and first-time misdemeanor conviction groups over the seven cohorts that have one or more of the following felony events within three years of the cohort-entering event (either the first MJACD or misdemeanor conviction that brought them into the cohort): felony arrest, felony conviction, violent felony conviction. These figures limit the time frame to three years after entering the cohort to make the time "at risk" comparable between the cohorts, as the late entrants to the 2010–11 cohort would have at most three years "at risk" by January 2015, after which the data is censored.

These figures display some notable trends. First, the earlier cohorts tend to have the highest proportions of later felony arrest and conviction, which is unsurprising given the fact that New York City hit record high violent crime rates and drug arrests in the late 1980s and early 1990s. Second, these figures show that at no point over the past thirty years have a *majority* of the misdemeanor arrestees that entered the low-end

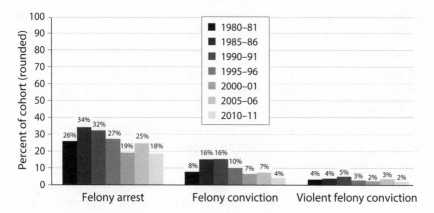

FIGURE 1.8. Percentage of MJACD Cohorts with One or More Felony Arrests, Convictions, or Violent Felony Convictions within Three Years of Entering Cohort
Note: Individual-level data from DCJS; author's own calculations.

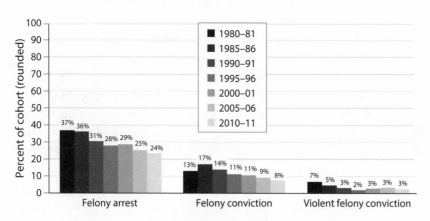

FIGURE 1.9. Percentage of First-Time Misdemeanor Conviction Cohorts with One or More Felony Arrests, Convictions, or Violent Felony Convictions within Three Years of Entering Cohort
Note: Individual-level data from DCJS; author's own calculations.

of the criminal justice system without a prior criminal conviction (using the only coherent groups that can be reliably tracked over time) gone on to be arrested, much less convicted, of a felony offense within three years of entering the cohort. The proportion of these cohorts that were convicted of violent felony offenses is even lower over the thirty years of misdemeanor cohorts spanning the years 1980 to 2011. The highest proportion of a cohort to be convicted of a violent felony is 7 percent for the first-time misdemeanor conviction group in the 1980–81 cohort. Recent cohorts in both groups hover around a 3 percent violent felony conviction rate within three years after entering the cohort. So it is apparent that many people caught up in the dragnet of Broken Windows policing stay in misdemeanorland. They are neither cycling back and forth between felony and misdemeanor arrests nor initiating a felony criminal career with misdemeanor arrests.

It is important to note that this data cannot identify the extent to which the tactics embraced under the rubric of Broken Windows policing succeed in identifying individuals who have outstanding felony, parole, or probation warrants, are in the course of a more serious felony (such as weapons possession), or have been deterred from doing so. Despite extensive anecdotal evidence offered by the NYPD and prior mayors contending that aggressive enforcement against low-level offenses interdicts serious offenders or people with outstanding warrants for violent offenses, it is difficult to ascertain with any rigor from currently available administrative data how many serious arrests (such as gun possession) were made possible by a stop or arrest for a low-level offense or how many people with serious outstanding warrants were identified in the same manner.[94] This is because aggregate arrest statistics reported by the state are grouped by the top arrest charge, so lesser counts are not visible.[95] Even if we could examine the entire docket to see all arrest charges for each incident, absent access to the narrative of the arrest, it would be impossible to tell from court data which charges or what incident precipitated the arrest.[96] Claims regarding the deterrent effect of misdemeanor arrests on nascent felony offending are more complicated to specify, both theoretically and methodologically, than most proponents seem to grasp.[97]

The difficulty of actually knowing the causal impact of these police tactics or court disposition practices is exactly the point that I will return to in chapter 3 to argue that we should not think of the patterns as being the result of their anticipated effects, because no one knows their effects. We should instead try to understand the disposition patterns in misdemeanorland as a set of practices innovated in the face of particular practical constraints and persistent uncertainty, practices that seemed institutionally viable given the social meaning of the infractions and defendant profile at hand. And that social meaning is inflected by the racial and ethnic status of the majority of the defendants and the spaces from which they hail.

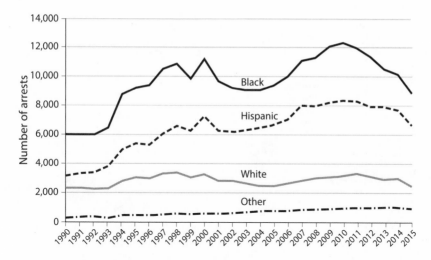

FIGURE 1.10. Misdemeanor Arrests by Race or Ethnicity of Arrestee,
New York City, 1990–2015
Note: Data from DCJS.

RACE, ETHNICITY, AND SPACE

One of the most marked features of our carceral state is its concentrated impact on communities of color. The same is true of the largely noncarceral expansion of low-level enforcement. Figure 1.10 displays the proportion of annual misdemeanor arrests accounted for by persons classified by DCJS as white, black, Hispanic, or other.[98] It illustrates that the dramatic expansion of misdemeanor arrests has been hyperconcentrated on first, black, and second, Latino, individuals. Taking 1990 as a baseline, the increase in misdemeanor arrest levels of white individuals peaked in 1998 at a 144 percent increase over 1990 and hit its second-highest increased level in 2011 at 142 percent.[99] The expansion of misdemeanor arrests of Hispanic and black individuals peaked later, hitting a high of 259 percent over the 1990 levels for Hispanics in 2011 and 206 percent for blacks in 2010.[100] The ratio or disparity in black to white and Hispanic to white misdemeanor arrests also rose over the past decade. In 1990, there were about 1.4:1 misdemeanor arrests of Hispanic individuals to white individuals; by 2007, the ratio peaked at 2.8:1, and in 2014, it sat at about 2.4:1. The black to white misdemeanor arrest ratio started at about 2.5:1 in 1990, peaked at 3.9:1 in 2007 and 2009, and in 2014 sat at about 3.2:1. In 2015, 46 percent of misdemeanor arrests were of black individuals, 35 percent of Hispanic individuals, 13 percent of white individuals, and 5 percent of other racial or ethnic individuals.

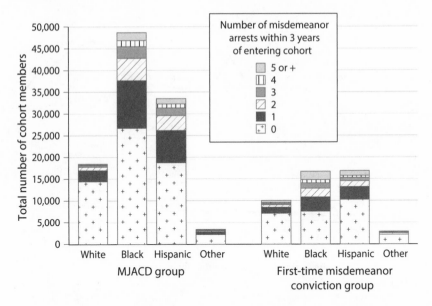

FIGURE 1.11. Number of Misdemeanor Arrests within Three Years of Entering 1995 and Later Cohorts, MJACD and First-Time Misdemeanor Conviction Groups by Race or Ethnicity
Note: Individual-level data from DCJS; author's own calculations.

Not only are more black and Hispanic individuals brought into misdemeanorland; they experience more misdemeanor arrests than white individuals after entering the misdemeanor justice system as recorded in the individual-level cohort data. Figure 1.11 looks just at the post–Broken Windows era by tracking the proportion of all post-1995 cohorts in both the MJACD and first-time misdemeanor conviction groups that experienced any New York State arrest within three years of their initiating disposition. The bars represent the size of all post-1995 cohorts by recorded race or ethnicity and the relative proportions of each group that experienced later arrests after either their first MJACD or their first misdemeanor conviction. Approximately 78 percent of the white individuals in all of the post-1995 MJACD cohorts and 71 percent of the post-1995 first-time misdemeanor conviction cohorts were not arrested within three years after their initiating disposition (MJACD and first-time misdemeanor conviction, respectively). A much smaller proportion of black and Hispanic cohort members were not rearrested within three years of their initiating disposition. Only about 55 percent of both black and Hispanic individuals in the post-1995 MJACD cohorts and about 45 percent of black individuals and 61 percent of Hispanic individuals in the post-1995 first-time misdemeanor conviction cohorts did not experience another arrest within three years after their initiating disposition.

One reason that black and Hispanic *individuals* make up such a high proportion of misdemeanor arrests is that quality-of-life policing is intensely focused in black and Hispanic *spaces*. Figures 1.12 and 1.13 show that misdemeanor arrests have been overwhelmingly concentrated in precincts that have 60 percent or more black or Hispanic population.[101] Arrests from these spaces have a social meaning, one that translates into a presumption of need for social control over the people who are brought from them to misdemeanorland. Precincts with high concentrations of minority residents tend also to be low-income spaces marked by other forms of social disadvantage.[102] Therefore, misdemeanor arrests are not only concentrated by gender, race, and ethnicity but also by socioeconomic class. The state DCJS does not keep income data on defendants, but according to the New York City Criminal Justice Agency (responsible for interviewing defendants to make bail recommendations), only about 46 percent of males interviewed by the agency in 2015 and 38 percent of females reported being full-time employed or in a full-time school or training program at the time of their arrest.[103] During my study, I observed very few defendants who did not qualify for public defender services. Therefore, we need to look at the social and economic characteristics of the spaces where misdemeanor arrests are concentrated.

Figure 1.14 is a collection of scatter plots where the unit of analysis is the precinct and the variables are demographics such as black or Hispanic population, percentage of the population below the poverty line, and the unemployment rate. The plots pool all of New York City's precincts over two post–Broken Windows census years, 2000 and 2010, when it is possible to generate related socioeconomic information, and they show that there tend to be more misdemeanor arrests in precincts with higher measures of social and economic disadvantage. Unsurprisingly, spaces that have higher rates of social and economic disadvantage also tend to have higher crime rates. Figure 1.15 shows that misdemeanor arrests are highly correlated with violent felony complaints and the overall "seven major felony" complaints, which include violent and property crime.

To what extent is the concentration of misdemeanor arrests in black and Hispanic neighborhoods "explained" by the concentration of violent or serious property crimes?[104] Well, it depends what one means by "explained." They are certainly not mechanically induced by serious felony

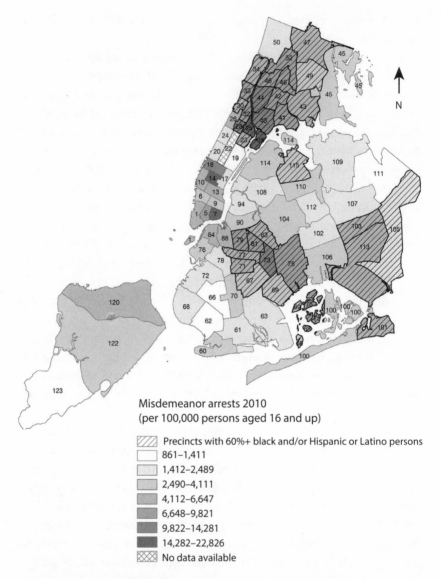

Misdemeanor arrests 2010
(per 100,000 persons aged 16 and up)

▨ Precincts with 60%+ black and/or Hispanic or Latino persons
☐ 861–1,411
☐ 1,412–2,489
☐ 2,490–4,111
☐ 4,112–6,647
☐ 6,648–9,821
☐ 9,822–14,281
☐ 14,282–22,826
▨ No data available

FIGURE 1.12. Population-Adjusted Misdemeanor Arrests per New York City Police Precinct, 2010

Notes: Arrest data from NYPD. No demographic data were available for the 22nd Precinct (Central Park). Total population aged sixteen and over is from the 2010 US Census. Population by race/ethnicity and age was not available in either the American Community Survey or the census data, and therefore the percentage of black and/or Hispanic or Latino persons in the precinct was calculated using total population proportions: adding "Non-Hispanic black persons alone" and all Hispanic persons from the 2010 US Census and dividing by the total population.

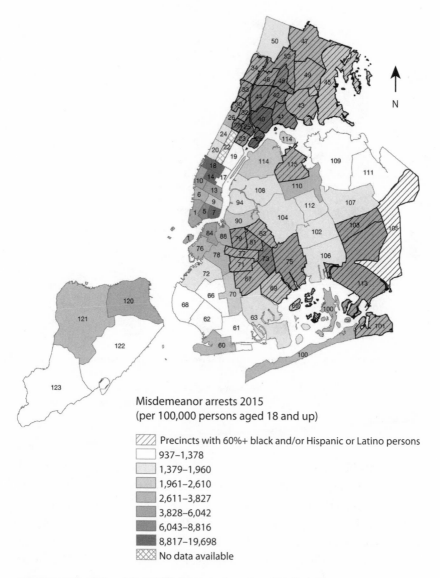

Misdemeanor arrests 2015
(per 100,000 persons aged 18 and up)

- ⧄ Precincts with 60%+ black and/or Hispanic or Latino persons
- ☐ 937–1,378
- 1,379–1,960
- 1,961–2,610
- 2,611–3,827
- 3,828–6,042
- 6,043–8,816
- 8,817–19,698
- ⧆ No data available

FIGURE 1.13. Population-Adjusted Misdemeanor Arrests per New York City
Police Precinct, 2015

Notes: Arrest data from NYPD. No demographic data were available for the 22nd Precinct
(Central Park). Total population aged eighteen and over is from the 2011–15 American Community Survey, US Census ("2011–15 ACS"). ACS age groupings required using eighteen and
up, instead of sixteen and up, for population adjustments. Because of the creation of the 121st
Precinct in 2013, populations for Precincts 120–23 (Staten Island) were calculated based on the
2010 Census Tract population distributions as applied to the 2011–15 ACS population. Population by race/ethnicity and age was not available in either the ACS or census data, and therefore
the percentage of black and/or Hispanic or Latino persons in precinct was calculated using
total population proportions: adding "Non-Hispanic black persons alone" and all Hispanic
persons from 2011–15 ACS and dividing by the total population.

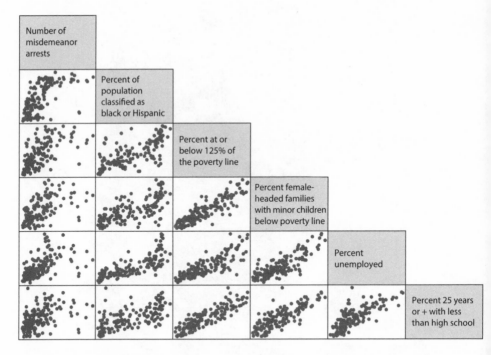

FIGURE 1.14. Precinct Misdemeanor Arrests and Socioeconomic Characteristics, New York City, 2000 and 2010
Notes: Arrest data from NYPD. Socioeconomic characteristics from 2000 and 2010 US Census, compiled to the precinct level by Infoshare Online, http://www.infoshare.org/main /public.aspx.

complaints because, as the first part of this chapter shows, recent levels of misdemeanor arrests and summonses are the result of extensive discretionary policy changes, most of which took place well after New York's index crime rate began its precipitous decline. The NYPD's public explanation for the spatial distribution of low-level enforcement in largely black and Hispanic neighborhoods is that more police are deployed to areas with serious violent crime, and more police mean more misdemeanor arrests, as they are by in large proactive arrests. They also cite more service calls complaining of drug activity or assault in minority neighborhoods.[105] It is difficult to sort out the relative importance of the many forces driving these racial disparities because residential segregation patterns in the city mean that most black and Hispanic residents live in spaces with much higher crime rates than white residents, which are also neighborhoods with other types of socioeconomic disadvantage. Consider the fact that in 2010 one-third of the city's entire black and Hispanic population lived in precincts that have

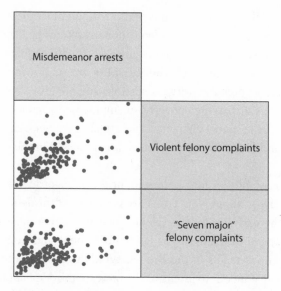

FIGURE 1.15. Precinct Misdemeanor Arrests vs. Felony Complaints,
New York City, 2000 and 2010
Notes: Arrest data from NYPD. The seven major felony complaints are
murder and non-negligent manslaughter, rape, robbery, felony assault,
burglary, grand larceny, and grand larceny of a vehicle.

a higher violent crime rate than *any* majority-white precinct. More than
52 percent of the city's white residents lived in precincts that had a lower
violent crime rate than *any* majority-black or Hispanic precinct. Therefore,
the social and spatial history of the city make it such that even if police
deployment patterns perfectly mirror violent crime rates, the net of Broken
Windows enforcement will necessary entangle more minority residents.

Most of the city's white population does not live in spaces that have a
significant police presence, and therefore they will have a much lower risk
of arrest for misdemeanor crimes. There is substantial evidence, however,
that the underlying behaviors of some of the largest arrest categories over
this period, such as marijuana and narcotics possession, are fairly evenly
distributed across racial and class groups.[106] Some criminal conduct might
be more likely to translate into an arrest because it occurs in communities
where police have become an established institution of not only social
control but also interpersonal and household control, or because of the
conscious or unconscious biases of police officers shaping their discretion
to make arrests for low-level conduct.[107] Other types of behaviors may be
unequally distributed.[108] Research of a different type would be needed to

apportion the relative contributions of those different factors to the clearly documented concentration of misdemeanor arrests among black, Hispanic, and low-income communities. But in any case, the preceding figures show that the spaces supplying the majority of the arrests flowing into misdemeanorland have high minority populations and are also characterized by social handicaps such as high poverty, unemployment, and low educational attainment. These spatial characteristics attach certain social meanings to these cases and these defendants, which are discussed in the next chapter.

This chapter establishes four points about the changes in the policing regime that brought about New York City's era of mass misdemeanors. First, starting in the early 1990s, the valence of enforcement against low-level offenses changed dramatically as law enforcement and political leaders embraced various tenets of the Broken Windows theory. Therefore, secondly, the police set out to intentionally increase misdemeanor arrests and summonses. Third, the new tactics increased not only the frequency but also the formality of subfelony enforcement. The NYPD expanded the types of arrest and ticketing procedures that allowed for more record keeping in order to classify, track, and monitor people the police encountered for low-level offenses. These records were carefully maintained and shared with other criminal justice agencies, especially courts and prosecutors. Fourth, the publicly expressed motivation behind quality-of-life policing tactics was not to identify and punish the maximum number of low-level offenders because the conduct was inherently and intolerably morally deplorable. Rather, it was to use the tactics to reduce major street crime and to abate certain quality-of-life issues, neither of which necessitates punishing every person identified through these tactics.

The policing changes were intentional and based on an explicit theory that was publicly presented and defended in political, policy, and media venues. However, little attention was paid to what *ought* to happen—much less what did happen—to the people arrested as part of these policies once they were delivered to courts. I argue in the following chapters that the judicial response to these arrests was less the result of planned and purposeful policy design than adaptive emergence of practical strategies adopted by front-line legal actors in the shadow of the intentional policy choices made by the police and local and state governments. The theory of Broken Windows never specified a philosophy of punishment for those accused of low-level offenses, much less demanded brute retributivism or severe sanctions. And the practice of quality-of-life policing populated misdemeanorland with people who presented as uncertain risks as opposed to obvious threats to public safety. The greatest proportion of arrests it generated was of people who had no prior criminal conviction. But, at the same time, space, race, and ethnicity infused the arrests with a special set of meanings that would shape how legal actors would process those arrests. The following chapter describes the aggregate trends in misdemeanorland court dispositions of the arrests since the rise of Broken Windows policing and puts forward a model to make sense of them.

2

Managerial Justice

> From beginning to end, from the police officer who arrests a persistent offender, to the prosecutor who asks for bail, to the judge who imposes sentence, to the probation officer who monitors his or her release, everyone is going to be focusing on the career misdemeanor offenders.
>
> —MAYOR MICHAEL BLOOMBERG[1]

New York City's Broken Windows policing initiative was designed to enhance enforcement against low-level offenses. Because the city offers a boundless supply of targets for such enforcement, it is hardly surprising that these tactics resulted in a steep increase in the number of misdemeanor arrests and summonses. What is surprising, however, is that while misdemeanor arrests dramatically climbed as part of a deliberate law enforcement strategy, the rate of misdemeanor convictions markedly declined. A person arrested for a misdemeanor crime has a *lower* probability of being convicted of a misdemeanor offense in the era of Broken Windows policing than he or she did in the decade prior to its rise. This outcome is particularly surprising given that one of the most common allegations levied at lower criminal courts by higher courts and academic commentators is that of "assembly-line justice"—mechanically churning out convictions and imposing one-size-fits-all punishments.

If lower criminal courts are not systematically convicting and formally punishing the people hauled into court as part of quality-of-life policing tactics, what are they doing? Was the sweeping, coordinated law enforcement effort just described stymied or thwarted by criminal court actors who processed the flood of misdemeanor cases? This chapter argues that the declining rate of criminal conviction and formal punishment appears less puzzling if we understand that the city's lower criminal courts are not adhering to the model of criminal law administration taught in law schools and represented in popular culture: that the role of court actors is to adjudicate the factual guilt or innocence of a defendant in a particular case. Rather, the way in which court actors are using their official powers is best understood by formulating a different model of criminal law administration, one that uses the assorted tools of substantive law and procedure to sort and assess the general rule-abiding propensities of defendants.

The traditional understanding of the function of courts in the social control project of criminal law is that they sit between the proscriptions of substantive criminal law and the hard treatment of punishment to employ the criminal process to select the right people for punishment and to determine the proper punishment. In this model, courts serve a vital sorting function by determining the legal issues pertaining to investigation and arrest and factual questions pertaining to guilt. Prosecutors (or, in rare cases, judges or juries) in criminal courts decide whether it is proper to attach the label "convicted" to a particular defendant. If they do so, the court sends the convicted to some formal punishment site where the real social control action takes place. I call this the *adjudicative model* of criminal law administration.

This model does not capture the operations of criminal law in misdemeanorland.

New York City's Criminal Courts in the era of Broken Windows have largely moved away from the adjudicative model of criminal law administration toward what I call the *managerial model*.[2] Under the managerial model, the practical orientation of criminal court actors and their regular operations are largely organized around the supervision and regulation of the population that flows through misdemeanor courts, often with little attention to questions of law and facts in individual cases. The vision of criminal law's social control role in the managerial model is to sort and regulate people over time. The criminal process is deployed to figure out the rule-abiding propensities of people and to calibrate formal regulation accordingly. This model is at odds with the received wisdom about how lower criminal courts have operated in other times and places.

Assembly-Line Justice in Lower Criminal Courts

Denunciations of assembly-line justice and the "shocking fact-finding deficiencies of lower courts" have been nearly constant over the past century, notwithstanding substantial changes in the procedural and substantive laws under which these courts operate.[3] In the 1930s, Roscoe Pound famously complained of the "bad physical surroundings, the confusion, the want of decorum, the undignified offhand disposition of cases at high speed, the frequent suggestion of something working behind the scenes, which characterize the petty criminal courts in almost all of our cities, [and] create[s] in the minds of observers a general suspicion of the whole process of law enforcement which, no matter how unfounded, gravely prejudices the law."[4]

The substance of this assessment was largely unchanged over the first half of the twentieth century. In 1951, Samuel Dash conducted a study of Chicago's municipal courts to assess their operations twenty years after a major court administration reform effort in Illinois. He concluded that, at least in the administration of misdemeanor cases, "[s]peed and the resulting careless handling of facts remain important evils," and "[a]long with the hurried atmosphere is the confusion which dominates most of the stages of the proceedings."[5] Around that same time, Caleb Foote conducted his well-known study of how Philadelphia's magistrates' courts handled vagrancy-type criminal cases, concluding that "[p]rocedural due process does not penetrate to the world inhabited by the 'bums' of Philadelphia." Foote observed, for example, four defendants who "were tried, found guilty and sentenced in the elapsed time of seventeen seconds from the time that the first man's name was called by the magistrate through the pronouncing of sentence upon the fourth defendant."[6] He noted that many defendants were quickly adjudicated guilty on the basis of appearance, ascribed status, or minimal statements from arresting officers and then rapidly committed to the House of Corrections for a term of months. But he also noted that many others were quickly discharged with orders to leave Philadelphia, to go back to the part of town "where they belonged," or allowed to avoid being processed at all if they could produce evidence of an outbound bus ticket or steady employment.

As Foote noted, even if there had been a more robust process in place, it is not clear that it would have altered the fates of the defendants that he observed. The substantive criminal provisions at play—the penal "law being applied" to most of the cases such as vagrancy or disorderly conduct—was so broad that the legal elements of the offense could not operate as a limiting principle on the exercise of the state's power to punish. Many of the offenses handled in lower criminal courts were status-type offenses such as vagrancy or being a "drunkard" that did not turn on proving that the defendant committed a particular act, but rather was a particular type of person. Others were specific acts of wrongdoing, such as disorderly conduct, but the definition of the act was so expansive or vague that it could mean almost anything in practice.[7] Furthermore, there were few levers for defendants to pull in an attempt to force an unwilling court to undertake a careful factual inquiry into guilt before a judgment was rendered.

Indeed, it was precisely these twin critiques—first, that the most common low-level offenses charged were so broad that there was little fact-finding work for lower courts to do and, second, that defendants had unconscionably little leverage to demand fact-finding work—that led reformers in the next two decades to challenge both vague statutes and sparse procedure. The first of these critiques was that certain criminal statutes, such as vagrancy or drunkardness, criminalized a status as opposed to a specific wrongful act. Therefore, these statutes provided patrol officers with virtually unbridled discretion to make arrests and judges and prosecutors with similarly unbridled discretion to impose convictions and penalties.[8] The second set of critiques was that once defendants were arrested for low-level public order offenses, criminal courts lacked regular procedures to accurately sort the guilty from the merely socially despised.[9] These twin assessments of lower courts were central to the reform movements of the 1960s and 1970s. As Deborah Livingston has argued, the "assembly-line justice meted out in lower criminal courts for offenses like drunkenness, disorderly conduct, vagrancy, gambling, and prostitution . . . was itself one of the surest signs that the criminal sanction was being misapplied."[10]

And those reform movements were largely successful, at least in reaching their immediate goals. Between 1960 and the early 1970s, many "status" offenses were struck down as either unconstitutionally vague or lacking a constitutionally required intentional act and, over much of the same period, the Warren Court's due process revolution unfolded.[11] In the criminal justice domain, this consisted of elaborating a series of procedural rights that the defendant could invoke between accusation and penalty and also limiting the state's use of evidence collected in methods declared unconstitutional. Many of the cases extending rights to state criminal defendants, such as jury trial or appointed counsel, were felony prosecutions.

Scholars and courts continued to worry that assembly-line justice thwarted procedural fairness for misdemeanor defendants.[12] The Supreme

Court even picked up on the assembly line metaphor in the 1972 land-mark case *Argersinger v. Hamlin*, which extended to indigent misdemeanor defendants the right to counsel in cases where jail time is imposed.[13] Reviewing the evidence of how lower courts processed misdemeanor cases, the Court concluded, "There is evidence of the prejudice which results to misdemeanor defendants from this 'assembly-line justice.'"[14] In sum, one of the most widely held understandings about lower criminal courts over the first two-thirds of the twentieth century was that they operated in a rote fashion, mechanically churning out convictions and imposing undifferentiated punishments.

In the late 1970s, Malcolm Feeley undertook what is probably the most famous study of misdemeanor courts at precisely the moment when the extension of procedural rights and the restriction of vague criminal statutes seemed to promise a more procedurally engaged and substantively circumscribed administration of criminal law. Commentators and activists hoped that the new rights and duties (especially the right to counsel when jail time is imposed) and limits on substantive criminal law would force courts to fairly adjudicate guilt and innocence of people accused of specific prohibited acts, as opposed to railroading the despised and disreputable into guilty pleas on vague or broad statutes. But that is not what Feeley saw happening in his extensive study of the lower court in New Haven, Connecticut, in the late 1970s. The motivating puzzle of Feeley's book was why, in the "full bloom" of the due process revolution, had so little changed about the operation of lower courts? Why did so few defendants take advantage of their newly awarded rights to demand a more rigorous process between arrest and penalty?[15]

The answer comes from the fact that the due process rulings did not so much direct legal actors to do something as they imposed a set of costs and constraints on how they did business. They consisted of, for example, the noncompulsory right of a defendant to demand a certain process before a certain determination could be made, or the right to challenge the state's use of evidence at trial if it was obtained in unauthorized ways. For example, *Mapp v. Ohio* held that a defendant could move to exclude evidence obtained by searches and seizures in violation of the Constitution in state criminal trials; *Argersinger v. Hamlin* held that the Sixth Amendment right to counsel in criminal cases extended to petty offenses when a jail sentence is imposed.[16] *Mapp* did not demand that any case involving unconstitutionally obtained evidence be tossed out, nor did it instruct prosecutors to shield their eyes from such evidence; *Argersinger* did not require lower criminal courts to provide attorneys to all misdemeanor defendants. Rather, the decisions changed the strategic incentives of courts, prosecutors, and defendants in negotiating pleas or pursuing trial, in seeking custodial versus noncustodial sentences, and in other discretionary acts. Feeley found that defendants rarely decided to invoke their newly granted rights, and prosecutors rarely sought to use evidence in trial. In fact, few cases even reached the pretrial hearing stage.[17] He found that prosecutors were often satisfied with conditional dismissals or noncustodial sentences that did not activate these new procedural rights and that defendants were willing to accept these early and quick dispositions without attempting to activate their procedural rights.

Feeley argued that most defendants did not invoke their procedural rights or engage in a protracted adversarial process simply because it was very often not in their (at least short-term) interests to do so. He famously concluded, "In essence, the process itself is the punishment." He argued that in the lower criminal courts, procedural costs—in the form of pretrial detention, missed work for court appearances, and attorney's fees—more often than not outweighed the formal sanctions imposed by early and quick case disposition.[18] Thus, despite a significant change in the legal rules structuring lower criminal courts during the due process revolution, the fact that the criminal process was not being used to sort the guilty from the innocent persisted.

Nonetheless, Feeley is one of the few observers of lower criminal courts to challenge the assembly-line metaphor as inapt. He argued that it failed to capture the complicated—although rapid and informal—calculus that went into misdemeanor case disposition. By his account, defendants did not forgo trials and due process rights merely because they were too burdensome. He argued that defendants declined them *in exchange* for a disposition proposed by prosecutors and ratified by judges.[19] Therefore, the second-level question raised by his findings was: What were those legal actors getting out of the exchange?

Feeley argued that most prosecutors and judges were concerned with what he termed *substantive justice*: delivering some appropriate response given a quick, yet individualized, assessment of the alleged criminal act and the defendant as a person. The very fact that defendants had experienced costly impositions and burdens was interpreted as a conclusion—indeed as a *punishment*—sufficient to satisfy the immediate goals of the frontline actors administering criminal justice. Key to his explanation was that, in that particular space and time, these subfelony cases were "universally labeled as 'garbage,' 'junk,' 'trash,' 'crap,' penny ante,' and the like" by the legal actors processing the cases.[20] So legal actors deemed the costs of being arrested and processed through court for such "junk" cases as, at least in the majority of the cases, an adequate punishment.

The institutional and political landscape of misdemeanor courts has shifted considerably in the more than thirty years since Feeley's study. These changes include a decidedly "punitive turn" in the overall tenor of criminal law and several waves of drug wars.[21] More recently, misdemeanor arrests are presented as the linchpin of urban crime control strategies in the order-maintenance policing models that have swept the nation. These tactics have flooded urban courts with low-level cases and enhanced the local political import of misdemeanor case processing. The valence of these cases is thus radically transformed from the time of Feeley's study: no longer mere "junk," they are held out as the key to maintaining order and safety in public spaces within the policing models pioneered in New York City. Furthermore, the relative costs of the dispositions have changed for misdemeanor defendants. The depth and quantity of collateral consequences flowing from a criminal conviction have in fact increased. This is partially because of the widespread availability of data on criminal records and partially because of a proliferation of rules and statutes tying determinations about housing, student loans, child custody, immigration, and employment to criminal justice contacts or convictions.[22]

Perhaps because of these changes, a small but growing number of legal scholars are directing renewed attention to misdemeanor courts, and the assembly-line justice critique has reemerged.[23] The metaphor, although intuitively appealing, conflates distinct features of misdemeanor processing.[24] One understanding of the assembly-line justice trope is that misdemeanor courts do not make significant differentiations in their legal treatment of defendants. In this view, everyone who is arrested pursuant to low-level policing priorities is mechanically convicted and punished, even if the sanctions are minor. Prosecutors indiscriminately charge all cases and reflexively seek convictions while courts robotically convict and issue standard sentences without regard to the individual characteristics of cases or defendants. This version understands the assembly line as a rushed and inaccurate method of adjudication, one that fails to take the requisite time to do the job of properly sorting cases based on legal and factual questions.

A second understanding maintains that the administration of justice in misdemeanor courts is rapid and impressionistic, but not random or mechanical. Misdemeanor courts do not perfunctorily and automatically impose convictions. They *do* distinguish among defendants and cases. However, the process by which cases are decided involves relatively little time or other judicial resources that the traditional adjudicative model defines as the mechanisms by which factual questions of guilt are determined. By this account, lower criminal courts do engage some mechanisms of differentiation, but the grounds for making distinctions among cases and defendants involve some logic distinct from sorting based on legal and factual merits.

Given the multiple meanings that could attach to the assembly-line metaphor, it might be best to abandon it altogether and look for a concept that better captures the operations and social control logic of these criminal courts. But before I proffer a replacement, the following section presents some descriptive data about disposition trends to discredit the mechanistic version of the assembly-line model in New York City's Criminal Court.

What Happens When Broken Windows Arrests Arrive in Misdemeanorland?

Because it is generally assumed that lower criminal courts produce assembly-line justice, we would expect that mass misdemeanor arrests would yield mass misdemeanor convictions or at least a roughly proportionate increase in convictions and punishments. We might even expect an increase in convictions proportionate to arrests if court actors interpreted the Broken Windows imperative to take low-level offenses seriously on the street to mean that courts ought to take them seriously with convictions and jail sentences.

The following figures show that neither increased convictions nor jail sentences came to pass. In many ways, the New York City Broken Windows experiment embarrasses our traditional understanding of how an expansion of criminal enforcement should work: as misdemeanor arrests climbed dramatically as part of an intentional law enforcement strategy, the rate of criminal convictions fell sharply. And as the police and elected officials talked about getting tough on low-level offenders, the proportion of low-level arrests that resulted in a jail sentence also fell.

Figure 2.1 shows the total number of misdemeanor dispositions each year from 1980 to 2015.[25] It also shows the number of each of the top three general disposition types: dismissal, noncriminal violation/infraction convictions, and misdemeanor criminal convictions. Even as the total number of misdemeanor case dispositions more than doubled between the start of the Broken Windows policing in 1993 and its height in 2011 (an increase

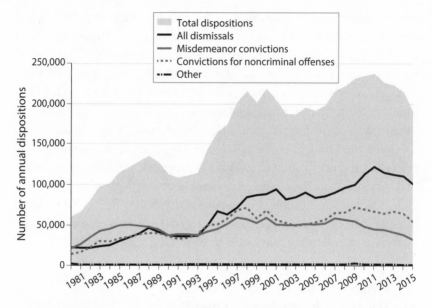

FIGURE 2.1. Select Disposition Types from Misdemeanor Arrests, New York City, 1980–2015
Notes: Data from DCJS. "Convictions for noncriminal offenses" include adult and youthful offender convictions for noncriminal and unknown offenses. "Other" dispositions include those covered by another case, acquittals, and dispositions marked "other" by DCJS.

of 107 percent), the number of misdemeanor convictions went up by only about 22 percent. The absolute number of dismissal dispositions increased by over 233 percent between 1993 and 2011.

Figure 2.2 shows more dramatically that the significant increase in misdemeanor arrests did not translate into proportionate convictions. The misdemeanor justice system converted an ever-decreasing share of misdemeanor case filings into criminal convictions as the total volume of cases increased. In 1985, approximately 44 percent of misdemeanor arrests terminated in misdemeanor criminal convictions, while in 1993 the percentage was 33 percent, and it has not exceeded 20 percent since 2010. In 1993, about 31 percent of misdemeanor dispositions resulted in some form of dismissal, but that figure has been above 50 percent since 2010.

In 2015, almost 54 percent of the misdemeanor cases in New York City's Criminal Court resulted in some form of dismissal. This disposition category masks significant variation in the type of dismissal and exactly what that form of dismissal means for defendants' experiences and the ability of courts and prosecutors to track or engage defendants. The chapters in part 2 discuss at length exactly how these various dispositions work and

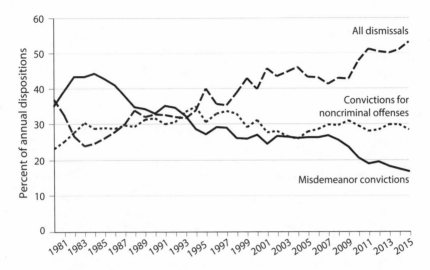

FIGURE 2.2. Select Disposition Types as a Percentage of Total Annual Misdemeanor Case Dispositions, New York City, 1980–2015
Notes: Data from DCJS. "Convictions for noncriminal offenses" include adult and youthful offender convictions for noncriminal and unknown offenses.

how they operate to allow prosecutors and the court to trace, classify, and engage defendants over time, even without imposing a formal probation or jail sentence. But for the purposes of this discussion, it suffices to say that in recent years almost *half* of all dispositions were some form of dismissal, such as declining to prosecute, an adjournment in contemplation of dismissal, or a speedy trial dismissal. The other half of misdemeanor dispositions are convictions, the vast majority of which are noncriminal. Since 2010, the percentage of misdemeanor arrests that terminated in such a conviction has hovered between 28 and 30 percent (which is 58–62 percent of misdemeanor arrests terminating in any conviction), almost all convictions for disorderly conduct. Over that same time period, no more than 19.5 percent of misdemeanor cases have terminated in a criminal conviction for a misdemeanor.

Although the number of people in New York City jails briefly went up after the rise of Broken Windows policing, the proportion of misdemeanor cases that result in a prospective jail sentence has declined in a fairly steady fashion since the late 1980s. Figure 2.3 tracks the sentences imposed (as well as nonconvictions) as a proportion of yearly misdemeanor case dispositions. The most common sentence to be imposed from a misdemeanor arrest is noncustodial, namely, a conditional discharge. The conditions imposed

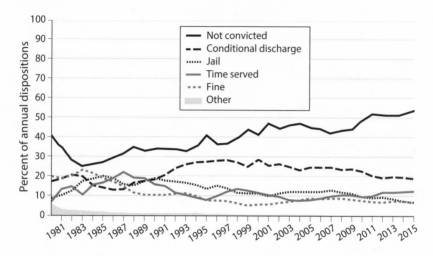

FIGURE 2.3. Sentence Types as a Percentage of Total Annual Misdemeanor Case Dispositions, New York City, 1980–2015
Notes: Data from DCJS. "Other" sentences include probation, jail and probation, prison, and others unspecified by DCJS.

are various—community service, abiding by an order of protection, or just avoiding police contact. A "time served" sentence means that the person is sentenced to the time that he or she already spent in custody before entering the plea (or, in very rare cases, before being convicted at trial). The time is usually the twenty to thirty hours spent in custody between arrest and arraignment, but it could also be lengthier if the defendant was held in on bail prior to the plea. Figure 2.3 also shows that at the highest point, in the mid-1980s, only about 20 percent of misdemeanor cases terminated in a prospective jail sentence; that number fell and then rose again to about the same level in the early 1990s. After that time, there were some periods when jail sentences as a percentage of misdemeanor case dispositions increased briefly, but the general trend over the past twenty-five years has been a decrease. Since 2010, no more than 10 percent of misdemeanor cases resulted in a prospective jail sentence, and in 2015, that number was closer to 7 percent.

Figure 2.4 shows that misdemeanor jail sentences on average are fairly short. In recent years, just under half of the jail sentences imposed were ten days or shorter; between 70 and 85 percent were thirty days or shorter. The actual time spent in custody is less than the imposed sentences; absent serious infractions, the defendant serves two-thirds of the term.[26]

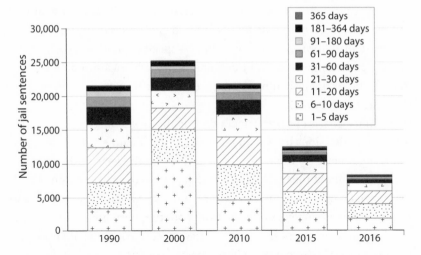

FIGURE 2.4. Range of Jail Sentences Imposed from Misdemeanor Arrests, New York City, Select Years, 1990–2016
Notes: Data from DCJS. Patterned (vs. solid) fill indicates jail sentences of thirty days or shorter.

The Adjudicative and the Managerial Model

In place of the assembly-line metaphor, I propose that we think of misdemeanor courts as instantiating a particular model of criminal law administration—what I call the *managerial* model—which is distinct from the conventional *adjudicative* model. Such models are ideal types.[27] They are analytic tools precisely because they distill the extreme complexity and concrete variety of everyday activity in courts, allowing us to discern the patterns of action, the overarching practical orientations of actors to their tasks, and the logic of the regular functions performed by the courts. Furthermore, we can ask to what extent traces of each model are present in different criminal law venues and what factors enhance or suppress the intensity of the model's manifestation in those venues.

Under the conventional adjudicative model, the animating task organizing the work of criminal justice actors is to determine whether the defendant in fact committed the criminal act of which she is accused. The defining features of this model are twofold: (1) the courts embracing it are primarily engaged in *adjudication*, and (2) the subject of this adjudication is guilt and punishment premised on a finding of guilt. The word "adjudication" cannot be used to describe just any activity in which courts engage to decide *what to do* with a case or defendant. To be useful, the term must pick out a particular set of decisional activities. I draw on Lon Fuller's renowned notion of adjudication to give precision to this concept as a particular "form of social ordering," a specific mode of "reaching decisions, of settling disputes, of defining men's relations to one another," that can be distinguished from others (such as contracts or elections) on the basis of certain formal traits.[28]

Criminal courts operating under the adjudicative model employ a mode of reaching decisions by way of receiving and evaluating "proofs and reasoned arguments" in the form of evidence about the facts of the case and information about the legal standards that pertain to an accusation of guilt for a specific offense. The relevant principles by which those proofs and arguments are evaluated are drawn from both the substantive criminal law, which defines what acts and mental states constitute specific offenses, and from the law of criminal procedure, which lays out permissible forms of police conduct for gathering evidence and approved methods for conducting the inquiry and assessment. For criminal courts to fit the adjudicative model, they must approach the decision about *what to do* with a case by eliciting and evaluating facts about the conduct alleged by the arrest and then applying legal rules that define prohibited conduct with approved procedures for establishing a violation thereof. However, this model does not require that courts adjudicate the question of guilt and punishment according to any specific type of formal or adversarial process.

Much of the activity of lower criminal court actors in misdemeanorland does not fit this conception of adjudication. Of course, few living organizations track their formal plans, as scholars have long noted.[29] And some have argued that we should no longer be surprised by the finding that real courts are "uncourtlike," if by "courtlike" we mean an independent adjudicator presiding over adversarial proceedings using established legal rules to find or dispel guilt or liability for one party.[30] But misdemeanor courts, for reasons that are detailed in the following chapter, are uncourtlike in very particular ways and for very particular reasons. It is helpful to have a model by which we can see their uncourtlikeness not as a deviation from an ideal, but as a patterned method of operation that follows a discernable logic.

The central issue that concerns misdemeanorland prosecutors and judges, in the preponderance of cases, is not the factual dispute before them: Did the defendant commit the act alleged on the criminal complaint? Rather, the driving question—the one that determines how prosecutors and judges will deal with the case—is about the type of person before them: Is this defendant a manageable person? The weight of evidence indicating whether the person committed the crime may enter into how that question is answered. But it is not the central inquiry. Thus, the principle that is brought to bear on the proofs and arguments presented by the defendant is, in practice, not aligned with the official question of the court as an adjudicative institution. It is not necessarily a determination of guilt or innocence, but rather a notion of governability and responsibility applied to an administratively generated assessment of a person.

The managerial logic has both a forward- and a backward-looking component. The future-oriented component appears to fit the model of what Feeley and Simon call "new penology" or "actuarial justice," defined as being "concerned with techniques to identify, classify, and manage groupings sorted by dangerousness."[31] Court actors in misdemeanorland rely on the record-keeping practices of the police, courts, and other partner agencies to construct a profile of the defendant based on the type, number, and outcomes of his or her prior criminal justice encounters. They consult that profile to determine which defendants they believe pose a risk for future offending and what type of offending. This, in turn, grounds their assessment of who is in need of closer monitoring or perhaps formal sanctioning. An orientation toward risk management, however, does not mean the actors operate with scientifically constructed, group-based, or validated actuarial tools.[32] Prosecutors, judges, and defense attorneys largely invoke folk heuristics indigenous to misdemeanorland about how to judge defendant risk, but their predictive capacities are rarely, if ever, exogenously validated in any systematic way. Some of these rules of thumb have an intuitive appeal as predictors of future criminal offending, such as getting rearrested during the trial period of a conditional dismissal; others seem more like personal affronts to the dignity or status of officials, such as showing up late to court or missing community service days. But both are treated as meaningful performances in this site without any systematic inquiry into what precisely these nonconforming behaviors predict or indicate. Therefore, although a managerial approach to criminal law administration entails a logic of risk management, court actors do not necessarily adopt and refine their techniques based on an external confirmation that their actions achieved any specific outcomes or objectives.

Yet, the managerial model cannot be reduced to a forward-looking risk management approach. It also incorporates a substantive principle of proportionality, which is that people do not necessarily *deserve* to be punished for every incident of low-level offending. Thus, the backward-looking component of the managerial model has a moral logic. It relies on marks of prior encounters and information collected from the procedural hassles of engagement with the court or performances discharged over the course of this engagement to form a composite of who the offender *is* and therefore what he or she deserves. Judges and prosecutors frequently say that one of the most important determinants of case disposition is the record of a defendant's prior criminal justice encounters, such as arrests, bench warrants, compliance with court mandates, and other indications of governability, including steady employment, family, or housing connection. Information from court records about the defendant's prior contacts informs a moral judgment about who the defendant is and how much penal engagement he deserves, whether it is in the form of tracking, testing, or punishing.

So, for example, if a person with no prior convictions is arrested for petit larceny, the prosecutor might offer a conditional dismissal not merely because she believes the defendant is not a serious risk to society, but also because she believes the defendant does not deserve to be marked with a criminal record for life on account of a single act of shoplifting. Alexis, a longtime supervisor in Borough A's district attorney's office, explained the moral logic behind offering a conditional dismissal: "We're evaluating the case and saying that based on the fact that maybe you have never been arrested before, or based on the fact that you are young and it's your first offense, or based on the facts of this case—this is a case that is worth us dismissing it, *if* you don't get in trouble again. That's all we're saying. That you are entitled to that clean slate. That we're going to give the opportunity to have this clean slate, despite this case."

The practice of offering conditional dismissals in so many cases is not about weak evidence, bad police stops or searches, or a position of unconditional mercy. Rather, it illustrates a sentiment that it is morally unnecessary for the heavy machinery of criminal justice to come down on every defendant accused of a low-level offense if the person can prove himself to be responsible and governable. The prosecutor simply declines to adjudicate the allegations of the crime altogether. Instead, she decides to do something else: track the defendant to see if he gets in trouble again soon. This approach to processing cases in misdemeanorland is what I call the managerial model.

Before proceeding, it is helpful to further specify what, precisely, the managerial and adjudicative models are and are not models *of*, that is, which aspects of the courts they are designed to illuminate. These are neither operational models (about who has power in the adjudication process) nor normative models (about what values ought to animate the adjudication process). First, the adjudicative and managerial models can be distinguished from operational models of who adjudicates guilt and punishment or how they do so. Courts can vary along operational dimensions without necessarily moving away from the adjudicative model of criminal law administration. There is near consensus that felony courts, and in particular federal felony courts, do not operate according to "the idealized model of adversary justice described in the textbooks."[33] Gerard Lynch, for example, proposes that we currently have an "inquisitorial" process in which "the locus of adjudication" is not the court through formal judicial proceedings but rather prosecutorial decision making.[34] Rachel Barkow conceptualizes the criminal justice system as an "administrative system" where the prosecutor's office—unlike what is permissible in administrative law—combines adjudicative and enforcement functions.[35] The claim, hardly disputable given the small fraction of criminal cases determined at trial, is that judges and juries do not play the primary role determining guilt and punishment in our criminal justice system. That role is played by prosecutors.

These operational accounts are about the party in the criminal process with the effective power to adjudicate the facts of guilt and the appropriate punishment (the prosecutor); the site where these decisions are made (the prosecutor's office); and the process by which the decision comes to be made (not through formal hearings and independent fact finding, but by relying on law enforcement records with some, perhaps minimal, input from the defense). I do not take any of these accounts to argue that the quasi-administrative/quasi-inquisitorial operations in felony courts means that they are no longer serving an adjudicatory function.[36] Courts could be characterized as adjudicative under many different modes of making adjudicative decisions, including full-fledged formal adversarial, quasi-inquisitorial, or administrative settings. This is because the adjudicative model focuses on the central animating task of the courts, not the location or relative power of agents in carrying out that task. Of course, the managerial model is also made possible by the near structural impossibility of a formal adversarial operational model in lower criminal courts. Nevertheless, the difference between the adjudicative and managerial model cannot be reduced to the difference between formal adversarial proceedings and pervasive plea bargaining. To do so would misapprehend much of what is distinctive about how social control is exercised in misdemeanorland.

Second, the adjudicative and managerial models are not normative models of what the criminal process *ought* to look like given a set of foundational values. Two of the best-known normative models are Herbert

Packer's "due process model" and "crime control model." Packer conceptualized his models as two idealized accounts of the criminal process that "give operational content to . . . conflicting schemes of values" about both "what the criminal law is good for" and how it ought to be used as a scheme of social control. The crime control model holds "repression of criminal conduct . . . [as] the most important function to be performed by the criminal process," whereas the due process model holds respect for individuals and restraint of state power from its natural authoritarian tendencies as its cardinal values.[37]

Both models hold that what criminal courts *ought to do* is adjudicate guilt and impose appropriate punishment. However, the models diverge on how to organize the criminal process to promote other competing values consistent with this function. Packer describes the crime control model as an "assembly line," in contrast to the "obstacle course" of the due process model, because the former holds that the efficient and uniform routine screening functions performed by actors at various phases of the criminal process, from arrest to sentence, produce reliable findings of guilt.[38] The crime control model rests on what Packer calls the "presumption of guilt," a faith in the accuracy and reliability of summary administrative fact-finding that makes it unobjectionable to graduate defendants from one stage of the criminal process to the next. This model nonetheless purports that "what the criminal law is good for" is punishing the maximum number of people for charges of which they are most likely guilty.[39]

The managerial model is not a normative model of how the criminal process ought to be organized given certain designated values. It functionally does, however, put forward a vision of "what the criminal law is good for" that animates lower criminal court actors, a vision different from both of Packer's models. The managerial model holds that "what the criminal law is good for" is to provide an opportunity to sort and test people hauled in from policing of so-called disorderly places, to see over time what sort of people they are, and to keep records on them in the process.

Three Defining Features of the Managerial Model

The managerial model I propose has three defining features. First, it operates on the basis of what I call (borrowing and altering Packer's phrase) a presumption of the need for social control over the population brought to misdemeanorland. Second, criminal court actors use various penal techniques beyond conviction and custodial control to exercise varying degrees of social control over defendants. Third, those penal techniques are combined in greater strength with each successive recorded encounter or failure to live up to the procedural and performance demands of misdemeanorland.

PRESUMPTION OF NEED FOR SOCIAL CONTROL

The first defining feature of the managerial model is a presumption among most legal actors of a need for social control. This presumption is conceptually and practically distinct from a factual presumption of guilt.[40] The assumption, to draw again on Packer's apt description, is "not . . . a thing" or a "rule of law," but rather "a complex of attitudes, a mood," that pervades the legal field, a dispositional basis to the logic of action that takes place there. In Packer's crime control model, the presumption of guilt serves as the factual justification for pushing defendants deeper into the criminal process without multiple stops at time-consuming evidence-testing stations, because the value to be promoted is punishing the maximum number of (probable) lawbreakers. The motivating assumption is that the fact-finding done by the police to justify the arrests and by the prosecutor's office to justify the charges are an efficient and reliable way of identifying lawbreakers.

But managerial courts often purposefully produce dispositions at odds with fact-finding reported in administrative records of police and prosecutors, especially with respect to early encounters. The enabling assumption in managerial courts is that once someone is brought into the system, the person is presumed to be eligible for some level of social control, even if the precise level is yet to be determined. The assumption is practically and conceptually distinct from the assumption of guilt—it is ultimately a broader and more enabling assumption. The presumption of need for social control justifies some social control action even if legal actors remain under significant uncertainty about the facts of the case at hand, as opposed to justifying punishment *because* a defendant is most likely guilty of an offense. The latter would require actors to affirm subjectively the fact-finding reliability of arrest and charging decisions earlier in the criminal process and rely on that affirmation as the basis for imposing punishment. But the assumption of need for social control can be grounded in prosecutors, defense attorneys, or judges affirmatively embracing administrative indications of guilt, remaining agnostic about factual guilt, or not even considering it prior to embarking on a course of action. As a practical matter, the assumption of need for social control obviates the requirement to establish according to any specific standard "what happened in this case" prior to deciding "what I should do with this case."

Many prosecutors, judges—and, to some extent, even defense attorneys—may actually assume the majority of defendants hauled into misdemeanorland are factually guilty of the offenses of which they are accused. It is also possible—and I would venture to guess more likely— that these actors might say most defendants are probably guilty most of the time only if they were explicitly asked to reflect on the question. This is an important distinction. The daily work of most of these actors is organized in such a fashion that they rarely face a practical imperative to truly confront and definitively settle the question of factual guilt. Court actors and defendants often come to a disposition with little discussion of evidence and law. Nonetheless, the fact that many legal actors would say upon reflection that they believe most defendants are probably guilty most of the time might be what enables them to inhabit the managerial model. Legal actors have been taught that the criminal law is an adjudica- tive system and have been socialized into adversarial roles. Yet, they find that their daily work does not consist of providing adjudication through formal adversarial roles. A post hoc affirmation of probable guilt may be what allows legal actors to fashion an acceptable subjective account of their actions.

Another reason I insist on the distinction between the assumption of need for social control and assumption of guilt is that the latter does not shed much explanatory light on what I hope to illuminate: the established, recurring patterns of dispositions in lower courts and the logic by which criminal law is deployed to produce those patterns.[41] Court actors may assume that most defendants are probably guilty most of the time, but they do not try to convict and formally punish most defendants most of the time. The assumption of need for social control sheds some explanatory light on observed disposition patterns. It is the drive to figure out what level of social control is appropriate for a particular defendant—not the desire to figure out what level of punishment is appropriate for a given offense—that animates the practices in this field, and it is the manifest rule-abiding pro- pensity of defendants—not the strength of evidence indicative of guilt—that determines disposition practices in most misdemeanor cases.

Furthermore, the presumption of need for social control spans the larger field of criminal justice in which misdemeanorland is embedded, because it animates the very policing policies that gave rise to the influx of subfelony cases, which, in turn, define the practical conditions facing court actors. The policing experiment dedicated to increasing low-level enforcement had two stated aims: to indirectly bring down serious street crime and to abate designated quality-of-life conditions. The law enforcement tactics were never conceived to punish the maximum number of people who engage in low-level criminal conduct. Instead, they were meant to sort people in designated "disorderly" places to see who was engaged in more serious offending and who could be dissuaded from engaging in certain types of "disorder."[42] Thus, the basis of the presumption of need for social control is not tied to the adjudicative project of sorting out which people violated specific legal rules. It extends to the entire category of people who are targeted by Broken Windows policing. The grounds for assuming the need for social control over defendants in misdemeanorland mirrors the grounds for extending the policing tactics over the people and spaces where they are concentrated. Thus, the populations that are most heavily targeted by Broken Windows policing, namely, low-income men of color, become a population with an ongoing burden to prove governability in lower criminal courts.

VARIED PENAL TECHNIQUES

The second defining feature of the managerial model is the use of varied combinations of penal techniques by legal actors to seek a measure of social control over the population netted into misdemeanorland. I classify those into three categories of techniques: *marking, procedural hassle,* and *performance.* Each category is a conceptual schema, as opposed to an objectively identifiable discrete type of action or type of motivation. Just as one can define a spoon by what it is used for (a spoon is a small eating instrument used to get liquidish things into one's mouth), these techniques are defined by how criminal court actors use legal rules and procedural tools available to them to exercise social control in this field.[43]

Part 2 is dedicated to exploring how these techniques are used and experienced. Here I briefly introduce them to explain how they are used to foster social control ends in the managerial model: to sort and test people over time, to determine the capacity of defendants to be certain types of people, and to see if they appear to be governable in various domains of social life. Sorting, testing, and monitoring are—more often than not—the point of the encounter, as opposed to the means of assessing guilt or imposing formal punishment.

Marking involves the generation of official records about a person's criminal justice contacts and behaviors. Many of the marks in misdemeanorland are temporary and conditional, often by explicit design of legal actors. Yet, even temporary marks have a host of significant effects in different arenas, especially for later criminal justice encounters. For example, in New York City, one of the most common outcomes of a misdemeanor arrest in recent years is an adjournment in contemplation of dismissal, or ACD, which means the case is technically adjourned for some period of time (usually six or twelve months) and then dismissed and sealed if the defendant is not rearrested. Prosecutors and judges agree to such a disposition in tens of thousands of cases each year at the very first court appearance, irrespective of the strength of evidence in the particular case. This disposition does not mark a person as guilty or innocent during the adjournment period, but it does allow the court system to keep track of later arrests and ratchet up social control measures if the person fails to prove governability.

Procedural hassle entails all of the burdens attendant on complying with the demands of legal proceedings—the degradation of arrest and police custody, the stress and frequency of court appearances, and the opportunity costs of lost work and other social responsibilities to make court appearances or to comply with court orders. These experiences are something more than a set of inconvenient burdens that dissuade defendants from pushing the adjudicative route, or an informal means by which judges and prosecutors punish defendants. Although procedural hassles can be both costly outlays that structure strategic decisions and informal instruments of punishment, they are also a set of active productive tools in the ongoing relationship of social control that lower courts have with defendant populations.

Defendants do not merely withstand the procedural hassles of misdemeanorland; they are evaluated on how they do so by legal actors who decide what to do with the defendant's case. The penal technique of performance can encompass a wide range of activities—from in-patient drug treatment to sitting quietly in court waiting for the case to be called. The unifying logic behind disparate performance activities is evaluating *how* a defendant has executed the act. The assessment of performance seeks normalization but does not involve constant supervision and retraining. Instead it involves irregular commands with sanctions for noncompliance.

These penal techniques are oriented toward the goal of social control by sorting (the one-time errant citizen from incorrigible misdemeanant or budding serious offender), testing (the capacity to respond to official directives or to be deterred by official penalties), and regulating (enforcing norms of order through rewards and sanctions). But the practices are modified to the limited resources of misdemeanorland, relying on technologies of audit, cursory assessment, and moderated sanction. These techniques can extend over significant populations without long-term removal, total control, or permanent marking.

The patterns of dispositions and regular practices in misdemeanorland are produced by a variety of actors, often working at cross-purposes—sometimes in ways intended in an adversarial system, sometimes as a result of poor institutional design—only loosely coordinated or sharing a substantive goal or normative understanding about the ends and value of the criminal justice encounter. Sometimes criminal justice actors intentionally rely on marking, procedural hassle, and performance when conviction is either too costly or legally difficult to secure, or when they believe that conviction or a custodial sanction is inappropriate or unjust. In other instances, these techniques emerge as the unintentional upshot of the uncertainty and transaction costs inherent in the criminal process.

In any case, criminal justice actors usually understand that marking, procedural hassle, or performance result directly from their choices and actions. This is true even if the proximate motivation behind the action was not to use the technique as a means of sorting, testing, or regulating. At various strategic points, actors make use of these techniques and look to information about the defendant and his behavior that was revealed through a prior imposition of these techniques to obtain a measure of regulation over the defendant or to update what they think is an appropriate formal disposition.

For example, consider a misdemeanor assault case where the complaining witness will not cooperate with the prosecution and both the prosecutor and judge assume that the case will eventually be dismissed on speedy trial grounds. The prosecutor might not intend to test a defendant's capacity for rule-following by demanding multiple court appearances when she refuses to dismiss the case at an early court appearance, even when she believes at that time that the case is headed toward dismissal. However, she is cognizant of the fact that the defendant will have to make many court appearances and comply with an order of protection during the pendency of the case until it is dismissed. And, she will likely calibrate what she deems an appropriate level of social control for this defendant to any information that is revealed about the defendant's capacity for rule following based on how he performs under the procedural hassle of making court appearances and complying with the order of protection. A similar opportunity to mark, test, and regulate is present when a defendant refuses a standard plea offer at arraignment and decides to fight her case. If that defendant is rearrested during the open case, the prosecutor on the second case will look to information in court records about how the defendant performed during the open matter when making relevant decisions, whether or not the first prosecutor intended to induce the defendant to reveal such information about herself for the later prosecutor's use.

In sum, penal techniques emerge from a mix of motives, intents, and strategic actions. Marking, procedural hassle, or performance are defined by how legal actors can use a range of records, rules, and processes to social control ends, irrespective of whether they wanted to establish a way to sort, test, and regulate defendants through their choices. To say, for example, that social control in misdemeanorland involves a technique of marking means that prosecutors and judges, on the one hand, might seek a particular disposition with the intent of only short-term marking of the defendant's criminal record, or, on the other, they might simply make a decision that has the short-term effect of marking the defendant's criminal record because other actors (the defendant and defense attorney) are taking other strategic actions to limit the marking. Different intentions might produce similar marking outcomes. To say that social control in misdemeanorland involves a technique of procedural hassle is to say that while the burdens imposed on defendants from multiple case adjournments may reflect poor court administration, they actually constitute a familiar and indeed useful tool in the ongoing project of social control that actors in the system intentionally use and upon which they rely.[44] And, to identify performance as an operative technique in misdemeanorland means that opportunities to observe a defendant's propensity to adhere to the demands of the case processing or to follow other official instructions are alternatively intentionally sought and opportunistically appropriated as an index of responsibility.

ADDITIVE IMPERATIVE

The third defining feature of the managerial model is the deployment of the penal techniques identified above in ascending strengths as defendants have more frequent contact with misdemeanorland or fail to conform to its demands—what I term the "additive imperative." The understanding is that, absent mitigating circumstances, a defendant should be subjected to more marking, procedural hassle, or performance for each subsequent encounter or failure to successfully discharge some requirement of the current encounter. Courts *do not* merely ratify the arrest decisions of the police by stacking progressively more onerous sanctions on each successive arrest. Rather, courts are sites where defendants are actively tested and evaluated, where criminal justice actors commensurate and trade off different types of penal techniques in the process.[45]

Consider, for example, the use of the adjournment in contemplation of dismissal. Many early encounters in misdemeanorland do not involve a conviction or formal punishment. In fact, the standard offer in most DA's offices on many types of first-arrest cases is an ACD, sometimes with community service or some short "program," such as introduction to drug treatment or an anti-shoplifting class. The court is not merely ratifying the assessment of a police officer that a particular defendant broke the law by demanding a guilty plea and imposing punishment. Instead, the judge and prosecutor are agreeing to temporarily mark the defendant and see if he or she can avoid arrest or perform other court mandates to their satisfaction. An explanation of the ACD disposition from the Court of Appeals (New York State's highest court) elegantly lays out the logic of marking and testing that early granting of the ACD offers to courts: "[It is a] means of disposing of relatively minor charges on a 'nonmerits adjudicatory basis.' . . . Provided that the defendant, the prosecutor and the court agree, this procedural path makes it possible for such charges—often family or neighbor related and usually involving an individual facing his or her initial encounter with the criminal justice system—to be kept in a state of suspense for a period of six months, *during which the subject's habitual behavior pattern can be tested by time.*"[46]

If the defendant fails to show improvement in his or her "habitual behavior pattern," such as by being rearrested or not performing the assigned program or community service, then the offer on the next case will involve more onerous conditions, or the prosecutor and judge will reopen the current case and impose more conditions. Thus, marking, procedural hassle, or performance are added either for later rearrests or for failure to adequately withstand procedural inconveniences or to perform successfully.

Prosecutors discuss the additive imperative in a variety of ways, but when I explicitly asked them about how they formed offers, each one consistently expressed the same logic: that the quantum of penal burdens must increase with subsequent encounters or observed failures to perform responsibly. Stacy, one of the top deputies in the DA's office, explained that she tells her assistant district attorneys to ask two questions when a case comes in: "Can I prove it?" and "Has he done it before?" She explained, "We look at the crime first and second who did the crime." Jill, another supervisor in the DA's office, said, "We try to build on prior cases." Samira remarked that whenever she sees an ACD on the rap sheet, even one that should have been sealed but was not because of some administrative error (which is surprisingly common), she "knows not to offer the ACD again." She continued, "You are not making an offer just on a charge, you are making an offer on the person, on the record that person has. You don't say, 'Oh well, this is just theft of services,' because if this is his one hundredth theft of services, then he is sentenced on that fact."[47] Al, another longtime prosecutor said, "Our offers are progressive; first the ACD, then the violation, then the misdemeanor, etc. etc., etc." Ryan, another supervising ADA with over two decades of experience explained, "We do progressive pleas; we think everyone deserves one bite at the apple. An ACD is a dismissal, but one way to phrase it is it involves a six-month probationary period." A former district attorney of Borough A explained the central importance of a prior record in the disposition process for subfelony cases as follows: "I think that—by and large—the misdemeanors, the violations, are driven by priors. If you've got someone who spends their career committing misdemeanors, I no longer consider that a small problem. That someone has got to have some incarceration."

Penal burdens will also increase along one dimension or another if the defendant does not conform to the procedural demands of case processing, such as coming back to court on time, or fails to successfully execute a performance, such as complying with court-mandated programs. For example, another common disposition in misdemeanorland is a plea to a noncriminal violation, usually "disorderly conduct," and what is called a conditional discharge. A violation is a less serious mark because it is not permanently recorded on a person's rap sheet and it does not trigger a host of collateral consequences that result from many criminal convictions, such as license suspension.[48] The conditional discharge allows the prosecutor or judge to set conditions that the defendant must fulfill to get the violation disposition. Conditions might include attending a class or program, doing community service, abiding by an order of protection, or avoiding police contact. If he or she fails at those conditions, the court can resentence the defendant to up to fifteen days in jail or allow the defendant to re-plead to a misdemeanor criminal conviction. Judge Kato explained that violations with conditional discharge dispositions had the value of allowing prosecutors and courts to monitor defendants for right behavior and avoid marking them with a permanent criminal record if they successfully performed:

> Another good thing with a plea like that [to a disorderly conduct violation], too, is it's known as a conditional discharge. And part of the conditional discharge is that the defendant has to promise on the record to live a law-abiding life and not be arrested for twelve months, or otherwise he could face the fifteen days' jail. So I like that kind of plea. You're getting community service out of the person. You're getting a promise on the court record, with the pain of possibly facing jail in this case. If you stay out of trouble for twelve months. At the same time you're not giving the defendant a criminal conviction, and you're not taking away driving privileges.

With the above understanding of the managerial model in mind, the next section offers evidence from my individual-level data to show that this model captures the current operations of New York's lower criminal courts better than the traditional adjudicative or the assembly-line models.

Evidence of the Managerial Model from Misdemeanorland Cohorts, 1980–2010

The policing changes collected under the Broken Windows banner yielded a significant increase in the total number of people brought into misdemeanorland who had no prior criminal convictions at the time of arrest and a significant increase in the proportion of misdemeanor arrests that did not terminate in a criminal conviction. Given these two trends, we might ask: Were the courts processing misdemeanor cases differently, or were they processing different types of misdemeanor cases? I hypothesize that as the lower criminal courts were flooded with cases from Broken Windows policing, they drifted toward a managerial model. Many of these new entrants were summarily offered standard nonconviction dispositions that allowed the courts to test and monitor them for limited periods of time. This would be consistent with the presumption of need for social control and a desire to mark and test defendants instead of imposing punishment for factual guilt. If this is the case, we should see different misdemeanor disposition patterns for people without prior convictions before and after the Broken Windows era.

The expansion in misdemeanor arrests of people without prior criminal convictions is reflected in the growth in the MJACD cohort size, from about 1,500 in 1980–81 to almost 40,000 in 2000–2001 and almost 34,000 in 2010–11, which percentagewise substantially exceeded the population growth in the city over the period.[49] I can exploit the fact that the individual-level data for the MJACD group track all later arrests and dispositions of people who come under observation from an initiating *dismissal* disposition to look at the arrest outcomes for people with no criminal records in different historical periods. To have a comparable amount of observed time at risk for each cohort pair before and after the rise of Broken Windows, I limit the analysis to just the 1980–81 and 1985–86 cohorts to represent the period before the courts were flooded with these arrests, and I then compare their experiences with those of the 2000–2001 and 2005–6 cohorts.[50]

The following analysis counts the disposition outcome of every arrest that occurred within five years after the initiating MJACD for the two pairs of cohorts before (1980–81 and 1985–86) and after (2000–2001 and 2005–6) the Broken Windows era. I limited the analysis to the arrests experienced when members of these cohorts had no prior criminal convictions to see how apparent new entrants to misdemeanorland were treated on average in the two periods. I also compare the felony arrest outcomes of the same cohort members to see if any differences in misdemeanor disposition patterns are limited to misdemeanorland, or if these same people also have systematically different outcomes in felonyland. If the difference in disposition patterns pre– and post–Broken Windows is due to a difference in the types of defendants entering misdemeanorland reflected in court practices, then this difference should also show up in differences between the two periods in the dispositions from the cohort members' felony arrests.

Figure 2.5 presents the results as bars that sum to 100 percent, meaning that the differently shaded segments show the proportions of misdemeanor or felony arrests for each cohort pair that terminated in a nonconviction disposition, a violation conviction, a misdemeanor conviction, or a felony conviction.[51] The figure shows a striking difference before and after the Broken Windows era in the pattern of misdemeanor dispositions. Of the misdemeanor arrests experienced within five years after the initiating MJACD when the person still had no criminal convictions on his or her record, approximately 27 percent resulted in a nonconviction disposition for the 1980–81 and 1985–86 cohorts compared to 45 percent for the 2000–2001 and 2005–6 cohorts. More than 30 percent of the misdemeanor arrests experienced by the 1980–81 and 1985–86 cohorts within

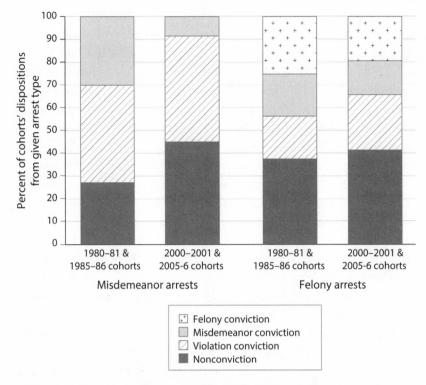

FIGURE 2.5. Five-Year Disposition Patterns from Misdemeanor and Felony Arrests of Persons with No Prior Convictions in the 1980/1985 and 2000/2005 MJACD Cohorts
Note: Individual-level data from DCJS; author's own calculations.

five years after the initiating MJACD when the person still had no criminal convictions on his or her record terminated in a misdemeanor criminal conviction, compared with less than 9 percent for the 2000–2001 and 2005–6 cohorts.

The evidence from the MJACD groups shows that people without criminal records arrested for misdemeanor crimes *before* the Broken Windows era were much *more* likely to have their cases result in a criminal conviction, while people without prior convictions arrested for misdemeanor crimes *after* the Broken Windows era were much *less* likely to have their cases result in a criminal conviction. The change in disposition patterns seems to suggest that lower criminal courts were not just processing a higher volume of defendants without prior criminal records; they were actually processing those people differently.

Nonetheless, it is very hard to tell from administrative data if people without criminal convictions arrested for misdemeanor crimes in the pre–Broken Windows cohorts were systematically different from those in the post–Broken Windows cohorts. One way to look for signs of average differences between cohorts is to see if these same groups also had different disposition patterns from felony arrests during the same five years after the initiating MJACD. The second set of bars in figure 2.5 represents the dispositions from the felony arrests that anyone in the cohort pairs experienced within five years after the initiating MJACD, as long as the person had no prior criminal convictions at the time of the felony case disposition. It shows there was a much smaller difference between the 1980–81 and 1985–86 and the 2000–2001 and 2005–6 cohorts in terms of the proportion of felony arrests that terminated either in a nonconviction disposition (37 percent and 41 percent, respectively) or a felony conviction (25 percent and 20 percent, respectively) in comparison to the misdemeanor case outcomes. It appears that the significantly higher rate of dismissals for the post–Broken Windows MJACD cohorts in comparison to the pre–Broken Windows cohorts is confined to misdemeanorland, consistent with the rise of the managerial model during this era.

It is somewhat counterintuitive that in an era when police and public officials declare their allegiance to a policing philosophy that takes enforcement against low-level offending to be the linchpin of maintaining urban order, a lower proportion of misdemeanor arrestees are convicted of the low-level offenses for which they are arrested. My explanation is that legal actors are still doing social control work, but not in the traditional way summarized under the adjudicative model with conviction and formal punishment. Under the managerial model, legal actors do social control work even in the cases that result in a nonconviction disposition by using limited-duration marking, procedural hassle, or performance to sort and monitor defendants en route to eventual legal dismissal of the case.

As discussed at length in chapter 3, prosecutors and judges report that it is currently standard practice to offer conditional dismissals to many people arrested for misdemeanor crimes when the defendant's criminal record reveals no prior convictions. Such a practice embodies various aspects of the managerial model, such as an assumption that the people of misdemeanorland ought to be subject to some monitoring and testing using varied tools, instead of an assumption that they are guilty on the basis of the arrest records and therefore ought to be subject to formal punishment.

Another constitutive aspect of the managerial model is reliance on marks of prior arrests, open cases, convictions, or failures to live up to the demands of misdemeanorland—instead of reliance on legal doctrines and evidentiary inquiries—to determine disposition outcomes in specific cases. This final section uses the individual-level data to document a series of associations for two purposes: first, to show that these associations over many cases and many years are of the type we would expect from the managerial model; and second, to shed some light on the question of transformation between the pre– and post–Broken Windows era where my qualitative data is lacking.

I do this by modeling the probability of what I call "on-par" conviction in different time periods separately for misdemeanor and felony arrests as derived from a series of multinomial logit models.[52] An on-par conviction means a misdemeanor conviction for the misdemeanor arrest models and a felony conviction for the felony arrest models. I model the likelihood of on-par conviction for two separate time periods, pooling all dispositions from 1990 and before and then all dispositions from 2000 and after. The precise division is somewhat arbitrary, but the pre-1991 period is meant to capture a time before the lower courts were flooded with Broken Windows arrests (which had started even by 1991 when Bratton was head of the NYPD Transit Bureau), and the post-2000 period is meant to capture a time when the courts were well entrenched in their post–Broken Windows arrest-processing routines. I display only the predicted probability of on-par conviction over the number of prior on-par convictions, meaning for the misdemeanor model, the relationship between prior misdemeanor convictions and the probability of conviction to a misdemeanor crime from a misdemeanor arrest, and for the felony model, the relationship between prior felony convictions and the probability of conviction to a felony crime from a felony arrest, because those values can be directly compared in a meaningful way.[53] Before proceeding to the results of the analysis, let me briefly discuss the promises and limitations of this quantitative analysis.

The managerial model would predict a positive association between the likelihood of on-par conviction from a misdemeanor arrest and the number of prior convictions. But the adjudicative model could predict the same relationship. The two models diverge on the mechanisms they posit behind such a relationship. Under the managerial model, the association is driven by, first, the fact that prosecutors and judges interpret the mark to signal many things about the defendant's person or deservedness independent of legal and evidentiary strength of the case. They see the mark as evidence that the defendant has used up his "bites at the apple," that he has been given prior chances to perform as governable and failed.

Therefore, prosecutors view the mark itself a reason not to offer a conditional dismissal or violation plea even if, seeing an otherwise similar case, they would have. Second, the association would be driven by the fact that the mark of prior misdemeanor convictions signals something about the defendant's behavioral propensities relevant in a system that doles out rewards and sanctions based on performances of governability. Defendants with prior misdemeanor convictions *can* earn nonconviction dispositions in subsequent misdemeanor arrests, but those who were unable to adequately perform court demands or withstand the procedural burdens of the first arrest are likely to be those who will fail to do so in later arrests. Third, defendants who already bear the mark of a prior conviction are more willing to accept a conviction disposition in comparison with defendants who have no prior conviction, other things being equal, because they are already laboring under the collateral consequences of a criminal conviction.

Note that the mechanisms driving the association in the managerial model are largely about what is called "self-selection," because people select into conviction histories based on what they do, who they are, or other aspects of their person or circumstances. The entire logic of the managerial model is to create and store records about certain defendant behaviors that tend to show ungovernability or risk. Court actors consult marks such as prior police contacts, records of timely court appearances, community service performance, or strength of family or employment ties to help them determine the proper disposition in a case. They are therefore actively looking for signals that the defendant is or is not the type of person who can withstand the ordeals of misdemeanorland or who is generally stable and rule-receptive. Statistical evidence of the managerial model does not require us to purge self-selection; self-selection *is* the very mechanism that drives the association.

The adjudicative model, on the other hand, would also posit a mechanism of self-selection driving the association between prior misdemeanor convictions and on-par misdemeanor conviction, but of a different type. If certain people have either bad luck or poor skill at committing crimes— say, they continually commit crimes in front of police officers—then the adjudicative model predicts that they are likely to get convicted because of the strength of factual evidence. They will continue to get convicted if they consistently demonstrate similar behavior over later arrests. Thus, associations consistent with the adjudicative model might look a lot like associations consistent with the managerial model.

The bad news is that it is nearly impossible to definitively sort out which mechanisms are driving an observed association using only this administrative data. The good news is that there are various ways we can conceptually and methodologically triangulate which model is a better account of the underlying social processes at work in lower criminal courts. The following section starts that process by using the individual-level data to answer five questions. First, does having a higher number of prior misdemeanor convictions at the time of disposition increase the likelihood of conviction to a misdemeanor crime from a misdemeanor arrest, holding other measured characteristics about the defendant and arrest charges constant? Second, has the strength of the relationship between the prior number of misdemeanor convictions and the likelihood of conviction to a misdemeanor crime from a misdemeanor arrest increased between the pre–and post–Broken Windows era, such that having a higher number of misdemeanor convictions is associated with a larger increase in the predicted probability of conviction to a misdemeanor crime from a misdemeanor arrest? Third, are nonconviction marks associated with an increase in the likelihood of an on-par conviction, and has that association changed over time? Fourth, does having a higher number of prior felony convictions at the time of disposition increase the likelihood of conviction to a felony crime from a felony arrest, holding other measured characteristics about the defendant and arrest charges constant? And last, has the strength of the relationship between the number of prior felony convictions and the likelihood of conviction to a felony crime from a felony arrest increased between the pre–and post–Broken Windows era, and if so, was the change in the same direction and of the same magnitude of any changes registered in the misdemeanor models?

Figure 2.6 addresses the first two questions regarding the relationship between prior misdemeanor convictions and likelihood of on-par conviction from a misdemeanor arrest and how that relationship has changed over time. I display the predicted probabilities of on-par conviction assuming different levels of prior misdemeanor convictions at the time of case disposition—from zero to five or more—holding the other predictor variables constant at their mean values from the underlying models because it is impossible to draw meaningful conclusions from naive comparisons of different multinomial logit model coefficients.[54] The dotted line is derived from the misdemeanor model limited to pre-1991 disposition events, and the solid line is the same model limited to post-2000 events.[55]

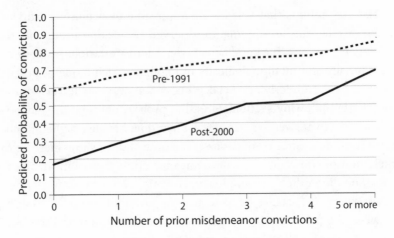

FIGURE 2.6. Pre-1991 vs. Post-2000 Predicted Probability of Conviction to a Misdemeanor Offense from a Misdemeanor Arrest by Prior Conviction, All Other Variables at Means
Note: Individual-level data from DCJS; author's own calculations.

These figures show that there is a positive relationship between the likelihood of misdemeanor conviction and prior misdemeanor convictions, controlling for measured differences about the arrest and arrestee, including prior number of arrests, age, ethnicity or race, and arrest charge. In both time periods, increasing the number of prior misdemeanor convictions is associated with an increase in the probability of conviction to a misdemeanor crime from a misdemeanor arrest, holding all other measured characteristics constant. Nonetheless, predicted probability of conviction to a misdemeanor crime from a misdemeanor arrest is notably *higher* in the pre-1991 period—before the courts were inundated with subfelony cases from the quality-of-life initiative—than in the post-2000 period—after processing high volumes of these cases was routinized into the courts' work. Consistent with figure 2.5, showing that a much lower proportion of the 2000–2001 and 2005–6 MJACD cohorts who lacked prior criminal convictions were criminally convicted from misdemeanor arrests relative to the 1980–81 and 1985–86 cohorts, figure 2.6 shows that the predicted probability of on-par conviction from misdemeanor arrests for those with zero criminal convictions is significantly lower in the post-2000 models, even after controlling for measured differences. In fact, the probability of criminal conviction from a misdemeanor arrest remains higher in absolute terms at every level of defendants' prior misdemeanor convictions in the pre-1991 period than it is post-2000.

However, the slope of the solid line—the rate of increase of predicted probability over increasing numbers of prior convictions—is appreciably steeper for the post-2000 era. Substantively, this means that having an additional prior misdemeanor conviction at the time of disposition for a misdemeanor arrest increased the predicted probability of criminal conviction at a faster rate post-2000 than it did pre-1991, holding constant other measured characteristics of the defendant and the case. Figure 2.6 shows that the mark of a prior misdemeanor conviction was associated with increased probability of conviction in a later misdemeanor arrest even before the Broken Windows era. But after the courts were flooded with these arrests, the association became stronger, such that each subsequent conviction became associated with a larger bump in the predicted probability of misdemeanor conviction.

These results do not prove that the adjudicative model has been thoroughly vanquished from misdemeanorland, nor is it my claim that it has been. This association could be consistent with the adjudicative model if the mechanism driving it is what we could call legal or evidentiary self-selection, that is, the people who get convicted the first time are people who commit crimes in ways that produce strong evidence for the state to use to convict them, and they continue to do so in subsequent arrests. My observations and interviews indicate that lower courts maintain some adjudicative traits such that facts, evidence, and legal doctrines play a role in some case outcomes. I do, nonetheless, contend that the managerial model better describes the vast majority of the operations in New York City's lower criminal courts. One way to try get at which mechanism is driving the results in figure 2.6 is to use the same multinomial logit models to predict the probability of an on-par conviction based on marks that do not reflect an adjudicated determination of the defendant's prior guilt, but do reflect his or her failure to satisfy the demands of the managerial system. One of the few marks I can access from this administrative data set is that of an open case.

The analysis below addresses three questions. Does the presence of an open case on the defendant's rap sheet at the time of disposition increase the predicted probability of conviction to a misdemeanor crime from a misdemeanor arrest, holding other measured differences, including prior arrests, constant? Does the presence of an open case on the defendant's rap sheet at the time of disposition increase the predicted probability of conviction to a felony crime from a felony arrest, holding other measured differences constant? And, finally, has that relationship changed before and

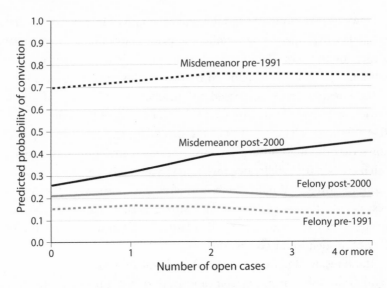

FIGURE 2.7. Pre-1991 vs. Post-2000 Predicted Probability of On-Par Conviction over Number of Open Cases, for Felony and Misdemeanor Arrests
Note: Individual-level data from DCJS; author's own calculations.

after the Broken Windows era? Figure 2.7 shows the predicted probability of an on-par conviction over different values of open cases visible on the defendant's rap sheet at the time of conviction, holding other independent variables at their means (except for number of prior arrests, which was set to six to match the predicted probability calculations in the prior figures).

Figure 2.7 shows that in the pre-1991 period—represented by the dashed lines—there was almost no appreciable relationship between the predicted probability of conviction and the number of open cases in either the misdemeanor or felony models. The post-2000 models are represented by solid lines. The solid gray line shows no appreciable relationship between the predicted probability of on-par conviction from a felony arrest and the number of open cases on the defendant's rap sheet at the time of disposition. However, the solid black line shows there is a significant relationship between the probability of on-par conviction from a misdemeanor arrest and the presence of open cases on the defendant's rap sheet at the time of disposition. These results are consistent with the dominance of the managerial model in the post–Broken Windows era, because even marks that merely reflect unresolved arrests—not necessarily a determination of guilt—were associated with increasing the probability of misdemeanor conviction, but not felony conviction. They are also consistent with the explicit description offered by prosecutors of their offer policies. For example, Farid,

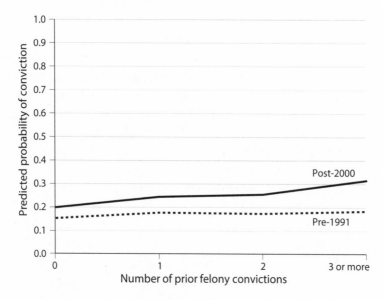

FIGURE 2.8. Pre-1991 vs. Post-2000 Predicted Probability of Conviction to a
Felony Offense from a Felony Arrest by Prior Conviction, All Other Variables
at Means
Note: Individual-level data from DCJS; author's own calculations.

a supervisor in Borough B, explained, "But we do treat people differently
who have prior arrests but no convictions yet. Compared to people who
have convictions. But we also treat them differently than the people who
have no prior arrests at all—it looks like a first arrest to us—from the person
that we know has three open cases in the last month. We're going to be a
little tougher on the person with three open cases in the last month than
we are with the person who just came in off the street for the first time."

A final way I will use the individual-level data to try to disentangle
the various mechanisms driving the observed role of prior convictions in
misdemeanorland is to look at the role of prior convictions in felonyland.
Figure 2.8 was derived from multinomial logit models similar to those
explained at the start of this section, except the observations were limited
to the felony arrests experienced by cohort members during the same
time periods. For the pre-1991 and the post-2000 periods, it displays the
predicted probability of felony conviction from felony arrest over numbers
of prior felony convictions.

The slopes in both time periods are noticeably flatter than those from
the misdemeanor models. In fact, increasing the number of prior felony
convictions does not increase the probability of on-par conviction from a

felony arrest by an appreciable magnitude, holding constant other measured variables. If there is some evidentiary self-selection mechanism driving the observed positive relationship between prior misdemeanor convictions and later misdemeanor convictions, it should show up in both the misdemeanor and felony models unless there is a theoretical reason to believe the same people consistently commit crimes in a manner that creates strong admissible evidence only when engaging in conduct that constitutes offenses of the penal law classified as misdemeanors, but not when engaging in conduct that constitutes offenses of the penal law classified as felonies.

The much steeper slopes in the misdemeanor models are evidence that marks are more important in driving disposition patterns in misdemeanorland than in felonyland, consistent with how prosecutors and judges describe their disposition practices in these two case types. Prosecutors have standard arraignment offers based on the level of prior convictions or arrests for misdemeanor cases. These offers are sometimes memorialized in officewide written policies and sometimes disseminated informally. Pleas are almost never offered at arraignment for felony arrests.[56] A defining aspect of misdemeanorland for defendants is that the process costs of trying to "fight a case" or secure a better plea offer often outweigh the cost of dispositions offered early on. But in felonyland, the specter of a felony conviction and prison time are often sufficient to incentivize legal actors and defendants to engage the heavy machinery of the criminal process. This does not mean that they engage the formal trial adversarial machinery in felonyland or do so fairly or accurately; in fact, the method of adjudication may be carried out exclusively through plea bargaining. The results presented in figures 2.7 and 2.8 are consistent with the theory that legal and factual characteristics about cases, unmeasured in this data, are stronger mechanisms driving felony case dispositions, whereas administrative records easily accessible to court actors are stronger mechanisms driving misdemeanor case disposition.

Prosecutors must decide who "deserves another bite at the apple" and who does not in a very rapid procession of cases, under severe resource constraints (time being the most limited resource, but also investigative capacity) and uncertainty (conflicting accounts of the events from police paperwork, the defendant, and the complainant). In these conditions, the prior record of the defendant becomes one of the most important determinants of the outcome. Even if early marks, such as the ACD, have a limited lifespan, they can be "built upon" if a person is rearrested before the expiration of the mark or does not discharge the conditions attached to the disposition. Certain individuals, namely, young men of color, tend to have many police contacts over short periods because, among other reasons, these policing tactics are highly spatially concentrated. These same individuals often face severe hardships in performing the demands necessary to earn a conditional dismissal. These individuals may use up their bites at the apple quickly. Leslie, a public defender, explained the dynamics of intensive policing practices in certain neighborhoods, combined with the additive logic of the managerial misdemeanor justice system and the incentive structure of lower courts:

> [D]on't forget a person can be stopped and searched fifteen times before they're arrested. And often are. People are getting stopped and searched their whole lives. And then they get an arrest. And then they get an ACD. And then they get a second arrest. And it's a dis con [disorderly conduct]. And then once your fingerprint even reflects contact with the system, you're in a different posture. . . . You get a dis con and then you get a misdemeanor, and then you get jail time. . . . But I think that the dis con resolution is underrated, in terms of the effect that it has on people's lives. Especially for young people getting arrested . . . because a dis con appears on your rap sheet. So you think a dis con is no big deal—it's a violation, it's not a crime. But it appears. And it will turn into a misdemeanor if you are at all at risk at having the increased police contact—which lots of our clients are. So if you have a bullshit arrest, right, but you decide to take a dis con to get it over with. Next time you don't have a bullshit arrest, and you have less truth—less real exclusionary power or whatever. And you can't litigate it, because you're going to lose. You're not going to get the dis con because you took it on your bullshit arrest, which you should have litigated . . . especially for, like I said, people who are getting stopped and searched all the time.
>
>   . . . [T]hat's how a criminal record builds, and that's how the population that's affected by unreasonable and unlawful searches and seizures is getting crushed by it. Because they have no leverage, because they've taken so many pleas. Good pleas, bad pleas. They were guilty, they weren't. The main thing is to get out of jail.

This incisive summary illustrates a number of important features of the managerial model in misdemeanor justice. First, the people targeted by the policing techniques that emerged in the mid-1990s have frequent low-level contacts. Second, there is a range in the formality and intensity of those criminal justice contacts, but the records and marks created by the formal contacts have profound implications for how a person is treated in later encounters. Third, the incentives created by the costs of dispositions relative to the process costs of court proceedings largely structure outcomes. Once a defendant is in a certain posture vis-à-vis the managerial system as a result of his prior marks, it is much harder to push the adjudicative framework, because a new set of constraints surfaces. A person with a criminal record is less likely to be credited as truthful in the abbreviated administrative fact-finding by police, prosecutors, and judges when they do inquire into facts or evidence of the charge. A person with a criminal record also has significantly diminished incentives to withstand process costs because she already has the mark of a conviction, and many defendants would rather take another conviction than stay in jail or come back to court for months to fight the case.

The managerial model as I have proposed it here has three key operational features. First, to borrow Packer's phrase with a slight twist, it is premised on a presumption of need for social control over the population targeted in quality-of-life policing. Second, it employs a toolbox of qualitatively varied penal techniques beyond conviction and carceral sentences for social control purposes. Criminal justice actors deploy those techniques in different combinations toward ends that are not reducible to punishing specific acts of lawbreaking. Third, there is an additive logic in the use of these various penal techniques, meaning that the regular practice in misdemeanor court is that successive criminal justice encounters or failures to live up to court demands is accompanied by an increase along one vector of the three penal techniques: marking, procedural hassle, and performance.

The managerial model explains the pattern of dispositions detailed here because the rules of criminal procedure and criminal law are used as tools for the social regulation of populations over time, as opposed to punishing for individual instances of lawbreaking identified through factual adjudication. Not all criminal court actors subjectively ascribe to a set of values that make maintenance of the managerial model possible, nor do they necessarily describe their choices as seeking managerial ends. The following chapter proposes that to understand how the managerial model came to dominate misdemeanorland, we should look toward understanding the practical constraints facing actors, how patterns of activity emerge from the interaction among them, the structure of constraints they encounter, and the ways actors collectively make sense of the problems they face in their daily affairs.

3

Working in Misdemeanorland

How does it happen at all that formations arise in the human world
that no single human being has intended, and which yet are anything
but cloud formations without stability or structure? . . . It is simple
enough: plans and actions, the emotional and rational impulses of
individual people, constantly interweave in a friendly or hostile way.
*This basic tissue resulting from many single plans and actions of people
can give rise to changes and patterns that no individual person has
planned or created. From this interdependence of people arises an order
sui generis, an order more compelling and stronger than the will and
reason of the individual people composing it.*
—NORBERT ELIAS, *THE CIVILIZING PROCESS*[1]

Criminal law unfolds in a concrete social and material setting. The rules
that constitute criminal law and procedure exercise their real social effect
and force under particular practical circumstances: inside a courthouse
made of old wood and steel; teeming with human bodies, some captive,
some semi-free, almost all wishing to be someplace else; stuffed to the
gills with papers and files that must be moved and processed by people
in jobs with definitive resource constraints and pressing time limitations,
who have homes to return to, where they have families to be cared for and
Netflix to be streamed. The practical circumstances of daily work inside
lower courts are the building blocks by which criminal law and procedure
are constructed as an actually existing social practice for the simple reason

that abstract legal rules come to have specific meanings only in real action settings.[2] These practical circumstances encompass the defining characteristics of the types of cases and defendants processed there; the time and resource constraints under which processing is done; how transactions and relations among actors are organized; and the structure of important decisional moments in the processing of cases.

We can understand why the managerial model flourishes at this time, in this site, only by carefully documenting the practical circumstances facing actors in misdemeanorland. This is because substantive rules of criminal law and formal procedure are not an instruction manual detailing exact tasks necessary to achieve clearly established ends. Rather, substantive and procedural rules are tools provided for the contested and always underspecified endeavor of social control. Frontline actors in organizations must both make sense of *how* they ought to use those tools and *what* exactly—at this time and site—the social control ends of criminal law are in the first place. To assume that criminal justice actors invariably seek conviction and punishment whenever legal rules enable them to do so, or merely *because* legal rules enable them to do so, is to confuse the empirical question of what legal rules mean to real legal actors doing actual work with the abstract question of what legal rules ought to mean "unlocated in any on-going course of activity in the organization in question."[3]

Therefore, this chapter analyzes the practical circumstances of lower criminal courts to explain why increased political and law enforcement emphasis on low-level offenses resulted in lower rates of conviction and formal punishment. This outcome is less puzzling if we suppose legal actors in the field of misdemeanor justice are still doing social control work, but in a different way—one that is captured by the managerial model, where social control is sought by sorting, testing, and regulating over time populations that appear as defendants. The managerial model is not defined by the manner of processing cases—that is, with little formal and adversarial procedures and a lot of plea bargaining. Both misdemeanor and felony courts alike have long handled cases in that manner.[4] The model is defined by the logic that structures the activities of legal actors in the field, by the very principles, goals, and understandings that organize how they approach the decision-making situations they encounter.

The managerial model cannot be found in the formal goals of organizations or the constitutive rules of the court. It was not necessarily the result of deliberate policy initiatives of organizational leaders or purposeful, value-guided change. In fact, I found little evidence that the judges, prosecutors, or defense attorneys in charge of their respective organizations intentionally sought to bring about the managerial model as a wholesale transformation of how lesser crimes would be processed. Nor did I find evidence that, prior to practicing the managerial model, these actors consciously embraced the constitutive elements of the model as a guiding vision for how they ought to process the influx of low-level cases generated by policing changes in the early 1990s. Nonetheless, many of the actions and decisions were purposefully directed at trying to secure *some* measure of social control over defendant populations, and they consciously embraced using the techniques of marking, procedural hassle, or performance—instead of conviction and jail—when the actors deemed those methods a suitable solution to the types of cases they faced. Although these intermediate goals were quite often purposeful and intentional, legal actors did not necessarily intend the larger goal of bringing about a wholesale transformation in the very logic of lower court administration. Frontline legal actors and managers of misdemeanorland's composite organizations had to engage in creative problem solving in the face of the practical circumstances generated by Broken Windows policing, and these adaptations and strategies brought about a new logic of action.

Law from the Ground Up

What is it about the practical circumstances of work and experience in misdemeanorland that leads actors there to use or invoke legal rules in the patterned way that, when viewed systematically, is captured under the managerial model? This question is particularly interesting because adjudication is what criminal courts are, officially, set up to do. The design of our system embodies a prototypical adversarial dispute resolution "triad"—two parties (the prosecution and defense) on opposing sides of an issue (the question of the accused's guilt of a given charge) and neutral third party (a judge or jury) whose job it is to apply preexisting rules to settle the dispute.[5] The penal law lays out what conduct is proscribed—for example, larceny as defined in NY PL § 155. The criminal procedure law lays out how the actors in the system may go about determining whether the defendant has violated the law. For example, New York's Criminal Procedure Law says that "a criminal action is commenced by the filing of an accusatory instrument with a criminal court" (NY CPL § 100.05) and further defines the different types of accusatory instruments that can be filed and precisely what form each must take.

Many classic studies of criminal courts approach the study of courts *from the top down*, assuming that the rules of criminal law and procedure direct legal actors how to act. They take the formal bureaucratic plan or structure of the procedural rules as a starting point from which to explain deviation, informal adaptations, or what institutional sociologists have called the "decoupling" of formal structure from actual practice.[6] But patterns of activity on the ground do not spontaneously and naturally emerge from the formal goals articulated at the top of an organization or from its abstract constitutive rules. The top-down approach to legal action is ill suited to the study of criminal courts (and perhaps to many organizations) for various reasons.[7] First, it is not clear what the formal goals of a criminal court are or where those goals are memorialized. The overarching goals can, at best, only be stated at a fairly high level of abstraction in terms of either a value to guide operations—to "do justice"—or a very general type of activity—to "resolve cases." Second, it is not clear where the top of the organization is located. Courts do not resemble the classic Weberian goal-orientated bureaucratic organization—a hierarchical set of offices rationally ordered to achieve a well-defined goal through explicitly authorized means, where decision making is assigned to offices of circumscribed jurisdiction that confine the exercise of official power, especially at the lower reaches of the organizational hierarchy.[8] Courts are populated by a multiplicity of actors working at cross-purposes. They offer a spatial and functional venue for the operation of several organizations and parties, such as the prosecutor's office; defense attorneys and public defender organizations; judges and judicial administration; court officers, clerks and other court administrative personnel; defendants; complainants; and witnesses. Each has its own goals and interests. Criminal courts are more like an open strategic action *field*—a social and physical space where different individual and organizational actors with their own respective (and sometimes divergent) interests interact recurrently on the basis of widely understood, although often contested, rules and norms.[9]

And finally, it is not clear that the abstract constitutive rules of criminal court set up any clear expectation about *how* the ground-level actors will in fact use them. The rules of criminal law and procedure are not a manual that tell legal actors specifically what to do. These rules are not "indeterminate" in the classic sense of not prescribing a unique outcome in contested cases, leaving room for political, policy, or other interests to fill in the intestacies. They are just not duty-imposing rules.[10]

The rules of criminal procedure are what legal philosopher H.L.A. Hart called "power-conferring" laws, rules that establish a menu of authorized actions or set forth a "manner and form" by which a delegated power must be exercised.[11] Power-conferring rules enact a menu of legal options from which actors can choose as they do their work, such as authorizing a range of sentences by conviction type (time served, fine, conditional discharge, jail sentences authorized for different levels of offenses) or designating the maximum allowable periods of time a prosecutor has to prosecute a case by charge type (ninety days for a Class A misdemeanor, sixty days for a Class B misdemeanor, or thirty days for a violation).[12] Or they set forth a formula for how an action must be performed if an actor wants to realize a certain outcome or to confer a specific status, such as how to file an accusatory instrument that will successfully initiate a case (it must be in the form authorized by NY CPL § 100), or how to convert an accusatory instrument to one upon which a guilty plea can be entered (it must not contain hearsay statements and must conform to the requirements of NY CPL § 100.10). A prosecutor is not instructed by NY CPL § 100 on pain of sanction to file an accusatory instrument for every arrest brought to her by the police. But, if she wants the case to proceed to arraignment, she must file an accusatory instrument in the form designated by that article. The rule designating how to file an accusatory instrument does not set up an expectation about why or under what conditions a prosecutor will do so.

Defendants' procedural rights from state statute or constitutional case law are also best understood as conditional power-conferring rules instead of commands to state actors. Prosecutors and judges have strategic power to trigger or not trigger many of the protections according to their choices. For example, the method by which evidence was gathered by law enforcement is not evaluated against constitutional and statutory standards unless the case actually proceeds to pretrial hearings and the state seeks to introduce the evidence at trial. If the case is resolved by a guilty plea, the defendant has no mechanism to effectuate his Fourth Amendment rights and keep unlawfully gathered evidence from decision makers. The federal constitutional right to a jury trial for a misdemeanor crime is not triggered unless the defendant is being tried for a crime for which imprisonment in excess of six months is authorized.[13] If the prosecution reduces the charges from an A to a B misdemeanor on the day of trial, the defendant has no ability to force adjudication by a group of her peers. Most of the defendant's rights are also waivable, and the prosecutor's charging and offering decisions can make the defendant's "choice" to waive such rights irresistible. In the actual practice of criminal law, defendants' procedural rights are not dictates to state actors; they are resources that the parties can use to impose costs and consequences to courses of action that must be strategically negotiated.

Nor does the content of penal law direct legal actors how to use it. The penal law in the hands of prosecutors is necessarily power-conferring in terms of how they decide to deploy it as a tool of social control, especially in the context of what has been called the current era of "overcriminalization," where much conduct could be charged under any number of many penal law proscriptions. Prosecutors have almost unreviewable power to decline charges, select charges, and essentially decide sentence because of their relative leverage in plea negotiations.[14] Prosecutors are not instructed by NY PL § 70.15 to seek and impose a jail sentence of one year for any conduct that could fit under the description of a Class A misdemeanor crime and three months for any conduct that could fit under the description of a Class B misdemeanor crime. The provision simply authorizes a determinate maximum jail sentence, should they chose to pursue one.[15] Thus, the content of the legal rules that structure misdemeanorland offer little guidance for the empirical regularities of existing criminal courts and criminal punishment.

These considerations lead me to propose that a better approach to understanding why the managerial model flourishes in this place, at this time is to study law *from the ground up*, asking how the practical circumstances of situated legal work lead actors to understand the ends and purposes of the rules of criminal law and procedure. This approach takes as an analytic starting point a strategic action field populated by various actors, many working at cross-purposes, under legal rules that are, by and large, of the power-conferring instead of duty-imposing variety. I invoke the practical circumstances of the field to explain why actors there have developed certain "ends-in-view" for the uses and purposes of criminal law and procedure that, taken together over time, reveal a pattern more consistent with the managerial model than the adjudicatory model.

"Ends-in-view" is a term taken from John Dewey, who argued that we should not model social action as being guided by ultimate ends, something "outside-and-beyond [what is] necessary to induce action and in which it terminates."[16] Rather, he argued, actors deliberate on ends only when they encounter dilemmas that disrupt established means of doing business or that present an impediment to habitual patterns of activity. Such obstruction inspires an assessment of *what* is valued and *how* it might be best to realize that value.[17] Encountering a problem situation motivates an actor to appraise how a course of action (means) relates to desired future states (ends-in-view) and to adjust behavior accordingly in a dialectic fashion.[18] Ends-in-view are provisional plans and aids to understanding that actors develop in the course of creative problem solving in a specific ongoing project, as opposed to predetermined values or well-defined goals that exist prior to the activity of actors.[19]

This theory of action is particularly helpful for the study of ground-level court actors, because the legal rules that structure misdemeanorland do not have meanings that are clear and immediately available to guide and direct them in the concrete dilemmas they encounter in their daily work. Legal actors do not encounter power-conferring rules as directions to realize specific values in prescribed ways. The powers conferred open up a wide variety of creative uses, especially in new or demanding circumstances. We should therefore look at the environment in which these rules are applied to understand why legal actors do or do not use their powers and when defendants do or do not invoke their rights in the patterned ways that we see here.

The Practical Circumstances of Misdemeanorland and the Managerial Model

The following sections explore what it is about the practical circumstances of misdemeanorland that shapes legal actors' "ends-in-view." The first details what and who is processed, because the social *meaning* of the low-level infractions and the defendant profile in this site make possible certain substantive ends-in-view for the criminal justice encounter. The second section details the resource constraints facing actors in the field—the exigent demands, the time, the caseloads—because these tangible limitations specifically shape how actors can pursue their ends-in-view. Prosecutors and judges are not just trying to clear cases so they can get out of court; legal actors must look for a way to manage the practical demands to clear cases in a manner that is compatible with the institutional imperative to do social control work, but calibrated to the precise composition of defendants and cases they face. These sections show how one of the defining features of the managerial model—ratcheting up social control mechanisms based on information displayed in the future as opposed to investigation into the alleged past crime—looks like a particularly rational adaptation to the profile of defendants and the resource constraints that actors face.

The last sections detail the key decisional moments in case processing—arraignments and adjournments—to explain why the choices actors make at those moments end up in the aggregate looking like the managerial model, even if individuals did not act with the intent of conforming to this model.

TYPES OF DEFENDANTS AND TYPES OF CASES

Broken Windows policing in New York City yielded a substantial increase in the absolute number of people flowing through misdemeanorland for relatively minor criminal offenses who had no prior criminal convictions. A supervisor in Borough B recalls his experience in the late 1990s: "So, going back to when I was in Criminal Court, I had 300 to 350 cases at any given time. A lot of it was the low-level stuff; people jumping turnstiles, people possessing marijuana, people possessing crack pipes, people trespassing in buildings. Quality-of-life crimes." The types of defendants and cases that legal actors face in their daily routine are key features of doing work in this field that shape the ends-in-view legal actors form regarding how they can and ought to use criminal law. Misdemeanors are, by definition, less serious than felonies, as they designate offenses for which a jail term of not more than one year is authorized by law.[20] The penal law contains an official, letter-graded offense classification system that determines the level of statutorily authorized penalties and ordinally ranks the seriousness of offense conduct, at least as determined by the legislature.[21] Misdemeanors are classified, from highest to lowest, as A misdemeanors, B misdemeanors, and unclassified misdemeanors.[22] The least serious offenses, such as spitting on the sidewalk or public consumption of alcohol, are classified as infractions or violations.[23] More severe sanctions are authorized by the penal law for A-1 felonies than for B misdemeanors, reflecting the public judgment that crimes such as intentional murder are more harmful and blameworthy than unlawful trespass.

Thus, the legal definition of the types of crimes being processed in misdemeanorland reflects a public judgment that the conduct at issue is categorically less serious than felony crimes. But in order to understand how legal actors approach processing these cases, we should look beyond the legal definition of the crimes to the substantive social meaning of the proscribed behavior. Misdemeanors are classified as criminal offenses, but the actual conduct behind the largest arrest categories over the past two decades does not have the same cultural status as other categories of penal offenses.

Émile Durkheim famously argued that the defining characteristic of penal law was that it addressed acts occupying a particular cultural status in our collective conscious reflecting deep-seated sacred values. He distinguished penal law from what he called restitutory law, such as civil, commercial, procedural, administrative law, not by the level of harmfulness of the acts it proscribes, but by the nature of the collective sentiments that motivate it and that it functions to reinforce. Durkheim believed that "we should not say that an act offends the common consciousness because it is criminal, but that it is criminal because it offends that consciousness." Because violations of criminal law offend "strong, well-defined" shared values, punishment is an expressive act whereby collective sentiments are "conspicuously reinforced." Demanding expiation from the offender is "a sign indicating that the sentiments of the collectivity are still unchanged." Restitutory laws, in contrast, ensure smooth functioning of the division of labor.[24] They are still enforced by the state's coercive power to sanction, but because the rules embodied by restitutory law are about coordination and organization of social tasks, they "do not strike us with the force of sacred entities."[25] As a society, we do not call for expiation when there is an established infraction of restitutory law; we are content with reestablishing the status quo.[26]

Whether or not we accept Durkheim's overarching theory of punishment, his distinction offers an important insight to move beyond juridical definitions in making sense of the actual operations of criminal courts dealing in lesser offenses. Many of the criminal prohibitions addressed in misdemeanor court are acts that straddle the line between restitutory and penal, occupying a liminal status between coordination rules and foundational moral values. Consider, for example, that narcotics possession and marijuana possession together accounted for 25–30 percent of all misdemeanor arrests for much of the past fifteen years.[27] The other largest misdemeanor arrest category is for minor assault, defined as contact that causes an injury less than the "serious physical injury" necessary to make out assault in the second degree, a large number of which are domestic incidents between intimates, prior intimates, or family members.[28] The other top arrest charges in recent years were for theft offenses, most commonly for theft of services (NY PL §165.15, the statute regularly used to prosecute turnstile jumping or otherwise riding on Metropolitan Transportation Authority [MTA] vehicles without proper payment); larceny, most commonly petit larceny (NY PL §155.25, typically shoplifting of any amount under $1,000 worth of goods and most commonly for very minor amounts); and trespass (NY PL §140.10 Criminal Trespass in the third degree or §140.15 Criminal trespass in the second degree, many of which come from the NYPD's enforcement in public housing). The other common arrest categories include minor weapons possession (NY PL §265.01, criminal possession of a weapon in the fourth degree, most commonly for a folding knife charged as a "gravity knife"); misdemeanor driving while intoxicated (NY Vehicle and Traffic Law §1192); and criminal mischief (NY PL § 145). These offenses made up about 87 percent of the misdemeanor arrests in 2014. Most of the conduct at issue in misdemeanorland does not strike legal actors as violations of deeply held, widely shared sacred values that are constitutive of our very social collective. Thus, it should not be surprising that such conduct does not call forth the passionate ritual enactments of punishment that Durkheim theorized reconstituted the norms of cultural cohesion.

Legal actors often reference the substance of the conduct in misdemeanorland to explain why they do not feel an imperative to impose formal punishments on most offenders. For example, Judge Muñoz explained that the type of offense at issue always influences her thought process on setting bail in Criminal Court arraignments: "Do I really want to put someone in jail? Go through the expense at the taxpayer's expense in keeping someone housed for five days or ten days, or until the case is resolved? . . . Do I want to put someone that warranted three times in a period of ten years, sporadically and the charge is for not paying a subway fare? Or for taking a pack of gum, or for taking a pair of earrings in Macy's?"

But the type of offense is always evaluated in light of *who* judges or prosecutors think they have in front of them. A turnstile jumping case where the defendant has an extensive history of violent or property crime convictions is likely to be seen as a troublesome disregard for society's rules, whereas the same crime by a person without a criminal record might be seen as a minor transgression. Discussing his process of taking dispositions at arraignment, Judge Kato explained that he looks first at the charges on the complaint and then the rap sheet: "The other major component [other than the complaint] would be *who* are we dealing with. . . . And that's where that rap sheet of criminal history comes in. You know, are we dealing with an eighteen-year-old and this is the eighteen-year-old's first time through the criminal justice system? Or are we dealing with someone who is fifty and has eighty-seven prior misdemeanor convictions and seven felonies, including five violents? So we look at that. Who and what?"

Thus, legal actors feel more leeway to do *something* other than investigate and formally punish every act, because of the types of cases and types of defendants in misdemeanorland. But they also—both in their actions and reflections—express discomfort about throwing cases out just because the charges are minor or because the defendant has no record. Consider, for example, Judge Marcos's reticence to outright dismiss cases at arraignments. He said that he rarely grants a defense motion to do so on the basis of factual claims, because "there's always two sides to the story," nor on the basis of legal claims, because he does not have time to adequately research the law in the middle of a typical shift when there are 80 to 150 cases to be arraigned. Explaining why he made an exception in the case of a woman arrested for walking between the subway cars (a violation of MTA rules), he noted that in making these determinations he looks both at the type of person and the type of offense:

> I did dismiss one quickly, where the woman said she was trying to get away from someone that was chasing her. And you know what? I could have looked into that a little bit closer before I dismissed it. But what she went through? She had photocopies of the posters that are displayed in the subway station [which stated "No Passing between Cars Except in Emergency"]. I mean, for someone to go through all of that. And they [the prosecution] were offering her an ACD. . . . So I granted the dismissal. . . . [It was] a first arrest, and she was like in her fifties. And those things come into play, too. Those things come heavily into play. Also, a lot of times . . . why . . . a person made one mistake. Why should they even have an ACD on their record? . . . Because you've got to remember the crimes that we're talking about. *We're not talking about crimes of the century.*

In sum, the offense and defendant profile generated by Broken Windows policing is a practical circumstance of doing legal work in misdemeanorland. The particular offenses and defendant profiles authorize a wide range of practical ends-in-view that legal actors could adopt for the uses of criminal law's tools beyond factual adjudication and formal punishment, because the most common cases and defendants these actors process do not trigger deep-seated moral opprobrium inherently deserving of formal punishment.

RESOURCE LIMITATIONS AND CASELOADS

Resource limitations are another key, practical circumstance of legal work in misdemeanorland that shape the ends-in-view legal actors form regarding the uses and purposes of criminal law. As Michael Lipsky has argued, *time* is always one of the most important constraints shaping the actual work of street-level organizational actors.[29] Organizational actors must make determinations on matters with limited information and with limited time to gather more information. For court actors, time constraints are usually felt in the form of caseload pressures. For defendants, caseload pressures are usually felt in the form of delay and neglect.

Changes in low-level police enforcement on the street increased the flow of new cases for Criminal Court arraignment and the volume of cases to be processed in courtrooms. There is a long and contentious debate over how caseloads affect the operations of criminal courts. Some cite heavy caseloads to explain the prevalence of plea bargaining instead of trials; others see them as leading to an excessively administrative mindset, where norms of cooperation overpower norms of conflict, thereby eroding the adversarial roles of defense and prosecuting attorneys.[30] These claims can be criticized for assuming the "goal model" of organizations, presuming that, absent high caseloads, criminal court actors would somehow invariably and naturally fall into adversarial roles and practices as provided for by the formal rules of the criminal procedure law.[31]

I conceptualize caseloads as a factor that leads actors to embrace a forward-looking goal of testing and managing defendants instead of a backward-looking goal of investigating, adjudicating, and attempting to punish every offense. My argument is not that the process was scarified because caseloads made formal adversarial adjudication too expensive as a means to accomplish convictions and punishment, but rather that caseloads shape the very ends-in-view animating legal actors. Given the volume of cases flowing into courts and the lack of matching resources, legal actors must evaluate if conviction and formal punishment are essential for *doing something* satisfactory with the types of cases and defendants they encounter every day.[32] Various other means are available to court actors that make it possible to do something other than adjudication, something that is not so radically different in its function from what criminal law has always been about—social control—by using different tools, or familiar tools in different ways.

Figure 3.1 shows the annual volume of cases arraigned, classified by the top arrest charge.[33] Citywide arraignments increased substantially between 1992 and 2015, driven by nonfelonies. In fact, felony arraignments decreased by almost 50 percent. If the case does not go to final disposition at arraignment—either by being dismissed, conditionally dismissed with an ACD, or with a guilty plea—it is sent to what is called an "all-purpose" part to be "calendared." An all-purpose (AP) part is just the

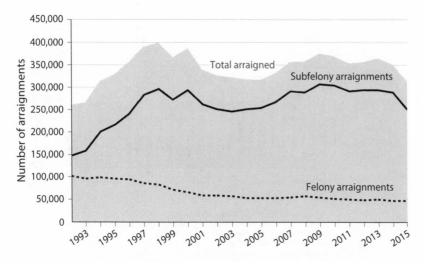

FIGURE 3.1. Total, Felony, and Subfelony Arraignment Volume, New York City, 1992–2015
Note: Data from Criminal Court of the City of New York, Chief Clerk's Office.

courtroom where the case is pending before it is in the posture of being trial ready. This is where the charging document is "converted"—if it was not so deemed at arraignment—from a "complaint" to an "information," meaning all hearsay allegations must be affirmed by first-person affidavits or supporting depositions.[34] This is also where motions requesting pre-trial hearings on the legality of stops, searches, or statements are filed; discovery is exchanged; and pleas are negotiated and entered. When a case is "calendared," it simply means that it is scheduled to be heard on the record before a judge.

Figure 3.2 shows that court resources—measured in terms of the aggregate budget for Criminal Court, the number of judges assigned, and the average number of AP parts open daily—did not keep up with caseload pressures—measured in terms of arraignment volume, total cases calendared in AP parts, and an overall measure of total cases calendared. Neither the number of judges assigned to criminal court nor the number of open all-purpose parts rose substantially during the years that subfelony arraignments or court calendared cases increased. The average number of AP parts operating throughout the city stayed virtually unchanged during most of the Broken Windows era; somewhere between twenty-one and twenty-four criminal courtrooms were typically open each day for processing misdemeanor cases. Figure 3.2 also reports the average number of cases calendared per day in an all-purpose part—the

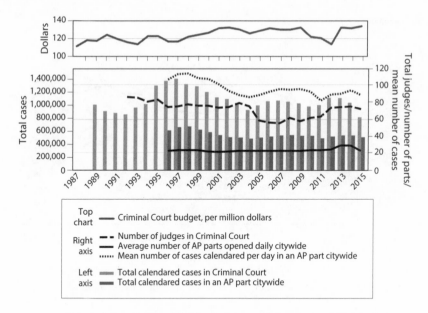

FIGURE 3.2. Criminal Court Budget, Calendared Cases, and Judges Assigned, New York City, 1987–2015

Notes: Calendared cases and judges assigned are from the Criminal Court of the City of New York, Chief Clerk's Office. Budget data are also from the Chief Clerk's Office, specifically Legislative Authorization (Final Budgets) from 1987–88 through 2003–4 and Universal Budget System from 2004–5 to 2012–13. Budget amounts are reported by fiscal year and normalized to 2016 dollars with CPI Inflation Calculator (https://data.bls.gov/cgi-bin/cpicalc.pl). Bronx data are excluded from 1994 until 2012 on citywide measures because of the merger of the Supreme and Criminal Courts during that period; they are included after 2012.

number of cases that judges must hear on an average day. The lowest number was in 2011, with an average of 82 cases per day in AP parts, and the highest was in 1998, with an average of 114 cases per day; over the entire period for which data were available, the average was 96 cases per day per courtroom.

These numbers are experienced as real demands on courtroom actors in their daily work. Judge Muñoz explained the pressure she feels as new cases are added to her docket faster than she can dispose of old ones: "With more judges we would be able to deal with the cases better. It's not so much that we need to devote more time to the cases because, as you said, a lot of the cases are dealt with at arraignments. But there are a large number of cases that come to every single part. And if you dispose of ten cases today and at arraignment you receive twenty—you are not balancing anything. Because you always have that extra. And if I dispose of five cases today, tomorrow I get fifteen, it's going to add to it."

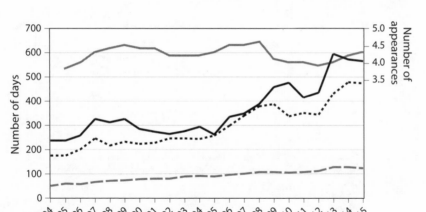

FIGURE 3.3. Criminal Court Time-to-Disposition Measures for Subfelony Cases, New York City, 1994–2015
Notes: Data from Criminal Court of the City of New York, Chief Clerk's Office. For the mean ages of dockets at bench and jury trials, Bronx data are included after October 2012.

As more cases entered criminal court as a result of the new policing regime and additional courtroom resources failed to keep up with demand, backlogs developed that made it more costly for defendants and court actors alike to invoke adjudicative procedures such as hearings and trials. One measure of delay is the average age of a case at the time of disposition, meaning how long cases are typically pending in an all-purpose courtroom if they are not disposed of at arraignment. In 1994, as shown in figure 3.3, the citywide mean age of a case surviving arraignment that terminated in any disposition in one of the courthouses' AP parts was 50.4 days, and by 2013 and 2014 (the first full two years that the Bronx is again included in citywide data), the mean age was 127 days. This means that, on average, defendants whose cases did not terminate at the first court appearance spent about a month and a half with an open case in an all-purpose part at the start of the Broken Windows era, and recently that average his risen to more than four months. Interestingly, the average number of court appearances has not increased dramatically during this era, which means the increase in open case time is largely a function of longer time between adjournments.

Almost all cases go to disposition either at arraignments or in an all-purpose part, because trials are exceedingly rare in misdemeanorland. A case is

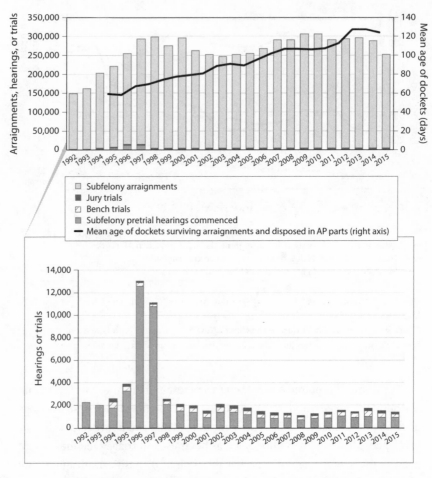

FIGURE 3.4. Criminal Court Subfelony Arraignments, Pretrial Hearings, and Trials with Detail of Subfelony Pretrial Hearings, Bench Trials, and Jury Trials, New York City, 1992–2015
Notes: Data from Criminal Court of the City of New York, Chief Clerk's Office. Trial data are available only after 1993.

"sent out" to a trial part only when both sides declare they are ready and if a courtroom is available to conduct hearings and trials. As figure 3.4 shows, the number of misdemeanor or violation trials did not increase substantially as the influx of subfelony cases increased (measured by annual subfelony arraignments), but the age of dockets that did go to trial—either bench or jury—increased substantially over the Broken Windows era. Pretrial hearings and trials are so rare that they are not perceptible on a figure scaled to the volume of subfelony arraignments.[35] Figure 3.4, therefore, plots these metrics standing alone.

Court delays and backlogs have been covered sporadically in the local media.[36] But even when the issue is not in the public spotlight, many judges say they feel an ongoing concern with keeping down docket numbers and clearing old cases. Caseload pressures create practical dilemmas in the pragmatist sense of presenting actors with problem situations in which they must consider what they want from, or value in, the encounter (for example, is a criminal conviction necessary to impose a measure of social control appropriate to the prosecutor or judge's assessment of the case and defendant?). Problem situations also occasion the creative reworking of conferred powers, a moment when familiar tools can be deployed in new ways (for example, might future monitoring of this defendant be accomplished by simply holding the case open, or is there a reason to insist on a formal probation sentence?).

Judge Henry discussed the change in his practical concerns when he became a judge after being supervisor in the DA's office for many years: "The old joke is that ADAs become more liberal once they are on the bench, and the former defense attorneys become more conservative. It is not about the person, but rather the situation you face." He went on to explain his practice at arraignments with cases that were designated "Operation Spotlight," a citywide initiative (now largely defunct in some boroughs) that targeted persistent misdemeanor recidivists.[37] The DA's policy in Operation Spotlight cases in this borough was to refuse to plea-bargain at arraignments and to recommend a plea to the top charge and a sentence to the maximum statutorily allowed jail time. Judges can, however, make their own sentence offer within the range authorized by the top charge on the docket. Judge Henry said, "When you're an ADA you implement the DA's policy of asking for an A misdemeanor and the year in Operation Spotlight cases [recommending the highest sentence], but when you're judge, you undercut that offer." He discussed the practical necessity of judges' making offers on Operation Spotlight cases as a function of both docket pressures (if the offer is one year, all defendants have an incentive to take everything to trial because they have nothing to lose) and substantive justice (one year in jail is not a fair sentence for petit larceny, even if the defendant did it three times this year). In the context of explaining why he was pressuring his old colleagues at the DA's office to "dispo" old cases that were on his calendar that day, he showed me assorted detailed paperwork about his court part that he regularly consulted, listing the number of open cases, the number of adjournments in each case, and the age of each docket.

The administrative pressures this judge felt precipitated a reconsideration of whether additional judicial resources in the form of further adjournments were necessary to accomplish the social control ends of the regular types of cases pending in his part. Judge Henry explained that when he took over, there were 1,250 pending cases, and he was able to get the number down to about 1,000 by adjourning cases for shorter time periods, pushing dispositions, and forcing old cases out to trial (or threatening to do so in order to get a disposition). But the practice of strongly encouraging dispositions when neither the prosecution nor defense has done significant legal or investigatory work has the obvious implication of reducing if not eliminating the role of judges (and certainly juries) in adjudicating factual or legal questions. Many judges are keenly aware of this diminished, if not transformed, role in the administration of criminal law.

Judge Felix, for example, believes caseload pressures prevent important legal issues raised by quality-of-life enforcement from being settled by courts "[b]ecause the volume is just such that—if all of those cases were litigated, the courts would come to a standstill." He noted that most of the quality-of-life arrests he sees "tend to happen *not* in Brownstone Brooklyn." He went on to recount a story about an arrest of "someone *in* Brownstone Brooklyn, sitting on their stoop, drinking a bottle of beer," about which there was a "pretty big uproar" because the person publicized the story about receiving a summons for drinking on private property. The judge noted "all these other legal and constitutional issues that could have played out there. It could have been a very interesting case, but it wasn't litigated. It just went away, the way all of those cases do." The person was offered and accepted an ACD. There was no pretrial hearing, where the defense attorneys can challenge the legality of the stop, arrest, search, statement, and other police action, which often produces written opinions further clarifying the legal standards for these actions.

Pretrial hearings are exceedingly rare in Criminal Court. Over the past ten years, there have been as few as 741 and never more than 1,077 annual hearings, and over that same period, there were somewhere between approximately 230,000 and 320,000 new subfelony cases arraigned each year.[38] The rules of reasonable stop, search, and seizure will only shape the disposition of arrests if there is a mechanism to trigger evaluation of police practices against those rules, and such mechanisms are rarely invoked in misdemeanorland.

Hearings challenging police action were rare even for marijuana possession arrests, the category that for more than a decade exceeded all other arrest

categories and about which there were constant reports of unlawful stops
and searches. Former Mayor Ed Koch inquired of every DA's office in New
York City in 2012 how many suppression hearings on "open to public view"
marijuana cases they conducted in 2011 and year-to-date 2012. The district
attorneys for the Bronx, Kings, and Queens Counties reported *zero* suppression
hearings; the Manhattan DA replied that his office was "unable" to determine
that figure; and the Richmond County DA (Staten Island) replied that they
conducted eight suppression hearings—over a time period when there were
more than sixty thousand arrests for this offense.[39] An initiative by the Bronx
Defenders even dedicated substantial resources to fifty-four marijuana arrest
cases with the aim of pushing them to hearing and trial. After more than a
year, the organization reported: "Not a single hearing on the constitutionality
of the NYPD's practice was ever completed, due to delays and pressure from
judges to resolve cases before trial, despite the fact that, on average, clients
came to court 5 times over the course of 8 months."[40]

Although caseload pressures can dissuade defendants from challenging the legality of police action, they can also incentivize judges to make
sentencing offers on cases where the prosecutor refuses to reduce the top
arrest charge. Jared, a public defender, talking about how arraignment
judges deal with Operation Spotlight cases, where the prosecutor's policy
is to recommend a plea to the top charge and the maximum allowed jail
time, said, "It's important to understand judges also have an incentive to
make reasonable offers. . . . The DA's office wants to take a position to look
harsh and pin responsibility on the judge. But the judges do not want to
let a case for some petty offense sit on their docket for a long time and
perhaps venture to go to trial. They have an incentive to make reasonable
offers to resolve the cases."

Aggregate caseloads in the entire Criminal Court system are only part
of the practical context of misdemeanor justice. The other part of the story
is the caseloads carried by the individual actors, which affect how they perform their assigned roles. Not only did the funding for the administrative
structure of Criminal Court fail to keep pace with the added volume of
subfelony cases; the funding and capacity of key actors in the system, especially defense attorneys, also failed to keep pace with the added caseloads.

Starting in the mid-1990s, as the mass misdemeanor case rush hit the
courts, New York City's Legal Aid Society lost significant resources to devote to indigent defense because of severe cuts in Mayor Giuliani's budget
for public defender services. Between 1995 and 1996, its appropriation
from the city was decreased 16 percent, from $79 million to $66.4 million,

without any decrease in caseloads.[41] The city began expanding contracts to alternative, non-union indigent defense providers after a strike in 1994, but caseloads continued to be an ongoing issue for all indigent criminal defense organizations.[42] According to 2011 testimony from Steven Banks, the then-chairman of the Legal Aid Society, the organization had about 435 criminal defense attorneys who handle over two hundred thousand cases annually (both misdemeanors and felonies) and who on average have about one hundred open cases, about 30 percent of which are felonies.[43] In 2009, the state passed a measure that would phase in caseload limits for New York City public defenders, capping the load at about seventy at a time. Nonetheless, public defenders argue there is no enforcement mechanism inside the workplace, and many carry loads well above the case cap, especially newer attorneys who primarily handle misdemeanor cases.[44]

Leslie, a supervisor at a criminal defense organization in Borough A, discussed how she believed Broken Windows policing practices led to organizational pressures that displaced traditional goals of criminal law—such as rehabilitation or even retribution—as driving considerations in Criminal Court operations. Rather, she said,

> It's like everyone is totally obsessed with how many people we can process. And to me, it has to do with policing policy; it always starts with the arrest. If you're arresting three hundred people a day . . . then you have all the bodies in the back, so you have to get them out. And then you need lawyers who are willing to get them out for the least amount of money. And it's just a big machine, really. It really has nothing to do with those things [traditional goals of criminal law]. And the majority of the people who are coming through are addicted to drugs or crazy. . . . For misdemeanors practically no one coming through is really violent, except maybe the DV [domestic violence] people—and those cases all get dismissed.

Samantha, a public defender with three years' experience when I met her, said that the most important aspect of good lawyering is "taking enough time to look at every single one of your cases. Taking enough time to read through the paperwork on your cases. To listen to your clients when they do have a story. To listen to what your client wants or needs." She went on to say that she often feels that she cannot do that type of lawyering, given that she was carrying almost one hundred open cases: "But, realistically we don't have that much time. We are constantly running around like crazy people, you know?"

Defense attorneys are responsible for all aspects of case investigation, legal research and writing, staying in touch with clients and their families, and negotiating plea offers with the assigned ADAs.[45] The average day of a defense attorney is spent in court all morning "calendaring cases," which basically means calling the case for thirty to ninety seconds, reporting on progress to the judge and setting a new adjournment date, and, if they have time, talking with the client and family about the status of the case. This means that on most days, their time at the office to work on motions, research legal issues, return phone calls from clients and family, do investigations, and organize files starts at the earliest around 1:00 p.m., when court parts go down for lunch.

Although it has received decidedly less attention, caseloads of prosecutors are also a significant factor in shaping how cases are processed in misdemeanorland.[46] Assistant district attorneys often carry even more cases than public defenders, because ADAs do not personally appear for all calendared adjournments of the case and because their investigative work is largely conducted by the police. New cases are assigned every month either at arraignment shifts or by supervisors. Once a case is assigned to an individual prosecutor, he or she is responsible for many things, including "converting" the charging document by substantiating any hearsay statements with signed supporting depositions or affidavits from those with firsthand knowledge of the alleged criminal act, gathering evidence by talking to the arresting officers or other witnesses, serving relevant notices on the defense, writing and responding to any legal motions, coordinating with witnesses for hearings and trial, and otherwise making sure the case is "ready."

The term "ready" is a term of art. It refers to the various milestones that must be met by the prosecution to advance a criminal prosecution and the time periods allowed to do so under NY CPL § 30.30. Dismissals granted pursuant to this statute are called "30.30 dismissal," or alternatively, it is said in courtroom vernacular that the case "30.30'd." Put very simply, the case must be dismissed if the prosecutor is not "ready" for trial within ninety days for an A misdemeanor, sixty days for a B misdemeanor, or thirty days for a violation.[47]

But, as is always the case in the law, that does not actually mean that cases are dismissed if the prosecutor is not ready for trial within these time periods. Several milestones must be met for the prosecution to declare "ready," and these stop the clock, so calendar time can pass even if 30.30 time is frozen; and, confusingly, the clock can start ticking again if the prosecution declares "not ready" even after having declared "ready."[48] The first milestone is "conversion," meaning all statements of fact in the accusatory instrument must be sworn to by someone with firsthand knowledge of the events.[49] The next is that the prosecution must be "trial ready," which usually means at a minimum having all witnesses available or on standby. There are various excludable adjournments between conversion and potential trial, such as discovery, motions, if the defendant has warranted on the case, unavailability of trial parts, or any "exceptional circumstances," that prosecutors often rely on to give them sufficient calendar time beyond the 30.30 time to prepare their many misdemeanor cases.[50] ADAs' caseloads make it difficult for them to manage all the aspects of their cases required to make them "ready" under the speedy trial times.

Ethnographers of other street-level organizations under severe load pressures have documented that frontline actors come up with what I would call "heuristics of desert," conceptual shortcuts that identify salient features of cases in order to distinguish the neediest cases and to rationalize how services are rationed.[51] Alexis, a former prosecutor, explained that when she started working in the early 2000s, misdemeanor caseloads were at an unmanageable high, necessitating a private ordering scheme: "I may have topped out at four hundred cases at one time. How can you not let them 30.30? . . . What I would do is I would get my manila files and on the tab, if it was important I would write it in red. If it was less important I would write in blue. So it would typically be assaults and domestic violences in red. Blue would be like DUIs. And then everything else was black. And quite frankly, if it was a black, the case often 30.30'd."

Official plea offer policies are one way prosecution offices try to deal with persistent organizational load pressures by giving frontline prosecutors a formal directive regarding acceptable dispositions for defendants with given charges and prior arrest records. As Alexis explained, "[T]here was a big push to get the first-years and second-years to start thinking about misdemeanors a lot more seriously and not let them 30.30. Guidelines became a lot more stringent. . . . In my opinion the guidelines became less suggestions and more mandates. That's just my sense. That's not based upon anything anybody said to me or anything I heard a supervisor say to anybody else. That was just the energy, kind of."

Farid, a supervisor in Borough B's Criminal Court said, "In the past, like 40 to 50 percent of these cases would get dismissed on 30.30. Just speedy trial. Because we couldn't get our shit together on time." He explained that his office has undertaken a number of different reforms, including changing arraignment offer policies, to reduce backlog and to keep 30.30 dismissal numbers low: "[W]hen I was a Criminal Court supervisor, just supervising maybe ten of these misdemeanor assistants—they had caseloads up to four hundred in 2008 or so. . . . That was the height. So they were struggling. . . . It was volume. Also arraignment dispos were not as high. And you can change arraignment dispos, right? Just by changing guidelines." And instituting offer guidelines is precisely what most offices have done, especially for first or second arrest cases, where the defendant does not have any prior criminal conviction. As Farid explained, "We base it on prior history. We try to reward if you've never come through the criminal justice system before. We don't even want you in the criminal justice system. . . . So, we give guidelines for first and second arrests. And for an example, it says if you're charged with petit larceny and it's your first arrest—and it's up to $500 worth of theft, and it's not some organized theft or whatever. Offer an ACD with the Stoplift program or a day of community service. That's the first arrest."

Nonetheless, guidelines do not eliminate all load pressures. Actors still must make discretionary calls about case priority and figure out tricks of the trade to manage their caseloads. This is especially felt among new prosecutors, handling primarily misdemeanors; some say they regularly carry upward of 150 cases at any given time, and some report between 200 and 250 cases at a time. Another way most DAs' offices have addressed the logistical costs of high caseloads is by not requiring prosecutors to personally appear in the courtroom for each of their assigned cases on every court date. The offices regularly staff each courtroom with "line attorneys," who manage the massive box of files that are calendared for the courtroom that day.[52] Caseloads impose a daily regime of mere administrative upkeep, which quickly eats up time and resources available for factual and legal investigation.

Caseloads and court backlogs are a burden legal actors must manage. But they also can be a strategic resource that court actors draw on in their daily work. Both the defense and prosecution talk about court delay being used by their adversary to strategic ends. Alice, a longtime supervisor in the DA's office of Borough A, complained about the "stalling tactics of defense attorneys." She said, "Delay never is in our interest. It never benefits the prosecution; it only benefits the defense. People get worn down, evidence gets stale, the complaining witnesses doesn't like to keep coming in, and people lose interest in pushing the case forward." During a June 2011 group interview with experienced and new ADAs in Borough A, all five attorneys stated the number one thing they would change about misdemeanor court was the availability of trial parts and judges. They wanted "the ability to actually have your case go forward when you're ready." But, given the number of cases ADAs have to manage, it is often difficult to be "ready" within the amount of time allowed under the state's speedy trial statute.

Leticia, like many defense attorneys in Borough A, claimed that the ADAs game the speedy trial clock by relying on the lack of courtrooms where bench or jury trials can be conducted. She explained that the prosecution is only charged against the 30.30 speedy trial clock for the time between the court date they declare "not ready" and the date they request for the next adjournment instead of the real calendar time the case is adjourned. So, for example, if a prosecutor declares, "not ready" on a particular court date and asks the court for a two-week adjournment, but the court adjourns the case for two months, then she will only be charged for two weeks against the speedy trail clock, even though everyone in court that day knows that the case would never actually be calendared for only two weeks after the current court date. Leticia contends that "ADAs announce 'ready' when they are not really ready all the time because they know there are no trial parts," or, "admit they are not ready at a court appearance but then serve and file a supporting deposition (to convert the information) or a certificate of readiness off-calendar." Hence, court congestion is a feature of misdemeanorland that all parties factor into their work strategies.

Whether or not anyone intends to delay case processing, it is the upshot of resource limitations, caseloads, and administrative backlog, or some combination of these factors. And what it means in practice is that defendants come back to court over a much longer period of time than what the speedy trial statute states as the allowable time. Judge Felix marched through a hypothetical misdemeanor case to explain:

> So, pre-readiness time—which is pre-conversion time—it's calendar days. So, you get arraigned on November 1st—until they convert, every single day is counted. Once they convert, let's say they convert on November 15th—they have fifteen days of chargeable time. . . . Now, if it goes to discovery, that time is not chargeable, because you have chargeable time and not-chargeable time.
>
>   And, so it gets adjourned for thirty days for discovery—well, that's thirty days that didn't count. Then, on that court date, the People [the prosecution] serve the discovery, and the case isn't solved by a

plea—then it gets set for a hearing and trial thirty days from that. That time from that court date to the next court date is not chargeable . . . so that's sixty days of nonchargeable—you only have . . . the case has been alive for seventy-five days, and only fifteen are chargeable. On that seventy-fifth day—now it's on to hearings and trial. If the People announce that they are not ready—let's say they request two weeks to get more paperwork, whatever the case may be—but two weeks is Christmas, so we're not going to do it on that day so, we adjourn it to January 5th. So, the time from which they requested—let's say they asked for December 24th—from the day that it was on in November to that day was chargeable, let's just say it was another ten days. And then the time from December 24th to January 5th is not chargeable. Because that time is a result of sort of "court congestion," and the calendar—we can't calendar on the day that they're asking. So, you could see how a case could go on; it could go on *for a year or longer.*

Under these circumstances, one can see how the strategies of provisional marking, procedural hassle, and decoding performances that unfold throughout the course of processing cases emerge as a rational means for achieving a measure of social control over a substantial volume of misdemeanor defendants. Getting to adjudication is quite costly, and in many cases the legal actors might not think it is worth it if they can achieve sorting and testing through other means. The adjudicative model hit a dilemma in the era of Broken Windows, in the sense that fully investigating the factual guilt of each allegation demanded substantial resources and time legal actors increasingly lacked. In addition, faced with a defendant profile heavy on people without extensive criminal records, legal actors had to decide if it would be *worth* their limited resources to adjudicate each defendant's factual guilt when accused of relatively minor crimes.

The practical difficulty of insisting on adjudication of factual and legal disputes of every misdemeanor arrest opened up new and creative uses of old tools and powers for legal actors who had to do something with this flood of cases. For example, the right to insist on a trial is converted into a tool to force prosecutors and judges to make more reasonable offers by imposing caseload costs on them. And the power to file an accusatory instrument and mark the start of a criminal proceeding against a defendant was converted into a tool to monitor future performance of that defendant, even when the legal actors did not intend to secure a conviction or think it would be possible, given the weak evidence. Various formal dispositions

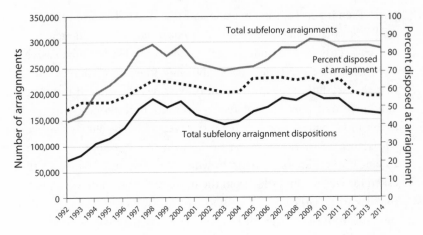

FIGURE 3.5. Number of Misdemeanors, Violations, and Infractions Arraigned and Disposed at Arraignment, New York City, 1992–2014

Note: Data from Criminal Court of the City of New York, Chief Clerk's Office.

(such as the ACD) and uses of procedural rules (such as merely adjourning cases multiple times) allowed criminal court actors to instead provisionally mark the defendant and observe future behavior, and then ratchet-up social control measures if he exhibited signs of being unmanageable. The possibility of exerting social control with tools in the criminal process *other* than formal punishment opened up a new set of justifications and explanations for actions, even if an overarching change in motives did not precede the choice. Immediate practical solutions become institutionalized as actors post hoc make sense of certain strategies in the normative currency of the field. Collective action, "especially highly public actions in a collective context, drive the formation of beliefs, goals, worldviews, and so on, rather than the other way around."[53]

THE PRESSURES OF ARRAIGNMENTS

One of the interesting upshots of the influx of misdemeanor arrests is that it did not significantly increase the number of cases calendared in courtrooms (see fig. 3.2). What did increase substantially was the number of cases disposed of at arraignments. As figure 3.5 shows, a full two-thirds (66 percent) of all misdemeanor, infraction, or violation arrests were disposed of at arraignments at the height of misdemeanor arrests.

What are the practical circumstances under which legal actors are resolving somewhere between 115,000 and 200,000 subfelony cases annually at the very first court appearance, usually within twenty-four hours after arrest? A typical arraignment part may have between one hundred and two hundred cases to be arraigned on a shift that has about six hours of operational court time (day shifts runs from 9:30 a.m. to 5:00 p.m. with about 1.5 hours for lunch; night shifts run from about 5:30 p.m. to 1:00 a.m. with typically about 1.5 hours of downtime for dinner). The essential paperwork in the criminal court file that the prosecution, judge, and defense receive before arraignment is the "complaint," which is the criminal court charging document with the charges and a brief description of the facts that make out the offense, and the defendant's criminal history (NYSID) sheet—informally known as a rap sheet.[54] The prosecution's file also contains additional paperwork, such as the police arrest report, which often contains more details of the occurrence.

Prosecutors typically flip through the paperwork for somewhere between two and five minutes before marking down a plea offer on the front of the file, if an offer is going to be made at arraignment. In the two boroughs where I did most of my fieldwork, the DA's office had standard offers printed on a sheet that listed the office policy for arraignment offers by charge type and number of prior arrests. Since a substantial volume of misdemeanor arrests are of people without prior criminal convictions, the noted offer on the file is usually just the standard offer for that offense type for a "first or second arrest" defendant. In most boroughs, the policy is to not make any plea offers at arraignments on certain types of cases, for example, any case with a complainant (especially domestic violence cases) or driving under the influence. In those cases, the prosecutor will make a bail recommendation note on the file.

Defense attorneys meet their clients for the first time at arraignments, either in a small, caged-in interview room separated by metal grating off the holding cells in the case of arraignments of online arrests or in the hallway in the case of DAT arraignments. Sometimes interviews are very short (if, for example, the attorney tells the client the offer will be a conditional dismissal, and he readily accepts); sometimes interviews last for ten to twenty minutes. Attorneys are focused on getting essential information about the arrest circumstances but, more important, getting information relevant to the bail application, such as employment and family connections, the type of factors relevant to showing what is "necessary to secure [the defendant's] court attendance" at future proceedings.[55] Defense attorneys know that a client is better placed to fight a case successfully if he is not being held at Rikers Island (the largest city jail) on bail.

Attorneys are also focused on speed. The longer all parties take to move arraignments along, the fewer people arraigned during that shift, which means defendants sit in the holding pens longer waiting to see the judge. During a night shift, if defense attorneys do not make it through the arraignment load, those defendants will have to wait another eight hours in custody before seeing a judge. Since the majority of defendants whose cases continue past arraignment are released on their own recognizance (that is, without bail), minimizing the prearraignment detention is a driving concern.

Some arraignment shifts have defense attorneys dedicated to "disposable" misdemeanor cases, which means the cases will likely go to disposition at arraignment. The fact that clerks and paralegals can guess which cases will be disposable simply by looking at the charging documents and rap sheets indicates that something other than facts relating to innocence and guilt are driving this process, and they know that the standard offers will be readily accepted at arraignments. The standard offer for many charge types where a defendant's rap sheet indicates no prior arrests—meaning no open cases and no prior convictions—where the charges do not involve a complainant is an ACD. The New York City Criminal Justice Agency reports that somewhere between 42 and 48 percent of arraignment dispositions in Criminal Court are ACDs.[56] Sometimes the ACD is conditioned upon the defendant's completing a short "program" or a few days of community service.

This arraignment offer policy does not distinguish between cases with strong evidence and cases with weak evidence, and, at this point in the case's life course, it would be very difficult to do so. The only factual information the actors in the system have at arraignments is the limited paperwork in the file described above. Prosecutors and judges rarely attempt to differentiate on the basis of facts at arraignments. Their regular actions demonstrate not a desire to prove guilt and impose punishment accordingly, but rather a desire to figure out if the person is generally governable. Offering conditional dismissals allows the state to mark defendants for a limited amount of time to see whether the person cycles back into the criminal justice system or can instead provide other indications of "responsibility."

An ACD offered at arraignment—usually within twenty-four hours of the arrest—might seem functionally equivalent to declining to prosecute the case. In both instances, the prosecution is not seeking a conviction and formal punishment; the case will eventually be sealed off the rap sheet; and the defendant is not required to come back to court (unless there are conditions attached that require proof of compliance). But, as a supervisor in the DA's office of Borough A explained, the ACD allows the prosecution to do something with the defendants at a first court appearance that relates to the familiar goals of criminal law but does not engage the heavy (and costly) machinery of the adjudicative system:

> I would explain the difference as that when the person takes an ACD, they are basically saying . . . we are basically saying to them—okay, as opposed to prosecuting this case and going through the regular prosecution channels, we are willing to dismiss this case in six months if, within those six months, you don't get rearrested and everything is fine. We are going to dismiss this case and seal it. And that's it. It's like it never happened. Whereas a Decline to Prosecute, we are saying outright we are not prosecuting this case. With an ACD we will prosecute this case, and if you violate the terms of the conviction [i.e., the adjournment in contemplation of dismissal], if you get rearrested, we can bring this case back, and we can try this case. And we *can* prosecute this case. So you could still face penalties for that. Whereas when we decline to prosecute, you're not facing any penalties. There is nothing hanging over your head, so to speak. Whereas with an ACD, technically there is.

Occasionally, the defense and prosecution argue about facts of innocence and guilt at arraignment, and sometimes the facts that emerge from those discussions affect some aspect of the offer. Yet, the imperative to exert some marking from the encounter can rarely if ever be overcome at arraignments, so if the defendant wants to secure outright dismissal, he or she must return to court multiple times to try to do so. As one supervising ADA explained, "There are very few outright dismissals at arraignments; at that point we have our police paperwork and version of events, so we can't just dismiss the case." The following two stories illustrate this dynamic.

In April 2011, in the desk appearance arraignment part, John, a young black man dressed in business casual, was being arraigned on charges of theft of services. The arresting officer accused him of using a special MetroCard that provides discounted rates to people with disabilities for which he was not eligible. Because John had been given a DAT, he had time before arraignment to procure a letter from his employer, a social service agency, stating that one of his job duties included accompanying disabled people on outings. John explained to his defense attorney, who explained to the judge and supervising arraignments ADA, that the day he was arrested he was with a group of disabled people and he was helping them swipe their cards. He insisted that he swiped a regular MetroCard and claimed that the arresting officer must have mistaken which light went off on the turnstile when he went through it because they all went through the turnstile in close succession (different color lights are illuminated for different types of MetroCards, such as student, senior, or disabled-discount cards).

After a brief discussion, the prosecutor agreed to offer a "straight ACD" instead of the initial offer of an ACD with one day of community service. In response to my question about why she would not move for an outright dismissal after seeing the employer's letter indicating the young man did indeed work for an organization supervising disabled people, she explained: "I can tell you that we don't dismiss cases. I mean we do, but we have to have proof that he is not guilty. The offer was an ACD with one day of community service, and he did bring proof that he works for that organization, so I dropped the community service. I still don't have proof that he was not using the disabled card on that day of arrest, so I gave him the benefit of the doubt with the ACD."

Ray, an attorney for the largest public defender organization, recounted the following story about a white man in his mid-thirties who had been arrested for having oxycodone. The arresting officer had recovered it from his pocket, not a prescription container.

The attorney speaking to the client determines and discovers that the client has a prescription for oxycodone. . . . We sent the individual home at 10:00 in the morning to go get the prescription to bring back to show to the court. Because we knew we were going to have to have this argument. And he made it back by about 12:00 in the afternoon. And between 12:00 and 1:00 we argued about the fact that this case should be dismissed. And the district attorney's office . . . determined that—well, the prescription that he was issued for whatever his ailment was for oxycodone was issued in July of 2010 and he was arrested in November of 2010 or December of 2010—and he didn't have it in the bottle. And the prescription bottle says "no refills." . . . In their perspective, because he had a prescription bottle that was issued in July of 2010 that said "no refills" that he must have been doing something illegal with carrying the pill in his pocket. . . .

We argued for an hour until finally the judge decided to—you'll excuse my expression—"grow a set," and just dismiss the case. . . . It took an hour to get past that . . . that alleged perspective from the

DA's office. And as we exited the courthouse—because this is what stuck in my mind—exit the courthouse, the DA was still arguing with me about that case. How it shouldn't have been dismissed because you don't know; he had no refills that were supposed to be issued on that.

In both cases the prosecution was willing to offer an ACD but not to dismiss the case outright. The judge was not willing to do so either in the first case, and finally agreed to do so in the second case after extended argument and after it was clear the prosecution was not willing to do so on its own motion. To state the obvious, I have no way of knowing if the claims of these defendants are true. I did not conduct any more of an investigation than the people in the courthouse that day deciding the fate of those cases at the first court appearance. In this and many other arraignment negotiations, prosecutors and judges are not maximizing punitive response or conviction. They are operating on the assumption of need for social control—seeking, even in the context of limited facts indicative of guilt, *some* ability to track the person for later encounters.

As many prosecutors explain, even if defense attorneys present facts suggestive of factual innocence at arraignments, it is very difficult to verify those facts in a way that makes them feel comfortable straying from standard offers at arraignments. Sticking to guidelines provides a measure of professional insulation. As former prosecutor Alexis said, "I don't think any supervisor in [Borough B] would ever tell an ADA you absolutely have to stick to these guidelines. They would say every case is unique; these are the guidelines. Stray as you see fit. But there is really no time in the space of a thirty-second arraignment call to see how this case is different from any other case."

Prosecutors seek, and judges almost always grant, the same ACD disposition in many other cases where there *is* most likely sufficient evidence to show guilt or where the judge or prosecutor would assume the defendant is factually guilty. In June 2011, a group of six men were brought out in front of the judge on assorted violation charges—disorderly conduct, public open container of alcohol, loud music. The judge is widely known as one of the most punitive judges in Criminal Court in this borough. All of the men had been held in Central Booking since early that morning because they had been picked up on outstanding warrants for not appearing on their summonses at the appointed time. As soon as the court officer finished reading the charges, the judge immediately granted an ACD to all defendants en masse without any discussion. No party to this proceeding had conducted any investigation of the underlying facts, nor did the judge or ADA indicate that he had any reason to disbelieve the police officer's account of the violation. Rather, the ACDs were granted because there is an established practice of agreeing to a conditional dismissal after a period of provisional marking on these types of cases.

Note, all actors can agree on a disposition at arraignments even as they remain far apart on their subjective assessments of facts of the case. John, the young man accused of swiping a disabled-discounted MetroCard, insisted to his attorney he was innocent. The defense attorney urged John to accept the ACD offer, even with one day of community service. John had shown his attorney the employment letter to prove that he worked for the social service agency, but the letter also indicated that he was paid over $30,000 a year in that job, which meant he would not qualify for public defender services. The defense attorney explained to John that he would have to hire a private attorney to come back to fight the case if he wanted to be acquitted at trial and most likely that would take over a year of court appearances. Furthermore, the arresting officer signed a supporting deposition saying he saw the defendant swipe the card that indicated by the lights of the turnstile it was a MetroCard for a disabled person. The attorney warned his client it was far from assured that a judge would believe the defendant over the arresting officer at trial.[57]

John also told his attorney that he had lost his job because of this arrest. His defense attorney explained that, in terms of employment collateral consequences, taking the ACD today was a better bet than fighting the case. If he took the ACD today, it would only appear on the publicly accessible WebCrims database for six months, and it would indicate the case was adjourned in contemplation of dismissal. If he chose to fight the case, it would remain as an "open" matter on the website for the entire period of time it would take to push the case to trial. It is worth noting that the defense attorney was not exaggerating his estimate of how long it would take to fight the case; in that borough, the mean age of cases at trial is well over four hundred days.[58] If the defendant lost at trial, he would then be marked with a permanent criminal record and all the attendant collateral consequences, all for a case where the prosecution offered a conditional dismissal at arraignment. The miniscule trial rates for misdemeanor cases make clear that few defendants find it in their interest to take this chance.

Not all cases disposed of at arraignment terminate in a form of dismissal. The New York City Criminal Justice Agency reports that somewhere between 52 and 55 percent of all Criminal Court arraignment dispositions are guilty pleas.[59] Although arraignment plea offers are based largely on prosecutorial practice and policy, and only minimally on factual or legal investigation, some defense attorneys report the difficulty in trying to convince clients to reject arraignment guilty pleas. Leslie, the supervising public defender from Borough A, said:

> Well, you can say, "give me one chance to do better." . . . You can almost always do better. Sometimes you can't. Sometimes your back is against the wall. But an offer at arraignment is based on what? Nothing. It's based on absolutely zero. It's based on an accusation and the degree to which someone's rap sheet is developed. That's it. It's like taking a plea in a vacuum. It's like taking a plea out of thin air, just because someone said something. You know what I mean? . . . So I get not wanting to come back. And I get that it takes a long time sometimes for justice to prevail or whatever. But the truth is that most of these cases are not what they seem at arraignments. Especially misdemeanors. Sometimes they're worse, sometimes they're better. . . . There is almost never a basis [at arraignments] upon which to make an informed decision to resolve your case—which is really an assessment of the evidence and the accusations, and all of that stuff against you. That's not when you should make a plea determination. Not like, "I want to get out of here, I'm really tired—I just want to go home." . . . I'm sorry; you have to come back to court. Because this happened. You shouldn't have been arrested. Okay. But you did. So if you're going to take a plea, we're going to really think about it and assess what's really going on. But that can wear people down.

Clearly a substantial volume people arrested for misdemeanor crimes in New York City in recent years did not decide, for one reason or another, to come back to take the route Leslie urged. The Criminal Justice Agency reports that somewhere between 62,000 and 92,000 cases *annually* resulted in a guilty plea at the first court appearance between 2010 and 2015.

The consequences of taking an arraignment misdemeanor plea for those with open felony cases can be significant. Anthony, a long-time supervisor in a public defender organization in Borough B, told the following story from an arraignment shift:

> [T]here was a man last night. It broke my heart. It takes a lot to break my heart, because it's been broken so many times. But here is a kid. He's twenty-two. Foster care since the age of fifteen. Completely alone in the world. Finally gets himself involved in a situation where he has a

Supreme Court case [a felony charge—carrying significant prison time that will be suspended if he successfully completes a program with the Fortune Society—on which he had been held in jail on bail pretrial]. It's his second day out [of jail]. And he has to go for the first time to Fortune Society. He's obviously at the beck and call of the shelter system. So he's at the Atlantic Men's Shelter, which is a reasonable distance [from] where Fortune Society is, in Queens Plaza. . . . So the night before . . . he's waiting for his bed assignment at Atlantic Men's Shelter. And lo and behold, oh; we're out of beds. What do they do? They put him on a bus, along with a whole bunch of other men, and they take them to the Bellevue Men's Shelter, at 30th and 1st. He keeps telling them, "I need a MetroCard, I need a MetroCard." . . . They swore to him, "Don't worry about it. You'll get it."

Anyway, the morning comes. He's got to be there at 9:00. No Metro-Card. "Ah, get the fuck out of here, bla-bla-bla." You know, he said they just didn't give a shit. He goes to [subway station] and he says he proceeds for a half-hour begging for people to help him. . . . He finally jumps the turnstile. A cop comes out of nowhere and arrests him. . . . [W]here is this homeless person, who has no income, where is he going to get $2.75 to go back and forth from the shelter, if somebody doesn't give it to him? And what do we do? We put him in jail, where it's $161 the Vera Institute said; $161 a day to house a person at Rikers. Versus $2.75. . . . This kid's whole modus operandi for seven or eight hours was how am I going to get to that program? How am I going to get $2.75? And the result [of pleading at arraignment] for him could have been devastating. Because had he pled guilty last night he would have blown his agreement with the Supreme Court judge. He would have ended up doing years.

It is not infrequent for jail sentences to be imposed at an arraignment plea. Again, the defendant's record largely dictates both the incentive to take the plea at arraignment and the sentence. In October 2010, Rita, a middle-aged black woman with a persistent tremor, was arraigned for petit larceny. Because of her recent arrest history, she was deemed Operation Spotlight. The DA's policy in these cases in this borough was to refuse plea bargaining (at least at arraignments) and recommend a plea to the top charge and a sentence to the maximum statutorily allowed jail time, which in this case was one year in jail on an A misdemeanor.

The defense attorney told the judge that his client had a serious drug addiction, asking the court to consider sending the defendant to the specialized drug treatment part where the case would be dismissed if she successfully completed intensive drug treatment over eight to twelve months. Flipping through her extensive rap sheet, the judge indicated that he would send her to the drug treatment part and instructed his clerk to give her the screening consent form, but he also indicated he would make an offer of thirty days in jail on a plea to the top charge on the docket. Without speaking to her attorney, the defendant quickly answered the judge directly, "I'll take it." After a brief exchange of words with his client, the defense attorney entered her plea, and she was sentenced. When I asked the defense attorney why he did not push his client into the treatment option, he explained, "Look, she had some thirty-plus convictions for shoplifting and other things, and although drug treatment would be best for her, it's hard. You might wait two weeks to six weeks on the inside to be evaluated and placed, and if you just take your straight thirty days, you will be out in three weeks or so (you do two-thirds of city time), and then she will be out with no strings attached. When you get someone who has been through the system so many times, they know what they want."

As this case illustrates, even substantial jail sentences can be imposed at the first court appearance. Defendants with experience in misdemeanorland are often familiar with the various costs and consequences of different dispositions or ways of dealing with a case—seeking a program, fighting the case, taking a plea. In a case like Rita's, the defendant's arrest and bench warrant history made it almost certain the judge would impose bail, and the defendant most certainly could not have made bail. I have no idea if this defendant had any legitimate defense to the charges. But I do know that the structure of incentives Rita faced in this encounter, in combination with her "preference" (for lack of a better term) for jail time over programming, made the offered sentence the most expedient way of resolving the case.

These are practical pressures under which the majority of New York City's Broken Windows arrests are resolved by the criminal courts—in arraignment courtrooms, often packed and rushed, with just the information available from the defendant's court file and arrest paperwork. The legal actors disposing of these cases do not have adjudicative accuracy as their ends-in-view; rather, they are seeking a practical resolution of the case that will satisfy the institutional imperative to *do something* along the lines of social control with the population flowing through misdemeanorland.

THE USES OF ADJOURNMENTS

Although a majority of cases in misdemeanorland are disposed of at arraignments, a significant number—somewhere between 86,000 and 130,000 annually—are adjourned and resolved after arraignments. Those cases pass to the all-purpose parts, where they are added to the dockets of pending cases and at some point terminate in a plea, dismissal, or rarely, *very* rarely, in a bench or jury trial. Cases survive past arraignments for various reasons. The DA's office may have a policy of not making offers at arraignments in certain types of cases, for example, if the case involves a complaining witness or driving while intoxicated. Sometimes the standard arraignment offer would entail significant collateral consequences for the defendant that outweigh the cost of protracted adjudication; for example, pleading to a misdemeanor can have serious immigration consequences or could trigger imprisonment if the defendant is on parole or probation. Some defendants decide to fight the case either because they are claiming innocence or a legally deficient search, seizure, or arrest, or simply because they or the defense attorney thinks the offer made at arraignments is not fair.

Most pleas are to charges below the top arrest charge, which only prosecutors can reduce, and the sentence is almost always well below the most severe authorized penalty. Therefore here, as in other criminal courts, prosecutors operate in a quasi-administrative or quasi-inquisitorial fashion, because they are almost always the final arbiter of guilt and sentence. What this means for defense attorneys is that much of their work in securing pleas on cases that survive arraignment consists of gathering factual information about the case or personal information about the defendant to present to the assigned ADAs and haggling—or sometimes supplicating—for better offers. And if they believe the current offer is unreasonable, usually all they can do is wait: adjourn the case and see what happens.

Explaining her frustration with the DA's policy in Borough A of only offering a disorderly conduct violation plea (a "dis con") in all trespass arrests made in New York City Housing Authority (NYCHA) units, Mary, a long-term public defender, said:

> From a defense attorney's perspective, what can you do? If you have a difficult case, one of the few powers you have is to adjourn the case. Of course you are going to have done your investigation. Of course you are going to research it and see if you can do any motions. And of course you are going to talk to your colleagues about the best way

to present this case to the district attorney's office. But we really have very limited power. We can't enforce a policy, like saying, "Oh, in every trespass case in the projects I am not going to take a plea." The way that they can come in and say, "In every trespass case in the projects we are only going to offer a dis con." That is the difference.

Sometimes plea offers get better with later court appearances. Other times prosecutors threaten higher offers if the arraignment offer is not accepted, putting a serious price on the attempt to fight a case. For example, in Borough B, certain designated "quality-of-life" cases are assigned to a specialized courtroom where the apparent policy is to offer a more punitive offer than the one proposed at arraignment.

The majority of defendants whose cases continue past arraignments are "out," the colloquial term for not being held in jail on bail. Bail is set in about 20 to 25 percent of the misdemeanor cases surviving arraignments in recent years.[60] Because about half of all misdemeanor cases were disposed at arraignments over the past decade, this means bail is only set in somewhere between 8 to 15 percent of all misdemeanor cases. The number of individual misdemeanor arrestees for whom bail is set in a misdemeanor arrest is most likely lower than 8 to 15 percent, because bail is usually set only for individuals with multiple arrests in the year. In the remainder of cases surviving arraignment, defendants are released on their own recognizance, colloquially called "RORed."

Although bail is not statistically common in misdemeanor cases, it is practically determinative of the outcome when it is in play. The overwhelming majority of misdemeanor defendants are indigent, so despite the fact that the average bail amount is about $1,000 or less, only about 10 to 13 percent of defendants in recent years make bail at arraignments, and another 27 to 29 percent make bail after arraignments.[61] Defense attorneys summarize this dynamic as "bail means jail." Defendants are much more likely to take a plea to get out of jail than they would if they were outside fighting the case.[62] This is because the time a defendant would wait inside to push a case to trial is usually much longer than the jail term being offered if he or she agrees to take a plea. Even if there is some legal or factual issue to be litigated, there are strong incentives to take a plea to be released from jail.

For those cases that continue past arraignments, case adjudication is just as rapid and resource-constrained as disposition at arraignment. All-purpose courtrooms processing misdemeanor cases may have between 40 and 150 cases calendared each day, with thousands of open dockets.[63] Although cases are often adjourned for four to six weeks between court appearances if the defendant is "out," both the defense attorney and the prosecution have limited time and resources to devote to additional investigation and litigation in adjourned cases. Furthermore, aside from assault in the third, the largest misdemeanor arrest categories (marijuana possession, drug possession, turnstile jumping) are cases where there is no complaining witness. The facts of these cases largely turn on conflicting accounts between the arresting officer and the defendant.

In March 2012, Trevon was arrested for theft of services, a Class A misdemeanor that carries the potential penalty of one year in jail. He was accused of entering the subway platform without paying. He was given a DAT, and at his arraignment in April, he was offered a plea to disorderly conduct and one day of community service. Trevon told his defense attorney that he had swiped his "unlimited" MetroCard to enter the subway platform on the day of arrest. He also presented the attorney with the "unlimited" MetroCard he purchased from the bookstore of his community college with his student identification. Trevon and his attorney rejected the arraignment offer because Trevon insisted he was innocent of turnstile jumping and because pleading guilty would carry significant collateral consequences for him. The case was sent to a specialized "quality-of-life" courtroom in Borough B, where the standard practice is to make a higher offer than what was offered at arraignments.

At the time of arrest, Trevon had an open felony case for possession of a controlled substance in Borough C. His March arrest occurred during the final stretch of a year-long alternative drug treatment program for which, upon successful completion, his felony case would be dismissed and sealed. The program required him to go to weekly office visits with a social worker, attend group therapy and support sessions twice a week, give urine for a drug test once a week, be in school or employed, and go to monthly court appearances. According to Trevon, he had successfully completed all of these requirements and was slated to "graduate" from the drug treatment program and have his felony case dismissed the week after his new theft of services arrest. However, because of this new arrest, the court in the Borough C would not dismiss the felony case until the theft of services case was resolved. According to Trevon, he was attending a technical college, studying industrial electronics. He successfully graduated from that program weeks after his misdemeanor arrest. However, he we was told that he was ineligible for a position at a local transit authority because he had an open felony matter and was told to return when his felony case had been dismissed and sealed, which was contingent on the misdemeanor being resolved.

The defense attorney representing Trevon in the Borough C subpoenaed the swipe history of Trevon's MetroCard to present to the felony court and also supplied those records to the defense attorney in Borough B, where his arrest occurred. The defense attorney in Borough B also verified the purchase of the unlimited MetroCard with a re-printed receipt from the college bookstore. The felony court in Borough C kept Trevon's felony matter open for an additional five months as he attempted to fight his misdemeanor arrest in Borough B, and he was required to continue his monitoring and program attendance during this time. In October, the felony court in Borough C dismissed the felony matter, finding he had been in substantial compliance and that the new theft of services case was weak in light of the evidence of Trevon's MetroCard swipe history.

The defense attorney in Borough B presented all this evidence to the assistant district attorney assigned to his case two months after his arraignment. He asked her to dismiss the case because it showed that the young man was both in possession of an unlimited MetroCard and also that at the time of arrest he had swiped it at the location in question. More than four months after Trevon's arraignment, the supervising prosecutor in the specialized quality-of-life courtroom in Borough B told the defense attorney that she had conferred with the arresting officer and she would not dismiss the case. She recounted to the defense attorney that the arresting officer insisted that Trevon attempted to jump the turnstile, but then, according to the officer, noticed the police mid-jump and only after that swiped the MetroCard. She offered a plea to a charge of a B misdemeanor with the sentence of time served.

Trevon eventually made fourteen court appearances on the misdemeanor case over a period of eight months, spending most days waiting between two to four hours for his case to be called, only to be adjourned again for a later date. Eventually in December 2012, the case was set for trial. On the first day of the trial, the prosecution offered the defendant a plea to a disorderly conduct violation and one day of community service, which he declined. After two days of a bench trial, which included four witnesses—the arresting officer, an MTA records custodian, Trevon's college bookstore manager, and Trevon—he was acquitted. Watching the two supervising DAs and the law student who had tried the case walk out of the courtroom, he said, "It's hard not to hate the DA after that. I mean a lot of black youth like me just take it. . . . We don't take the case to court, don't want to fight them petty charges, so many people I know just don't want to go through the system, don't want to get up and come back to court so take those little charges, take time served to go home and get it over with. That's why officers get away with petty stuff; they throw a lot of cases at you and you get used to it."

This rare trial case is the exception that proves the rule. Almost always, administrative fact-finding is the first and final venue of fact-finding. Even when prosecutors do have the time and opportunity to investigate or talk to relevant parties, many contested misdemeanor cases just come down to a credibility question between the defendant and the arresting officer over the events surrounding the arrest. Prosecutors often say that defendants have a manifest interest in telling a particular version of events that absolves them of criminal liability. A longtime supervisor in Borough A said, "I am not going to say that all defendants lie, but defendants do have an interest in not admitting guilt, and I assume that when you hear a defendant telling you a story, you take that into consideration—that they have an interest to not be fully truthful sometimes." It is hardly surprising that, given their professional role and daily contact with police, ADAs most often find the officer's account more compelling in contested cases. As Alexis explained, "My default is to believe the police officer, unless I have reason to otherwise. In a perfect world . . . what do you do? You, yourself, talk to both of them. Right? I talk to the police officer. I talk to the defendant with attorney post-arrest; without the defense attorney pre-arrest. You talk to everybody involved. But unless I have a reason, I assume the officer is telling the truth."

Trevon's case also shows that defendants and defense attorneys are not overestimating the costs of invoking adversarial due process. Pushing a misdemeanor case to trial involves significant time, willingness to make numerous court appearances, and the costs of having an open, pending criminal matter readily accessible to the public and potential employers. When, as in this case, the charge comes down to a credibility contest between the arresting officer and the defendant in front of a judge, it is a significant gamble for defendants to attempt vindication through trying facts in an adjudicative venue. It should be noted this was not an obvious win; the judge made a number of legal rulings against the defense, and, in a post-trial discussion with the judge, prosecutor, and defense, he indicated he thought this was a "tough case." This case also shows that prosecutors are often willing to offer dispositions that secure some marking of the defendant but minimal formal sanction, and defendants risk serious costs (namely, a permanent criminal record) by going to pretrial hearings or trial.

Sometimes prosecutors will keep cases open knowing they will eventually be dismissed under the speedy trial clock and make no attempt to prosecute them in the interim. This practice serves the goal of marking and risk management. The statutory time allowed to prosecute a case is therefore not only a guarantee to the defendant; it is a tool for the state to monitor and sometimes to punish the defendant. For example, Joan, a defense attorney in Borough A, discussed her client who was accused of misdemeanor assault against a woman who was his girlfriend at the time of arrest. They had subsequently broken up and were no longer involved romantically. The woman was, however, pregnant with the defendant's child, and she had been refusing to participate in the prosecution and had requested that the court modify the temporary order of protection from a full to a limited order. According to Joan, the woman wanted the man to be present at the birth of their child so they could immediately and automatically establish paternity and he could assist in child care and pay child support.[64] So, "the problem," she continued, "is if the child is born and he wants to claim paternity, he has to be present at the hospital to sign the birth certificate with her, with the mother. Which he is forbidden from doing because of the order of protection. If he doesn't do it that day and they go home and she has to initiate paternity . . . you know, they have to settle the paternity through the courts, which takes at least six months. So it's just . . . forever and ever and court involvement before they can both see their kid. Which is kind of ridiculous."

The defendant was on parole for life, and, according to Joan, the ADA would not make an offer to anything below a "letter" misdemeanor because of his parole status. The defense attorney did not want her client to plead to a misdemeanor criminal offense because that would open him up to reincarceration on a parole violation, most likely for a time between one and three years.

Joan: So that case was "ready" forever. I've had it for four months now probably, and it was on for hearings and trial last week, and they finally announced "not ready," so the clock started ticking.

Q: So why did they announce "not ready?"

Joan: Well, she said the officer wasn't available, but she told me off the record too that she would rather let the case 30.30 out than agree to a limited order of protection, for example, which is what my client and his ex want, or dismiss it.

When asked why she thought an ADA would agree to let a case become dismissed, but not agree affirmatively to dismiss, Joan opined, "I mean because it covers, they see it as covering their backs. You know, they're not on record as agreeing to dismiss a case; they're not on record as agreeing to adjust the order of protection to be limited. . . . On the off chance that something happens again, it's not their fault; they tried to prosecute it, [but] they ran out of time because of the statute."

These examples demonstrate what I have largely observed in my field-work: Sometimes a defendant comes to accept the offered disposition because it appears to be a genuinely fair offer, given the conduct at issue. Sometimes it is the only rational choice, given the structure of incentives and risks. Although adjournments are sometimes used to investigate or develop legal and factual questions, they are also used as a period "during which the subject's habitual behavior pattern can be tested by time."[65]

Legal actors may not have set out to formulate a new, comprehensive managerial approach to dealing with the influx of people into criminal court generated by the policing changes initiated in the 1990s. But they faced a practical reality of limited information about the allegations that brought defendants to misdemeanorland and limited resources to figure it out, both at arraignments and over multiple adjournments. However, they have at their disposal various tools from court records, criminal law, procedure, and informal practices that can be used to evaluate the defendant's overall rule-following disposition and to manage social control measures based on how the defendant bears up under the criminal process. Prosecutors and judges make creative use of the power-conferring rules of criminal procedure to *do something* with the cases they face daily, something that responds to the institutional imperative to exert a measure of social control over the people hauled into court from Broken Windows policing but something that is also practically manageable and morally acceptable, given the profile of defendants and charges at issue.

The strategies selected to deal with the immediate pressing tasks and regular problem situations they face on a daily basis produced a pattern of handling cases that progressively enhances penal control according to their assessment of the defendant's overall rule-following capacity. And as that pattern plays out over time, it gives rise to collective justifications of the approach in ways that tie it to institutionalized ideas about the social function of criminal law. Part 2 details precisely *how* the various practices, records, and strategies that legal actors use in the managerial model to seek social control operate in misdemeanorland.

PART II

The Tools of Lower Courts

4

Marking

I forgot to ask you; what sort of acquittal is it you want? There are three
possibilities; absolute acquittal, apparent acquittal and deferment. . . .
[D]eferment consists of keeping proceedings permanently in their
earliest stages. To do that, the accused and those helping him need to
keep in continuous personal contact with the court, especially those
helping him. . . . You must never let the trial out of your sight, you have
to go and see the appropriate judge at regular intervals as well as when
something in particular comes up. . . . If there's an absolute acquittal
all proceedings should stop, everything disappears from the process,
not just the indictment but the trial and even the acquittal disappears,
everything just disappears. With an apparent acquittal it's different.
When that happens, nothing has changed except that the case for your
innocence, for your acquittal and the grounds for the acquittal have
been made stronger. Apart from that, proceedings go on as before,
the court offices continue their business and the case gets passed to
higher courts, gets passed back down to the lower courts and so on,
backwards and forwards, sometimes faster, sometimes slower, to and
fro. It's impossible to know exactly what's happening while this is going
on. Seen from outside it can sometimes seem that everything has been
long since forgotten, the documents have been lost and the acquittal
is complete. No one familiar with the court would believe it. No
documents ever get lost, the court forgets nothing.

—FRANZ KAFKA, *THE TRIAL*

Criminal justice systems keep records. They do not keep records for the sake of mere posterity, to maintain repositories of factual and legal findings. Record keeping is a dynamic organizational practice. It involves the construction, constant refinement, and maintenance of a resource. This resource is continually consulted and used because it contains information that criminal court actors rely on to make decisions. Other criminal justice actors, state agencies, and private actors, such as employers and landlords, seek access to this resource to get information about the people with whom they deal. One of the primary penal techniques in managerial misdemeanor courts is that of *marking*—the practice of indexing certain behaviors and status determinations about individuals. The import of the mark is determined both by the content of the mark—what it designates—and by how the mark is accessed—where and subject to what rules it can be retrieved by people who would consult the records in making important decisions.

Sociology has a long tradition of thinking about how the operations of the criminal law construct and convey the social standing of those it touches. The classic understanding of the role of marking is that conviction and punishment express social condemnation by designating that the offender's status has been degraded because he violated one of society's laws. At the macro level, Durkheim famously characterized the entire enterprise of punishment as a "meaningful demonstration" against the offender's transgression.[1] Punishment, in the Durkheimian understanding, is not enacted to inform the offender that he has brought upon himself a degraded status. Rather, it is enacted to share that message with the rest of society's non-offenders and to reconstitute collective solidarity and moral cohesion expressed in criminal law's prohibitions.[2]

Sociologists have also theorized how the concrete operations of criminal law construct designations of social standing at the micro level. Harold Garfinkel, for example, conceptualized the criminal court proceedings that transitioned a person from unmarked to marked as a "status degradation ceremony," accomplishing "communicative work . . . whereby the public identity of an actor is transformed into something looked on as lower in the local scheme of social types."[3] Once the status of criminal offender has been bestowed by a finding of guilt, that stigma must be managed throughout life.[4] Howard Becker, for example, theorized the mark of a criminal conviction as a deviant "master status" with "generalized symbolic value, so that people automatically assume that its bearer possesses other undesirable traits allegedly associated with it," and the bearer "will be regarded as deviant or undesirable in other respects."[5] Because a criminal conviction is a permanent and accessible record, it can be thought of as a negative credential as Devah Pager argues, where "[t]he power of the credential lies in its recognition as an official and legitimate means of evaluating and classifying individuals." The " 'credential' of a criminal record, like educational or professional credentials, constitutes a formal and enduring classification of social status, which can be used to regulate access and opportunity across numerous social, economic, and political domains."[6]

But the marks produced in misdemeanorland frequently have a limited lifespan or are restricted from open public access, often by design and consent of the parties to the legal process. The marks typically designate a provisional suspect status or indicate minor transgressions of social rules, not full-fledged transition into a denigrated caste. This chapter shows that conviction is only one of the many ways that marking in the criminal justice system produces status designations and public credentials. In order to understand how marking functions as a penal technique, it is necessary to detail how marks are generated in misdemeanorland and how they circulate and have import there and beyond.[7]

Marking in the managerial model is not necessarily a conclusion of guilt. Is not the final determination indicating that court actors are satisfied that some evidentiary standard has been met sufficient to conclude that the defendant transgressed a specific penal law provision. Nor is it the predicate finding of guilt that triggers the state's lawful imposition of hard treatment. In the subfelony world, marking is a dynamic practice that sorts and classifies the people moving through misdemeanorland, often into provisional or conditional statuses. Marks document a range of behaviors and accomplishments, including the fact and frequency of prior encounters, whether defendants have properly complied with the prosecution's demands, court mandates, if fees and fines have been paid, if court appearances have been missed, or how defendants have performed various tasks. These marks are consulted by court actors to determine what level of social control response is warranted and what other sorts of testing or punishments ought to be imposed if a person cycles back through the system. Criminal court actors are also well aware that many criminal records are accessible outside the court system and can trigger extensive social and economic consequences. Marking—independent of it signaling the state's authority to lawfully impose a formal punishment—is itself a penal technique, even when the mark is temporary and its accessibility limited.

Far from a system mechanically marking masses of defendants with convictions that systematically fails to make distinctions between people brought into its orbit, as the assembly-line justice story would have it, the actors in misdemeanorland consistently make distinctions between the subjects they encounter. One way they do so is through the graded use of marking. To understand how this is done, we need to unpack *how* defendants are marked and the import of those marks in the managerial enterprise.

Dismissal

One of the most common outcomes from a misdemeanor arrest is that there is no outcome. At least no formal legal outcome. Somewhere between 45 and 51 percent of all misdemeanor cases in recent years terminated in a dismissal of one type or another (see fig. 2.2). The disposition category of "dismissal" masks significant variation in the type of dismissal and how defendants are marked in the process. The shortest marking period in the dismissal category occurs when the prosecutor decides not to prosecute the case.[8] Colloquially, these are called "DP'd" cases, for "decline to prosecute." After the police make an arrest, they fill out paperwork (mostly into the NYPD's "online" computer system) at the precinct and then fax (yes, fax) the paperwork to what is called in most boroughs the Early Case Assessment Bureau (ECAB). There, assistant district attorneys and paralegals work to screen cases and prepare the "complaint," which is the charging instrument for arraignment. Because defendants are supposed to be arraigned within twenty-four hours after arrest,[9] ADAs and others working to screen and "write up" cases must work quickly to identify cases that they do not think they want to prosecute, either as a matter of policy or fairness or where there was a constitutionally suspect stop or search. If the assistant district attorneys working in ECAB decide to decline to prosecute the case, the defendant is not arraigned, and the arrest should not print on future rap sheets.

Somewhere between 7 and 12 percent of misdemeanor case dispositions over the past ten years have resulted in a decline to prosecute. The DA supervisors I spoke to typically underscored that it would be rare to DP a case with a victim or complainant, or where there are questions about the facts of the arrest. As Angela, a supervisor in the DA's office of Borough A explained, "We have to speak to the officer, if we can. We're going to interview a witness if need be. We wouldn't want to just decline to prosecute something without speaking to someone, because there may be information that's not in the paperwork."

A common example of cases Angela said they would DP are those where they believe the arrest itself was sufficient punishment because of some special circumstance:

> There are cases where we decline to prosecute, and it's based on our discretion. Those DPs are different, right? So if it's Mother's Day and the NYPD has arrested twenty people for selling flowers, I don't know that after they've taken the flowers that we want to compound that with a prosecution for being an unlicensed vendor. I'm not criticizing the police department. But I'm saying that's a case where we would exercise discretion.... It's 97 degrees and this guy is selling water, right? So technically, yes. It's illegal. Actually I don't know if there's an ordinance about water. But let's say they did a sweep on water, and it was a sweltering hot day. That's a DP'd that it would be at our discretion to say we don't want to prosecute this case, we don't want to prosecute this guy who is out there with a cooler selling water.

As the DA makes clear, these are discretionary choices, not firm office policies. An ADA, intern, or other worker writing up the case would have to bring it to the attention of a supervisor to get permission to DP the case.

By far the most common mechanism for dismissal in New York City is called an adjournment in contemplation of dismissal, which represented roughly 23 to 30 percent of all misdemeanor arrest dispositions in recent years. An ACD is authorized by statutory provisions in the state criminal procedural law allowing the court to grant the motion of either party (prosecution or defense), with the consent of the other party, to adjourn the case for a specific time period, after which the charges are dismissed and the arrest and prosecution are deemed a "nullity." Two different criminal procedure law provisions authorize an ACD, one specifically for marijuana offenses (MJACD) and the other general (ACD).[10] These statutes specify different maximum adjournment times—for marijuana offenses (and family offenses) the adjournment period cannot be longer than one year; for other offenses, no longer than six months. As a practical matter, these statutory maximums are the usual adjournment times.[11] The mark of the ACD is itself an intent to put the defendant on notice of the potential for more formal court control. Judge Henry explained the ACD disposition as, "a low-maintenance form of probation; you don't have to report because you monitor yourself."

The court can set all sorts of conditions on the defendant during the adjournment period, but most judges just say "stay out of trouble," or "lead a law-abiding life." Other examples of conditions include a temporary order of protection, an educational or therapeutic program, restitution, or community service. If there are no conditions attached to the ACD, the defendant is not required to come back to court. If there are conditions, the defendant must come back to court to prove compliance before the case is dismissed and sealed. During the adjournment period, the arrest charges and the ACD disposition are available to the court, prosecution, and defense attorney if the individual is arrested again, because open cases print on rap sheets. Unless the prosecution makes a motion to restore the case, the charges are automatically dismissed after the adjournment period and the record is sealed.[12]

For thousands of defendants each year whose cases terminate with an ACD at arraignments, marking is one of the primary penal techniques they experience from their misdemeanor arrest. This is the case for some of the largest arrest categories in New York during the Broken Windows era, such as marijuana possession. Over a fifteen-year period, marijuana arrests skyrocketed from about 8,000 in 1994 to over 56,000 in 2010. In somewhere between 45 and 66 percent of all cases since 2004 where the top arrest charge was simple possession of marijuana, the arrest resulted in an adjournment in contemplation of dismissal.[13] Although the NYPD has drastically reduced marijuana arrests since late 2014, the way that marking operates as the primary penal tool is perfectly illustrated in this class of arrests.[14]

On a Tuesday in November 2010, in an overcrowded courtroom, there were 185 cases on the court calendar to be arraigned on a desk appearance ticket. Defendants scheduled to be arraigned that day spilled out into the hallway to wait for their attorney or a court officer to tell them their case would be called. That day, as on most days during that time period, the most common penal law arrest charge was misdemeanor criminal possession of marijuana. Ray, the supervising arraignment lawyer for one of the public defender organizations, walked over to the prosecution table with stacks of files, saying, "all of these will be marijuana ACDs" to Samira, an arraignment supervisor from the DA's office. Ray can assume, without asking, that she will offer an MJACD for each of the first-time arrestees because it is the normative practice in the borough. Using the technique of marking to summarily dispose of substantial volumes of misdemeanor arrests immediately after arrest with no additional factual or legal inquiry is standard practice in misdemeanorland, even if the frontline actors processing the cases believe that the defendants are probably guilty or that the charged conduct is not trivial.

Samira, for example, does not have a reputation for being particularly progressive or lenient; in fact, I have seen her be quite strict in plea nego- tiations on many occasions. Later that day, Ray complained about being overwhelmed "with so many bullshit arrests," and I pointed out that Samira does not think of the cases that way, as she had just told me that defendants need to be more responsible and not do things to get themselves arrested. Ray responded, "[Samira] is a nice, smart, competent lawyer and whether or not she expresses the belief that these people should not be putting themselves in the position to be arrested and not be doing these things is more an expression of a personal opinion—you don't see her opposing the ACDs, but granting them. So, it is not really about what she thinks of these people's behavior but how she deals with the arrest." Ray knew that certain types of misdemeanor cases are granted ACDs at the first court appearance as a matter of course, irrespective of whether the prosecution could easily secure a conviction. And as Ray's actions demonstrate, he had no question that Samira would deal with the files he handed her that day by granting a marijuana ACD.

Not only can Ray assume that the prosecutor will consent to the MJACD; he can assume that the judge will consent. In order to streamline the backlog of cases for arraignment, many judges agree to have multiple defendants called up to the podium for arraignment if they will all be receiving the marijuana ACD. In some courtrooms, judges issue MJACDs without requiring defen- dants to even walk up to the podium: their names are called, they stand up in the audience, where they had waited for hours, while the judge issues the order, practically yelling it from the bench. On that November day, there were six groups consisting of four to six individuals summoned as a group to receive an MJACD. The court officer called out the list of defendants' names, and they took their places in a huddle around the assigned defense attorney. The judge said, "Your cases are being adjourned in contemplation of dismissal; you need to stay out of trouble for one year, and then your case will be dismissed and sealed." They silently filtered out of the courtroom.

The defendants granted marijuana ACDs en masse left the courtroom with the expectation that their cases were behind them, as they were told that their cases would eventually be dismissed and sealed. But they also left with a marker—albeit one with a limited duration—a trace of this encounter. The criminal record is tied to the physical body of the offender: the unique criminal justice identifying number, the New York State Identification (NYSID), is generated and matched to the defendant's fingerprints. For any person convicted of a criminal offense (that is, the case is not dismissed, and the defendant is not convicted of a noncriminal violation), the DCJS maintains a digital image of the fingerprint linked to the offender's name, NYSID, and other identifying information. From that point forward, if the person is arrested, his prints are taken and matched to the NYSID, and the criminal record is generated based on this match. Thus, the marker of the ACD will follow the defendant after he leaves the courtroom. If the defendant had no prior convictions, he can shed the marker (if no conditions were imposed on the ACD) based on his performance in the outside world without having to return to court.

The residual category of "other dismissal"—constituting between 12 and 15 percent of misdemeanor case dispositions over the past five years—includes various legal grounds for dismissal and can occur at any point in a case's life course. For example, a case can be dismissed because the charging instrument is facially insufficient at arraignment or "in the interest of justice" after many months of court appearances. As long as the case is open, it will appear on the defendant's rap sheet and also be available to the public on the court's website, called WebCrims. Once the case has been dismissed by a judge, it should (absent an administrative error) be sealed, meaning it ought not to print on court rap sheets or be presented to the public on background checks done through the state agency (DCJS).

One of the most frequent grounds for dismissal included in this "other dismissal" category is the speedy trial dismissal, often referred to as a "30.30 dismissal" because it is provided for by section 30.30 of the New York Criminal Procedure Law. A case must be dismissed if the prosecutor is not "ready" for trial within ninety days for a Class A misdemeanor, sixty days for a Class B misdemeanor, or thirty days for a violation. Cases that are eventually dismissed "30.30" are often open for much longer in real calendar time in excess of the statutory speedy trial times because many adjournments are excluded.[15] Until dismissal, the case is "open" on the defendant's rap sheet and available to the general public.

Having an open case marks the defendant in a number of arenas beyond criminal court. Depending on the charges, an open case could keep a lawful permanent resident from traveling outside the United States and an undocumented person from making any immigration moves.[16] An undocumented immigrant who is put in on bail during a case could be detected by Immigration and Customs Enforcement (ICE) and deported, even if that case is eventually dismissed.[17] The conduct alleged in a dismissed case can be, and often is, the subject of a parole violation (and sometimes a probation violation), even if the criminal case based on that conduct is dismissed. Open cases are more readily available to the general public than cases that have gone to disposition. Anyone can access the state's online criminal court system, WebCrims, and find an open criminal matter by searching a person's first and last name. The arrest charges, disposition, and court appearances made in the case can all be viewed on WebCrims while a case is open, which includes the adjournment period in an ACD or MJACD disposition. In contrast, to view someone's criminal record, a person must pay a fee of $65 to the state or use some other private firm that accesses state data, and only final, nonsealed criminal convictions should be printed. An open case is often an outright bar to many license applications or professions or significant impediment to many others, such as security guard, police officer, firefighter, or member of the military. Those who are employed may be suspended from their jobs, often without pay, while a case is pending.

Kima was arrested in November 2010 after she sent a text to her boyfriend of eighteen years during a tumultuous breakup to the effect that if he tried to hurt her, she would kill him. He went to the police to, in her words, teach her a lesson. According to Kima, he did not understand the implications of making the complaint and signing a statement of events. Kima was arrested and charged with aggravated harassment. Her boyfriend expressed his wishes to the DA's office to not have the prosecution go forward, and he refused to participate, but they were able to proceed with the prosecution and stop the 30.30 clock by relying on his prior signed statement.

Although the assigned prosecutor refused to affirmatively dismiss the case, she informally agreed to let the case 30.30 out because, according to the defense attorney, the assigned ADA believed Kima's account that it was a one-time incident and there was no risk of future violence. While keeping the case open for the entire statutory period may or may not necessarily have been intended by the prosecutor as a punishment, it allowed her to monitor Kima through regular court appearances, assess whether she was correct in assuming there would be no further problems, and maintain the order of protection as a point of leverage. Furthermore, because Kima had an open case for almost eight months, she was forbidden from working as substitute teacher or even applying for jobs for the following school year until the case was dismissed 30.30 in late June 2011.

Many criminal justice actors are cognizant of the potential collateral consequences of even the most minor and short-lived markers. Debbie, a longtime supervisor in the DA's office, explained: "A huge factor that we always take into consideration is whether or not the person is employed. We don't want to see people losing their jobs, especially not in today's economy. We do not penalize someone for not having a job, but it certainly is a plus, and we always take it into consideration in forming dispositions." They can therefore adapt their use of the tools available to them if they think it is merited for particular defendants.

For example, in March 2011, Herman, a man in his late forties, voluntarily returned to Criminal Court on a warrant from a 1991 misdemeanor arrest for turnstile jumping. The prosecutor had agreed to offer the man an ACD, but the defense attorney asked for immediate sealing, meaning the case would not be perceptible to the public during the six-month adjournment period. The defense attorney simply stated, "He is applying for a state job in Pennsylvania," and the judge agreed, smiling at the defendant as she said, "Well, it was a theft of services case in 1991, and he's going to pay taxes soon!" The assumption that Herman would soon be "paying taxes" seemed to ease the imperative to insist on the six-month mark before eventual dismissal.

Often criminal court actors understand even better than defendants the relevance of various markers. Judge Muñoz explained that she has granted immediate sealing in certain cases if there will be serious repercussions— such as immigration consequences—from an open disposition: "If it's the first time, I go along with it, but I tell them: 'You are putting your life in jeopardy. Make sure this doesn't happen again. Because the second time it's not going to be sealed—it's going to be open, and your future could be [jeopardized].' . . . So you tell people things like that, because sometimes . . . I don't know what it is, but people don't realize the seriousness of being arrested and having even an ACD."

The details of *how* these various forms of dismissal work are essential for understanding how nonconviction, noncustodial dispositions to misdemeanor cases operate in the managerial model. Defendants are marked—sometimes for a very short time and sometimes for a very long time—even if the eventual outcome of the case is a dismissal. This marking serves an important function, even if it is not to trigger the capacity of the state to impose a formal sanction. It allows the state to record the fact of an encounter and to use it as a data point in later encounters. The next prosecutor and judge who encounter a defendant can know whether there was a prior allegation of criminal conduct, and this marking is accomplished without demanding all the time and resources necessary to secure a conviction.

Conviction

Between 2010 and 2015, somewhere between 46 and 51 percent of misdemeanor case dispositions have resulted in a conviction.[18] Here again, the disposition category of conviction masks variation in the type of conviction, the types of records generated, who may access those records, and by what means. Conviction can occur at any point in a case's life course: defendants can plead guilty to a misdemeanor crime at arraignment or after years of court appearances.

The major fault line lies between a criminal and a noncriminal conviction. In criminal court vernacular, that distinction is described as the difference between taking "a letter" criminal conviction—meaning a Class A or Class B misdemeanor—or a noncriminal violation or infraction conviction—usually a "dis con." In recent years, approximately 30 percent of all dispositions in which the top arrest charge was a misdemeanor crime resulted in a conviction for a violation or infraction (that is, approximately 58 to 60 percent of all cases terminating in a conviction).[19]

Table 4.1 displays the top conviction charges resulting from a misdemeanor arrest in five-year intervals from 1985 to 2015.[20] Comparing these conviction charge counts to the arrest charge data presented in chapter 1 (see fig. 1.5) shows that people are rarely convicted of the specific offense for which they were arrested. For decades, the majority of the convictions from a misdemeanor arrest have been to NY PL § 240.20, disorderly conduct, commonly called a "dis con." During the Broken Windows era, there have been somewhere between 2.5 and 5.2 times more disorderly conduct violation convictions than the next most common conviction charge.

The statutory definition of disorderly conduct is very broad. In practice, the mark of a "dis con" conviction does not indicate that the defendant is guilty of any specific illegal conduct.[21] Rather, it serves as an all-purpose generic charge to mark the defendant for a specific length of time at a specific level of seriousness—above the ACD but below the level A or B misdemeanor criminal conviction. As Ivanna, a supervisor at the DA's office, explained: "A lot of the fighting in criminal court between the defense bar and prosecution is over the 'letter.' Defense attorneys do not want their clients to take the letter if they don't have a criminal record, or if they are on parole or probation, taking the letter often means violating them and opening them to more exposure on the VOP [violation of parole or probation]."

TABLE 4.1. Top Fifteen Conviction Charges Resulting from a Misdemeanor Arrest, 1985–2015

1985

Top conviction charge	Number of convictions	Rank	Percentage of total convictions
PL 240.20 Disorderly conduct	23,002	1	27
PL 240.37 Loitering for prostitution	14,877	2	18
PL 155.25 Petit larceny	5,895	3	7
PL 220.03 Criminal possession of controlled substance–7th	5,137	4	6
PL 140.05 Trespass	4,812	5	6
VTL 1192 Driving while intoxicated	3,713	6	4
PL 221.40 Criminal sale of marijuana–4th	3,604	7	4
PL 230.00 Prostitution	3,215	8	4
PL 165.15 Theft of services	2,987	9	4
PL 221.10 Criminal possession of marijuana–5th	1,912	10	2
PL 240.25 Harassment–1st	1,636	11	2
PL 165.40 Criminal possession of stolen property–5th	1,512	12	2
PL 221.05 Unlawful possession of marijuana	1,491	13	2
PL 220.45 Possession of hypodermic instrument	1,290	14	2
PL 225.05 Promoting gambling–2nd	830	15	1
All others	7,785		
Total convictions	83,698		

1990

Top conviction charge	Number of convictions	Rank	Percentage of total convictions
PL 240.20 Disorderly conduct	30,999	1	37
PL 155.25 Petit larceny	8,203	2	10
PL 220.03 Criminal possession of controlled substance–7th	7,285	3	9
PL 240.37 Loitering for prostitution	6,228	4	7
VTL 1192 Driving while intoxicated	3,463	5	4
PL 165.15 Theft of services	2,468	6	3

PL 230.00 Prostitution	1,849	7	2
PL 140.05 Trespass	1,693	8	2
PL 240.25 Harassment–1st	1,264	9	2
PL 221.40 Criminal sale of marijuana–4th	1,254	10	1
PL 145.15 Criminal tampering–2nd	1,006	11	1
PL 165.40 Criminal possession of stolen property–5th	875	12	1
PL 145.00 Criminal mischief–4th	793	13	1
PL 120.00 Assault–3rd	630	14	1
PL 220.45 Possession of hypodermic instrument	540	15	1
All others	5,727		
Total convictions	74,277		

1995

Top conviction charge	Number of convictions	Rank	Percentage of total convictions
PL 240.20 Disorderly conduct	40,368	1	48
PL 165.15 Theft of services	10,442	2	12
PL 220.03 Criminal possession of controlled substance–7th	10,113	3	12
PL 155.25 Petit larceny	6,347	4	8
VTL 1192 Driving while intoxicated	5,432	5	6
PL 140.05 Trespass	4,115	6	5
PL 240.26 Harassment–2nd	3,426	7	4
PL 240.37 Loitering for prostitution	2,414	8	3
PL 221.40 Criminal sale of marijuana–4th	1,332	9	2
PL 140.10 Criminal trespass–3rd	1,310	10	2
PL 140.15 Criminal trespass–2nd	1,206	11	1
PL 120.00 Assault–3rd	1,043	12	1
PL 215.50 Criminal contempt–2nd	943	13	1
PL 165.40 Criminal possession of stolen property–5th	667	14	1
PL 230.00 Prostitution	624	15	1
All others	7,231		
Total convictions	97,013		

Continued on next page

TABLE 4.1. (*continued*)

2000

Top conviction charge	Number of convictions	Rank	Percentage of total convictions
PL 240.20 Disorderly conduct	49,634	1	59
PL 220.03 Criminal possession of controlled substance–7th	18,790	2	22
PL 165.15 Theft of services	6,966	3	8
PL 221.10 Criminal possession of marijuana–5th	6,381	4	8
PL 240.26 Harassment–2nd	6,300	5	8
PL 140.05 Trespass	6,096	6	7
PL 155.25 Petit larceny	6,080	7	7
PL 221.05 Unlawful possession of marijuana	4,091	8	5
PL 140.15 Criminal trespass–2nd	3,647	9	4
VTL 1192 Driving while intoxicated	2,827	10	3
PL 221.40 Criminal sale of marijuana–4th	2,804	11	3
PL 240.37 Loitering for prostitution	2,525	12	3
PL 140.10 Criminal trespass–3rd	2,053	13	2
PL 230.00 Prostitution	1,955	14	2
PL 120.00 Assault–3rd	1,520	15	2
All others	7,503		
Total convictions	129,172		

2005

Top conviction charge	Number of convictions	Rank	Percentage of total convictions
PL 240.20 Disorderly conduct	35,453	1	42
PL 220.03 Criminal possession of controlled substance–7th	14,249	2	17
PL 155.25 Petit larceny	7,056	3	8
VTL 1192 Driving while intoxicated	6,474	4	8
PL 240.26 Harassment–2nd	4,855	5	6
PL 140.05 Trespass	4,539	6	5
PL 221.10 Criminal possession of marijuana–5th	4,307	7	5

PL 165.15 Theft of services	4,236	8	5
PL 221.05 Unlawful possession marijuana	4,234	9	5
PL 140.15 Criminal trespass	3,610	10	4
PL 120.00 Assault–3rd	1,941	11	2
PL 140.10 Criminal trespass–3rd	1,620	12	2
PL 230.00 Prostitution	1,352	13	2
PL 221.40 Criminal sale of marijuana–4th	1,032	14	1
PL 240.37 Loitering for prostitution	1,013	15	1
All others	9,915		
Total convictions	105,886		

2010

Top conviction charge	Number of convictions	Rank	Percentage of total convictions
PL 240.20 Disorderly conduct	49,564	1	59
PL 220.03 Criminal possession of controlled substance–7th	10,861	2	13
PL 155.25 Petit larceny	7,663	3	9
VTL 1192 Driving while intoxicated	7,064	4	8
PL 140.05 Trespass	6,676	5	8
PL 165.15 Theft of services	5,688	6	7
PL 221.10 Criminal possession of marijuana–5th	5,610	7	7
PL 221.05 Unlawful possession of marijuana	5,147	8	6
PL 140.15 Criminal trespass–2nd	3,505	9	4
PL 240.26 Harassment–2nd	2,754	10	3
PL 120.00 Assault–3rd	1,900	11	2
PL 140.10 Criminal trespass–3rd	1,699	12	2
PL 221.40 Criminal sale of marijuana–4th	1,147	13	1
VTL 0509 Unlicensed driver	1,008	14	1
Local laws	802	15	1
All others	9,020		
Total convictions	120,108		

Continued on next page

TABLE 4.1. (*continued*)

2015

Top conviction charge	Number of convictions	Rank	Percentage of total convictions
PL 240.20 Disorderly conduct	40,612	1	49
PL 155.25 Petit larceny	7,862	2	9
PL 220.03 Criminal possession of controlled substance–7th	6,947	3	8
VTL 1192 Driving while intoxicated	5,670	4	7
PL 165.15 Theft of services	5,182	5	6
PL 140.05 Trespass	3,482	6	4
PL 221.05 Unlawful possession of marijuana	2,187	7	3
PL 240.26 Harassment–2nd	1,867	8	2
PL 120.00 Assault–3rd	1,355	9	2
PL 140.15 Criminal trespass–2nd	1,306	10	2
PL 140.10 Criminal trespass–3rd	1,219	11	1
PL 221.10 Criminal possession of marijuana–5th	1,193	12	1
VTL 0509 Unlicensed driver	964	13	1
PL 221.40 Criminal sale of marijuana–4th	688	14	1
Local laws	614	15	1
All others	5,859		
Total convictions	87,007		

Source: DCJS.

The marking period of a noncriminal conviction depends on the sentence imposed. If the defendant is convicted of a violation or infraction and sentenced to a conditional discharge, then the case remains on the defendant's rap sheet for one year, after which the case should be sealed.[22] If the defendant is convicted of a violation or infraction and is sentenced to time served, a fine, or other sentence short of a conditional discharge, then the record may be sealed as soon as the defendant completes the sentence and pays the fine and court-imposed surcharge, *if* the court transmits the seal order.[23] The sealing statute covering noncriminal convictions differs in one important respect from the sealing statute that governs dismissals: court records do not seal. Prosecutors and judges can search the Office of

Court Administration database with a defendant's name, birthday, or other identifying information. As a practical matter, this means that although the case will not print on a rap sheet, judges and prosecutors often look for these sealed cases and use them in forming plea offers and sentences.[24]

The most serious marking that can occur from a misdemeanor arrest is a criminal conviction.[25] A criminal conviction never seals, and New York State has only recently provided a limited expungement mechanism.[26] Once a person has a criminal conviction, his fingerprints will be maintained by the state and linked to a stable NYSID number, and all later arrest events will be linked to this number. Arrest charges, disposition, sentence imposed, and warrants issued because of failure to appear during the pendency of a case will all be listed on a defendant's rap sheet. Any guilty plea, even to noncriminal violation or infraction charges, triggers mandatory court surcharges. There is no "waiving" of surcharges, even upon showing of indigence. Rather, the court can enter civil judgment, which will then be reported on the person's credit rating. Figure 4.1 summarizes the marking effect of various dispositions.

Even the jail sentence entails an element of marking. Any portion of a day spent in custody is credited as a full day toward sentence time, including the day of arrest, and city jail sentences are reduced by one-third for "good time." A five-day sentence, for example, means four days in custody. A defendant arrested on a Tuesday and sentenced to five days on a Wednesday would be released two days after the plea. A defendant arrested on a Thursday and sentenced to five days in jail on a Friday will be immediately released, because the New York City Department of Corrections does not release on weekends, and consequently if a release date falls on a Saturday or Sunday, the defendant is released on the Friday prior. However, this does not mean that the noted jail sentence is meaningless. It sets a floor, and, as Judge Alfred explained it, "most judges conform to the folkways of the system," which is "this mechanical ratcheting of sentence length," often in five-day increments for each subsequent conviction. As one defense attorney explained, even when a jail sentence of a specific length is in fact equivalent to a time-served sentence, many prosecutors will seek the day-denominated jail sentence because it is "a note to future prosecutors not to offer less time on the next case."

Additive Imperative

The marks generated from criminal justice contacts classify and credential people in various realms, perhaps most importantly in later criminal justice encounters. The additive imperative does not mean there is a mechanical

Type of disposition	Marking period on rap sheet		Arrest and prosecution records seal?	Court records seal if case seals?	Sealing happens automatically after the marking period unless…	Court fees and surcharges
	Pending disposition	After disposition				

DISMISSALS

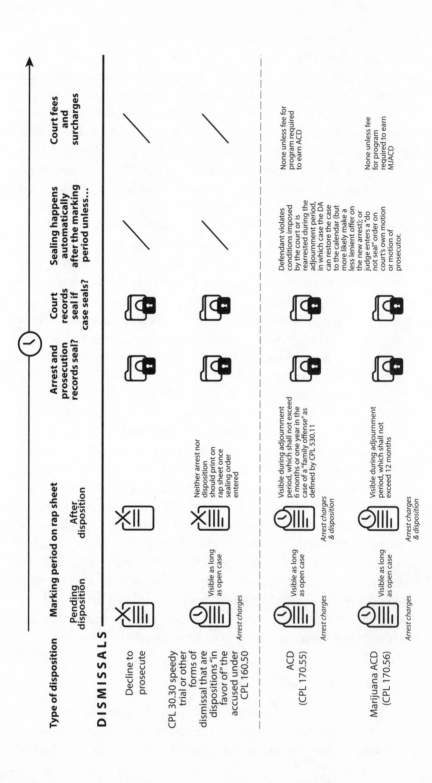

Type of disposition	Pending disposition	After disposition	Arrest and prosecution records seal?	Court records seal if case seals?	Sealing happens automatically after the marking period unless…	Court fees and surcharges
Decline to prosecute			🔒	🔒		
CPL 30.30 speedy trial or other forms of dismissal that are "in favor of" the accused under CPL 160.50	Visible as long as open case *Arrest charges*	Neither arrest nor disposition should print on rap sheet once sealing order entered	🔒	🔒		
ACD (CPL 170.55)	Visible as long as open case *Arrest charges*	Visible during adjournment period, which shall not exceed 6 months or one year in the case of a "family offense" as defined by CPL 530.11 *Arrest charges & disposition*	🔒	🔒	Defendant violates conditions imposed by the court or is rearrested during the adjournment period, in which case the DA can restore the case to the calendar (but more likely make a less lenient offer on the new arrest); or judge enters a "do not seal" order on court's own motion or motion of prosecutor.	None unless fee for program required to earn ACD
Marijuana ACD (CPL 170.56)	Visible as long as open case *Arrest charges*	Visible during adjournment period, which shall not exceed 12 months *Arrest charges & disposition*	🔒	🔒		None unless fee for program required to earn MJACD

CONVICTIONS

NONCRIMINAL

Sentence: time served
Arrest charges

Neither arrest nor disposition should be visible (once court transmits sealing order) if surcharge is paid or civil judgment entered on court surcharges

Total mandatory fees and surcharges $120 = $95 mandatory court surcharge + $25 victim assistance fee. In addition, program fees might apply if a program required as part of the disposition. Traffic civil penalties and additional mandatory surcharges might apply for vehicle and traffic offenses.

Sentence: conditional discharge
Arrest charges

Arrest charges & disposition

Visible during adjournment period, which shall not exceed 1 year

Exempted under CPL 160.55; defendant violates the condition of the conditional discharge sentence; or judge enters a "do not seal" order on court's own motion or motion of prosecutor.

CRIMINAL

Misdemeanor
Arrest charges

Arrest charges & disposition

Never*

Total mandatory fees and surcharges $250 = $175 court surcharge + $25 victim assistance fee + $50 DNA databank fee.** Additional fees or civil penalties might apply for sex offenses and vehicle and traffic offenses. Applicable program fees if program is required as part of disposition.

Felony
Arrest charges

Arrest charges & disposition

Never*

Total mandatory fees and surcharges $375 = $300 court surcharge + $25 victim assistance fee + $50 DNA databank fee.** Additional fees or civil penalties might apply for sex offenses and vehicle and traffic offenses. Applicable program fees if program is required as part of disposition. Felony sentences might entail incarceration, probation, and/or parole supervision fees.

* Effective October 2017, the state's first general adult discretionary conviction sealing authority went into effect, allowing individuals with up to two convictions and only one felony to request the sealing, upon application to the court and with comment from the prosecutor, of the records of conviction for all crimes other than sex offenses and Class A and violent felonies after a ten-year waiting period. See NY Law 59, Part VVV, § 48 (2017) (to be codified at NY CPL § 160.59).

** A DNA databank fee of $50 is assessed for anyone who commits a crime defined in NY Executive Law §995(7), which includes all felonies and most misdemeanors. For example, criminal possession of marijuana in the fifth degree is exempted unless person is (a) found in possession of more than 25 grams; or (b) caught with marijuana in a public place after having been previously convicted of a crime. NY PL § 60.35(1)(a)(v).

FIGURE 4.1. Marking Effect of Various Dispositions

Date of Earliest Arrest: December 2008   Date of Last Arrest: March 2011

Total Arrests Charges:	20
Felony:	0
Violent Felony:	0
Firearm:	0
Misdemeanor:	15
Other:	5

Total Convictions:	5
Felony:	0
Violent Felony:	0
Firearm:	0
Misdemeanor:	0
Other:	5
YO Adjudication(s):	0

Warrant Information:		Revocation Counts:		Miscellaneous:	
Failure to Appear Counts:	1	Probation:	0	Escape Charges:	0
Open Warrants:	0	Parole:	0	Sex Offender Convictions:	0

FIGURE 4.2. Redacted Section of a Rap Sheet

imposition of a higher severity mark for each successive arrest. But it does mean that the records of prior criminal justice encounters are an important resource consulted to determine what level and combination of penal techniques a prosecutor or judge will deem appropriate in a given encounter.

The additive imperative is expressed and demonstrated in various ways, including the paperwork that criminal court actors rely on in their fast-paced workflow. The essential paperwork in the criminal court file that the prosecution, judge, and defense receive before arraignment is the "complaint," containing the charges and a brief description of the facts that make up the offense, and the defendant's rap sheet. The most salient marks—the prior arrest, conviction, and bench warrant history—are not consulted to disambiguate the circumstances of the arrest or to settle contested versions of the alleged violations, but rather to determine the disposition for which the defendant is eligible. To illustrate, figure 4.2 reproduces that portion of a rap sheet that summarizes all contacts associated with a particular NYSID. This redacted selection is taken from a young man who had experienced twenty arrests, five violation convictions, one bench warrant (listed as a "failure to appear counts"), and zero misdemeanor or felony convictions over about a two-year period between the ages of eighteen and twenty.

Prosecutors and judges must decide on plea offers or recommendations, sometimes up to one hundred cases a day, by flipping through this limited paperwork. A substantial portion of misdemeanor dispositions are reached on the basis of this paperwork alone. In recent years, *over 57 percent* of all dispositions occur at arraignment, when no additional investigation by defense or prosecution has been conducted beyond what is available at arraignments.[27] Defense attorneys realize how important quick glances at the marks of prior encounters are for both prosecutors and judges in setting offers and bail. As Ray, a supervisor at one of the largest public defender organizations, explains, "There is also on the NYSID sheet a section that, for purposes of making things easy for the court and for the judges, indicates how many arrests a person has had . . . how many bench warrants they have, how many open cases they have. And inevitably that shorthand section is incorrect . . . so we train our attorneys how to read those sheets very carefully."

Temporary markers en route to dismissal allow criminal justice actors to mark and classify recent police contacts. While visible, these marks are often "built upon" by successive arrests. For people living in highly policed neighborhoods, there is a high risk of rearrests for misdemeanor offenses in short time periods. In late June 2010, Al, a long-time arraignment supervisor with the DA's office of Borough A, was seated in his usual spot reviewing files. In the summer months, law school interns often stood at the podium on the misdemeanor arraignments. Al would quickly look over a file and note the offer and bail request (if applicable) for the intern to read at the podium when the defendant was brought out for arraignment. With more than a decade of experience, Al could efficiently run through a stack of more than sixty misdemeanor files with a quick look at the complaint and the rap sheet. In one of those files, the top arrest charge was graffiti. Al scribbled "ACD + 5 CS" on the folder, indicating the arraignment offer would be an ACD with five days of community service. After another look at the rap sheet, he crossed it out and changed it to "dis con + 5 CS," a violation and five days of community service. I asked Al why he changed the offer, and he replied, "Why would you want to keep giving ACDs?," showing me that the ACD from this young man's prior arrest was still open and explaining that the standard practice is to not offer another ACD if there is an open ACD. Samira, another supervisor in the DA's office, explained that whenever she sees an ACD on the rap sheet, even one that should have sealed but did not because of some administrative error (which is surprisingly common) she "knows not to offer the ACD again."

Later that day, Al came across a man arrested for misdemeanor marijuana possession. Al flipped through his charging document and rap sheet in about ninety seconds and scribbled an offer on the file: "B misdemeanor and 10 days jail." He explained to me that this is the man's third marijuana case; he had already been given a marijuana ACD and a violation within the year and did five days of community service on the last arrest, so this time he thought a conviction for the misdemeanor offense was appropriate. The defense attorney asked if Al would "come off the misdemeanor" and Al replied, "His last [criminal justice] contact was August of 2009, less than a year ago, and he got the violation last time; that's why I went up. He got the violation last time." After negotiating with the defense attorney, Al agreed to "come off the misdemeanor" and offer a violation plea, but the accused would have to do fifteen days of community service this time.

This exchange illustrates another aspect of the additive marking regime in the managerial model: the time between cases is important for evaluating the mark. Certain types of marks are difficult or legally forbidden to access (for most purposes) after specific periods of time. In addition to the impediments to access, the ascribed import of accessible prior marks attenuates over time. In January 2011, a judge addressed Wilbur, a black man in his mid-thirties, who had missed his prior court appearance for an open misdemeanor case. Wilbur had voluntarily returned on the warrant and stood before the judge explaining that he missed the last court date because his girlfriend was giving birth to their baby, who was born with severe health problems. Wilbur's defense attorney argued to the judge that it was not necessary to set bail, repeatedly highlighting that Wilbur's last conviction dated from 1995. Defense attorneys regularly bring up the length of time since a defendant's last conviction if their client has not been arrested in a number of years. It is not always an availing argument, but the logic that the person in court today should be perceived as having wiped the slate clean if he or she has not been arrested in many years is well understood.

Although the judge in this case agreed to not set bail, the mark of the bench warrant will remain on this man's rap sheep as long as the case is open or if it terminates in a conviction. Bench warrants are one of the most important marks judges consult in setting bail. If, for whatever reasons, a person chalks up a number of bench warrants over a series of arrests, a conviction is much more likely for a later misdemeanor arrest because bail will be set on that new arrest. Most defendants will accept a guilty plea when they are being held in on bail, even if they would not have if they were out on their own recognizance—for the simple reason that taking the plea is usually the fastest way to get out of jail, as most sentences do not involve *prospective* jail time. Judge Marcos explained that even if he believes the eventual disposition in a case he sees at arraignments will not involve a prospective jail sentence, he feels obligated to set bail if the person has a record of bench warrants. "Record is the first primary thing that you look at. And this is one of the frustrating parts. You know that chances are a person is not going to be . . . is not going to do any jail time on [the case], or if they are, it's going to be very little jail time. But they have a huge record of bench warrants. You're pretty sure they're not going to make bail no matter what you set. So now you're torn. . . . But they have a history of bench warranting. How can I not set bail on the case?"

Even the import of a bench warrant mark can fade with time. Mary, a defense attorney of several decades, explained the counterintuitive fact that, if a defendant warranted on a minor case many years ago, the evidence of a successful life performance can overcome the otherwise fatal mark of an open case and active bench warrant.

> We get cases ten, fifteen years old. What do you think you're going to do in the AP part? Dismiss them. It's amazing, right? Those people will get rewarded for bench warranting. As long as you don't get arrested for fifteen years. They should have gotten the ACD in the first place. . . . They want civil obedience. Not only not going to do it again, but they don't want to . . . if you are a functioning, productive member of this society. A lot of judges don't want to screw up your chances of remaining so, with a record of some sort or something that is going to prejudice your employment. Except for DWIs. They don't have that feeling then.

It might seem surprising that a defendant who has bench warranted for more than a decade would be offered a conditional dismissal almost immediately instead of a jail sentence. But inside the logic of the managerial model, judges and prosecutors essentially decide to forgo the future mark because they have seen evidence of a successful performance over an extended period of time in the past, as reflected by the fact that the person has not had police contact. Thus, the mark of an old bench warrant becomes less potent in a later encounter not simply because it has aged, but because legal actors believe something relevant about the defendant has been reveled over time.

Notwithstanding that the value of marks depreciates over time, once a person has chalked up his or her first criminal conviction, it is difficult to secure a nonconviction disposition in later arrests for several reasons. First, a defendant's conviction record is one of the most important determinants of the standard plea offers in misdemeanorland. Prosecutors' misdemeanor offer policies are often reduced to a sort of matrix, crossing the arrest charge with the defendant's criminal history to delimitate the range of pleas authorized for line ADAs, which can be departed from only with supervisor approval. Certainly, prosecutors and judges also take into account the facts of the charges and the strength of the evidence in forming offers. Nonetheless, it is difficult to distinguish between cases of the same charge type in the abbreviated time devoted to each case. Therefore, if the standard office policy is a plea to the top charge for defendants with prior convictions, then even if there is some possibility of securing a better plea—by litigating the factual or legal issues or by presenting mitigating evidence about the offense or about the defendant's life to the assigned prosecutor or judge—the practical meaning of that possibility is structured by the defendant's incentives and resources.

Valery, a public defender who has worked in Boroughs A and B, recounts that she often has to explain to her clients that there are strong institutional biases against offering noncriminal dispositions to defendants with prior convictions. She explained how this dynamic works by discussing the advice she gives clients who claim factual innocence of the current misdemeanor charge but who have one or more prior criminal convictions at the time of arrest. If she can secure a plea to a noncriminal violation, normally disorderly conduct, she explains to the client: "Dis con is what they offer innocent people with records"—meaning that even on a very weak case, an offer of disorderly conduct is often the best that a defendant with a prior conviction can expect. Valery said that much of her job as a defense attorney is explaining that contesting charges and seeking trial is both time-consuming and risky. In practice, this often means she feels challenged in her professional role because she feels as if she is dissuading her clients from "fighting their cases."

Defendants with prior criminal convictions struggle to secure a noncriminal conviction disposition for two other related reasons: it is difficult for defendants to marshal the resources to defeat the standard offer presumption and because they often do not withstand the process costs necessary to do so. Much of the literature on plea bargaining in the felony context concerns whether insufficient legal and factual investigation will lead innocent defendants to be convicted and punished unjustly because the finders of fact (judges conducting sentencing or prosecutors with the power to set the plea offer) do not have the relevant information. Those same concerns are of course present in the misdemeanor context. Both public defenders and prosecutors are overloaded with cases and have limited time and resources to investigate cases or to research legal issues before pleas are taken. But, in addition and perhaps more important, in misdemeanorland defendants often perceive the *time* it takes to do legal research or factual investigation as more burdensome than the plea offer available early in the case's life course. This raises questions not just about the accuracy of pleas in terms of factual guilt or innocence, but also about the fairness of institutional design when one party in an ostensibly adversarial system lacks leverage to contest the unilateral assessment of the other party regarding guilt and proper punishment. Judge Marcos explained that he sometimes felt uncomfortable about how this dynamic played out in his court:

> I did the AP part yesterday. And I'm getting cases that are just out of arraignments. The person has been in jail a week. The offer is an A or a B [misdemeanor] and time served. So the person is getting out anyway. And you know what? Is this fair—this person sat in jail. And you know that they've taken the plea to get out.
>
> Time served, they can walk. You also know that a lot of pleas that are taken in the arraignment parts are taken for a matter of convenience. It's . . . you feel bad, because you don't want people taking pleas just for a matter of convenience. But then you look and you understand what could happen. Bail can be set.

The marking dynamics in misdemeanorland make it very difficult for defendants to overcome the presumptive offers authorized for each designated status. In February 2011, a thirty-something black man was arraigned for petit larceny. He was accused of stealing a package of Cracker Barrel cheese. He was deemed subject to "Operation Spotlight" because of his recent arrest history. The DA's policy in these cases is to not engage in plea bargaining (at least at arraignment), and instead to recommend a plea to the top charge and the maximum statutorily allowed sentence, which in this case was a conviction for a Class A misdemeanor and one year in jail. Judges can, and often do, make their own offers on these cases, but they are limited to sentencing within the range of the top charge. In this case, the judge offered a plea to the A misdemeanor with five days in jail, and the defendant readily accepted.

What actually transpired with the Cracker Barrel cheese was uncertain not only to me as an observer of the court, but also to the legal actors processing the case. But what was readily apparent to all actors, including the defendant, was the structure of incentives. Had the defendant not accepted the judge's jail offer, the judge most likely would have set bail because of the defendant's substantial recent arrests and bench warrant history. If the defendant accepted the judge's offer to plead to a misdemeanor with a five-day jail sentence, he, as discussed above, would have then been held in custody for only three additional days. However, if the defendant did not accept the judge's offer, he would likely have been held in custody at least five additional days. An in-custody case is typically adjourned for at least five days, excluding Sunday, to allow the prosecution the statutory time to convert the charging document.[28] Therefore, assuming the defendant could not make bail (his attorney stated he was homeless), the jail sentence offered at arraignment was *shorter* than the time he would spend in custody just to make his very first appearance in an all-purpose courtroom. The incentive to plead guilty at arraignment in order to minimize time in custody is fairly obvious in cases like this.

Furthermore, this defendant, like most who plead to misdemeanor crimes with jail time at arraignments, was already marked with prior criminal convictions. Many defendants tend to apprehend a lower marginal cost to incurring an additional mark of a misdemeanor conviction when they have already been living with the collateral consequences of a prior criminal conviction. They are forced to weigh the future costs of another conviction not only with the immediate salient threat of longer jail time, but under the time constraints and pressure of an abbreviated arraignment. The incentive structure illustrated here helps make sense of the quantitative trends documented in chapter 2, which shows that the probability of conviction on a new misdemeanor arrest increases substantially with the number of convictions the defendant bears at the time of arrest, even holding constant the number of actual arrests not visible to court actors.

Judge Muñoz, a former supervisor in the DA's office and current Criminal Court judge, explained the significance of the defendant's record in the dynamics of accepting plea offers:

> Most of these people are very poor and they don't have the time or the energy to litigate. And, as you see, they don't want to come to court. If there is a [criminal] record that they have or a history of arrests, they have the tendency to believe that no one is going to believe them. And in situations like that, when they come up to me to my part, and those types of allegations are put on the record, I ask the People to look into it. But I tell the People if those factual allegations are going to come up going to trial, you probably will not have a good case. Or

maybe they will have a case. I have no idea. It depends what type of jury you pick. Maybe you pick a jury that will believe the police officers no matter what. And maybe you pick a jury that you might not believe the officers, no matter what. You never know.

So based on all of those situations, the defendant tends to plead more often than not, as opposed to litigate those cases. Because it's their word against the police officer. You just have to make a decision as to how they're going to handle that case.

This illustrates not only the importance of the defendant's record in determining the plea offer. It also illustrates the limited role of judges in the pretrial period to encouraging, but not forcing, consideration of factual and legal questions about cases in their courtrooms. However, this does not mean that judges have no role in the dynamics of managerial justice. Even if judges cannot force prosecutors to reduce charges, they can take various actions that influence plea-bargaining dynamics, including setting bail, setting the tone in the courtroom for what they deem an appropriate disposition for a given case, urging the prosecution or defense to look into issues in the case, and deciding motions on the admissibility of evidence.

In addition, it is the specter of a *bench* trial—and not a jury trial—that makes the fact of the defendant's prior record so important in plea negotiations. The standard practice with A misdemeanors (the majority of misdemeanor arrests) is to keep the cases as Class A during the pendency of the case in order to gain the benefit of the longer speedy trial time allowed for A misdemeanors, but then to reduce the charge to a B misdemeanor on the trial date in order to ensure a bench trial. The expectation to reduce for purposes of ensuring a bench trial is so pervasive that one specialized quality-of-life offense courtroom in Borough B is staffed almost exclusively by judges with limited jurisdiction who cannot legally perform jury trials, despite the fact that most cases pending there are A misdemeanors. Whether or not defendants are in fact less likely to win acquittals at bench trials, prosecutors have a manifest preference for trying cases to judges over juries. One defense attorney called this practice "an end run around the constitutional and due process right to a jury trial."[29] Nonetheless, defense attorneys are largely powerless to resist it. New York Criminal Procedure Law exempts New York City Criminal Courts—and only New York City— from the statewide rule providing for jury trial rights for all misdemeanor cases, limiting the right only to only A misdemeanors.[30]

What this means is that the bodies of law intended to give defendants fair and impartial adjudications by limiting the state's use of evidence collected in violation of law or that is more prejudicial than probative are of limited, perhaps even theoretical, import for almost all misdemeanor defendants. There are, for example, extensive statutory and common law rules that govern when and to what extent a defendant's prior bad acts or convictions ought to be admitted into evidence: prior convictions are not to be admitted for the purpose of proving the defendant's criminal propensity—that is, because he has been convicted of crimes in the past he is likely guilty of the current charged offense. Sometimes, however, some or all of the defendant's prior record can be admitted into evidence for an alternative purpose, such as showing proof of motive, opportunity, intent, absence of mistake or accident.[31]

In a jury trial, a judge holds what are called *Molineux* pretrial hearings to make a legal determination if evidence a prosecutor seeks to introduce about the defendant's prior criminal record should be admitted into evidence and for what purpose.[32] If she decides certain evidence is not admissible, the jury will never hear about it. In a bench trial, however, the same judge presides over the pretrial hearings and the trial, deciding both the admissibility of evidence and serving as the finder of fact. Judges in bench trials still must hold *Molineux* pretrial hearings to determine which of defendant's alleged prior bad acts would be admissible in the trial and for what purposes, but they are of course aware of all of the alleged bad acts in the fact-finding portion of the trial. Defense attorneys and defendants often express skepticism that the judges can effectively "un-ring the bell" from the pretrial phase. Therefore, the entire nonsealed criminal histories of defendants in lower criminal courts are visible and salient at each of the key decision-making points in their cases, from setting bail, to the administrative decision in the prosecutor's office regarding the plea offer or recommendation, to the finder of fact if the case goes to bench trial.

In sum, prosecutors and judges often discuss the value of rendering individualized justice and taking case- and defendant-specific character-istics into account in case disposition. But the marks defendants bear as they enter and traverse misdemeanorland trigger a series of organizational, professional, and political pressures on court actors and activate standard responses in the field. Once a defendant is in a certain posture vis-à-vis the managerial system because of his prior marks, it is much harder to push the adjudicative framework, because a new set of constraints pops up. A person with a criminal record has a significantly diminished likelihood of being believed in the abbreviated administrative fact-finding pervasive in misdemeanor courts. Prosecutors do not want to risk professional reputations diverging from standard offer policies, and judges do not want to be on record not setting bail or imposing non-jail dispositions. A person with a criminal record also has significantly diminished incentives to withstand process costs, because he or she already has the mark of a conviction, and many defendants would rather take another conviction early on in the case than stay in jail or come back to court for months to fight the case.

Criminal court actors, especially prosecutors and judges, often explain their adherence to the additive imperative in terms such as "deterrence." But, interestingly, they also often claim that by the time a defendant has cycled through misdemeanorland enough to qualify for a criminal conviction, much less jail time, he or she has been acclimated to the penal burdens such that the addition of marks or even jail time has minimal deterrent effect. Jill, a supervisor in the DA's office in Borough A, explained that she believed the humiliation of a first arrest or the collateral consequences of a first conviction might have a deterrent effect—but, she said, "for the people with like forty or fifty arrests, it [the criminal conviction] means nothing to them, and neither does the time. The jail time does not mean anything to them."

Certainly, being incarcerated means something to the human being who experiences it. But, I understood the ADA's statement to essentially concede that by the time prosecutors and judges are adding five-day increments to jail sentences for the umpteenth misdemeanor conviction, the practice is done more out of observance of the marking ritual in order to give an internal consistency to the managerial logic than out of a belief that incremental jail time has any effective exogenous function such as deterring future criminal activity. Mark, a public defender of about five years said, "Jail time only gets imposed in this building on those people for whom it doesn't matter. I mean, it matters *for* them, but it does not matter *to* them. They are going to keep using drugs and being an addict if you impose ten days, thirty days, ninety days. The jail time is not going to change that." Even those who do say that they believe incremental marking and sentences accomplish something would have no way of scientifically verifying the intuition—or at least I have never encountered anyone who offered anything other than folk understandings about some vague notion of "deterrence" in defense of the practice. This is not to claim that it does not does not have those effects; I don't know either. But the incremental approach to marking is a ritualized, perhaps even ceremonial, aspect of the managerial model whose adoption predated any possibility of knowing its effects and whose persistence is quite independent of evidence of its effects.

Dynamic Marking

The Broken Windows policing regime has resulted in more arrests but fewer convictions. This means that the people targeted by these policing tactics, largely young men of color, have increasingly experienced cycles of temporary marks, such as open cases or conditional dismissals, or marks of limited accessibility, such as noncriminal convictions from misdemeanor arrests. To illustrate, compare the five-year trajectories of those individuals who received their first MJACD in the years 1980–81 and 1985–86 with those receiving their first MJACD in the height of the Broken Windows regime during the years 2000–2001 and 2005–6.

A strikingly similar proportion of the pre- and post–Broken Windows MJACD cohorts were not rearrested within five years of the initiating MJACD disposition: 43 percent of the combined 1980–81/85–86 cohorts had no later criminal arrests, and 46 percent of the combined 2000–2001/05–6 cohorts had no later criminal arrests within five years. But the average outcomes for those who *did* experience another arrest varied substantially, most strikingly in misdemeanorland. Figure 4.3 counts all arrests experienced by cohort pairs (for those that had one or more rearrest post-MJACD) at any point within five years after entering the cohort separately by type (misdemeanor versus felony) and by disposition—no conviction, violation conviction, misdemeanor conviction, felony conviction—and displays the disposition patterns from all of the misdemeanor and felony arrests, separately for the 1980–81/85–86 and 2000–2001/05–6 cohorts. The relative sizes of the shaded portions show the proportion of each arrest type that ended in each type of disposition. What this figure means experientially for the people who traversed misdemeanorland is that a much higher proportion of the cohorts entering with an MJACD during the Broken Windows regime experienced one or more later misdemeanor arrests that did *not* terminate in a conviction.

Figures 4.4 and 4.5 show the misdemeanor arrest and conviction patterns for the 1980–81/85–86 and 2000–2001/05–6 cohorts, respectively, broken out by the number of arrests the person had experienced within five years of entering the cohort. For example, 13 percent of the people in the pre–Broken Windows MJACD cohorts who experienced

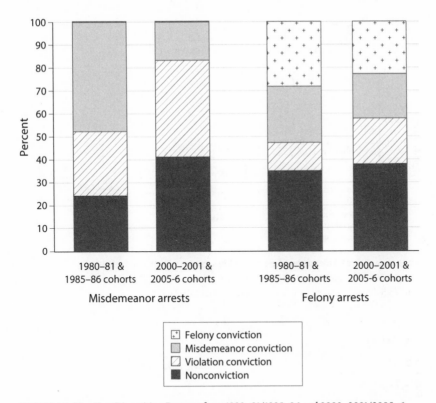

FIGURE 4.3. Five-Year Disposition Patterns from 1980–81/1985–86 and 2000–2001/2005–6 MJACD Cohorts, Misdemeanor and Felony Arrests
Note: Individual-level data from DCJS; author's own calculations.

four or more misdemeanor arrests within five years of entering the cohort ended up with zero misdemeanor convictions, whereas fully 52 percent of the people in the post–Broken Windows MJACD cohorts who experienced four or more misdemeanor arrests within five years of entering the cohort had zero misdemeanor convictions. About 65 percent of the people in the pre–Broken Windows MJACD cohorts who experienced two misdemeanor arrests within five years ended the five-year period with zero misdemeanor convictions from misdemeanor arrests, whereas 89 percent of the people in the post–Broken Windows MJACD cohorts who experienced two misdemeanor arrests within five years ended the period with zero misdemeanor convictions. These figures show that a much more common experience for the people drawn into the orbit of misdemeanorland during the Broken Windows era is to experience a series of arrests resulting in open cases, conditional dismissals, speedy

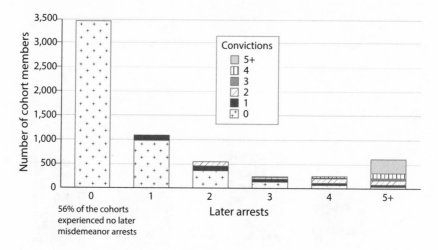

FIGURE 4.4. Later Misdemeanor Arrests and Misdemeanor Convictions within Five Years of Entering 1980–81 and 1985–86 MJACD Cohorts
Note: Individual-level data from DCJS; author's own calculations.

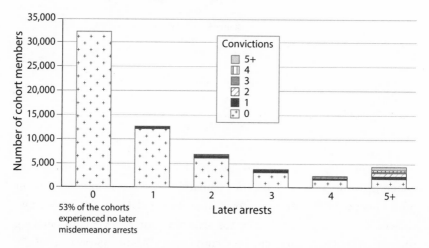

FIGURE 4.5. Later Misdemeanor Arrests and Misdemeanor Convictions within Five Years of Entering 2000–2001 and 2005–6 MJACD Cohorts
Note: Individual-level data from DCJS; author's own calculations.

trial dismissals, violation noncriminal convictions, and other types of temporary or limited-access marks, as opposed to the permanent mark of conviction.

Because the later cohorts are so much larger than earlier ones, these provisional marking experiences have touched a much wider swath of city residents over the past two decades. Notice the scale of figure 4.5 is *ten times* that of figure 4.4. Fully 83 percent of the combined 2000–2001/05–6 cohorts who were arrested for a misdemeanor at least once more after their first MJACD were never convicted of a crime, meaning that the only later encounters with the criminal justice system they experienced generated temporary or limited-access marks.

Marks are an unavoidable part of case processing, but those that emerge out of misdemeanorland are not merely the passive upshot of bureaucratic court processes. Nor are the arrest decisions of police officers merely ratified by courts recording arrests as convictions. Criminal court actors understand the varying degrees of severity, accessibility, and consequence of different marks, and they actively use marking as a penal technique in the managerial logic. Criminal court actors engage marking in a dynamic process of sorting, testing, and assessing defendants. Committed to the additive imperative, judges and prosecutors actively guard their ability to retain and access marks, and defense attorneys actively try to guard their clients against it.

Take the recent Human Trafficking Intervention Initiative, initiated in 2013 by then–Chief Judge Lippman with the aim "to promote a just and compassionate resolution to cases involving those charged with prostitution—treating these defendants as trafficking victims, likely to be in dire need of medical treatment and other critical services."[33] The disposition practices in these specialized parts (which are usually a designated day in a regular domestic violence court part) involve offering an ACD upon completion of five to ten counseling sessions. Prosecutors in one of the largest boroughs insisted that defendants execute a waiver of sealing of the prosecutor's internal records in order to qualify for the disposition. This means that although the defendants would benefit from the public suppression of the record of the arrest, the prosecutors would maintain access to the information so that they could engage more mechanisms of social control if the defendant is rearrested. Defense organizations strenuously resisted the concession. After extensive negotiations, they agreed upon a waiver for a limited number of years.

An increasingly common practice in some boroughs, especially Manhattan, is demanding that defendants "waive" sealing altogether to receive certain noncriminal conviction dispositions. So even when the apparent consensus surrounding arrests of sex workers is an approach keenly tuned to improve their basic welfare by averting the deleterious consequences of records from prostitution arrests, prosecutors are disinclined to give up access to the marks that would allow them to classify people in later encounters. Even if they agree that a mark should be inaccessible to the outside world, criminal court actors guard their own ability to preserve records so they can use them in the managerial pursuit of evaluating compliance over time and ratcheting up social control for later encounters.

The marks that matter for people's lives generated from low-level arrests are not just the final disposition or conviction that signal to the world the defendant's absolute, final achieved status. Rather, marking is an interactive process that responds to how the defendant performs after accepting the mark. The marks associated with a particular person can change over time, and interim marks are often accessible to various entities beyond the court. If, for example, an ACD or disorderly conduct violation conviction is conditioned on a program or community service, the defendant is required to make a court appearance to prove compliance. The court records will show that the defendant has a particular disposition during the allotted compliance time period, which is accessible to the public during this time, but that can change if he fails to make the compliance court date and provide verification of completion. Thus, conditional marks like the ACD can transform into permanent marks if a person fails to discharge a mandated performance or cannot withstand the procedural demands of misdemeanorland.

In February 2012, a middle-aged Latino man stood before the court for arraignment on a new assault charge, but he also had an outstanding warrant for not making a court date to prove he had completed two days of community service on an ACD granted more than a year prior. Before being released without bail on his new arrest, he was resentenced to a noncriminal disorderly conduct violation with the sentence of "time served," which was the two days he had spent in custody on the new arrest awaiting arraignment. The new disposition would impose a more serious mark than the ACD that he failed to secure because he did not perform the community service or make the compliance court date, but it did not involve any prospective jail time. Exchanges like this one show how quickly seasoned criminal court actors can commensurate and trade penal burdens: a failed performance and inability to conform to procedural requirements was exchanged for a more severe mark.

Provisional marks accumulated from one open case often have important consequences for a subsequent arrest. This dynamic is pronounced for people with frequent arrests because of mental health or drug problems.

For example, most defendants are released on their own recognizance on a first arrest. However, if they fail to show up to their court appearance for that open case and are rearrested, it is much more likely bail will be set on the new arrest. Mary, a public defender in Borough A, said that she had a client with severe paranoid schizophrenia who also was struggling with a drug problem: "He was accused of taking a drill from a storehouse, which he was going to sell for drugs. His mental problems are complicated by drug problems. He had been arrested five times." Mary explained that she supposed that the prosecutor and judge understood this man's criminal conduct was the result of his mental health and drug problem, but she believed they felt constrained to ask for bail because of the marks of the prior arrests and bench warrants.

> They are not looking to punish him, but they are more looking to keep him out of . . . protect society. They like the warehouse idea. They're big on warehousing. And you said that to them, "Why are you asking for so much bail?" They just didn't want to let him out. And you're looking at someone who is a street person. You could say $50, and the guy would stay in. $5,000? $10,000? $15,000? What's the point? Talk about overkill. And then you ask them, and they'll say stuff like, "I always ask for that much bail in those cases." [Laughs.] So then you know you're not going to get anywhere. It's all about covering your ass. Nobody wants anybody to get out.

There are strong professional and organizational reasons that prosecutors and judges ask for bail when a person has a record of past bench warrants, even if a prospective jail sentence is an unlikely disposition from the arrest. Once bail is set, the defendant is much more likely to take a plea to a criminal conviction. And in this case, taking a plea to a criminal conviction was a much more expedient way to resolve the case than having the defendant evaluated for mental fitness to proceed.[34]

One cannot really understand the marks people traversing misdemeanorland accumulate without understanding the other challenges facing those who are most frequently brought into its orbit. Consider the following account from Martha, a public defender for several decades, about her client who was a young man living with his grandmother: "I did have a case in [Borough C] [where] the [NYPD] officers would come into the home to make sure that the family was in compliance with the order of protection—that the [kid] who had been ordered to stay away. . . . Now, this was a kid. . . . He lived with his grandmother, and the grandmother would periodically call the cops on him and get him out. Then they would resolve their differences, and she would invite him back. And the mother was sort of in the mix, but the kid had custody taken away from her and given to the grandmother. How old was he? A teenager. At this point he was like seventeen, but it had been going on for years."

Upon arrest, the mark of the open case and the order of protection are available to the NYPD, who is charged with enforcing it. In this case, the court imposed a full stay-away order of protection in favor of the grandmother. The NYPD has a dedicated Domestic Violence Bureau (all *family* offenses are classified as DV) that makes random house visits to addresses listed on orders of protection. If a defendant successfully abides by the order of protection, or avoids detection for violating it, he or she might be able to earn a less restrictive order or even the willingness of the prosecutor and judge to be less than diligent in trying to prosecute the case. But the order itself opens the defendant up to a new charge. A defendant is guilty of criminal contempt in the second degree, an A misdemeanor, if he intentionally violates an order of protection by making in-person, electronic, or third-party contact, and a defendant is guilty of criminal contempt in the first degree, an E felony, if he violates the order by placing the protected party in reasonable fear of physical injury.[35] Contempt is often much easier to prove than the underlying case, in which complainants often become unwilling to cooperate with the prosecution, because all the prosecution needs to show to prove contempt is communication in violation of the order. Young men and women living in poverty with few other residential options and whose families have few resources to secure the young person alternative housing are at risk of building a criminal record because the police are one of the few resources their families can reliably call on if they feel worried or threatened. At the same time, families are often unwilling to force young men or women into homelessness, so they allow them to come back into the home with a pending order of protection.[36] Martha explained how this dynamic plays out in Criminal Court:

> Martha: The only record he had was from these DV cases. The pleas of guilt that he had to do, to get out [of jail because bail was set]. You know, when he had all this time in. And it was so tragic. I got to know the whole family. They really wanted to help him. One time he got arrested because they showed up and the family hid him in the bathtub. But the cops came in and they

found him. It was just wrenching. It was really wrenching at that
point. And I know that there needed to be more services for the
family, to help them reunite as a family. Because that's what they
really wanted. But they had these things that were imposed on
them, that prevented them from doing it. And it was just so . . .
a wrong-headed approach to it. It was horrible. And then the kid
ended up with a major record.

Q: All on contempt cases?

Martha: Yes. . . . Three. But he had a contempt case, and the cop
testified. They can make out their case without the family, then.
Because the cop is going to testify that he was there [at the house
in violation of the order of protection]. And then you get these
judges who . . . when the family doesn't want to go forward and
the DA doesn't want to go forward, right? The DA doesn't want
to go forward. . . . And then the frigging judge on the bench says,
"Well, you don't need your witnesses to prove this case; get the
cop." And all of a sudden it's a case they wanted to die, because
it was some kind of family matter, has a new life. It's resurrected,
with the cop testifying.

Marks emerge as part of a dynamic, ongoing process or relationship
with various arms of the criminal justice system, including courts, police,
and service providers, and their interactions with families and communities. A young man like Martha's former client ended up with three Class
A misdemeanor convictions because, owing to the family's inability to
provide other alternatives, he returned to the only home he had—one in
which his grandmother lacked tools other than the police to help her deal
with a grandson suffering from behavioral issues.

Many people have difficulty bearing up under the procedural requirements necessary to earn the conditional dismissals offered in misdemeanorland. Consider Michael, a young black man in his early twenties arrested
in the summer of 2011 for swiping a "student MetroCard" without a student
ID. When I met Michael, he had already been arrested twice before, once
for jumping a turnstile at age sixteen and a second time, at age seventeen,
for bringing a folding knife to school so that he could, in his words, "make
little necklace and things for girls," using fishnet string. When the officers
stopped Michael in 2011, he insisted that he had a seven-day unlimited regular MetroCard and asked the arresting officers to swipe his card to verify.
Michael said he gave the card to the arresting officer, who retained it but,

instead of verifying the type of card, instead ran Michael's name over the radio and found an outstanding warrant for an unanswered summons for disorderly conduct from the prior year. He recounted:

> They never even checked the card. They never went to the booth and asked the clerk to check the card and when it was last used. They didn't do that. I asked them could they do that, so I could keep going about my business. I was headed back home. But they sent me to Transit. . . . Yeah, they just sent me back to the Transit District [redacted]. Brought me there. Ran my name. Took my fingerprints. Took my photo. They said they were going to give me a "DAT," but I didn't really understand what that was, so I asked them. . . . But they didn't. The guy kept lying, "Oh, we're going to get you out of here." I already knew. I understand how the system works. How the law works.
>
> So basically, when I heard, "We're going to have you out of here in like an hour or so," I knew I was headed to Central Booking. So, I was really upset.

Per NYPD Patrol Guide regulations, Michael was taken into custody for the open summons warrant. He was also arrested and charged with criminal trespass in the fourth degree and theft of service for swiping a student MetroCard.

Michael was offered an ACD at arraignment, conditional on the completion of two days of community service. He insisted to his attorney that he had in fact swiped an unlimited card and there was no student MetroCard found on him when he was searched at the Transit precinct because, according to Michael, one of the officers at the subway station had taken it and forgotten about it, and it was not at the precinct. Nonetheless, Michael accepted the arraignment offer and signed up for two days to complete his mandated community service. His compliance date was set for September to bring proof of completion of the community service. He was also instructed to clear the summons warrant by returning to court with a picture ID.

Michael came back to court about a week after arraignment to clear his summons warrant. He did not have ID with him because he said it was at his sister's house and he was staying with someone else. The clerk would not give him the docket number on his case without ID, and he needed the docket number to take to the "war room" to pull the case file and ask a judge to call it and adjudicate the summons. The clerk pulled the docket numbers as a favor to me, using just a name and birthday search, which revealed not one but two unanswered summonses. Upon seeing the other summons, he recalled it was for selling water on a hot day at the beach in Queens the prior summer. He recounted that when the police officer approached him and said it was a violation to sell water without a vendor's license, he had replied, "Come on, man, it's for water, is not drugs. It feels good to get a dollar for selling something you ain't got a be like all [makes furtive movements] on the corner like this," and he added, "This is what my friends be doing," making more furtive movements acting out a drug sale. He said the cop told him, "Well look, you have to have the vendor's license, and it is better I give you this ticket as opposed to arrest you for it," and Michael agreed and took the ticket.

We proceeded to the "war room" with the summons docket numbers and were told they were "down for the day." The clerk instructed him to take those small slips of paper with the docket numbers home and come back on Monday at 9:00 a.m., and they would pull the summons dockets for him to get cleared by the judge. Next Monday he did not show up in court, and I was not able to reach him by phone. Next time we spoke, he said he had completed the assigned community service but lost the paperwork that proved compliance. He did not show up for his compliance court date in September. Michael had a cell phone, but it was regularly cut off or reactivated with new numbers. His aunt and cousin had better phone access, but he did not have a stable residence with either of them. When I finally reached him, he said he did not receive the warrant notices or reminder mailings or phone calls for his court dates because he did not have a stable residence and his cell phone was cut off. When he did come back to court, he again had lost his state ID, so he had trouble getting the community service clerk to release the court's copy of the paperwork proving completion of the community service (he had lost his copy from months prior).

The last time I talked to him, he said he had copies of the compliance paperwork to get his ACD, but he had picked up a new DAT for marijuana in November after walking with a friend who was smoking a joint. After that point, I lost track of him. I was never able to reach him on any of his cell phone numbers or at his aunt's or cousin's number. Somehow he must have succeeded in securing noncriminal convictions for both of his misdemeanor cases, because when I checked his criminal record in 2015, the only visible mark was an open warrant for a criminal possession of weapon in the fourth arrest in 2013.

Michael is an example of the type of experiences typical in the era of Broken Windows policing. He had, by my count, at least five misdemeanor arrests and two summonses over a five-year period. He likely had more summonses that I was not aware of after we lost touch. Not one of these encounters terminated in a criminal conviction. He cycled in and out of marked and semi-marked status, often with open cases that any landlord or potential employer could easily find on WebCrims without even paying for a criminal background check. He often had pending warrants, but not for things that would qualify him for prison or jail. Nonetheless, lacking ID, money for a cell phone, and a stable residence, he found it very difficult to execute the performances and bear up successfully under the procedural hassles required to earn conditional leniency.

Marking in misdemeanorland serves some of the same functions it does in the more familiar felony regions of the criminal justice system, namely, to record relevant facts of defendants' actions and status to be used by officials in various arenas of social life. However, in the managerial logic, marking is not always the upshot of a determination that a defendant has been adjudicated guilty of a precise crime and thereby an indication that his public self has been socially transitioned to a new master status of "convicted" or "felon." The most common marks produced in New York City's lower courts during the Broken Windows era are signals of temporally limited duration or limited public accessibility, often by design and consent of the parties. Criminal court actors use marking dynamically, to record how defendants have performed under the requirements of misdemeanorland, and they consult these records at punctuated moments of decision making about a defendant's case. Yet, precisely because actors often know and understand the collateral consequences of marking, they sometimes contest the type of mark or seek to limit its duration. Sometimes conviction is not even a desired or necessary part for the social control project in misdemeanor courts, which relies more on constructing a record of a person's behavior over time than assigning guilt for a specific transgression.

5

Procedural Hassle

"They don't show much concern for the public," he said.

"They don't show any concern at all," said the usher, "just look at the waiting room here."

—FRANZ KAFKA, *THE TRIAL*

Procedural hassle—the collection of burdensome experiences and costs attendant to arrest and case processing—is an inevitable part of the criminal process. By analyzing it as a *technique* of social control, I mean to propose that these experiences constitute something more than a set of inconvenient burdens that dissuade defendants from invoking their due process rights or even informal means by which judges and prosecutors punish defendants; they are also active, productive tools in the project of social control in the field of misdemeanorland. The set of experiences analyzed here are relevant in their content as well as form: the procedural hassles represent a series of opportunities to engage defendants in official encounters with symbolic meaning, construct their status vis-à-vis the court and its powers, and to discipline and reform their behavior.

The technique of procedural hassle is distinct from marking because it is not about tracing a potentially risky defendant in the outside world but rather about delaying, engaging, and compelling the defendant to conform to the institutional and organizational demands of the court and court actors. It encompasses the degradation of arrest and police custody; the stress and frequency of court appearances; and the opportunity costs of lost work, child care, or other family or social responsibilities to make court appearances or to comply with court orders during the pendency of the case.

Arrest and Arraignment

Every misdemeanor case begins with an arrest, and it is this "ceremony of degradation" that transforms a free person into a criminal defendant, with all of the attendant social meanings, physical discomforts, and civil burdens.[1] Misdemeanorland is not a total institution. There is no "barrier to social intercourse with the outside"; the great majority of defendants are "out" while the case is pending, either on their own recognizance or bail, freely traveling back and forth to court from home. The court itself does not establish all-encompassing control over every aspect of defendants' lives.[2] Nonetheless, procedural hassles are the rituals by which the people brought into misdemeanorland are initiated into a denigrated status vis-à-vis the coercive powers of the police and courts. A series of initiation mortifications serve the purpose of what Erving Goffman called "role dispossession," such that whatever status the person has in the outside world is stripped away and the only self that is maintained is that aspect relevant to the individual's encounter with the court: his or her record of transgressions and involuntary client status.[3] The arrest-to-arraignment process involves loss of physical autonomy and comfort, fears for one's safety, enactments of deference to the police and court officials, forced contamination with unpleasant and unwanted people and substances, and a violation of self and privacy in order to record and register the entrant into the system. Those initial mortifying experiences transform a free person into a criminal defendant.

Jannelle, a black woman in her early twenties, was arrested for theft of services when she entered a crowded city bus from the back door without swiping her MetroCard. She was in college, employed, and had never been arrested or issued a summons prior to this incident, although she had been stopped, questioned, and asked for identification at least five times over the past few years. Jannelle presented herself this way: "I'm not the type of person who is always in trouble with the law. I kind of look the part, but that's not me completely. I'm totally away from that."[4] According to Jannelle, she had a transfer on her MetroCard from the bus she had just ridden but did not want to miss the bus to which she was transferring, so she, along with some other people, entered the bus through the back door to avoid the late afternoon crowd rushing the front door. She described her arrest as both personally humiliating to her sense of self as a law-abiding college student and physically degrading:

> That's when the other officer came. And he is really big. . . . And he continued to grab me, like really grab my arm. Really pulling me off the bus. Like if I really stole somebody's stuff or if I robbed anybody. My books are all over the floor. . . . My papers destroyed. This is my schoolwork. . . . And like I said, I'm not small. And I know that. But at the same time, the way they handled me was that if I was a guy that robbed something.
>
> . . . And they pull up my hands behind my back. My arm is just killing me right now. They pushed me up . . . there's a bank on the corner, Chase Bank. They pushing me up against the bank and putting me on this wall, and if you don't shut up we're going to throw you on the floor. All of that for $2.25. All of that.

People with an extensive arrest history also often talk about the arrest as a painful and violent degradation of personhood. Destiny started engaging in prostitution to earn money as a teenager living in a group home after her drug-addicted mother could no longer take care of her. Over the years, she has had numerous arrests for drugs and prostitution, but contrary to some folk wisdom, she is not inured to the ordeal of arrest. In fact, she talked about the specific vulnerabilities she felt and humiliations she suffered when police make prostitution arrests:

> So one day I met a guy in a car, and he asked me some questions. And basically one of those questions was how much would it take him in order for us to go out. So I started asking him whether or not he was a police officer, or not. Because I was kind of trained to do that. He told me no. And then once I agreed to a sum that he actually kind of like quoted, he basically was like, "What's your name, what's your name?" And I was like, "My name is Destiny. Why? What happened?" And, "Oh, the cops is coming." So the cops rushed up like I was El Chapo. And they rushed up to the car, and they had their guns drawn. . . . One lady took her hand and just dug it in my bra. She snatched out. And at the time, because I was smoking drugs so heavily, I didn't have any breasts. So I was using some socks to fill out my clothing and fill out my bra. . . .

Because she was probably looking if I had a pipe on me, or some drugs. But they don't ask nicely. Once they catch you in a situation, they can strip you in the street if they want, and kick your ass if they want. You're lucky if they don't smash your head in. So it was just how they treat you. And then they threw me in the back of a van.

An arrest is a protracted affair. Sometimes the arresting officers keep people in a large police van for hours while they are making other arrests. Destiny explained:

There were some other women [in the van already]. Everybody was hog-tied. It was like five or six women already back there. One little woman had a black eye because apparently she tried to resist the arrest. First of all, you really don't know. These guys got plain clothes. You don't know if you're being kidnapped or if these guys are in fact the law. Who knows who these people are? So they come rushing up, and they smacked her to the ground and punched her in her face. So she was back there. We all hog-tied. So we ride around for hours, looking for more prostitutes, looking for more hoes or hookers in every neighborhood in [Borough A]. For hours. For hours. One girl had to do-do, and she hunkered up her ass and shitted in the van and just shitted on the side panel of the van. Because they wouldn't . . . I think she was on heroin and her stomach was turning. She just hunkered up, and she just took a shit right there in the van. It was disgusting. It was defiling.

The first stop after a person is taken into custody after an arrest is the police precinct to which the arresting officer is assigned (or transit district if the arrest is made by transit officers). At the precinct, he or she is finger-printed and photographed, and the police draw up the arrest paperwork. This process can take hours. The arrestee waits in one of the holding cells at the precinct, which are often crowded and squalid. The second phase is processing at Central Booking; there is one location in every borough, usually attached to the courthouse. Defendants are generally not trans-ported to Central Booking until there is a critical mass of arrestees, so sometimes defendants can wait hours at the precinct after the paperwork is completed if there are other arrests to be processed. During the prear-raignment detention, many defendants find that "the boundary that the individual places between his being and the environment is invaded and the embodiments of self profaned."[5]

Kima, whose case was introduced in chapter 4, was arrested after she sent a text message to her boyfriend to the effect that if he tried to hurt her, she would kill him. She learned that he had filed a report against her for the incident in November 2010. A few days later, after getting her son off to school, she went directly to her local precinct, thinking she could "sort it out." She thought that by going to the police herself she could clear up the matter by explaining it was an aberrant event and she meant no real threat. Upon identifying herself to the desk officer, she was immediately arrested.

She described being so traumatized by the filth and stench of the precinct holding cell that she would not sit down on the bench. Kima stood for approximately seven hours. A few hours into her detention, a female officer allowed Kima to use her cell phone to contact her mother to ask her to pick up her son from school and to explain that she had been arrested. Kima was arrested around 9:00 a.m., and around 4:00 p.m. a sergeant arrived and noticed that she was not sitting down. He asked her if she had been offered anything to eat or drink since her arrest, and when she said no, he gave her a bottle of water and brought her a slice of pizza. The sergeant warned her that she would be standing for at least four more hours before being moved to Central Booking. Kima replied, "Yeah, this place is filthy. Are you kidding me? I am not going to sit down." He said she should know that Central Booking is "even dirtier," and she replied, "Well, then, I will stand there too." He asked her, "Okay. What do you need?" She recounted, "I told him, 'I need bleach and ammonia, and I need paper towels.' And he brought everything to me. And he wasn't supposed to. 'Cause I could have thrown that stuff at him. That bleach and ammonia, I could have thrown that in his eye. But he let me clean everything. It took about thirty minutes, but I cleaned everything. It was like *so* clean! Compared to when I got there."

Typically, defendants are held anywhere from three to ten hours in the local precinct before being transported for arraignment. Kima was not moved until 11:30 p.m. from the precinct to Central Booking, where defendants wait for their fingerprints to be processed for rap sheets, for the district attorney's office to draft the complaint, and for the opportunity to be interviewed by their defense counsel in preparation for arraignment and bail determination. They are also interviewed by the New York City Criminal Justice Agency, the entity charged with collecting basic personal and demographic information for issuing a bail recommendation.

On a typical morning in Borough A's Criminal Court there are somewhere between 150 and 400 defendants "in the system"—sometimes referred to as the number of "bodies" that must be arraigned that day. These
individuals have "gone through the system"—they were arrested for a
felony or misdemeanor crime, fingerprinted at a police precinct, taken
to Central Booking for photographs, then transferred to the holding cells
behind the arraignment courtroom (called the pens) with a single toilet
in the corner open to view, where they wait to be called by a defense
attorney for a brief interview. Rats, mice, and roaches are a common
sighting, and smashed cheese sandwiches, the only food offered during the
entire arrest-to-arraignment period, litter the floor, in part because people
sometimes use the plastic-wrapped sandwiches as pillows if they need to
lie down. Kima explained that she was shocked that the police and court
officers who work in Central Booking and the holding pens area would
tolerate conditions infested with vermin. She said to one of the officers in
the pens area, "You are a police officer, which means you went to college,
at least for sixty credits. How does it feel that you paid sixty credits to work
with rats every day? . . . You went to college to work with rats." She spent
the night in Central Booking and was arraigned the next day around 4:00
p.m. and released on her own recognizance.

Defendants can wait anywhere from a few hours to up to twelve hours
in these pens. Michael, who did not make night court after his 2:00 p.m.
arrest and had to remain through the night in the pens for morning court,
described his overnight wait:

Q: Were there enough benches for you to sleep?
Michael: No, there was about a good twenty-seven or so of us, so I
　　actually stand up during the whole night. . . . Yeah, I didn't fall
　　asleep, not once. I am very tired right now.
Q: Wait, you stood up the whole night?
Michael: The whole night.
Q: Because it was just too gross to sit on the floor?
Michael: It's like, the sandwiches, the cheese, and whatever milk,
　　and they don't clean the toilets, the aroma from that is, uh, it's
　　killin'.
Q: There is one toilet in that room for twenty-seven people?
Michael: Yeah, basically, we got to ask people to move to the other
　　side. I'm not goin' lie, I am right here, the toilet is right there,
　　exactly let's say like nine inches away from me, I can still smell

it, so I am like this [plugging his nose] standing up, and you know when the guy uses the bathroom, you don't want to make it like you lookin' at them so, you know, they just ask, "Excuse me brothers, ya'll mind," and we got to all make a little space and turn our heads.

Sometimes defendants are moved to different holding cells while they await their arraignment. Carlos, arrested for trespassing while on parole explained:

Carlos: We call it bullpen therapy [Laughs].

Q: Why do they call it that? Because you don't understand why they keep moving you?

Carlos: To weaken you up. I don't know. To weaken you up or something. How are you going to take me from this bullpen, to this bullpen, to this bullpen, to this bullpen? You go to like five, six bullpens before you see the judge. You go to five or six bullpens before you see the judge. Why? I don't know. Some days there ain't no room to sit down. People standing up, people laying down. People sleeping under the bench.

The total arrest-to-arraignment time is, according to New York case law, not to exceed twenty-four hours, but every day numerous defendants are held in excess of this time limit. The courthouse keeps statistics on the number of people who have been waiting more than twenty-four and more than thirty-six hours to see a judge in an effort to minimize the number of complaints and identify bottlenecks. Jack, a black man in his late forties who has had a series of arrests for misdemeanor narcotics possession, explained: "I came in yesterday and got out today. Most times it'd be three days. See, this is new to me—getting out the next day. This is new. Usually you three days, bouncing around in the bullpen. Three days sleeping on the floor. Not washing. Not brushing your teeth. . . . Somebody come in there haven't bathed in months and they smell up the whole thing. It's always like that. And then the food they give you is not food. Two pieces of bread jammed together with nothing in the middle, and they call it a sandwich."

The time in custody for an arrest is often sufficient to trigger cascading negative consequences. Ernie moved to New York from Virginia, where he was on "unsupervised probation" for a drug crime. He was able to secure employment at a laundromat where he regularly worked twelve-hour shifts, but he complained of frequent arrests and summonses interfering with his attempts to get his life on track, even though none of his misdemeanor arrests had resulted in a criminal conviction over the three years he had lived in New York. He contrasted his experience with getting arrested frequently for small offenses (and often as collateral damage when someone near him was arrested) with his experience in Virginia: "When I first moved up here, I had a job. I was telling them that. . . . I mean, New York is kind of different. . . . They lock everybody. . . . That's what I've been thinking; some of the laws, they be a little bit harder. But on the up-and-up I just know that jail is probably getting tired of seeing my face. Me being here. They be petty charges; they're letting you go. They haven't really convicted me of a misdemeanor yet."

He explained his first arrest in New York City as being "in the wrong place at the wrong time. . . . Two dope fiends making a sale, and they [the police] know that these two people had a transaction, and just me being at the bus stop involved me. That was my first time." According to Ernie, he was arrested for possession with intent to distribute. He recalled being in the police van with the two people involved in the sale and asking them to tell the police he had nothing to do with the sale, showing the police that he had no money in his pocket, only a MetroCard: "Talkin' about possession with intent. I didn't even have no money on me, just my MetroCard. You know what I'm saying? Yo, if I made a sale, ain't I supposed to have some money? . . . I'm looking at this dude [the person with whom he was arrested], like *he did it*, you need to go ahead and tell these people [the police] what's goin' on, that I ain't have nothing to do with it. And he's like, 'You be all right, you be all right. This New York. They gonna let you go.' And they did. They did. But it's the process you go through."

No drugs were found on his person, so, as Ernie put it, "they gave me the back door," meaning he was released from police custody before arraignment. However, he continued, "I had to work twelve hours that night. And my job is working in a laundromat. So my Chinese lady, I'm not trying to be prejudice or nothing, she was a good Chinese lady, but she tight when it comes to that money. They don't want to hire other people. So when their relief doesn't come in, like when I don't come in—they got to stay there all night. So that's another twelve hours for somebody, just 'cause I ain't there." He spent so long in custody prior to being released that he missed his shift and was fired: "I missed it. I missed my job that day. They never let me use the phone call; they was tellin' me, 'sit down, shut up.' . . . I couldn't call my job. I was locked up." As Ernie's case shows, even an arrest that does not result in charges being filed creates significant procedural hassle. As he put it, "They just run you through the system, it's just a way to get your fingerprints, see if you wanted, you know—run you through the system. But running you through the system takes you a while. 'Cause it's packed. But people got lives out there."

If the DA does decide to file a complaint, the charging document that initiates a misdemeanor case, then the defendant will wait in Central Booking until the paperwork is ready for arraignment. Prior to seeing the judge, the defendant will meet with her or his defense attorney in pens behind the arraignment courtroom. Connected to the pens are a series of small (also filthy) metal interview booths where the defense attorney will speak with the defendant to gather information necessary to make a bail application. After the interview, court officers take defendants from the pens to hard wooden benches in the courtroom to await their arraignment. Malik, arrested for possession of marijuana and an alleged gravity knife, explained that after hours and hours of waiting, the attorney interview and arraignment are often quite speedy:

> Malik: So at one point it's like a whole bunch of attorneys showed up and then when they called up whoever case they had and that's when I met Mr. Stevens [defense attorney]. He asked me had I been arrested before, because apparently there was something in my rap sheet where somebody had used a name—my name—and had been arrested. So he said—you've never been arrested in . . . some state, Arizona or someplace like that. I said I've never been to Arizona. . . . He said—you're charged with possessing marijuana; did you have marijuana? I said no. He said—you're charged with possession of a weapon; did you have a gun? I said no. And then he kind of went down the list, and then he looked into the arrest report and saw that it was a knife. So I said—yeah, I had a knife. He said what type of knife? I said it's a pocketknife. And I demonstrated to him about how long it was, which is literally about this long. And he said okay. And that was it. The next time I saw him, we were in front of the judge for arraignment.
>
> Q: What did he say in front of the judge? Do you remember the application he made?
>
> Malik: Umm . . . I don't. It was a very brief exchange, and I was released on my own recognizance.

For many people, these legal encounters are their only direct experience with entities representing the state and therefore constitute an immediate source of information that they will draw on to form ideas and beliefs about state power and their relation to it. My data on defendants do not extend beyond the courtroom, but there is a wealth of social science exploring how encounters with the police shape the perceptions of state authority and influence later behavior. For example, Tom Tyler has argued that the perceived fairness of official actors, even in brief encounters, can influence beliefs about the legitimacy of police and legal institutions, which in turn shapes compliance with the law.[6] Vesla Weaver and Amy Lerman have shown that what people of color "come to believe about government [is] derived primarily from their interactions with" institutions of criminal justice such as police, courts, probation officers, and jails.[7] These inter-actions form their core beliefs about what to expect of state officials, the roles and values promoted by public institutions, and their status vis-à-vis these institutions—in short, their very conception of citizenship. These perceptions are not merely psychological states; they often translate, as Sarah Brayne has shown, into concrete actions such as "systems avoid-ance," the practice of "individuals avoiding institutions that keep formal records (i.e., put them 'in the system') and therefore heighten the risk of surveillance and apprehension by authorities."[8]

Jannelle's discussion of her arrest experience reveals some of these themes. She explained that the arraignment itself brought into relief the devastating shock to her identity formed by achieving significant academic and employment success, despite living in a low-income and high-crime neighborhood. The arrest and prearraignment detention despoiled the sense of self she had maintained for years, and that short encounter put her into an unfamiliar, degraded status: "Wow. Well, the courtroom . . . this is what's going on in my head. Like, I've seen this on TV! I watch *Law and Order*. What am I doing here? What exactly am I doing here? I don't deserve this. I don't need to see any judge. I don't need an attorney. Why am I here? And I'm watching everything, like—okay, this is actually a judge, these are actual criminals. And I'm here for $2.25. All night when I was in prison, playing in my head—$2.25. A transfer. This guy went hard on me for $2.25. Wow."

The arraignment is the first court appearance at which the criminal charges against the defendant are entered and an initial bail determination is made. And for a significant number of misdemeanor defendants, it is also the only court appearance, because a majority of subfelony cases go to final disposition at arraignments. Jannelle recounts being relieved that the judge did not even look at her when her case was called because she was humiliated by being in the position of an accused criminal. The police roughed her up during her arrest, and her clothes were torn and her arms bruised. She said that her lawyer told her she would most likely be offered an ACD, and she described how quickly the judge accepted the proposed offer from the prosecutor:

> Jannelle: Literally tossed a paper, like [mimicking throwing a paper with the flick of the wrist]. "Okay, six months. Okay, whatever."
>
> Q: So there was no discussion.
>
> Jannelle: No. Didn't even look at me or nothing. He just looked at the paper; six months, no arrests and you can go. And he just threw it. Literally threw it. And I'm like—thank you, your honor.

For Jannelle, the hurried and impersonal nature of the proceedings was a relief. She felt that she escaped being personally addressed and recognized by an official who she imagined would transform her into being "a criminal" if she were subject to protracted engagement, irrespective of the legal outcome of the case, just by virtue of being in the designated space and role of an accused. "Honestly, all I'm saying is I was just happy he didn't even look . . . he didn't look at me and say, 'You look like a criminal.' That was my biggest thing. I tried to . . . You know, they ripped my shirt up; they kind of ripped it. And I don't want to be up here as this person who does something like every day and is always in trouble. And I was just hoping he wasn't going to look at me and say—'Okay, you're a criminal.'"

Even the abbreviated experience of a desk appearance ticket, which involves a custodial arrest and processing at the precinct without transfer to Central Booking, entails significant procedural hassle. On top of the number of "in" defendants, there are typically one hundred to two hundred DATs in Borough A that must be arraigned most days. Each of these defendants is handcuffed and arrested, taken to a police precinct, fingerprinted, and detained there until his or her criminal history record is produced, usually a matter of hours. Later, the defendants also need to take off at least one day from work or child-care responsibilities to come to the courthouse at 9:00 a.m. and wait in a winding line outside the building for security for fifteen to thirty minutes. They must then sit patiently in a crowded courtroom, sometimes all day, watching the seemingly inscrutable logic of other cases being called and courtroom lulls, waiting for their 60–120 seconds in front of the judge. When defendants are arraigned, in both DAT and online arraignments, they are told to stand with their hands grasped behind their backs. The defendants thereby enact their own semi-captive status, binding themselves on command under the watchful gaze of penal authorities.

When lunch break is called at 1:00 p.m., the crowd of defendants who have been waiting all morning for their cases to be called invariably express what could be understated as discontent. Defense attorneys and court officers brace themselves for the rush of frustrated defendants demanding to know why their cases have not been called yet and exasperated because they don't know what to do if they cannot return after lunch for the 2:30 p.m. call. On a representative January morning, defendants told their attorneys they had child care only until 1:00 p.m. and could not return; they had to get back to work or risk getting fired; they had school exams; or they simply just did not know where to go to wait for an hour and a half with freezing rain coming down outside. If defendants fail to return for their case call after lunch, a warrant will be issued, unless a judge can be convinced to stay the warrant.

Prosecutors and judges understand the experience of arrest and arraignment to accomplish something by way of procedural hassle even for those cases dismissed or granted an ACD at arraignment. Jill, a supervisor in the DA's office, while discussing the deterrence value of the arrest-to-arraignment experience, said, "If the defendant is young and it is a first arrest, then yes. If it was someone like me, to have to be in a cell with all of those people urinating in front of me, I would be horrified and never do it again. But for the people with like forty or fifty arrests, it means nothing to them." According to this reasoning, the degradation and discomfort of arrest alone is meaningful only for those who are unaccustomed to its pains. The belief that there is a declining marginal pain, humiliation, or discomfort with each successive arrest is frequently invoked to make sense of or to justify a central feature of the managerial mode, the addition of more burdens and hassles beyond arrest for later arrests.

Furthermore, the procedural hassle of the misdemeanor arrest does not terminate at arraignment. Even dispositions that do not impose jail time can entail significant demands and entanglement. In March 2011, a man in his forties was being arraigned for misdemeanor drug possession, and he had an open warrant for failing to appear on a prior misdemeanor marijuana possession. The prosecutor refused to make a plea offer, citing his bench warrant history, and therefore recommended a plea to the top charge and one year in jail. Judge Muñoz offered a plea to a misdemeanor crime (recall that judges can't reduce the charges for purposes of a plea without the consent of the prosecutor) for both of the open dockets and offered a short drug treatment class, called the Treatment Readiness Program, instead of any jail time, saying to him, "You got to get your act together sir, you have to get your act together." During the allocution, she explained that the misdemeanor drug conviction will trigger a six-month license suspension and $200 in mandatory court fees. The defendant protested through his attorney that he needed his license for work. Judge Muñoz replied, "If he is concerned about maintaining his license, he should stop doing drugs, enter a drug program," before instructing him that he could go to the DMV to apply for a hardship waiver to restore the license. The defense attorney asked for civil judgment on the mandatory court fees, and the judge said, "It will be on his credit report for seven years. Does he understand that?" The defense attorney replied that his client understood that and still maintained that he could not pay the fees.

So even dispositions that happen at arraignment produce significant burdens going forward. For example, any misdemeanor drug conviction triggers a six-month license suspension and more severe sanctions for commercial licenses, which includes truck or taxi licenses.[9] If a person can't pay the mandatory court fees, civil judgment is disastrous for credit. This defendant will also have to return to court to prove compliance with the drug program. Therefore, the procedural hassles experienced by misdemeanor defendants are not limited to the processes entailed in resolving the legal disposition of case; they often can extend well beyond the day of disposition, even for those cases that terminate within a day of arrest. And for that portion of cases that are not resolved at arraignment, there are a myriad of ways the legal process—the ostensible means by which cases are resolved—works as a form of social control.

Keeping Cases Open

Although over half of misdemeanor cases are disposed of at arraignment, the remainder can drag on for months or even years for various reasons. The DA's office may have a policy of not making offers at arraignment in certain types of cases, for example, if the case involves a complaining witness or driving while intoxicated. Sometimes the defendant is in a position where he or she cannot take the standard offer at arraignment without significant collateral results that outweigh the cost of protracted adjudication, such as immigration consequences, or a potential violation of parole or probation triggered by a conviction. Some defendants decide to fight the case either because they are claiming innocence; a legal defect in the stop, search, or arrest; or simply because the defendant or the defense attorney thinks the offer made at arraignment is not fair.

Pay a visit to one of New York City's Criminal Courts on a weekday morning around 9:30, and you will see a line, sometimes stretching around the block, of people waiting to clear security and enter the courthouse. On busy mornings in Borough A, the line often spans two sides of the block, populated almost exclusively by young black and Latino men and women, often with their children in tow. A busy day at this courthouse during the periods of most of my fieldwork could mean as many as 400 defendants in custody in Central Booking and holding pens waiting to be arraigned, an additional 150 to 200 desk appearance tickets, and somewhere between 40 to 100 cases on the calendar of each of the fourteen active courtrooms.

One Tuesday in 2012 was a relatively slow day. The security line wait was only about fifteen minutes, and most of it could zigzag inside the courthouse atrium, with only the tail of the queue trickling outside into the February winter air. John, a tall black man in his thirties dressed in dark blue cargo pants and matching shirt under his winter coat, had been waiting for ten minutes: "The security line sucks, but it's not bad today, I mean, I can't complain; it's the system, and I gotta go through it." This is his fifth court appearance on his first arrest, misdemeanor driving while intoxicated. He explained that he always comes wearing his uniform so he can get to work at JFK airport if his case is called before lunch. "Once I see it's noon, I know I am going to have to come back after lunch and lose the entire day, so I have my lawyer call work to tell them I will be out for the day." As he reached the top of the line, he grabbed a small, gray, plastic box into which he placed his belt and emptied his pockets. One of four court officers manning metal detectors yelled "Next!," and he handed over the box and proceeded through the metal detector. A few of the other people behind him walked through the metal detector with their hands raised high over their heads, as if they had just been taken captive. After clearing security, they made their way to the elevators, where large crowds pushed onto a car as packed as the morning subway.

Most people in this security line are defendants in ongoing misdemeanor or violation cases, and most are here for the second, third, or even fifteenth adjournment in a case or to show proof of compliance with some court order such as a fine or restitution, community service, or completion of an educational program. In any case, most will wait about fifteen to thirty minutes to clear security and then proceed to one of the crowded court-rooms to wait, perhaps for an hour but more likely for several hours, for their case to be called. Either it will be "disposed of"—usually through a guilty plea or a dismissal—or adjourned to come back again. The vast majority of individuals who traverse misdemeanorland experience very little incarcerative time in the process of their case: most misdemeanor cases terminate in a type of dismissal or a noncustodial sanction, and pre-trial detention is the exception, not the rule. But in the process, iterative engagement with judicial bureaucracy is demanded, and conditions are imposed before people are sent back into their communities.

Defendants experience procedural hassles in materially felt ways in the physical site of the courthouse. As Piven and Cloward eloquently state, "People experience deprivation and oppression within a concrete setting, not as the end product of large and abstract processes, and it is the concrete experience that molds their discontent into specific grievances against specific targets."[10] Behind all of the defendants' inconveniences and felt humiliations are a series of political and policy choices: how the state funds policing versus education or social welfare or mental health services, the relative budgets for prosecutors and public defenders, the allocation of judicial resources, the priorities that dictate facility upgrading choices and limit budgets, and countless other social and political forces that cre-ate the actual conditions under which people experience misdemeanor justice. Piven and Cloward make a telling analogy: "Workers experience the factory, the speeding rhythm of the assembly line, the foreman, the spies and the guards, the owner and the paycheck. They do not experi-ence monopoly capitalism. People on relief experience the shabby waiting rooms, the overseer or caseworker, and the dole. They do not experience American social welfare policy. Tenants experience the leaking ceilings and cold radiators, and they recognize the landlord. They do not recognize the banking, real estate, and construction system."[11]

Misdemeanorland defendants do not encounter the abstract political values that prioritize a penal over social welfare approach to social control or the structural lack of equal concern and respect for poor and minority communities. They encounter handcuffs, squalid cells, and underfunded, overcrowded jails and courthouses. They do not always identify the demands put on their lives to conform to the procedural hassles of misdemeanorland as a form of social control. Often, they identify frustration with the actions of recognizable actors that they encounter: the violence of police officers, indifference of corrections officers, the inattention or incompetence of defense attorneys, the pettiness of prosecutors, or the unreasonableness and ineptitude of judges.

Ernesto, a forty-something Latino man arrested for trespass when he entered a public housing building to try to stay with a friend of an ex-girlfriend who lived in the building after being locked out of his apartment late one night. Reflecting on his experience, he identified injustice with the immediate actors who seemed to not value his time or personhood:

Ernesto: The cops stopping you for some bullshit, to put you in this predicament. When the case ain't serious in the first place, you know? But you're here. They put you through this. The back and forth to court. What happened last time I was here? Do you remember? I got here at 9:00 in the morning, and I left out of here at 3:40 when the courts closed. I was the last one to get called. . . . It's adjourned or something.

Q: You were just waiting the whole day.

Ernesto: Waiting. Waiting. Didn't see nobody. But I knew the case was supposed to get adjourned. . . . Basically, I see my lawyer—he was walking through the hallway—and . . . he said, "Yeah, I told them to put it down that you were supposed to be adjourned for today." . . . So we had keep waiting for the judge. Okay, you're adjourned. Could have told me that from the gate, as soon as I got there. I could have taken care of a couple of other things.

Q: So you waited from 9:00 a.m. to 3:40 for the case to be adjourned, and they didn't even need you.

Ernesto: They didn't even need me there. I wasn't supposed to even show up. But my name is on the paper. I don't show up, I'm wrong. You know?

Q: You get a warrant.

Ernesto: Yeah, I get a warrant. So I'm damned if I do and damned if I don't. You know. . . . Yes, it's so frustrating.

Thus, when John, the JFK worker, said with resignation, "It's the system, and I gotta go through it," or when Ernie, the laundromat worker, expresses frustration with the "process you go through" in New York for "petty charges," they identify the tangible burdens and felt indignities that are the result of the particular ways in which misdemeanor justice is organized and the role it plays in our social order. They do not, necessarily, identify the particular ways in which misdemeanor justice is organized and the role it is playing in our social order as the source of their burdens and indignities. The misdemeanor justice "system," like many systems, is an ongoing process that comes to look like a steady-state fact. Many of the processes that come to constitute the social control technique of procedural hassle are produced by legal actors making daily choices about their organizational roles under conditions of uncertainty and resource constraint, as opposed to being the product of an intentional strategy of social control by frontline actors. Nonetheless, the collective force of these recurrent decisions and organizational habits is the repeated deployment of procedural hassle as a form of social control.

These procedural hassles are not merely meaningless inconveniences. They are active techniques of social control: they transmit social and symbolic meanings to defendants, construct their status vis-à-vis the court and its powers, and seek to discipline and reform defendant behavior. Sometimes these practices are the unintended upshot of contested law or facts in a case, in which case observations about how the defendant bore up under the resultant hassles will be appraised to determine what level of social control is warranted. In other cases, judges or prosecutors resort to procedural hassle because they know they will not be able to secure a conviction and they can utilize an extended engagement with the criminal process to monitor the defendant, to maintain legal leverage over him or her with an order of protection, or to hedge against uncertainty inherent in the initial stages of the criminal process. And in other cases, criminal justice actors purposefully impose procedural hassle in lieu of formal punishment because it is a form of hard treatment that does not entail creating a lifelong criminal record, which they may believe is unwarranted, given the charge and the defendant's history.

Consider the way that procedural formalities are produced and traded off when cases are adjourned to inquire into factual or legal questions. In March 2011, Travis, a young Latino man, was returning to court for his second appearance for criminal possession of a weapon in the fourth degree, namely, a folding box cutter that was charged as a gravity knife. He had refused the arraignment plea offer in order to procure a letter from his employer, the owner of a bodega, to explain that he used the knife for work. When case was called, Travis came from the audience and stood with his defense attorney at the podium and handed her a letter. As Travis approached the front of the court, the prosecutor announced that the plea offer was a violation conviction (disorderly conduct) and three days of community service. Looking over the paperwork with her client standing next to her, the attorney asked the prosecutor to explain the legal basis for the stop that led to recovery of the box cutter, since the complaint alleged that it was recovered from her client's pocket. The ADA looked at the file and replied that the box cutter was recovered from the defendant's front coin pocket so that it was visible to the officer on the street because the top of it protruded from the pocket. The defense attorney replied by gesturing to her client's big, baggy tee-shirt that fell at least some six inches below the man's waist, and argued to the judge that the proffered explanation still did not make sense because, even if it was protruding from a smaller coin pocket, the officer could not have seen it through the type of tee-shirts he wears. She continued to argue that the complaint lacked any allegations from which to infer probable cause for the stop and search, because there was no statement that the knife was "open to public view," at the time of the stop. The judge insinuated she might consider deeming the complainant legally insufficient, and the prosecutor replied that any deficiency in the complaint was remedied by the supporting deposition of the officer who said it was in the coin pocket.

The defense attorney then read the letter that her client had given her, summarizing it to the court by saying that the man was on his way to work at the time of the arrest and the employer certified that he uses the knife daily at this job. In response, the judge said, "He uses it for work. How about an ACD?" The prosecutor replied, "If he uses it for work, why didn't he leave it at work?," and then agreed to the ACD, conditional on one day of community service. Travis readily agreed, and the disposition was entered.

Legal actors must decide how to deal with factual or legal issue presented in misdemeanor cases knowing that more clarity is almost always bought at the price of more procedural hassle, not just for the defendant but also for them. They must either seek adjudication of a legal or factual question, which necessarily entails costly undertakings, or come to a disposition that will trade off some quantum of penal burdens in the face of residual uncertainty. As this negotiation shows, legal actors can settle on a disposition even without resolving the animating factual and legal questions: no one was certain at the time the plea deal was struck at the second court appearance if Travis's box cutter was in fact a prohibited weapon or if the arresting office had legal probable cause for the stop and arrest. In fact, sometimes the procedural hassle that the defendant endures in pursuit of seeking adjudication of a factual or legal issue is used as a reason to reduce prospective penal burdens, because it is interpreted as a performance. Returning to court with a letter from the employer was not only a burdensome task; it was also a meaningful undertaking. The action demonstrated the defendant's capacity to respond to the demands of the court and also to procure evidence that he was part of other social control systems—namely, the formal labor market—making him appear less risky and more deserving of leniency.

For defendants, the only way out of misdemeanorland is through misdemeanorland. If the case survives past arraignment because of a contested legal or factual issue, defendants can pursue litigation of an issue over many court appearances in the face of an uncertain outcome. Or they can accept a disposition with a definite quantum of procedural hassle at an earlier court appearance. If Travis wanted to secure an outright dismissal or acquittal, he would have to come back to court many times to try to get the case to hearing and trial. Although Travis's ACD disposition meant that he will not have to come back to court to litigate the stop and search issue, he will have to do one day of community service and then return to court to show compliance.

Sometimes procedural hassle experienced by the defendant is the upshot of an intentional strategy by the defense attorney, who believes the prosecution's offer is unreasonable. In a system where defendants can rarely invoke their formal legal and procedural rights because they risk conviction and sentences far out of line with reigning notions of fairness, defense attorneys often resort to the only available tools beyond suasion and supplication: waiting. Mary, a long-term public defender in Borough A, explained that when an arraignment offer seems unreasonable, she just "puts them over, and they go to the AP parts." Summarizing what happens next, she said:

> It depends. If I have a DA who has too many cases, I have a judge who wants to help out, or I have a judge who doesn't want to help out. I have to adjourn the case for as many months as I can. . . .
>
> Sometimes a year or two, if I'm lucky. And eventually they get tired, or you'll get an assistant who doesn't care. Or you'll get an assistant who does care, and wants to take it to trial. So you've got to go either way. Sometimes you get lucky. Or the client will get arrested again, and then it gets disposed of too. Or the client will bench warrant and come back hopefully in ten years with a normal job and a normal person—and we can say, "Judge, please ACD this." Those are my favorite.

Defense attorneys can rarely credibly threaten to go to trial or invoke procedural protections, either because there is no viable legal defense or, even when there is, the "trial tax" is just too steep. Lacking other leverage to advance their client's interest if the standing plea offer is unacceptable, defense attorneys resort to imposing procedural hassle on other court actors, namely, prosecutors and judges. The defendant's procedural hassle is collateral damage.

In March 2011, Rashad, a public defender, stood in an AP part on a trespass case where a young man was arrested for being in a building that had signed on to the NYPD's program allowing them to patrol in the hallways of privately owned apartment buildings. After a brief discussion with the defendant, he said to the prosecutor and judge, "He knows people in the building. We are not taking any disposition except dismissal." Rashad also argued that the complaint should not be deemed to be converted to an information, because he did not see the trespass affidavit program agreement form that private landlords fill out to authorize the NYPD to patrol their buildings in the file. Judge Wilson retorted, "That is absolutely wrong," and found that the complaint had been properly converted. Dispassionately, the defense attorney said, "Fine, we will just adjourn for hearings and trial, wait for the speedy trial clock to run out." In response, Judge Wilson said, "Well, no time's been charged yet," pointing out that since he found the information converted, the next adjournment would not be charged against the prosecution's speedy trial clock. The defense attorney said, "I understand that. We are still going to wait. They will never be able to prove this case in court."

Rashad's exchange makes clear how procedural hassle can emerge as a penal technique in misdemeanor courts. The prosecution may not eventually be able to prove all of the elements of criminal trespass beyond a reasonable doubt at a trial. But they don't have to do so in order to keep the case alive and keep the defendant under an obligation to come back to court to fight the case. The defendant can therefore either accept whatever plea deal is offered at early court appearances or wait. By waiting, the defense hopes eventually either to get a chance to challenge the state's case at a bench trial, receive a better offer after many court appearances, or get a dismissal under the speedy trial statute. It is not certain that the defendant will himself be able to withstand the procedural hassle of this strategy. He might fail to show up at court or get rearrested. But if he can endure the inconveniences, the fact that he was able to make all of the court appearances reliably without getting rearrested is itself interpreted as a meaningful performance.

In other cases that survive arraignment, procedural hassle is sometimes intentionally imposed by prosecutors in order to monitor defendants or maintain leverage over time that would not be possible with a disposition, because the evidence is weak. In February 2011, two women were arraigned on what is called a cross-complaint assault case, meaning they each accused the other of assault, and the police arrested both participants. At arraignment, the women were asking for mutual dismissal, stating they would not cooperate as a complaining witness in the other's criminal prosecution on the understanding that both cases would be dismissed. The cases had been classified by the DA's office as domestic violence because the police paperwork indicated the women were either currently or formerly romantically involved.

One of the defense attorneys approached the supervising ADA at the arraignment and told him the case was misclassified: "Same-sex partners my ass! She says she has a live-in boyfriend!" he exclaimed, and pressed his case for mutual dismissal. The ADA responded that, live-in boyfriend or not, his police paperwork indicated that the women had referred to each other as "girlfriends" and that the fight started over a romantic issue, so he would not agree to mutual dismissal. The defense attorney replied that, even if they were girlfriends and even if the DA would not affirmatively move for dismissal, they all knew the case would be dismissed 30.30 because neither would cooperate in the prosecution of the other. He demanded, "So what? You schlep them back here for three months of court appearances and then you dismiss it? What's the point of that? Just to schlep them back here for months of court appearances?" The ADA responded coolly, "Yup, that's the point."

His response was not surprising to any party to this negotiation. Defense attorneys working in this borough know that the DA's policy is to almost never affirmatively drop a domestic violence case, but to allow the entirety of the speedy trial period to run and let the case be dismissed 30.30, even if the complaining witness repeatedly refuses to participate. A supervisor at the domestic violence unit of the DA's office explained: "We could close off the cases at the very beginning, knowing that victims were not cooperative—but the district attorney's philosophy is bring them all in because we want to be monitoring the perpetrators.... So if legally the case can remain open, then let there be an umbrella ... for the victim. Let there be an order of protection in existence.... Because victims change their mind. Intervening circumstances. There can be reoffending. So, the idea is that the law gives us this amount of time in order to prosecute a case, so we're going to keep the case open."

On this day, a supervisor from the Domestic Violence Bureau eventually came down to the arraignment courtroom to make a final determination on the case. The supervisor looked over the police paperwork and listened to the defense attorneys tell their clients' accounts. In this case, like so many others that go to disposition at arraignment, the ADA supervisor was left to make her decision using ambiguous police paperwork and conflicting accounts from parties that have an interest in painting a particular picture of the facts. She decided to offer ACDs to both women with six-month limited orders of protection—meaning they can have contact, but any assault or harassment would constitute a violation of the order and therefore be a contempt of court charge, on top of the underlying criminal conduct. The women agreed and walked out of the courtroom together, each clutching her printed order of protection.

All of the possible dispositions of this case that were being considered involved some form of marking, procedural hassle, and performance, and no party to the negotiations contemplated a conviction and formal sentence. The penal techniques are instruments that allow prosecutors to address issues presented by the criminal allegation in various ways—managing future risk by keeping tabs on the defendant over a period of time, maintaining legal leverage with mandatory court appearances or an order of protection, using the passage of time between adjournments to figure out whether the person really deserves to be punished by seeing whether this was a one-time aberration or part of a pattern of unruly behavior. They can do so without having to expend significant resources and time investigating the specific past incident alleged in the complaint or securing evidence sufficient for a conviction. Furthermore, they can see how events unfold to determine if they think it is fair or warranted to even seek a conviction. The statutory time allowed to prosecute a case is therefore not only a guarantee to the defendant of a speedy trial or resolution, it is a tool that allows the state to engage the defendant in a series of encounters with state authority.

Orders of Protection

One of the most common sources of procedural hassles for that subset of misdemeanor defendants in complainant-initiated cases is the order of protection: a court order to stay away from or desist from certain conduct against a protected person.[12] If the criminal complaint alleges the defendant harmed or threatened another individual, the prosecution will request, and a judge will almost invariably grant, a temporary order of protection. Most DA's offices have a written policy to request an order of protection in any case considered "domestic violence," a broad category including crimes and violations against any member of a household, even if no physical injuries are reported.[13] An order of protection can also be issued in favor of witnesses to a crime.

Orders of protection are issued, with few exceptions, axiomatically if there is a complainant in a case, whether or not the defendant knows the complainant. Once issued, they are sticky. As Mary, an experienced defense attorney, explained, they are often issued without much inquiry in the specifics of the case: "Cars. Busses. Houses. . . . I break into a car, and I steal something in there. Whoa; you've got an order of protection—stay away from that person. Like I'm going to know? Joe owns the car? I kick in somebody's door on Atlantic Avenue. I'm going to know that that's Joe's place? And I get orders of protection? These orders of protection are ridiculous."

A temporary order of protection will remain in effect for the entire pendency of the case unless the prosecutor or judge agrees to modify the order to a limited order or to remove it completely, both very rare. A final order of protection, lasting between one and five years depending on the disposition, can be included in plea deals or imposed at sentencing. These orders can imply absolutely no procedural burden whatsoever if the protected party is not involved in the defendants' social or work lives at all, immense burden if the parties previously cohabitated or worked together, and everything in-between. The procedural hassles imposed by orders of protection are a frequent method by which certain defendants are tracked, tested, and sorted on certain behaviors.

Orders come in two varieties: full and limited. A full order of protection is sometimes called a "stay away" order because it prohibits contact of any sort—e-mail, phone, in-person, and third-party contact. A limited order of protection allows for contact but prohibits harassment and assault, conduct that is also prohibited by the penal law but by the order's terms would be subject to an additional charge of contempt of a court order if violated. In many cases, the charges alleged at arraignment make out a clear safety risk for the complainant. However, in other cases, the safety risk to the complainant is not obvious from the charging documents.

In February 2011, a middle-aged woman with apparent mental illness was being arraigned for misdemeanor assault in the third degree for having a fight with another woman who lived in her YMCA shelter. The ADA asked for $2,000 bail. The woman started to speak directly to the judge, begging her to release her and saying that she would lose her housing, her SSI, and her SSDI. The judge set $500 bail and imposed a full order of protection in favor of the complainant who lived in the shelter. The defendant started to cry, ignoring her defense attorney's hand on her shoulder indicating that she should not speak directly to the judge. She supplicated the judge, saying: "I don't have $500. I live at the Y. If you set bail, I will lose housing, SSI, SSDI." The judge called the defense attorney and the ADA up to the bench, where they had a confidential conversation for a few minutes. When they returned to their respective podiums, the judge announced on the record that she would release the woman on her own recognizance with a full order of protection on the condition that the defendant not live in the same shelter where the complaining witness lived and that "she find somewhere else to stay." The judge ordered a police escort for the woman to retrieve her belongings from the shelter and calendared the next appearance three weeks out.

This exchange involved more specific inquiry into the circumstances of the accusation and the potential effects of pretrial conditions such as bail and a temporary order of protection than most cases I witnessed. But even with the dedication of a few extra minutes, it is almost impossible to sort out under the normal conditions of arraignment the level of risk the defendant actually posed to the complainant or what effect forcing the woman to leave her shelter spot would have on her mental health, benefits, or even her ability to return to court on a regular basis.

There is rarely much effort to distinguish cases where the safety risk to the complainant is minimal and the burdens substantial from those where there is substantial danger. Judges and prosecutors also have minimal incentives to do so because the professional risks are huge if they miscalculate, and their payoffs are minimal or nonexistent for agreeing to modify or remove an order of protection. Therefore, the temporary order of protection is largely taken for granted as a condition of most cases involving a complainant. The procedural difficulties it imposes must be negotiated during the entire pendency of the case.

Lester is a retired math teacher in his late fifties who had never been arrested before February 2011, when he was charged with unlawful eviction after he changed the locks on his apartment door in an effort to block access to the unit by Henrietta, a woman whom he had allowed to stay with him. In 2010, a single room occupancy apartment building located on the block where Lester lived burned to the ground. Henrietta, with whom he had a prior romantic relationship, was made homeless by the fire. Lester allowed her to stay at his apartment, and she remained there for about a year without paying rent.

According to Lester, their romantic relationship initially revived and then faltered as Henrietta began stealing his property and money to pay for her drug habit and also began to display a series of aggressive and disrespectful behaviors. In October 2010, Lester's landlord increased the rent, and he asked her to either help pay a portion of the rent or to move out, neither of which happened. After a period of frustrating exchanges during which Lester requested that she leave the apartment and return the key, Lester one day decided to buy a new lock cylinder for the apartment door and changed the lock. Later that same day, Henrietta returned to the apartment and demanded a key to the new lock. Lester refused and offered her an opportunity to remove her belongings. Early in the morning two days later, Henrietta returned and tried to jimmy the lock open. When Lester called the police and claimed Henrietta was breaking into his apartment, she informed the responding officers that she had lived there for almost a year and that Lester had changed the lock and refused to give her a key.

The responding officer demanded Lester provide Henrietta with a key and explained to him that under New York law anyone who has lawfully occupied a dwelling for thirty days or longer, whether or not she is on the lease, is considered a resident and can only be evicted through housing court proceedings. The officer arrested Lester for unlawful eviction, a Class A misdemeanor. Lester was still wearing his pajamas, had not eaten breakfast, and was not given an opportunity to take his blood pressure medication before being taken to the precinct. He did not know if the arresting officer had taken his keys and wallet or left them at the apartment.

The officers took Lester to the precinct for initial processing, where he sat in a cell with thirteen other people while he waited to be transferred to Central Booking. "I'm put in a cell with these . . . with dirty, nasty . . . umm . . . unfortunate people. . . . It's uncouth in there. Oh, my god. Plus I didn't get a chance to eat. I didn't have my medication. And my head was splitting. My head was splitting. I was going off in there, because I made sure the officer knew that I have high blood pressure and I could feel it; feel my head exploding in there." One of the officers eventually drove back to his apartment, where she, evidently, was able to retrieve his blood pressure medication from Henrietta. Although Lester felt he was in need of medical attention, he reported that another officer on duty advised him that asking to be taken to the hospital in advance of arraignment would only prolong the time before release. Lester took this advice and agreed to be transferred to Central Booking, and he was arraigned before the close of night court that day, around 12:30 a.m. He explains the shock of being told that a temporary order of protection would be imposed that would make it illegal for him to reenter his apartment:

> Upstairs now to see the judge. I think my emotions got the best of me when she said there is a restraining order and you cannot go back to your apartment.
>
> That hit me like a ton of bricks. How could I not go back to my . . . where am I going? "You are restrained from seeing this individual." What are you talking about? This is mine, I'm paying rent for my apartment. And I can't go back? How am I going to get my mail? I know I have bills to pay. How am I going to get all my stuff? How am I going to know that my property is safe in my apartment? Where am I going? Where am I going to spend the night? On the subway? What am I going to do? And I realized that I didn't have my phone and I didn't have my keys. Where am I going? And who am I contacting? I got a restraining order; don't go back to your apartment.
>
> . . . I cried in front of the judge. I remember wiping tears from my eyes because I couldn't control myself. I say she doesn't know what she's doing . . . she's telling me I'm evicted from my apartment that I'm paying rent for. How . . . what? I couldn't speak. The tears rolled. The tears rolled. The tears rolled. And the court officer says, "Stay standing!" I'm trying to hold it. I lost it. I was in full tears. Full tears, man. I was embarrassed. I was hurt. Mostly spent. . . . Oh, my god. I don't wish that on nobody. I don't wish that on anybody. Even if they're a criminal, but—I don't wish that on nobody, man. That's a life-changing experience. I'm not going through that again. God willing.

According to Lester, he was released at 1:00 a.m. from the courthouse with a full order of protection and a note that he could return to the arresting precinct at 9:00 a.m. the next morning to ask for an escort to retrieve his things. He was released with no money, no cell phone, dressed in his pajamas in March, and given a MetroCard with one swipe.

> When I was released I didn't have my phone, I didn't have my keys. I went to the precinct to access my property, which were my phone and my keys and my $10. The precinct said they did not have it. Where was I going? I couldn't tell anybody I was coming because I didn't have my phone. I walked—I don't know, it must have been . . . I think it was thirty blocks, to my house. Which is . . . I'm being restrained from the house here. But I had nowhere else to go. I walked there. I'm not

supposed to be here. I rang the bell because I had no keys, now. I didn't have no keys. I rang the bell. . . . Come on, man. Come on. What did the officers expect me to do? . . .

I know. The order. The arrangement was for me to wait until 9:00 in the morning to go back to the precinct to get an escort. But I'm released now. It's now 1:00 in the morning. What am I doing for eight hours? Where am I going for eight hours? What am I doing for eight hours? Come on, man. Come on, man.

Henrietta let him into the apartment, and he spent the night there. The next morning, he called his brother in New Jersey and went to stay with him for the remainder of the open case. By mid-March, Lester's attorney had helped him begin the process of lawfully evicting Henrietta. By the fourth court appearance, the judge finally agreed to modify the order to a limited order so he could begin moving out of the apartment. Because Lester was legally responsible for the rent, did not want to have an eviction on his record, and all of his property was housed at the apartment, he paid rent at the unit for March and April, even though he was forbidden from entering the premises and Henrietta was living there alone.

It is not clear that the various judges who saw his case or the assigned prosecutor actually believed that Lester posed any threat of physical injury to Henrietta or that they even thought about the question prior to imposing the order of protection. There was no allegation of physical harm to Henrietta on the charging document, and, to Lester and his attorney's knowledge, she never made any such allegation to the prosecutor over the course of the case. Yet an order of protection is essentially a default practice in almost every case where there is a complainant. It requires a significant showing by the defendant and defense attorney to overcome that presumption.

Here again, we must understand the practices of the criminal court actors not merely in legal terms, but also in terms of organizational incentives and institutionalized understandings in the prevailing legal field. The order of protection is the path of least resistance in a prudential sense but also in a professional and political sense. Prosecutors and judges always reference the fact that they would not want to be on record failing to issue an order of protection least the defendant ends up committing a serious act of violence. And the initial decision regarding issuing an order of protection must be made very early in the case's life course, when there is minimal information available to the legal actors or often divergent accounts of the underlying facts. Judge Taylor explained the default practice of issuing an order of protection even when it is clear it will create serious disruptions in the lives of defendants and in the lives of the protected parties:

> We had an arraignment case a couple of weeks ago. The mother was charged with endangering. The mother was observed with the three- or four-year-old child out on the street on one of those really brutal cold, snowy days without shoes and socks on. CPS [Child Protective Services] was called. The police were called. The police arrested the mother. She was charged with endangering. There is an order of protection—a full stay away order of protection. Now, you're talking about an infant of three or four years old, right? You're going to do everything in your power to make sure that kid is protected. You have no idea what's going on. You're sitting in arraignments; you are hearing the accusations being made. You are hearing another side of the story from defense counsel. But you know what? You better figure out what's going on. You've got to figure out the best way to protect that kid until everything has been figured out. Because don't forget—it's arraignments, so it's right after arrest. These have just come into play. There's no investigating, you know—no in-depth investigation at this point in time. I issued the full order of protection and put it over for a short date. . . . Because now, again, you separate the parent from the child. Put it over for a short date to the AP [all-purpose] part so the AP part judge, who has the time to schedule a hearing and hear what's going on and make a decision as to whether or not it safe to let this mother and this child be together again.

Once full orders of protection are issued at arraignment, they are rarely modified. Judges in the all-purpose parts are also concerned with being on record modifying an order of protection and infrequently agree to downwardly modify, absent an overwhelming showing from the defense attorney and defendant. They often reference the initial determination of the arraignment judge in refusing to do so. For example, Kima (introduced in chapter 4) was subject at arraignment to a full order of protection forbidding her from any contact with her partner of eighteen years with whom she had a teenage son. She said that for the first month she had no contact at all with him and forbade her son from speaking with him out of concern that it would be considered third-party communication. Kima's boyfriend expressed his wishes to the DA's office to not have the prosecution go forward, and he refused to participate, but they were able to proceed with the prosecution and stop the 30.30 clock by relying on his prior signed statement. She said around Christmastime she allowed her son to contact his father, and her ex-boyfriend offered to financially support her for almost six months, "working overtime every day," according to her, because the open case kept Kima from working at her job as a substitute teacher during the entire pendency of the case. Neither the DA's office nor the judge agreed to modify the order of protection from full to limited. Kima and her ex-partner merely ignored it to the extent they needed to communicate about their son and financial matters.

Explaining the rarity of modifying or removing a full order of protection, Judge Felix, who regularly presides over one of the dedicated domestic violence courtrooms, said:

> You know, probably the biggest issue of contention is the orders of protection. Basically, to issue the order of protection there basically has to be a finding that there's a threat to the complaining witness. And, at arraignment the allegations that are made . . . basically in the complaint and some of the information that's provided—you know, there's prior cases, prior DIRs [domestic incident reports]—the judges all take that into account and issue the orders of protection. You know, when it comes to me—in order to modify it, there would have to be some really significant change in circumstances. And, generally we don't see that because the same claim that was made before me was the same claim that was made at arraignments—which is that the [complaining] witness doesn't want the order of protection. But nothing has really happened since arraignments that would indicate that, in fact, that threat that the arraignment judge determined existed, that potential threat, has changed. So the orders of protection are maintained. Every once in a while, you know, you'll get a defense attorney that—for whatever rea-son—they just truly believe this complaining witness or the defendant, and will push it to try to get a modification. I would say most of them don't try, because it is so rare that there's a modification.

The imposition of complications in the form of an order of protection is a strategic resource, both for the complainant and for the prosecutor. Having the order in place gives the prosecution and judge an opportunity to observe if the defendant respects the order, or at least if the complainant decides to notify the authorities of a violation. The temporary order of protection is not only a legal device for directing and controlling behavior or for reordering interpersonal relationships.[14] It is also a method of testing and assessing the defendant's capacity to follow directives and his or her capacity for harmful behavior in cases where the facts are contested and the prosecutor and judge lack sufficient information to decide what level of penal intervention is warranted.

In June 2010, Clifford was arraigned for allegedly throwing a small family dog named Bella against the wall. The prosecutor informed the judge that his office was classifying the case as domestic violence because the incident happened during a fight with the wife. The ADA asked the judge to impose a full order of protection for the dog, and in addition, to impose a full order of protection for the wife. The defense attorney objected, saying the complaint contained no factual allegations of harm or intimidation to the wife, only an allegation of harming the dog. Therefore, he argued, there was no legal basis to impose an order of protection in favor of the wife. The judge said that he would second-call the case for the parties to look into the situation regarding the wife. At the second call, the defense attorney said he had talked to the wife, who was sitting in the audience, and represented to the court that she did not want an order of protection because they lived together and had children in common. The judge decided to issue a limited order of protection for the wife and a full order of protection for the dog. Later that day, another supervisor commented on the case, "It may seem silly, and it is easy to criticize, but the crazy thing is, it would probably be easier to get a conviction on the guy for injuring the dog than for hurting his wife. It is classic abusive controlling behavior to hurt something someone loves, and I bet there is abuse going on in the home, but often in these situations the woman would never testify against the man."

The case of Bella the dog was just one of over a hundred cases arraigned in the courtroom that day. Under these circumstances of rapid and resource-constrained processing of cases, legal actors are often left to make decisions about how to handle situations that they find problematic with limited information and also limited tools. After lunch was called, the defense attorney, supervising ADA Clarence, and the law clerk for the judge picked up a discussion of the canine order of protection before making their way out of the courtroom. Everyone concurred that throwing Bella against the wall was "bad"; however, they continued to debate whether the behavior was linked to an underlying pattern of abuse to other human family members. The court attorney offered a few hypotheticals, asking if we would consider the criminal act sufficiently linked to a domestic incident to warrant an order of protection for the wife without specific

allegations of harm to the wife if the defendant had lit a marijuana cigarette or assaulted a random guy on the street after a fight with his wife.
The ADA said no, but argued that the dog is an extension of the wife and
that the defendant harmed the animal to hurt her (assuming that the wife
loved the dog). It was only during this discussion that anyone bothered
to look up the order of protection statute, and a lively debate ensued as
to whether it was legal to issue an order of protection for an animal when
there was no allegation on the arrest-charging document of harming a
human member of the same family.

Yet, in the immediate context where these decisions are unfolding, the
legal actors feel rushed to process cases and often have little time or incli-
nation to research and debate the law, and even when they do, judges often
are disinclined to entertain such arguments for very long. I witnessed many
judges get impatient and even angry when defense attorneys put forward
either factual or legal arguments against issuing full orders of protection
at arraignments. The context of choice for the judge is that she has to
make a decision in a short time frame about whether to issue an order of
protection. She has limited information about the facts giving rise to the
arrest and only cursory knowledge about the defendant, the complainant,
and their relationship.

The order of protection is not just a direct response to allegations of
harmful criminal conduct to another person (or animal). It is also a tool that
provides more leverage over the defendant and that provides an opportunity
for information to unfold about the defendant: to observe how the defendant
bears up under the new constraint and to collect more data about his or
her behavior and relationship with the complainant. Legal actors will then
marshal the unfolding information to adjust their assessment of how and
to what extent the defendant has to be managed. Consider that in Lester's
unlawful eviction case, the judge eventually agreed to modify the order to
a limited order only after three court appearances and no complaints from
Henrietta in a situation where there was never any allegation whatsoever
of physical harm against the complainant.

In Clifford's case, the fact that the canine order of protection could
not serve as a means to gather information about his later actions was the
reason the prosecutor called the order "useless" and "ridiculous." Clarence,
the supervising ADA, expressed his frustration, less at the decision any
actor made in court but more at the limited powers the court had to really
do anything substantial about the situation that concerned him. He said,
"This is ridiculous, how can we enforce an order of protection for the dog?

Who is going to tell that he violated the order of protection for the dog? He could kill it and no one would know." He said he understood why the Domestic Violence Bureau wants the order of protection in place—because if the man was looking to harm the wife he could do so by hurting something she loves, like the dog. Nonetheless, because there is very limited ability to audit the man's compliance, Clarence did not think the order would be an effective leverage point to change what he believed to be an abusive dynamic. "Look at her. . . . She is not going to do anything about this," Clarence said, pointing to the wife of the defendant, who was sitting behind him in court as he waited for his paperwork, running her fingers through his hair.

Sitting and Waiting

Coming back to court means sitting and waiting once you get there. The inconvenience of waiting to be addressed in court transmits social meaning about the status of the subjects of misdemeanorland, and repeated encounters work transformations in those subjects. As is the case in many street-level bureaucracies, "Clients are typically required to wait for services; it is a sign of their dependence and relative powerlessness that the costs of matching servers with the served are borne almost entirely by clients."[15] But waiting and delay are not merely upshots of a service delivery design that prioritizes the convenience of established organizational actors over clients or even a method for rationing service. Waiting and delay allows court actors an opportunity to engage and monitor defendants over time and to learn more about them during that period.

As Megan Comfort's evocative examination of the security rites of prison visitation demonstrates for the intimates of inmates, "mundane actions [can] cumulatively signify and materialize their denigrated status," thereby subjecting them to "secondary prisonization."[16] The same is true for that set of misdemeanor defendants whose cases continue past arraignment, the majority of whom are "out" defendants, the colloquial courthouse word for those not being held in correctional custody on bail.[17] Even for "out" defendants, the procedural hassles of repeated court appearances entail subjugating and disciplining experiences, such as waiting in interminable security lines, whiling away hours in courtrooms gruffly policed by court officers and judges, and being kept in a constant state of confusion about how long they are going to wait that day and how long the case will continue.

Although criminal courts are not total institutions in the way Goffman defined the term, the way in which the court actors interact with defendants in misdemeanorland serves a function similar to boundary maintenance in total institutions of controlling and denigrating the "inmate" status. The legal actors and court staff maintain boundaries against defendants and families: "Just as talk across boundary is restricted, so, too, is the passage of information, especially information about the staff's plans for inmates. Characteristically, the inmate is excluded from knowledge of the decisions taken regarding his fate. . . . Such exclusion gives staff a special basis of distance from and control over inmates."[18]

In late December 2010, a middle-aged black man sat toward the back of the courtroom, looking with a confused face over crumpled, carbon-copied court papers he pulled out of his pocket. He got up and walked toward the rail separating the audience from the court with his papers in hand where a middle-aged white female public defender was sitting at a desk facing out toward the audience, reviewing files. As he drew close enough to speak, she peered out at him over the rims of her reading glasses without expression. Before he could get more than a whispered word out, the court officer yelled, "Do not approach the bench while court is in session!" and he returned to his seat looking exasperated and confused. From 10:00 a.m. until noon, he tried three more times to approach someone on the defense side of the bench to ask some unknown question, and each time his efforts were aborted by an abrupt reprimand from the court officer. The defense attorney sitting at a desk on the other side of the rail kept peering over her glasses at him as he approached, and no one ever sought him out to determine his concerns. Around 12:30 p.m., his case was called and covered by an attorney substituting for his defense attorney. In less than sixty seconds, the judge adjourned his case for another day.

The official legal actors in misdemeanor court often proceed around the defendant, rarely apprising him of the logic of their proceedings. Thus, the defendant's disciplinary experience extends beyond incarcerative custody into required waiting and enforced ignorance of how long he must wait and what is structuring the process.[19] Defendants are therefore not just beleaguered by the pains and privations of procedural hassle. They are constructed as having a particular status in the field through the particular way court procedures are structured, one that is inferior to legal and court actors. Defendants are disciplined and trained through their encounters with the court. Lines and publicly shared waiting spaces tell nonvoluntary clients that their desire for services and individualized treatment is undersupplied:

court actors must only point to physical signs of unmanageable backlog to defeat demands for prompt attention.

Defendants often have to wait hours for their case to be called. The timing and order of case calling is mysterious to those without significant experience in the court's inner workings and even to many legal actors new to the criminal courts. Defendants must abide by the rules of the courtroom during these periods of waiting. No cell phone use, including Internet use or texting. No talking. No standing. No sitting in the front row. No loud children. Some courtrooms impose a no reading requirement, or no reading of newspapers. No approaching the rail to ask questions of court officers, clerks, or attorneys. In many courtrooms there are signs forbidding various modes of dress: hats, du-rags, and sagging pants are common examples of forbidden attire.

Despite all of the waiting that defendants are expected to patiently endure, showing up at court late is often an opportunity for a court actor to instruct the defendant in the proper respect he ought to show the court. In December 2010, Judge Everett reprimanded a young man for showing up late. The judge's courtroom ran a special calendar once a week after lunch just for young people facing any criminal charges. This young man had been offered a conditional plea to a noncriminal violation upon completion of a drug and counseling program, and was returning to court to report on his progress. Judge Everett said, "Compliance has two parts, going to the program when you are supposed to and getting to court at 2:15 p.m. If you want to treat this like it is nothing, then you will end up back in jail." In the next case, she imposed a negotiated sentence of a violation conviction and a twelve-week outpatient drug program for a young man with a domestic violence case. The judge was allocating the plea, explaining to the defendant that after the program was completed, he would still face a two-year limited order of protection, and at some point she stopped talking. She said that she saw him smiling and that he was not "taking this seriously"; she instructed him to sit in the audience, saying she would second-call the case when he was properly attentive.

In many fields of action, the extent and conditions of waiting track the social status of constitutive members of that field. The front row of the courtroom is always explicitly reserved for attorneys or police officers (and sometimes the press). Attorneys are permitted to text and use the Internet on their cell phones, to talk (until the total volume upsets either the judge or court officers), and to read any materials they like while waiting. During court lulls, judges and court officers also regularly read newspapers, books, and other material. But defendants are regularly scolding for engaging in any of these activities being carried out by attorneys and officers just feet away.

Defendants and audience members engage in prohibited activities in courtrooms regularly. Sometimes there is an ebb and flow to the enforcement; as the conversational volume swells, court officers and judges lose patience and shut down all talking. It appears there is an element of randomness to the enforcement patterns. Certainly the inclinations, habits, and moods of the presiding judge and the court staff shape the conduct that will be tolerated or castigated. One afternoon in November 2010, the audience carried on sporadic conversations with each other in fairly hushed tones, and the court officers sporadically admonished them, "No talking in the courtroom," in mild tones. Then one court officer yelled to the audience with a surprising level of anger, "I am not babysitting! I have two small kids at home. Take your conversations outside!"

Thus, as Barry Schwartz observes, "in waiting, usable time becomes a resource that is typically nonusable. . . . This transformation is mediated by the power relations between server and client." That is, the client's time is "transformed during the waiting period into a resource that is governed only by the one whom the client attends." This resource is not only under the control of the people dispensing the service in terms of *quantity*, meaning that the legal actors who control access to court services determine how long a defendant must wait for his or her case to be called. In a criminal court serving nonvoluntary clients, it is also under their control in terms of *quality*, meaning the legal actors who control access to court services determine the conditions of waiting and just how nonusable the waiting time will be. The prohibitions on various activities—reading, talking, using text or Internet communication—makes the time lost to waiting feel like a complete forfeiture of productive capacity. It also further enhances the felt power of those imposing and structuring the conditions of waiting: "To be able to make a person wait is, above all, to possess the capacity to modify his conduct in a manner congruent with one's own interests. To be delayed is in this light to be dependent upon the disposition of the one whom one is waiting for . . . and by virtue of this dependency, find . . . himself further confirmed in his position of power."[20]

Court officers and judges not only police conformity with the rules limiting activities in the courtroom; they also deny information to defendants about how long they must wait, what accounts for the temporal ordering of court business, and express little concern or any willingness to address the problems caused by waiting. Sometimes courtroom actors purposefully withhold this information. Other times they fail to transmit information simply because it not a regular or valued practice to keep defendants and the audience apprised of how and why the court orders its business. This is a classic feature of how total institutions govern subjugated populations: "The incomprehensible order or rule is a basic feature of life in prison. . . . Some of the inmate population's ignorance might be described as 'accidental'; it arises from what we can call the principle of bureaucratic indifference, i.e., events which seem important or vital to those at the bottom of the heap are viewed with an increasing lack of concern with each step upward."[21] Although misdemeanor defendants are not thoroughly committed to the total control and custody of the court for extended periods of time, they must submit to its rules and schedule of activity in each encounter.

Each instance of procedural hassle is also an instance of being subjected to and disciplined by a set of rules and normalizing rites, including the actions required of defendants given conditional dispositions. For example, if the compliance component of the disposition involves paying a fine, surcharge, or showing proof of completion of community service or some other program, the defendants are given a court date at the time of disposition to return to the compliance courtroom. The courtroom in Borough A assigned for defendants to bring proof of compliance with community service and other programs or to pay fines and court surcharges is a specialized court part staffed by clerks and court officers. No judge presides, and assigned defense attorneys do not usually attend these court dates, so defendants must navigate the appearance on their own. On the left side of the courtroom is a small, handwritten sign reading "Cashier Files" posted on the wooden barrier separating the audience from the court well; on the right side the sign reads "ACS files."

In September 2010, a parade of defendants filtered into the courtroom throughout the morning for their assigned compliance date. They walked in clutching crumpled paperwork and looked around for some clue about how to get recognition from the court personnel in order to pay the required monies or present proof of compliance. Most tried to approach one of the two clerks sitting at the front of the court rail, facing the audience. Sometimes the clerks just ignored their glances or direct questions; other times they responded in very loud voices, seemingly to make sure as many people heard the answer as possible. Although I could not hear the exact questions, the answers were almost always the same: "Go outside and find your name on one of the calendars, then find the yellow highlighted number next to your name and sign in. Then wait until we call your name." In one instance a clerk told a defendant that showing compliance and paying the court surcharge fee is a condition of the "conditional discharge" sentence entered in his case. The defendant asked, "What is a conditional discharge?" "You should have been listening in court," the clerk replied. "Your lawyer and the judge explain what a conditional discharge is."

Defendants (and their families, lovers, and friends who come to court with them) are often construed by frontline actors—intentionally or not— as subservient and unworthy to make demands on state functionaries throughout misdemeanorland. In the desk appearance ticket arraignment courtrooms, court officers regularly warn audience members, "*Do not approach the bench!*" in bombastic tones when lunch is called at 1:00 p.m. The officer tells them that if their cases have not been called already, they must return at 2:30 or a warrant will be issued. In January 2011, one defendant approached the court officer, pointed to a clock above the doorway that already read 2:00, and asked if that was the correct time. The officer looked up at the clock and replied, "No, it's an hour fast. It's too high to change." Another group of defendants tried to approach the defense side of the bar to ask about their cases or to explain why they could not come back at 2:30 to wait in the afternoon. A young black man exclaimed, with evident frustration and concern, "I have been waiting here since 9:00 a.m.! Now I have to come back at 2:30?" The defense attorney barely looked up to register his comment, coolly replying, "So have I. I have been here since 9:00 a.m. too." Many defense attorneys understand that their lack of time to address the individual needs of clients has a profound effect on their clients' perception of the process. One described DAT arraignments as "institutionalized malpractice," explaining that she feels guilty every time she works a DAT shift, knowing that the volume of cases means she will necessarily rush conversations with every client she encounters and not have time to explain the legal and practical impact of the dispositions granted.

In early February 2011, in a misdemeanor arraignment courtroom, over thirty minutes passed with no cases being called (a lull longer than the usual breaks in business, but not unheard of in a normal arraignment). As audience members became increasingly restless and muttered openly about lazy court workers or speculated that the judge was outside smoking cigarettes, a lieutenant came out to address them. He tried to explain the mechanisms that generate the timing and production of defendants for arraignment: "Folks, what is going on is that we did not get the paperwork until recently, and the lawyers just got it. And they need to review it and then go talk to the defendants, which is who you are all here waiting for. So as soon as they do that, they give us paperwork to bring them [the defendants] out. It is not that the judge does not want to work; it is that there is nothing for him to do. So soon as we can, we will bring them out. We will." Some family members in the audience sighed, "Thank you," and shifted their posture with some apparent satisfaction in being acknowledged.

Procedural hassles of the misdemeanor process commence by putting defendants through mortifying experiences with incarcerative custody, transforming them from free persons into criminal defendants. The cases that continue past arraignment involve recurrent visits with judicial authority and the subjugation of waiting. The great majority of defendants are "out" during this time, living in their communities and making routine trips back and forth to court. The regular requirement to return to court on pain of warrant, the security rites of entering the building, the experience of waiting for unknown periods of time in policed courtrooms, and the enduring burdens of an open case—missed work, transportation costs, child care, and temporary orders of protection—these things "cumulatively signify and materialize their denigrated status . . . [as] people at once legally free and palpably bound."[22] Finally, these procedural hassles are not merely discharged but are also evaluated as a performance.

6

Performance

"I know," he said, "that my case can't be settled today, not yet, but
I've come in anyway, I thought, I thought I could wait here anyway,
it's Sunday today, I've got plenty of time, and I'm not disturbing
anyone here."

"There's no need to be so apologetic," said the information-giver,
"it's very commendable for you to be so attentive. You are taking
up space here when you don't need to but as long as you don't get
in my way I will do nothing to stop you following the progress of
your case as closely as you like. When one has seen so many people
who shamefully neglect their cases one learns to show patience with
people like you. Do sit down."
—FRANZ KAFKA, *THE TRIAL*

Some performances are scripted. Some are impromptu. Some performances
transpire as the unintended consequence of case processing and are then
reinterpreted as meaningful accomplishments only at some later point in
a case's life course. But what unifies the disparate activities I collect under
the rubric of *performance* as a distinct penal technique is that the defendant
has discharged some meaningful undertaking that is evaluated by court
officials. He has complied with some duty, assigned task, program activity,
therapeutic encounter, or proposed some other behavioral accomplishment
that court actors can interpret as expressive of the defendant's character or
worthiness. Sometimes defendants are instructed to go somewhere to do

something and to prove, at some later date, that they were able to execute the directive satisfactorily. They are told they will be subject to sanction if they fail. Sometimes defendants offer up performances of their own accord, actions that exhibit responsibility, reform, or regularity. The performance presents an opportunity for defendants to prove governability. Prosecutors and judges inspect defendants' performances for signs that they can be guided by official directives or are enmeshed in mainstream institutions, activities, and lifestyles.

The content of performances vary from an eight-month, court-mandated, in-patient drug treatment program to merely showing up on time at court and waiting quietly. Performance offers an opportunity for what Foucault called an examination, which "places individuals in a field of surveillances and also situates them in a network of writings," creating knowledge about the individual's status in relation to a standard of conduct and engaging mechanisms to normalize behavior.[1] Yet, like the other penal techniques in misdemeanorland, this instance of disciplinary power is structured to conserve police, court, and organizational resources. Instead of unremitting watching, evaluating, and reforming activities, the technique of performance involves the issuance of a command to participate in an encounter or the observation of behavior in an encounter, and then record keeping about *how* the defendant presented in the encounter.

Penal control is modulated in response to the records about how the defendant performed in discrete encounters, which are often arbitrary in terms of content or anecdotal in terms of representing the defendant's person. Rewards and sanctions are doled out according to the level of compliance gauged at these punctuated performances. Some performances are demanded *ex ante* with the express purpose of evaluating the quality of the defendant's conduct. Others are only recognized as such *ex post*; they are the upshot of intended or unintended procedural hassles of the criminal process. The manner in which the defendant endured the procedural burdens is revealed as a meaningful expression of the defendant's risk or worthiness at critical junctures when legal actors make decisions about what to do next with his case.

The role of performance as a penal technique inside courts has been relatively neglected because the traditional adjudicative model of criminal law holds courts to be "people processing," as opposed to "people changing" organizations. Yeheskel Hasenfeld famously contrasted organizations whose "explicit function is to process [people] and confer public status on them" from those seeking to "change the behavior of people directly."[2]

The adjudicative model understands courts be to people-processing organizations because their role is to determine a status and then convey the status to the external environment, "which in turn typically results in both societal and self-reactions."[3] By this account, courts use criminal procedure to determine guilt and impose a sentence. Status determinations are then transmitted to external sites of punishment and to civil society, where the people-changing takes place in reaction to received statuses. If courts are conceptualized only as people-processing organizations, then their import is limited to how they determine and circulate statuses to external sites. But lower criminal courts are not primarily adjudicative, merely processing people by resolving criminal cases.

Rather, lower criminal courts in New York City's Broken Windows era operate closer to the managerial model described in chapter 2 and are, therefore, also "people-changing" organizations. They actively engage their subjects in an effort to modify their behaviors or produce new sensibilities through various transformative techniques. It is important to note that many people leave misdemeanorland with the same formal legal status with which they entered: no criminal conviction. Nonetheless, even those who are never convicted of a criminal offense often make repeated trips through misdemeanorland. There are active feedback loops within and between encounters such that subjects are evaluated on *how* they engage with the processing mechanisms. For both those who end up with criminal records and those who do not, recursive classification, processing, and evaluation is not merely a series of independent and sequel adjudications. As Megan Comfort notes with respect to the frequent encounters with the security clearance rituals of intimate partners visiting loved ones in prison, "one can posit that recurrent exposure to this ordeal will itself become a transformative course," if not upon the subjectivities of defendants, then upon the person they are perceived to be by court actors.[4] The trip through misdemeanorland is productive of a social and political status by virtue of the experience, not just by virtue of the formal status determined by the court. The performances demanded, offered, and evaluated represent a mode of engaging defendants over time to evaluate their capacity for right behavior and to adjust official reaction and reform activities accordingly.

In this sense, the managerial court is like other street-level bureaucracies, such as welfare offices, that construct and reproduce social status through their engagement with applicants. Scholars of the welfare state have long argued that eligibility rules, along with the process of application, enrollment, and monitoring program compliance, have extensive uses in addition to their role in allocating the material benefits of the program according to official eligibility criteria.[5] They are also tools for curtailing any sense of entitlement in marginal populations and for rationing services more scarce than the demand produced by actual need and formal eligibility.[6] The content of eligibility rules conveys prevailing values about deservedness, and enforcement of those rules seeks to bring applicants into compliance with those values. Even if judging and evaluating welfare applicants according to behavioral rules does not actually transform subjects, moments of judgment and evaluation are meaningful enactments that express the diminished cultural standing of current and potential recipients and their degraded citizenship status.[7] As in welfare offices, the way performances are demanded and evaluated in misdemeanorland expresses the presumption of need for social control that arises from the social standing of the people subject to its power. The subjects of Broken Windows policing are almost exclusively poor people of color from the city's most disadvantaged neighborhoods. The penal technique of performance in lower criminal courts mirrors a theme that is repeated in multiple sites: that these populations are inherently disorderly and must affirmatively prove their fitness for freedom.

Coming Back to Court

One of the most common performances in misdemeanorland is the simple requirement to show up. Many of the procedural hassles documented in the prior chapters are a direct consequence of the criminal process. Contested cases are not settled without some expenditure of time and resources to sort out competing versions of events. Malcolm Feeley famously argued that defendants in lower criminal courts rarely have an incentive to invoke formal adversarial procedures to contest factual guilt or the legality of police stops, searches, or arrests because procedural burdens of doing so often outweigh the formal sanctions being offered for an early disposition. This is certainly still the case for many defendants in misdemeanorland. But in New York City's lower courts operating under the managerial logic, these hassles are also evaluated as a performance. Court actors evaluate *how* defendants bear up under the varied demands, which in turn, engages a diachronic process of updating the official penal response based on court actors' evaluation of the defendant's performance.

Consider Malik (briefly introduced in chapter 5), a black man in his mid-forties, arrested in May 2010 in one of Borough A's highest-crime, and most highly policed, neighborhoods. He was charged with misdemeanor marijuana possession and criminal possession of a weapon in the fourth degree, ostensibly a gravity knife. According to Malik, he was walking to the post office smoking a Beedi cigarette when an unmarked car pulled up in the sidewalk crossing and three plainclothes policemen jumped out of the vehicle and surrounded him. They asked him if he was smoking marijuana. He showed them the Beedi cigarette he was smoking and told them it was not marijuana. The police started searching his person when he said to them, "Now that you know it's not marijuana, why are you still fucking with me?" Malik said he was then handcuffed and the police continued to put their hands in his pockets, removing his wallet and a folding pocketknife. According to both Malik and John, his sixty-something white public defender, Malik maintained from his prearraignment interview that he never had marijuana and that the knife was not an illegal "gravity knife," which is defined in the penal law as any knife that can be opened "by the force of gravity or the application of centrifugal force" and in practice means any knife a police officer can open with the flick of the wrist.[8]

Malik was the rare defendant who was steadfastly determined to take his case to trial.[9] He explained that he had served time for a felony gun case almost two decades ago and had led a law-abiding life for almost twenty years with his wife and two sons. He had recently seen his sons stopped, frisked, arrested, and assaulted during an arrest. He said he wanted to fight against what he said was "a general acceptance in the black community of police's behavior." From May to November 2011, he made eight court appearances. His defense attorney showed up for three of the eight court dates; a substitute attorney covered the remaining five. For most of the appearances, Malik had to take an entire day off from his job because no attorney showed up to call his case until after the lunch break. By the third court appearance, the marijuana charges had been dropped. His attorney reported to me that he never received a field or lab test for the supposed marijuana. The prosecution had been offering a plea to a noncriminal violation with the condition of three days of community service, but at the penultimate court appearance they offered an ACD with one day of community service. Malik refused to accept any offer, as he maintained complete factual innocence. In October, the case was finally transferred to a trial courtroom, and on the third scheduled trial court appearance, the defense attorney and prosecution were finally ready to proceed to trial when the defense attorney mentioned to the judge that "there was some possible issue with the knife not being a gravity knife."

Upon hearing this, Judge Becca suggested to both parties that "it would be wise to look at the evidence before calling the case for trial." Clarence, a white ADA in his late twenties, responded that "it is not costless to look at the knife," to explain why he had not already done so. They were sent out of the courtroom to wait for the arresting officer to bring the knife to court so that they could test it before calling the case for trial. On the way out of the courtroom, the prosecutor angrily told the defense attorney and Malik that if the knife turned out to be a gravity knife, all offers were off the table.

After lunch, the arresting officer arrived at the courtroom with a vouchered evidence bag containing the knife taken off Malik's person in May. Prior to opening the evidence bag, the prosecutor stated in the presence of the arresting officer, the defense attorney, Malik, and me that, had the officer observed the knife outwardly displayed on a shirt or pant pocket on the defendant's clothing when he stopped him, Malik could be charged with a violation of a New York City administrative code violation that prohibits wearing any knife open to public view.[10] He proceeded to demonstrate various ways the knife could have been displayed such that it would have been open to public view by clipping his pen to the outer portion of this pants pocket so that the long end of the pen was visible. After the knife was removed from the evidence bag, the arresting officer and prosecutor took turns trying to open it with strong downward thrusts of the arm. Both tried a number of times, and neither could successfully open the knife with a forceful flick of the wrist or full arm. The officer then told everyone present that when he approached Malik on the street seven-and-a-half months ago he had seen the knife clipped to his outer right pocket such that the knife was open to public view. The prosecutor told the defense attorney that he would either offer an ACD with one day of community service or he would proceed to a trial on the violation. After conferring with Malik, the defense attorney addressed the prosecutor:

> Defense: Okay, one last question, in a semi-serious vein, what did they do with Cain? In a semi-serious vein, is not this a "Let my people go" situation?
>
> ADA: Well, we've never been asking for jail time.
>
> Defense: With no marijuana, with no gravity knife, and with him missing his work, missing his job . . .
>
> ADA: Does he work?
>
> Malik: Yes I do.

ADA: So he would rather go to trial on the administrative code than do the one-day community service?

Defense: He does not even want an ACD, he wants outright dismissal.

ADA: (emphatically) Now *that* I'm not going to do.

With no plea resolution in sight, everyone walked to the courtroom to have the case called a third time that day. The prosecutor informed the judge that he had to drop the misdemeanor charge because the knife was not a gravity knife but would like to proceed to trial on an administrative violation because the officer was claiming he saw the knife displayed to public view and the defendant refused the ACD. The judge said that in her view, "The officer no longer had any credibility" because he signed a sworn statement in May claiming he retrieved marijuana and found the knife to be a gravity knife, and now both of those charges had been dismissed. She said she had a hard time believing that today, almost eight months later, the officer recalled seeing the knife open to public view, as there was no such claim in the initial complaint. She then dismissed the case in the interest of justice.

Malik's case illustrates Feeley's point about the strategic incentives facing lower court defendants arising from the relative costs of process versus punishment. It is not clear that it was rational for Malik to choose to fight his case if he was only interested in minimizing the short-term direct costs and burdens from the arrest. Some thirty years after the publication of *The Process Is the Punishment*, the procedural costs of trying to adjudicate often outweigh the formal punishment being offered to resolve a case along the way.[11] But Malik's case also illustrates two further arguments about the role of procedural hassle in New York City's misdemeanorland. First, procedural hassle is interpreted as a performance by legal actors because it offers an opportunity to evaluate the manner in which the defendant endures it along the way. Second, it also demonstrates the presumption of need for social control. Criminal court actors evidence a desire to track and test, in *some* capacity, almost all defendants who enter the orbit of misdemeanorland, regardless of any specific allegation of criminal wrongdoing. As this case shows, it persists even in the face of clear evidence that the defendant had not violated any provision of the penal law. Sometimes the presumption is based on an assessment of individualized risk, usually because of the defendant's past criminal record. But it is also deeply intertwined with general understandings about race, space, class, and assumptions that most defendants hail from what Elijah Anderson has called the "iconic ghetto," a space that is "impoverished, chaotic, lawless, drug-infested, and ruled by violence."[12] It is often impossible to untangle which of those threads are undergirding the presumption in any particular case. Waiting for the defense attorney to confer with Malik, the prosecutor and arresting officer kept mentioning the number of stabbings in the precinct where Malik was arrested and explained that they evaluate the arrest allegations against the backdrop of the crime conditions in the neighborhoods where arrests happen. The arresting officer asked me multiple times, "You know there were five hundred stabbings in the [redacted] precinct last year?," and the prosecutor referenced Malik's gun conviction from twenty years prior.

Thus prosecutors engage in plea bargaining not just to keep defendants from activating their procedural rights and to maintain inquisitorial control over case disposition, but also because they themselves often don't know what punishment they believe a defendant deserves or what measures of social control are warranted. They must make case disposition decisions from a position of profound uncertainty about what actually happened to occasion the arrest, who the defendant is, what risks he might pose. Malik's prosecutor insisted that his plea offer to Malik was not designed to secure maximum punishment or even to mark him with another criminal conviction. Rather, Clarence insisted he was concerned with securing *some* measure of assurance that this person was not a risk, some ability to track him, some mechanism to test his rule-abiding propensity. Prior to reentering the court, I asked the prosecutor why he pursued the case by mentioning the administrative code possibility to the arresting officer before the knife was tested. He replied, "People with gun records having knives, smoking marijuana in public, or smoking something that turns out not to be marijuana. . . . I mean it's not something that we'd be like, 'Oh, that's totally okay, I have no problem with that.' It's just whatever the next level of official attention is from 'that's totally okay, I have no problem,' which is do a day of community service, and then we'll dismiss the case in six months if you don't get arrested again."

It is precisely at that "next level of official attention" above "no problem" that performance comes in handy. Although the defendant has been hauled into misdemeanorland because of some allegation that he violated the penal law, he can usually only make his way out by performing as a governable subject, often in ways unrelated to the underlying allegation. Performance is a tool that allows prosecutors and judges to observe some capacity of defendants to follow official directives in the face of profound uncertainty about what type of person the defendant is. Legal actors do not have to expend investigative and court resources to determine what in fact happened to occasion the arrest. They can let time pass and behavioral propensities play out while holding ultimate disposition in abeyance.

The performances they evaluate bear some rational relation to what might be imagined as propensities for law abiding in general. To be clear, no actor in the system has any idea if a person who can successfully complete one day of community service, show up to a compliance court date, and then avoid arrest for six months is a good predictor of future risk of using a knife to stab someone, or even of getting arrested for some other low-level nonviolent offense. To my knowledge, there are no studies, assessments, or any other rigorous exogenous validation of the predictive accuracy of the performances valued in the folkways of misdemeanorland. But court actors deem performance a satisfactory tool because it seems to bear some rational relationship to the goal of risk management.

The notion that reliably coming to court warrants credit in the case disposition is prevalent in courtroom exchanges. Prosecutors sometimes talk of "earning your 30.30" to indicate they might not put a lot effort into prosecuting a certain case if the defendant reliably shows up to multiple court appearances. They might even think a speedy trial dismissal is a fair outcome only because the mark of a criminal conviction has been traded against procedural hassle and a reliable series of performances. A former prosecutor explained her approach during the years when she had an unmanageably large caseload: "When you have four hundred misdemeanors and you have a fare beat case? Even if that guy had five previous convictions for fare beat, what are we talking about? We're talking about a fare beat, right? So if that gentleman who has committed a fare beat shows up to court five times? I feel like that guy has kind of . . . if we're talking about responses that are proportionate to beating a fare—showing up every day for five times, and waiting in court for maybe as long as five, six hours to get your case called? I mean, should cases 30.30? Probably not. But in that case do I feel like that was a horrible result? No, the guy showed up five times."

Defense attorneys regularly trot out the number of court appearances a defendant has made to ADAs and judges in plea agreements to urge dismissal. In Malik's case, the defense attorney repeatedly said to the ADA during the final negotiations, "This is a 'let my people go' case," citing the number of court appearances Malik made over the months without any bench warrants. He made the same argument to Judge Becca before she affirmatively dismissed the case.

A set of background understandings shared by legal actors in misdemeanorland make such utterances about performance intelligible, even if prosecutors and judges reject the logic in specific instances. One such belief is that legal actors have actually achieved or learned something by way of the performances generated by monitoring, testing, and imposing costly inconveniences on the defendant. Sometimes they marshal this fact to claim that the number of procedural burdens and the quality of the performances discharged are commensurate to a downgrading of a mark. Other times they showcase the performances attendant to the procedural hassles to argue that the defendant has been proven trustworthy and that the criminal allegation represents an aberration, not a persistent pattern of rule breaking. Or they cite the number of court appearances to show that the person demonstrated commitment to his case and takes the legal system seriously, and therefore he deserves mercy because of his respectful character.

Conforming to Court

Whether intentionally imposed or not, the demands to come to court and conform to its customs offers an opportunity to observe and judge an unfolding performance by the defendant. Court actors react to how defendants perform under procedural hassle not only because that performance might proxy general law-abiding character, but also because they interpret the performance as a meaningful demonstration of who the defendant is and therefore what he deserves. The performance might be interpreted as a respectful act of deference to official power, one that can be given only by someone who accepts his proper place in the social order as a "patient" of the state, to borrow Javier Auyero's term.[13] Or, as the "information giver" suggested in Kafka's *The Trial*, cited in the epigraph to this chapter, the performance might be interpreted as a heroically endured ordeal that demonstrates the defendant's worthy character. It might also signal other facts about the defendant that assuage a prosecutor or judge's presumption of need for social control. For example, the performance might present a picture of a man or woman subject to the demands of family, work, or religion and effectively regulated by these normalizing institutions.

The demand to perform is a familiar penal technique in carceral institutions, where performance of degradation and obedience rituals is central to socializing inmates into a new immersive culture or securing their compliance with an all-encompassing behavioral regime.[14] In contrast, performance in misdemeanorland is not about transitioning the offender into a new "society of captives" or breaking down his outside person or habits to be subject to a new and totalizing system of control.[15] Rather, the logic of performance is about demonstration of *continuity* with a generalized capacity for rule following, normalcy, and integration into mainstream institutions. It is not enforced as unremitting, constant evaluation but as punctuated audits. Performances are evaluated for evidence that the defendant is well integrated into mainstream institutions of social control, such as the labor force or traditional family forms, and that he or she is receptive to official directives.

The evaluation of performances extends to the entire affair of case processing. Here the logic and practice of all three techniques of marking, procedural hassle, and performance are deeply intertwined. Repeated court appearances are demanded for ongoing, contested cases. Sometimes procedural inconveniences are imposed purposefully to burden defendants, and sometimes they are the unintentional upshot of contesting the charges or holding out for a better disposition. In any case, procedural hassles allow the judge and prosecutor to test and monitor defendants. The evaluation of *how* the defendant performed under these stresses is known and transmitted to assorted criminal court actors because it is marked down in the various record-keeping practices. Court actors evaluate and discuss how well the defendant manages procedural demands when they engage in plea negotiations and debate the appropriate disposition. A defendant's failure to perform adequately, for example, by violating an order of protection, showing up late at court, or violating courtroom norms can have significant effects on the trajectory of the instance case and on the disposition of later cases.

Defendants delivering successful performances of self-discipline or personal responsibility are rewarded. Thus, if a defendant has made all of the court appearances on time, many judges will not require the defendant to attend the final court date if the case is scheduled for speedy-trial 30.30 dismissal. Conversely, defendants delivering performances demonstrating disregard or merely failing to satisfy the formal demands of the legal process are sanctioned. Ricardo, a defense attorney, recounted the story of a client whose poor performance derailed a probable 30.30 dismissal. His client missed one court appearance and showed up after the lunch break for the next two. Despite all this, the prosecution had used up seventy-two of the ninety allowable days on the speedy trial clock. At the fourth court date, she again showed up after lunch, and the judge told the defense attorney that he should urge his client to "strongly consider" taking the ADA's offer, which was a guilty plea to a violation, an anger management program, and a two-year order of protection. Ricardo explained to his client that the judge's suggestion was crystal clear: if she did not take the plea, the judge would set bail because of her poor court appearance record. She would be incarcerated for the remainder of the case unless she could post the bail, which she could not. She took the plea.

Child care presents a difficult set of performances, where defendants must navigate competing demands of presenting as responsible parents and as responsible court subjects with limited resources to do both. On the one hand, evidence that a defendant is playing an active role in his or her children's lives and that he or she is a responsible parent is often presented as positive evidence that the defendant is not in need of penal discipline. On the other hand, defendants can be sanctioned if they miss or disrupt court because of child-care issues. Recall Wilbur, introduced in chapter 4, who returned to court voluntarily on a warrant in January 2011, telling the judge that he missed the last court appearance because his girlfriend was giving birth to their baby who was born with serious health problems. He said he tried to come back another time, but the case was not called in the morning, and since the home health aide could only stay with his girlfriend and baby until 1:00 p.m., he could not stay for the afternoon case calls. His defense attorney pointed out to the judge that the man's last criminal justice contact was in 1995, and he therefore asked for the warrant to be vacated and that the judge not put the man in custody on bail. The judge agreed but warned, "This case *has got to* move forward. You need to have child-care plans and back-up plans in case those plans fall through."

Many defendants have to bring their children to court because they lack other child-care options. Some judges are tolerant and polite, others are short-tempered and rude, but most eventually react to the inevitable noises children make in the courtroom. These encounters provide an opportunity to discipline the defendant about his or her responsibility to the court or norms of comportment generally. In November 2010, in one of the specialized domestic violence court parts, a number of young children were sitting with their parents who were waiting for their cases to be called. In the back of the audience a baby was fussing and eventually began to cry. "The child needs to be taken outside!" barked Judge Leanne, and a court officer started to walk toward the mother and child. Before he reached them, the mother got up off the bench with her baby to wait outside of the courtroom in the hallway. Later that same day, Judge Leanne upbraided a young woman who showed up for her court appearance after missing the last appearance, at which the judge had agreed to stay the warrant. The defendant pushed a stroller with an infant up to the threshold of the well and left it there before approaching the podium with her attorney to explain that she missed the last appearance because she could not find child care. The judge addressed the defense attorney, asking with whom the young woman lived. The attorney conferred with her client and answered that the defendant lived with her mother. The judge told the defendant in a stern tone, "Your mother can take care of the child; that is no excuse for not coming to court," without inquiring whether the mother could, in fact, watch the child during an entire business day.

Orders of protection are another mechanism for performance evaluation. Warrants issued in cases classified as domestic violence are shared with an NYPD squad charged with doing random home visits. Failure to abide by the order of protection can result not only in a new arrest; it can also cause the prosecutor and judge to change their assessment about what level of social control and punitive measures are appropriate for the underlying case. All judges have a slightly different version of the order of protection speech, but most advise defendants of a few important things that let them know the court's power to punish and control them now has a basis outside of the accusations of the complaining witness. Judge Leanne, who regularly presided over one of the specialized domestic violence courtrooms, frequently delivered some version of this admonishment: "This is *my* order, not Ms.———'s order. She cannot change it. You will be arrested if you violate *my* order." Judge Felix, another DV judge, would say, "This is a court order, which means that even if the person named in the order invites you to have contact with her (him) and you were to do so, you would be in violation of the order and subject to additional penalty."

In mid-November 2010, Ted, a young black man, was arrested at his home for being in bed with a woman who allegedly was the complainant on his open domestic violence case during a random NYPD home visit of addresses listed on active DV orders of protection. The case was on route to 30.30 speedy trial dismissal because the complainant had not participated in the prosecution since the arrest and the case could not be proved without her testimony. Yet during the speedy trial time there remains in effect a full order of protection prohibiting the defendant from any contact with the complainant. Ted was arrested for contempt of a court order. Bail was set at his arraignment for this new arrest.

The defense attorney argued to the judge that this address was the defendant's legal residence and produced documents to show the defendant was the only person listed on the lease. Presumably, the complainant was staying or living with the defendant at the time of the incident and so gave this address to court officials making up the order of protection.[16] The defense attorney argued that the complaint should not be considered "converted" for purposes of stopping the 30.30 clock because the arresting officer had no firsthand information about the woman's identity. He was relying on hearsay, namely, the address listed on the order of protection, from which he inferred that the woman was the complainant.[17]

The judge summarily rejected the defense attorney's argument, merely saying that the issue of the woman's identity was an issue for trial. The ruling meant Ted would be held in custody until the disposition of the case because he could not afford bail. Ted eventually pled out on both the underlying case, which was clearly on track to dismissal prior to the new arrest, and to the contempt case. Again, I have no idea what the true facts were. But these facts were similarly opaque to the legal actors in the system, who readily accepted his plea without further investigation. This case illustrates how a defendant failing to successfully execute the performances demanded of him will change the course of probable disposition. No new facts or evidence changed the legal merits of the underlying case that gave rise to the order of protection. But the contempt arrest changed the structure of incentives for the defendant to take a criminal conviction on the underlying case because he was put in on bail. And it is the structure of incentives, not necessarily the legal or factual merits of the case, that more often than not drive disposition in misdemeanorland.

Orders of protection are sometimes modified if a defendant offers certain performances that lessen the felt need of judges or prosecutors to impose the full order. Judge Felix explained that it is rare for him to agree to modify an order.

But every once in a while you do find someone, and—I have modified them, on occasion. [For example, I had] an elder abuse, in this case— the complainant was now in a nursing home, and so—the defendant was the victim's . . . adult daughter. She had voluntarily started taking a program before taking a plea, and so the program represented that—they could escort her to the nursing home to see her mother. So, I agreed to modify it. I kept it as a full, but with allowing with escorts to go see the mother, who was ninety-something years old and in the throes of

Alzheimer's and had other health issues. For me, that was a change in circumstances—the person was in a program, was going to be with an escort, and . . . there was really a history. What was evident with that person was that there was a substance abuse problem. But they [*sic*] were in a program, and they [*sic*] did it without a mandate.

The performance was not just that the defendant had enrolled herself in a program but that she had done it of her own accord without a court mandate. However, even under these circumstances, the judge would not agree to change the legal status of the order from full to limited.

Judges also often strive to clearly establish their power to evaluate the defendant's performances during the case's life course, irrespective of the eventual, even certain, dismissal. In late November 2010, a number defendants in one of the specialized domestic violence parts appeared for what would, most likely, be their penultimate court appearance. The prosecution had not been able to convert these cases, and it was apparent to all parties the cases would be dismissed at the next court date, such that the judge announced the next date was for "conversion or 30.30 dismissal." That final court appearance was scheduled for early January 2011 in all of these cases, and Judge Leanne individually cautioned each defendant with some variation of the following: "Your next court date is in January, and the order of protection remains in effect until that date; there is *no exception for the holidays*. This order of protection will remain in effect for Thanksgiving and Christmas and New Year's, and the complaining witness cannot give you permission to violate it."

Another means through which failure to perform successfully, in conjunction with the marks generated by such failure, affects a defendant's trajectory is by acquiring bench warrants. If a defendant fails to make scheduled court appearances, or sometimes even to make appearances on time, a judge will issue a bench warrant. The NYPD warrant squad has its own set of priorities for tracking down such defendants, but if the person is encountered for any reason, his or her name will be flagged when the officer makes a radio ID check, which is standard procedure with street, transit, and traffic stops. If a defendant is brought back to court by a police officer, it is called an involuntary return on a warrant. Defendants can, and in fact most often do, return voluntarily on a warrant. New York City's Criminal Justice Agency has documented that, among the defendants who fail to appear at a required court appearance (about 14 percent of misdemeanor cases in 2015), about one-half voluntarily return to court within thirty days of the bench warrant.[18] Nonetheless, insofar as the case is recorded on the rap sheet (that is, it is an open case or a case that has not been sealed), the bench warrant history will always be visible to judges and prosecutors. Bench warrants therefore not only affect the trajectory of misdemeanor defendants by creating a status of being "on the run"; they are also significant marks that are consulted to determine what type of person the defendant is and how he or she should be treated in later cases.[19]

In November 2010, Judge Leanne admonished a defendant explaining his late appearance in court, saying he first went to the wrong floor and then a court officer sent him to another wrong floor before finding the correct courtroom. The judge replied, "9:30 means 9:30 in the courtroom," and said to the attorney, "your client is not excused on the next court date; if he is not here, I will not dismiss the case." This same judge regularly told defendants who returned to her courtroom, either voluntarily or involuntarily, on warrants that she would set bail if she ever had to issue a second bench warrant for not showing up at court. In another instance when a defendant made it to court in time for the "second call" of his case, which occurred around 11:30 a.m., she warned: "If I ever say the words 'warrant ordered' again, even if it is 'just' because you are late, you can rest assured I will set bail." Since most defendants are indigent, the threat of setting bail means the person will almost certainly be held in custody at Rikers Island pending the disposition the case.

Judges and prosecutors regularly name prior bench warrants as one of the most important factors they consider in making bail determinations or requests.[20] It is one of various factors listed as permissible considerations in New York State's bail statute.[21] In addition, the New York Criminal Justice Agency—the entity that interviews defendants before arraignment and makes release recommendations to the court—assigns significant weight to prior bench warrants.

Judge Marcos in chapter 4 attested to the importance of bench warrants when he said he felt compelled to set bail in cases where the defendant has a warrant history, even if he knows the current complaint "is not a case that the person is going to do jail time on." Even if a defendant performs the predisposition aspects of a case successfully, he can come out of misdemeanorland with a bench warrant history if he fails to properly execute postdisposition performances. Judge Kato discussed whether he differentiates the mark of a bench warrant when setting bail depending on why and under what circumstances the defendant failed to make a court appearance by considering a hypothetical (but commonly occurring) case.

The defendant was sentenced to a conditional discharge requiring five days of community service with a fifteen-day jail alternative (possible if the condition is not discharged); the defendant performed the community service but missed the compliance court date:

> Q: No harm, no foul? [T]he prosecution will say, "So-and-so has a warrant history," and the defense attorney will say, "Well, you know there are warrants and then there are warrants . . ."
>
> Judge Kato: Well, you know what? Even if . . . What I'm saying is if you show up and even if we vacate the warrant, and you present proof you've done your dates of community service, you're not going to jail for fifteen days. So that's going to be taken care of. But you still had an obligation to the court. You don't get to choose your own dates. So I mean, a bench warrant is a bench warrant when you look at it.

Marks recording that defendants have unsuccessfully performed the demand to conform to court orders therefore shape the trajectory of later cases.

There is no explicitly scripted, normative code consciously embraced by legal actors to guide the interpretation of performances. The indigenous moral economy that credits certain performances emerges in response to the particularities of misdemeanorland as field of action. Frontline legal actors face recurrent "problem situations" to form offers, resolve cases, and make other decisions under practical conditions characteristic of under-resourced street-level bureaucracies. In this context, legal actors interpret as meaningful performances that are elicited—intentionally or unintentionally—from defendants traversing the travails of criminal court case processing. This repurposing of procedural hassle is not unique to misdemeanorland.

Many observers of street-level bureaucracies—especially those serving nonvoluntary clients composed of marginalized populations—have documented how eligibility screening and application of administrative rules evolve into tools to winnow or even dissuade applicants.[22] Careful observation of how frontline actors use rules exposes the moral economy of those charged with administration. For example, Lara-Millán's ethnography of an overcrowded and underfunded public hospital emergency room shows how frontline actors faced with an onslaught of medically needy patients rely on heuristics of desert to make admissions decisions and to justify the pattern of admissions that results from their decisions. The admitting nurses face an immediate imperative to distinguish between applicants that present as similarly needy and to thin unmanageably overcrowded conditions. One way they do this is to observe *how* patients withstand the "harrowing wait." Essentially, they judge the performances of patients, seeing if they comply with the rules of the waiting room, if they can be located during random "reassessments" when names are called, how they react to police officers checking identification, and who is waiting with patients and under what conditions.[23] Hospital workers either allow patients to self-censure their demands for services in reaction to these circumstances or they adjust the official status of the applicant in reaction to the information generated.

Notably, it seems from Lara-Millán's account that neither police officers nor nurses set out to use these tactics to dissuade patients from seeking care. They might not even consciously endorse the specific heuristics of desert that seem to be structuring their admission decisions. Nonetheless, practices that have a formal, rational purpose—for example, checking patients' vital signs every few hours during protracted waits to see if symptoms have worsened—present new functional possibilities—an opportunity to see if the patient is continually present in the waiting room to use as a basis for exclusion—when situated actors must make a series of constrained decisions under conditions of severe scarcity. This is also the case in misdemeanorland. To my knowledge, no DA or judge sets out to intentionally conserve legal resources by not investigating cases and, instead, deciding dispositions by measuring behavioral propensities or moral worth from a series of performances. Nonetheless, legal actors are faced with recurrent problem situations under a set of practical constraints. On a daily basis, they must decide what to do with a large volume of judicial cases alleging low-level criminal conduct with limited time and resources to determine what in fact did happen or what type of person the defendant is.

Jonathan Simon has shown something similar in the context of parole supervision, where parole officers face the practical problem of managing people who all appear "indistinguishably dangerous." Parole officers usually have large caseloads, limited time, and perhaps most important, limited ability to draw on the "mainstream organizing forces of social life" in order to distinguish between parolees to see which are at the highest risk of reoffending, because so few are stably embedded in mainstream social control institutions such as formal employment or civil organizations. He notes that many parole officers resort to using drug tests and reporting compliance as a way to sort the parolee population for two simple reasons: these methods are readily accessible, and they present some rational connection to risk management. But although these techniques allow parole officers to distinguish between various parolees on a spectrum with some logical connection to their perceived dangerousness, they do not truly engage the structuring influences of employment and family that meaningfully reduce recidivism.[24]

Thus, frontline workers in many organizations facing severe load constraints reappropriate the upshots of constraint and scarcity to new uses. Ground-level actors rarely begin their endeavors with a coherent theory about the criteria of selection or basis of desert to distribute rewards and sanctions over which they have power. If pressed, many legal actors might provide an account of why they rationed services or made decisions based on how the subjects of misdemeanorland withstand procedural hassles. But these are often rationalizations of prevailing practices, not motivations for the pattern of action. Actors must make situated determinations about what broad rules and indeterminate selection criteria *mean* in complex choice situations. They improvisationally designate as relevant certain information that unfolds about the applicant over time under the specifically contoured constraints of the encounter. Many of the performances that are frequently evaluated in misdemeanorland have emerged as relevant in this way. One class of performances is expressly designated as a meaningful show of self and is often designed as a means of earning a reduction in other penal burdens: programs.

Programs

"Program" is a catchphrase for an assortment of classes, therapeutic interventions, informational sessions, and social services. The content of programs addresses the gamut of criminal conduct or, in some cases, the ascribed underlying problem of the offender. There is an anti-shoplifting program for first-time petit larceny arrestees, an anti–domestic violence program, a program to help people exit the sex trade offered to prostitution arrestees, a "John" program for men arrested for solicitation, anger management programs, numerous drug treatment, and various anti–drunk driving programs. These programs are an increasingly common element of case disposition practices in New York City's lower criminal courts.

Programs can be imposed as part of different types of dispositions—dismissal, conviction to a noncriminal violation, or conviction to a misdemeanor crime. Many ACDs are granted with program performance conditions. Indeed, it is more accurate to state that the dismissal is *earned* through the program, a phrasing often heard in misdemeanorland. Community service is a common condition precedent to ACD dismissal, usually requiring anywhere between one and fifteen days of service at a city park or cleanup site. The performance of community service is less about the content of the activity than the requirement to prove that the defendant can responsibly show up early in the morning at the site and at the compliance court date. Some prosecutors say mandating community service is silly because it does not engage the defendant in any particularly substantive way. Alvin, a supervising prosecutor in Borough A, commented:

> I don't think community service has much value because it costs the taxpayers a ton of money. . . . I mean you have to pay someone to supervise them as they sweep up the park. That person does not really care about the park, and the person supervising the defendant does not really care about how well they sweep up the park, they are just checking them off for attendance. And then they [the defendants] have to come back to court to show compliance. And if they did not do the community service, then they can get cycled back into the system, and it is costly for everyone. What is the end? You will see people argue for five days' community service, and we say no fifteen days' committee service. I often think, who cares?

But using community service as a way to earn a noncriminal disposition is a deeply entrenched plea practice partially *because* it is an empty task. It is a neutral currency of hassle and performance capacity that is traded to reduce other penal burdens such as marking. For example, when one borough was strapped for funding to conduct the half-day anti-drug classes that had been the standard mandate to receive an ACD for a first-time misdemeanor narcotics possession arrest, it seamlessly transitioned into requiring one to two days of community service instead.

Many ACD conditions involve a more content-specific program. Although DCJS does not have comprehensive records on the number of dispositions involving a program, the standard offers in most boroughs for certain types of arrest charges always involve a program. For example, an antiprostitution class or mandated counseling sessions designed for sex workers is the standard offer on a prostitution arrest with an ACD upon successful completion; many first-time arrestees for shoplifting are offered an ACD only upon completion of an anti-shoplifting program ("Stoplift"); in many boroughs, first-time arrestees for possession of misdemeanor-weight narcotics are offered an ACD only upon completion of short half-day session discussing the availability of treatment services called the Treatment Readiness Program.

Programs are also often part of conviction dispositions. Anti–domestic violence programs are standard offers for assault arrests where the complainant is an intimate of the defendant, and some sort of anti–drunk driving program is mandatory for almost all DWI convictions. The length of performance requirements can vary substantially, from a one-day, four-hour class to in-patient drug treatment for up to twelve months. Many of these performances involve not only enactments of responsibility and treatment, but also significant financial penalties in the form of mandatory program registration fees. The anti-shoplifting program fee is listed as $125, and the anti–domestic violence program is over $1,000, but most program operators say they offer a sliding fee scale based on income with a minimum fee.[25]

Programs to engage the values, attitudes, and character of penal subjects and to reform their errant behaviors through education, treatment, and retraining are hardly new.[26] The reformist penal projects of the nineteenth century were premised on the restorative promise of rehabilitative programs, both inside and outside of prisons. In fact, the era of mass incarceration in the United States, starting in the 1970s, is widely identified as the epoch in which the state retreated from welfarist approaches to crime and punishment.[27] Many scholars have defined the current criminal justice era in the United States in terms—such as punitive neoliberalism, new penology, or culture of control—that denote a rejection of an overarching commitment to rehabilitation and an embrace of punitive exclusion, segregation, and brute behavioral control.[28]

Despite these changes in the master narrative of criminal justice practices, programs are currently a central feature of case processing in misdemeanorland. Sit in any misdemeanor arraignment or all-purpose part in the city, and you will hear a veritable alphabet soup of programs being offered and accepted as part of case dispositions. And criminal justice actors often talk about their innovation and use of programs by appealing to welfarist rationalities, expressing concern with "root causes" of criminal offending or a desire to aid the psychological transformation of defendants.[29]

Jerome, a staff member of a nonprofit entity that pioneers programs in criminal court, said of the underlying social ills behind most of the arrests he saw, "We cannot just ignore these problems with impunity.... In theory, social services would be there in other ways outside of the criminal justice system, but they are not. So they show up at the courthouse doorstep." Discussing the mandated social services his agency designs and operates that are offered to earn a favorable criminal court disposition, he said, "We are not widening the net but breaking the cycle that could lead to many more arrests and convictions in the future."

Judge Barry, who worked with the DA's office in Borough A to design and implement a series of antiprostitution programs, gave the following presentation at an April 2010 event held at the courthouse to present the new (at the time) programs and services available for prostitution arrestees.[30] He began by recounting his time working as an arraignment assistant district attorney (before he became a judge) during what used to be called the "lobster shift" of night court, from 1:00 a.m. to 9:00 a.m., where a large number of prostitution arrests were arraigned. He told the audience that police officers would march the women into court, and he spoke of his discomfort seeing how their revealing outfits looked embarrassing and cheap in the bright florescent lights of the courtroom, and their faces looked tragic with makeup smudged and running from crying. When each woman was brought up to the well to be arraigned, the prosecutor and defense attorney would begin haggling over the case's worth: the line ADA would ask for thirty days, the defense would say she does not deserve more than ten, and the judge would give twenty days. He said that as the corrections officer took charge of the sentenced defendant and brought her back to the holding pens, he would try not to look at her face because he felt ashamed. He knew these women were young and often victims of terrible abuse and sex crimes. He felt ashamed because he knew that putting them in jail did nothing to reduce prostitution or improve their lives.

When he became a judge, he invited one young defendant to his chambers to tell her story after hearing her case at arraignment. He took it on himself to secure for her an assortment of services. Judge Barry proceeded to share with the room of attendees what he learned about sex work and why he became interested in figuring out how the criminal justice system could better to engage the women arrested for prostitution. After offering a number of personal stories about young women he had worked with, he concluded that these defendants should not be thought of as criminals, but as victims. The judge finished by explaining the new programs and noting some of the limits of using the criminal justice system to deliver services to this population. But, he insisted these programs were a vast improvement from when ADAs and defense attorneys were haggling over the number of days at Rikers Island. He concluded, "We have gone from 'let's make a deal' to 'let's make a difference.'"

Mike, a senior supervising ADA, discussing how criminal prosecution differs in this borough from other New York City boroughs, quipped,

"[Borough A] is unique; we have a program for everything. Some defense attorneys in Supreme Court joke with me saying, 'Hey Mike, can I get that murder program?'" Criminal court actors draw on welfarist rationalities grounded in a rehabilitative paradigm to talk about programs as a way to both *do something* with the case and the defendant while also addressing underlying criminogenic issues. The office has a "cheat sheet" listing over twenty-seven different programs it regularly uses, spanning a number of different nonprofits and agency service providers. Many of these programs were innovated by the DA's office and run by them in-house.

Criminal justice actors in misdemeanorland often explain their devotion to programs in terms of discomfort or disagreement with using traditional custodial penalties in response to certain crimes or defendants. Diane, a young lawyer recently hired at the DA's office in Borough A, said that the extensive offerings of programs is one of the reasons that she wanted to work in Borough A's prosecutor's office: "It's not like other offices where we have no autonomy to offer anything. Here you can go to the supervisor and say, 'This is this person's issue. Can we work on something like this?' It's the progressive dedication to programs and problem solving that made me want to work at this office."

Despite the declaration of welfarist rationalities, the design of most programs and the larger social and political context in which they are deployed make it hard to reasonably believe these programs are capable of achieving anything close to the transformative ideals espoused to support them.[31] Al, an arraignment supervisor for the DA's office, in response to a question about what he found frustrating about his job, said, "You cannot really address all the problems that bring people here, *but they all end up here with their problems.*" Looking around the arraignment courtroom filled with low-income people, mostly of color, he went on to say, "This place is not set up really to deal with the issues. They try, and you have to give Mr. [District Attorney] credit for that, but it is hard to deal with these issues in the courts."

One explanation for the persistence and revival of programs is that the rehabilitative impulse was not so much trampled as transformed in the current epoch.[32] Some scholars have argued that facially welfarist programs have explicitly given up on fundamental inner transformation or meaningful reintegration of penal subjects into a stable social and economic order.[33] Stanley Cohen, Malcolm Feeley, David Garland, and Jonathan Simon have argued that content-specific programmed interventions in the current era are more concerned with behavioral control or risk management than with knowing and modifying the subject's inner self.[34] These accounts tie operations in criminal justice to larger social and economic trends. But there are also meso-level dynamics that transform programs motivated by welfarist rationalities into mere disposition tools that seem more interested in control and surveillance than subjective or social transformation.

Although criminal court actors promote programs with welfarist trappings, their central operative features tend to become not their programmatic content but the form of performance. All programs require defendants to execute a series of actions and activities. Defendants are subsequently evaluated on their accomplishments. This form of performance allows criminal court actors to engage the defendant's general capacity for rule following, manage potential risks, or merely impose punitive burdens. As programs become established disposition tools in misdemeanorland, performance is commensurated with and traded off against other penal burdens in the ongoing enterprise of social control.[35] In the process, it is not clear that programs either increase *or* decrease the overall social control burdens experienced by defendants.

Any examination of so-called alternative criminal justice sanctions seems to lead inexorably to the question of "net widening." The term is sometimes loosely used to simply mean the expansion of penal social control. But the original meaning of the concept, first popularized by Stanly Cohen and Andrew Scull, refers to the process by which noncustodial, often community-based, forms of corrections supplement—as opposed to replace—incarceration by pulling in more "shallow end" deviants who would not have otherwise entered the system, thereby increasing the total volume, scope, and intensity of control institutions.[36] The concept is so well entrenched in critical criminological literature that it is almost axiomatic to assume noncustodial alternative programs mechanically induce an expansion and deepening of social control.[37] But to show that programs involve net widening in the classic sense entails a set of very complicated questions not only about counterfactuals (What would have happened to the relevant cases in the absence of programs in terms of sanctions and life outcomes?), but also about commensuration (How do we compare qualitatively distinct penal burdens such that it is meaningful to talk about *more* penal control?). These questions are precisely what legal actors are negotiating and strategizing about as they discuss programs in misdemeanorland (although they rarely use terms such as "counterfactuals" and "commensuration"!).

Insofar as welfarist programs are mandates arising from a criminal justice case, the power to require performance is limited by the leverage court actors have in the encounter. Marta, the social worker coordinator for the drug courts in Borough A, explained that the judge sitting in the misdemeanor drug part would rarely impose more than a ninety-day jail sentence for someone who repeatedly failed out of mandated drug treatment. She said that although she understood why that was a fair sentence, it made it hard to motivate misdemeanor defendants into intensive drug treatment programs, especially those with long histories of addiction and arrest:

> Our participants generally don't get any more than ninety days . . . [and] that's also the challenge with the misdemeanor population. One of the reasons that Drug Court is so successful is that—because it's the carrot and the stick approach. So the carrot is that your case is going to be dismissed, but it's also, like, a hammer. Like, if you don't do this—if you don't complete it, . . . it's the jail alternative, with felonies. . . . In addiction, you need that kind of motivation. Unfortunately, what we're finding with the misdemeanor population, especially misdemeanants who have been in and out of this system for so long they can do, and I should probably put it a different way, but they can do ninety days standing on their head, at Riker's Island. Unfortunately. So the threat of a ninety-day jail alternative isn't really a motivator for the misdemeanants.

Excessively burdensome programs are usually not considered for a misdemeanor arrest unless the defendant is facing some jail time, and even so, many defendants would rather take traditional sanctions over some programs. Fred, a middle-aged black man arrested for misdemeanor narcotics possession with an extensive history of misdemeanor drug arrests (but not a single felony), described the options:

Q: Are you going to fight the charge?
Fred: [Sighs] If I fight it, I'm going to go to jail. That's why everybody pleads guilty. You come, plead guilty, and go home. And if you try to fight it, they're going to lock you up.
Q: So what happens when you keep pleading guilty?
Fred: See, now they're talking about giving me some time. And I have to go to take this drug treatment thing program. And I don't have time for that. Eight months, going to this place two or three days. I don't have time for that.
Q: Do you work?
Fred: Yeah. I'm a plumber.

Fred admitted to struggling with a serious crack and heroin addiction since he was seventeen, but he reported holding down a steady job notwithstanding his addiction. Nonetheless, he explained that he refused to be subject to what he felt was degrading treatment, even to avoid another conviction or jail time:

> Fred: This place I was in. After dinner there would be pots, and they don't have a designated man to wash the pots. So the way they did it was that if you violated one of the rules—okay, you got to wash pots as a punishment. Say no one violated rules? Now they going to pick on somebody. "You have to do the pots." And that's not right. You know what they said? It builds character. Washing pots? You wash them fucking pots! [Laughs] What kind of character? . . . I'll accept the punishment if I've done something. Okay. But if I didn't do anything, you wash them pots. Okay? If I came in late—all right, fine. That's how you think it works, we'll do it. I can understand the discipline. But just because no one is in trouble at the moment and you need the pots cleaned? I think you should go wash them.
>
> Q: So it sort of feels like they think that if they punish you enough, it's going to help you get over your addiction? Is that the logic?
>
> Fred: Yeah. I've heard of ones where they sit you down in the chair and the other people that's in the program will scream on you. And say things like, "What you did was wrong! And you should never have done that!" Embarrassing them. What the hell is that going to do? And you can't say nothing while you're sitting in that chair.
> . . .
> Q: What do you think they're trying to do?
>
> Fred: I don't know. Make them jump up and punch somebody in their face. What else? What is that going to do, really? I can't get that. I tried. And I won't go to one of those programs. One of those "TC." That's what they call them.
>
> Q: What does that stand for?
>
> Fred: Therapeutic community.
>
> Q: Really?
>
> Fred: Yeah. That's some kind of therapy.

Like Fred, many people mandated by courts to participate in programs see the ostensibly welfarist intervention as punishment by the different name. By 2013, the programs Judge Barry had discussed were rolled into a statewide initiative to launch Human Trafficking Intervention Courts, announced as a "system of specialized criminal courts to handle prostitution cases and provide services to help wrest human- and sex-trafficking victims from the cycle of exploitation and arrest."[38] The standard offer for prostitution arrests in most boroughs is now some combination of individual or group counseling sessions, usually somewhere between three and ten.

Casandra, a senior public defender who has worked extensively with prostitution and human trafficking cases, explained that the offer practice in these programs looks a lot like it does in other cases in misdemeanorland: the defendant's record will provoke a higher offer along some vector of either mark, hassle, or performance. She explained that most defendants feel the added demand for programming as merely another punitive measure occasioned by their record, irrespective of the actual or stated motivations of court actors: "I don't know that my clients will say, 'Oh, it's amazing they want me to do ten sessions because they really want to help me,' as opposed to in the marijuana case or the crack case, [from which] 'they wanted me to do ten days of community service because they told me that's a wake-up call and I have to be accountable.' I don't think clients are appreciating that. . . . But it's the same essential record-keeping goal. I just think the way they describe it is a little bit different."

The fact that the defendant's record plays such an important role in determining the extent and shape of programs demonstrates that punitive burdens are being shifted from one frontier (the permanent mark of a conviction or custodial sentence) to another (restrictive program conditions or repeated court appearances) according to some rough metric of the level of social control the prosecutor thinks appropriate for the defendant. Casandra explained that, with welfarist intentions or not, institutional actors tend to focus on their practical goals in the immediate work of criminal court: "I don't know that anyone believes that the mushy therapy stuff is actually effective. I don't think it's harmful. I'm convinced it's not harmful. And I'm convinced that there are some very thoughtful, and dedicated, and conscientious people that are now interacting with our clients through these partner organizations. So I don't have a problem with it. But I don't think anyone is operating under the notion that we are somehow combating trafficking by doing this. So there has to be some other thing operating. So for us, it's about better dispositions for clients."

The practical brokering of programs also brings out key differences in the constituency of misdemeanorland: different defendants are willing to bear different types of penal burdens in order to avoid others. Defendants with extensive criminal records are sometimes less willing to take on procedural or performance penal burdens because they perceive those as more onerous than the additional marking weight of another criminal conviction. Many people struggling with longtime addition issues do not want to attempt rehab under the specter of a jail alternative. Defense attorneys often say that some of their clients with the most need for services are the ones they would be the least likely to enroll, because they worry they would be doing their client a disservice if the person cannot successfully complete the program. Leslie, a supervisor at a public defender organization in Borough A explained why so few clients went to the misdemeanor drug treatment court: "The main problem, from our client's perspective, I think—misdemeanor programs—is that the effort it takes to complete a drug treatment program for someone who is addicted to crack or heroin . . . the effort is incredible. It's almost impossible. And the benefit is to get your case dismissed. These people have . . . misdemeanor convictions anyway. So there is no real . . . the real benefit in misdemeanor court is your own personal triumph. What you're going to get if you decline treatment is between, I don't know, thirty days in jail and six months. Which, for a lot of people, is literally easier to do than doing treatment. Treatment is brutal. It's brutal."

But for other defendants, even those with prior criminal convictions, the cost of a new criminal conviction outweighs their valuation of the procedural and performance burdens of a program. Ernesto had been on parole for felony narcotics sale since 2010. In 2011, he picked up two new misdemeanor cases, one for trespass in November and one for petit larceny in December. Ernesto readily admitted the petit larceny offense, but told me at his first three court appearances that he intended to fight the trespass case because he was innocent. He claimed he was visiting a friend in the building and that this friend would come to court with a lease and notarized letter saying he had invited Ernesto to visit him in the building that evening but was not home to let him in before the police arrested Ernesto. At his third court appearance, Ernesto borrowed my phone to call his parole officer to ask if he would be violated (and possibly sent back upstate) if convicted on a new misdemeanor offense, and the parole officer said yes. The parole officer also indicated that he would not oppose Ernesto entering a drug treatment program through one of the specialized drug court parts to dispose of the cases, but that the parole office would take the position that he would have to do inpatient, as opposed to outpatient, treatment.

"That's all you got to tell me, one thing, now I'm taking it," Ernesto responded, meaning he would rather do the program than go back upstate.

On his fourth court appearance, in January 2012, Ernesto pled guilty to both offenses. He signed a contract with the treatment court agreeing to eight to twelve months of inpatient drug treatment (or in Ernesto's case, alcohol treatment, as he claims he never uses drugs, just drinks excessively). The contract stated that if he succeeded in treatment, both cases would be given ACDs. Ernesto entered a residential drug treatment facility in January 2012 and made more than fifteen court appearances after November 2011 in connection with his two misdemeanor cases and as part of the court supervision of his treatment program. (He had to switch inpatient providers three months into the program because the facility he was in was infested with bedbugs and refused to pay an exterminator. The facility threatened to issue the court a negative progress report if he told, but he told anyway and was moved to a new facility.)

Thus, Ernesto was able to avoid a violation of parole and the mark of another misdemeanor conviction in exchange for a weighty performance and repeated court appearances. But the performances entailed losing his job. Ernesto had been delivering pizzas for a high-end restaurant but was forced to quit in order to enter inpatient drug treatment, because residents are not allowed to leave the facility for extended periods of time during the first few months. "They don't recognize my job, since it's off the books," he said, explaining why his employment status did not sway the parole officer or court to allow him to do outpatient treatment. When asked if he would prefer a shorter jail sentence to a longer inpatient drug treatment program, he responded that he would take a month in jail "in a heartbeat," but went on to clarify, "If I accept the misdemeanor, I'm accepting the violation of parole. . . . I'll be up north, either way. . . . The whole thing was to avoid this violation."

Ernesto's case demonstrates the complicated ways that programs are transacted by many actors in the criminal justice system, including judges, defense attorneys, prosecutors, parole officers, drug treatment agencies, and of course defendants themselves, who sometimes have other entanglements with the system beyond misdemeanorland. The prosecutor and parole officer's insistence on intensive inpatient drug treatment was not clearly motivated by a clinical assessment, but rather by the imperative to exert more intensive social control over a longer period of time because of Ernesto's record and parole status. Ernesto was willing to undertake the procedural hassle and performance of drug treatment and extended court appearances to avoid the additional misdemeanor convictions only because those convictions would have triggered a violation of parole and, most likely, time in an upstate prison.

As programs become integrated into the everyday operations of courtroom practice, they circulate less as meaningful welfare interventions and more as devices to dispose of cases. Like other techniques in misdemeanor justice, they offer the potential for behavior monitoring and evaluation of responsibility-proving performances without deeply engaging the offender's soul. Patricia, one of the most senior prosecutors in the Domestic Violence Bureau talked about the anti–domestic violence class: "There is plenty of research that has been done on batterer's intervention programs, and no one is harboring the illusion that it changes anybody. But it's more about the compliance component—that it's used by the courts as a way of monitoring the behavior of individuals."

One of the most frequent complaints from defense attorneys about programs is that they are "setting up the defendant to fail." Defense attorneys regularly say they would not let a client plead or agree to a disposition if it involves more penal burdens—more procedural hassle, performance, marking, or financial penalties—than the case is worth. Discussing anger management or anti–domestic violence programs, Elise, an experienced defense attorney said, "I certainly know a lot of clients that could use it. But, I'm not going to take a program if the case is going to get dismissed. It's just at odds with the adversarial nature of our system." Mark, another veteran defense attorney discussing the rarity of misdemeanor defendants entering drug treatment programs explained, "No one is going to do an eight-month program unless they are facing jail time." Josh, the probation officer who represents the agency at court appearances, warned that defense attorneys ought to be careful in assessing whether their clients will be able to successfully complete noncustodial sanctions such as probation or programs before letting the client take a disposition that requires a lot of performance. He joked when we were looking a particular defendant's file with an extensive history of bench warrants and arrests, "Would you take probation?! Duhhhh! Would you take probation, as an attorney?! I mean, for someone with twenty-four lifetime arrests. I have seen a defendant in jail for two weeks, agreed to [a program], and two minutes later they had to recall the case because the defendant split."

Often defendants want to try a program as a means of case disposition but are unable to satisfy the conditions necessary to get the benefits of the plea arrangement. Ariel was homeless and struggling with a serious drug addiction when arrested in July 2010 for loitering for the purposes of prostitution, although she claimed she was buying drugs and not prostituting. She already had two open cases: one for crack possession and one for attempted assault against her boyfriend. The DA's office had recently introduced a new program designed to help women exit the sex trade, and she was offered an ACD on the prostitution cases if she completed the once-a-week program for six sessions. Ariel missed multiple court appearances for the other open cases and, although she signed up for the class, she repeatedly missed it. She was subsequently arrested two more times for drug possession. In January 2011, after being held on bail for her most recent arrest, the ACDs were withdrawn because she never completed the conditions, and she was sentenced to forty-five days in jail in satisfaction of all five open cases. She knew, and her lawyer knew, that the fastest way to dispose of all her cases would be to serve time as opposed to keeping up the cycle of failing at programs, warrants, and rearrests. Ariel had spent so much time in custody on her various arrests that by the time she was sentenced, she had less than a week of prospective jail time.

Performance involves normalizing and disciplinary rites defined by the content and form of the program. But in misdemeanorland, conformity with the *form* of program rites becomes more important than the initial purpose of its content. For example, the prostitution program Ariel was offered consisted of six two-hour meetings with different modules on sexual health and safety, mental health and trauma counseling service options, and trafficking and drug treatment services. Alicia, the supervisor in the sex crimes bureau who monitored the antiprostitution program, candidly explained that she was well aware that many of the women were still "prostituting on the side," during the program and in fact often showed up to the class directly from work. Whether or not the program causes a change in sex work practices, the performance offers an opportunity for defendants to prove compliance and governability.

If participants show up late or miss a class, they are in violation of their agreement and sent back to court. Defendants are often given a second and third chance to complete the program, but sometimes the ACD is withdrawn, and they can be resentenced to a violation or a misdemeanor. Alicia explained the rationale for reporting a defendant who has repeatedly showed up late for the program: "We have to stay strict with the rules because this is court; we are working with the courts." The social worker overseeing the program added: "The part about forcing them to be there on time for all sessions is therapeutic in and of itself; it's about establishing consistency and rules, like a job. Sometimes they come directly from work, so they're not dressed appropriately, and we obviously know some of them are still prostituting on the side, but it's important to model a routine and joblike circumstances."

Program compliance is evaluated as a performance; the defendant must execute it properly or be sanctioned. As Judge Taylor explained, "We give them compliance dates. If they don't do it, they don't comply, they don't show up—then we will bench warrant them and violate them all. At some point it will come up. At some point you get pulled over for a speeding ticket, you get pulled over for something stupid, and that warrant—in the state of New York [comes up]." He then described how he deals with a defendant coming through for failure to satisfy the condition or make the compliance court date: "One, you can say—look, I'm giving you a final opportunity. Or you can set bail, which for community service you try not to do. Some of it is repetitive. You know . . . you'll see bench warrant issued, bench warranted vacated, bench warrant issued. You see stuff like that. Then you're going to set bail. But you can increase a couple of things. One, increase the number of community service days. Fine, you got two days? Now you're doing four. You don't show up, a bench warrant is going to be issued and you're going to get picked up eventually. And then you know what? You're going to do fifteen days in jail." Or, he continued, sometimes failure to perform a program mandated as part of conditional dismissal means additional penal burdens are demanded from the next encounter: "I had . . . a petit larceny case where [the defendant] was supposed to do the Stoplift program for an ACD. And then she gets arrested on [a new case]. . . . She never did the Stoplift. . . . The only thing I would take would be a plea to the A [misdemeanor] on the new case. I said—you blew us off; now you're having increased punishment for this. Maybe they [the DA] would have given her a violation or a B with an attempted petit larceny, but I'm requiring you to plead to the A, or I'm not taking a plea."

Programs do not necessarily represent an attempt to withdraw or even reduce a penal response to the conduct or offender. The criminal justice actors promoting programs may embrace a welfarist rationality and may believe that jail and criminal conviction are not always appropriate sanctions for some offenses or offenders. However, they are not necessarily expressing a sentiment that criminal justice engagement with the conduct is itself improper or undesirable. To expect an overall retrenchment of penal power from these programs is to misunderstand the intentions and understandings of actors administering and innovating them. Explaining the policy regarding women who fail out of the antiprostitution class, one supervising prosecutor noted, "We have to answer to the community; we have an obligation to people who call up and complain that they do not want to just let prostitution exist in their community." She went on to say, "When the defendant just keeps bench warranting and not showing up to the program, we have to take a stance and offer a jail alternative. *We are a DA's office in the end; we prosecute cases.*"

And finally, welfarist intentions of programs are often working at odds with other punitive and exclusionary practices of other components of the criminal justice system. Consider Destiny, who had a history of misdemeanor prostitution and narcotics possession arrests over almost two decades. Her most recent prostitution arrest brought her into one of the Human Trafficking Intervention Courts, where she was offered a disposition of an ACD conditional on successful completion of six counseling sessions. Destiny unsurprisingly said she preferred counseling sessions to Rikers Island, but she also pointed out that the sessions did little to change her objective circumstances; her only source of formal income was a meager public assistance of $40 a month:

> Destiny: Listen . . . I told [my defense attorney] that I need a job, I need housing. Let's just say that I don't turn back into prostitution because I need some easy money, and now that I'm not using, my money could probably go to more beneficial elements.
>
> Q: What did you think [of the mandated treatment sessions]?
>
> Destiny: They really didn't do anything. They just gave me a MetroCard, really. And some snacks.
>
> Q: Do you feel resentful of what the court did, and what they mandated?
>
> Destiny: No, I don't. I'm happy about it. But it's just that these programs are experiments. They just need to take a survey, and they probably don't have the budget or don't want to put in the budget. But the women need more. You need at least a stipend once a week, about $200 of stipend or something like that. You know, to get people on their feet. People will come more. Because you just want to get out of jail initially, but when you see that it's not really doing anything . . . I don't know what these workers do, but they don't really have . . . They don't do this, they don't do that. They don't have the budget for that. I don't know what . . . it's an experimental program.

What Destiny really wanted to talk about was the fact that she had been made homeless by a drug arrest inside her public housing apartment the prior year. She explained that she had picked up a John on "the track," the street where people solicited clients, and they had bought drugs together. They then went back to her apartment to smoke, and, while she was in the bathroom, he opened the door to the police, and she was arrested. Although I did not see the paperwork from the case, she said she was charged with a drug sale and subsequently evicted from the NYCHA apartment she had occupied for the eight prior years. By the time of the prostitution arrest that brought her into the Human Trafficking Intervention Court, she had been living in a women's shelter for over a year. She also had been slashed in the face by a John who demanded his money back after an encounter. She said she never felt safe going to the police for protection and so was similarly concerned about her safety and general health. Destiny confirmed that the program was a more pleasant experience than doing time at Rikers, but it did not touch the deep and acute needs for essentials such as housing, employment, safety, or health care:

Q: And did you feel like it was helpful to talk to [the social worker/
     therapist]?
Destiny: Well, I think it was helpful to talk to the person, yeah. But I
     don't feel like they really did anything . . .
Q: Concrete?
Destiny: Yeah. Except to stop them from locking me up in jail. That's
     the only thing they did. But as far as my personal needs? . . . I
     am sick. You know, as far as me being an addict and me being
     mentally ill. . . . The things that I'm going through now, those are
     things that, like, I did myself. Me going to the doctor, me getting
     a personal permanent care physician, a foot doctor, breast exam,
     blood work. That's me doing that through WeCARE. Welfare is
     doing all of that for me right now. They ordered me to do that,
     because they're going to see [if she is eligible for disability].
     They got me unable to work right now because of my mental
     condition.
Q: So you're saying the person you talked to didn't help you get
     medical [treatment]?
Destiny: No, they didn't help me with medical. It's no kind of
     extra stipend for us. There's nothing for us. They had some used
     clothes, and that's about it. That's it. That's it. It's going to make

me cry. [Cries] Nobody doesn't do nothing for you. You have to
do everything for yourself.

Q: [I am so sorry.]

Destiny: I'm scared. Because I don't want to go back out there.
[Cries] I was almost killed.

Q: [I'm so sorry.]

Destiny: But this is what the court wanted. So I did what they told
me to do. Leave me alone, and I could be free. But you're never
really free.

Programs are not intended to free the subjects of misdemeanorland. They
are deployed and circulate in an adversarial criminal justice system where
they present as feasible disposition tools precisely because they demand
a series of performances. The technique of performance seeks normalization but does not involve constant retraining and supervision: it entails
a command and a sanction-backed compliance check. Sykes famously
identified the "defects of total power" inside of prison as lying in the limits of physical violence and the deficiency of the guard's legitimate moral
authority. In misdemeanorland, one of the defects of disciplinary power
lies in the inadequate capacity of police and courts to constantly monitor
and control the multitudes of people arrested for low-level offenses and
in the pushback of defense agents and defendants seeking to limit the
reach of penal power.[39] The penal technique of performance allows court
actors to ration scarce social control resources according to a logic of risk
and desert. Defendants must prove some capacity for self-governance by
performing certain actions terms laid out by the court—arrive on time, sit
and wait quietly, go to a program, complete community service—and earn
either leniency or sanctions depending on how they perform.

CONCLUSION

Many readers may arrive at this conclusion deeply disturbed by the account of misdemeanorland documented here, shocked that criminal courts charged with adjudicating guilt and innocence and protecting constitutional rights rarely do so, and disillusioned that these courts instead use the tools of criminal procedure to manage and control multitudes of the city's most disadvantaged populations. One might conclude from the data that New York City's misdemeanor courts are broken: they infrequently test accusations of guilt with any rigor, often fail to enforce the limits on police power imposed by the Constitution, compromise foundational values of criminal law, and make a mockery of due process principles.

Others might be heartened that New York City's misdemeanor courts are working so well. Flooded with substantial volumes of subfelony cases without a concurrent increase in court resources, one could see the managerial model as an efficient adaptation to the conditions generated by Broken Windows policing. Why spend scarce resources to investigate and adjudicate if someone has in fact committed a relatively minor infraction in the past when instead the court can mark, engage in procedural hassles, and wait for a defendant to exhibit meaningful performances in the future to determine if he or she deserves to be punished? One might conclude that misdemeanorland court actors—perhaps unwittingly—innovated not only a brilliantly efficient response to accusations of low-level offending, but also an inherently just one. If the punishment of minor crimes implicates moral and social values distinct from those at play in the punishment of serious crimes, then perhaps what we *ought* to do with minor crimes is not necessarily punish the act, but rather assess the person over time to see if he persistently disregards rules.

I concur with both assessments in some respects and contend that it is important to puzzle through why both can be simultaneously true. Therefore, this conclusion turns to what—to borrow from William James—I take to be the "cash value" of my theoretical and empirical claims for what most of us who study and read about criminal justice deeply care about: political and social change. I start the discussion as a lawyer and end it as a citizen. That is, I begin by highlighting what this study can tell us about the possibilities and limitations of legal reform and transition to emphasizing what this study exposes about the way most social problems are addressed in the United States. In the end, I argue that what should really alarm us about the operations of misdemeanorland is the way that this site, like so many others in criminal justice, functions to either reproduce class and racial inequality or manage the effects of class and racial inequality in a punitive fashion.

Ultimately, this book points to moral commitments we hold about the dignity due to those in our social community who have been accused—or even convicted of—violating laws and the to the political values that we demonstrate through the ways we address the very real social problems that gave rise to and sustain commitment to the Broken Windows policing model. Those issues cannot be remedied by legal reforms that target judicial practice. They can only be addressed by a larger transformative project, much like the one that brought our country to tolerate the current role that police and prisons play in managing social and economic ills.[1] The dominant social-ordering role presently accorded criminal justice institutions in the United States is neither natural nor was its development inevitable. It took a historical process to get to a place where we accept the current capacious operation of the penal state. It involved innumerable political battles fought at the local, state, and federal levels to direct resources to punitive social control while neglecting other integrative institutions. It is the result of intentional social movements to shift our cultural posture toward the appropriate roles of penal and welfare policies. Scholars of mass incarceration have carefully traced the historical process by which "we arrive at a political moment where indefinite solitary confinement in a concrete box is sound policy, but cash assistance to poor parents 'has corrupted their souls and stolen their future.'"[2] If we find ourselves uncomfortable with the vast operations of managerial misdemeanor justice extending over poor minority communities, we must address the political and cultural trends that brought us to accept such a social role for this and other criminal justice institutions.

Conclusions from a Lawyer

Commentators have long noted that lower criminal courts neither do much adjudication nor do it well. Accounts of municipal courts dealing in petty crimes and infractions of public order over the first half of the nineteenth century lamented the lack of concern with factual guilt, legal decorum, and procedural justice. These critiques played an important role in the due process revolution that extended new rights to defendants and curtailed expansive and vague criminal statutes that had been used to criminalize despised social statuses instead of specific acts. Despite these seemingly monumental changes, Malcolm Feeley noted in his seminal study of New Haven's lower criminal courts forty years ago that defendants seldom invoked their procedural rights and prosecutors and judges strategically pursued dispositions that avoided triggering these rights. The data in chapter 3 show this is still the case in misdemeanorland: trials have gone the way of the dodo bird, and pretrial hearings are on the endangered species list. Defendants rarely have a short-term incentive to invoke formal adversarial procedures to challenge questionable police search-and-seizure practices because the process costs of doing so usually outweigh the formal sanctions being offered to dispose of a case early on. In addition, they risk quite a lot by pursuing claims of actual innocence or challenging the legality of the police stop, search, or seizure that led to their arrest. Prosecutors regularly plea bargain in a way that makes invocation of the right to trial or to exclude illegally seized evidence intolerably perilous, such as stating that any lesser charge plea will be "off the table" if a defendant pushes a case to pretrial hearings.[3] Few defendants are willing to risk a criminal conviction in order to vindicate such rights when being offered a conditional dismissal or noncriminal violation plea. In many cases, judges are powerless to alter these incentives because prosecutors have exclusive discretion to select and reduce charges. In other cases, judges actively disincentivize legal and factual adjudication by imposing steep a trial tax, threatening or actually sentencing defendants who go to hearing or trial with a harsher punishment than the pretrial offer.

Fourth Amendment jurisprudence is built on the premise that substantive rights against unlawful police stops, searches, and seizures are secured by the mechanism of excluding unlawfully seized evidence and arrests. The overwhelming amount of police work is low-level enforcement activity, not serious violent felony arrests, where the exclusion of necessary evidence would seem salient and professionally important. It is questionable (at best) that this is an effective mechanism for the most common low-level arrests in a jurisdiction where less than 1 percent of misdemeanor cases proceed to pretrial hearing or trial. Furthermore, most of the police officers I have spoken to confirm that they either don't know or don't care what happens to most of their misdemeanor arrests (except for resisting arrest) after they have completed the booking paperwork. Therefore, the mechanism of excluding valuable evidence from prosecution that higher courts assume is the incentive for police to conform their conduct to constitutional standards it not at work if the police who collect evidence for prosecution are not informed about the outcomes of their arrests or professionally affected by judicial determinations about the lawfulness of their methods.

It would be hard to imagine that we *could* use exclusion of evidence as an effective mechanism to govern police conduct in the most frequent forms of police enforcement: low-level arrests and citations. There is just no way to get around the fact that procedures entail costs, resources, and time, and that low-level infractions have a different substantive meaning from serious infractions, such that legal actors and defendants will often feel that adjudicating them is not worth the trouble. Many defendants who are factually guilty are offered conditional dismissals precisely because actors in the system are content to monitor their later criminal justice contacts rather than incur the process costs necessary to convict them. And many defendants who are factually innocent plead guilty precisely because they are trying to avoid process costs. Over thirty years ago, Malcolm Feeley noted this tension and called it "the dilemma of lower courts. . . . Expanded procedures, designed to improve the criminal process are not invoked because they might be counterproductive. Efforts to slow the process down and make it truly deliberative might lead to still harsher treatment of defendants and still more time loss for complainants and victims."[4]

Therefore, one policy implication of this study is that if we are serious about bringing street-level police activity into line with substantive legal principles governing stops, searches, and seizures, then we must innovate other political and organizational mechanisms to do so. Beat officers may never care if a few of the hundreds of drug possession or fare-beating arrests they make in their career are dismissed in court. But they do care about vacation days, promotions, choice assignments, scheduling, and other aspects of job quality and compensation. A mayoral and police administration that took seriously enforcing the constitutional rules of police action would build internal mechanisms to audit for lawful street-level activity and build feedback loops between the data gathered there and the things that police officers care about.

The data in this book also suggest that the constitutional limits placed on vague and broad criminal statutes that target people on the basis of perceived status rather than violation of a proscribed act do not in practice seriously constrain the power of the police and prosecutors to control people. Take, for example, the so-called gravity knife statute passed in 1958 to ban a specific World War II weapon that opened effortlessly with mere inversion. The NYPD and city prosecutors currently interpret the statute to apply to *any* folding knife that can be opened by a forceful flick of the wrist by trained officers, despite the fact that such an interpretation makes illegal one of the most common work tools in the construction trade, sold everywhere in the state and city. Courts have countenanced this vague and expansive interpretation of the statute and even found that it is not necessary that the defendant *know* the knife could be opened in this fashion, making mere possession a strict liability offense.[5] The cases of Travis in chapter 5 and Malik in chapter 6 show the marking, procedural hassles, and performances imposed on just a few of the three thousand to five thousand New Yorkers who are arrested each year on this statute—overwhelmingly black and Latino men. The NYPD, the Manhattan DA's office, and the de Blasio administration have fought aggressively and successfully against changes in the statute that would make it clear that common work tools are not illegal weapons—with the assent of Governor Andrew Cuomo, who vetoed legislative reform of the penal law not once but twice—just as prosecutors and police have fought throughout other historical periods efforts to curtail the massive discretion afforded them by equivocal and far-reaching statutes.[6] Another example is loitering for the purpose of engaging in prostitution, one of the charges that brought Ariel to court in chapter 6, which seems to be enforced by the officers' having interpreted a particular person's motives or appearance as opposed to activities he or she engaged in at the time of the arrest.[7]

People are no longer arrested for status offenses such as being a vagrant, drunk, prostitute, drug addict, or unemployed. But for some people, the iterative logic of the managerial model has functional similarities to the way vagrancy statutes were enforced in prior eras.[8] This is especially true of those who live in highly policed neighborhoods and seem to occupy "suspect statuses," which can be as broad as being a young man of color or as specific as a looking like a drug addict or sex worker.

The content of the penal law checks police and prosecutorial power only if there is an effective mechanism by which one appeals to the law to challenge an arrest. But the managerial model is an iterative one. The vast majority of first- and second-arrest defendants are offered a conditional dismissal or noncriminal infraction without much attention paid to the strength of the evidence or circumstances surrounding the arrest, and most accept these deals. Prosecutors and judges can be agnostic about factual guilt or the legality of police action in the specific cases because they are not imposing a formal criminal conviction or punishment, and they can always point to the possibility of "fighting the case" to show that the defendant is freely accepting the disposition. Defendants can earn their way out of a criminal conviction from early arrests if they are able to outlive the conditional mark of an ACD without getting rearrested, withstand the procedural hassles of coming back to court, or adequately perform by doing community service or some other program. However, those who lack stable housing, struggle with drug addiction, are not good at performing responsibly in court, or who live in highly policed neighborhoods quite often fail these conditional leniency offers.

In subsequent encounters, prosecutors usually seek a conviction or demand more performances. Most people who are arrested for specific misdemeanor crimes in the Broken Windows era and eventually plead guilty to an offense are convicted of disorderly conduct, a broad and vague statute indeed.[9] In 2015, disorderly conduct violations outnumbered the next largest penal law conviction offense by a factor of 4.6. The "dis con" conviction is used to mark defendants for a specific amount of time (usually the default year for a conditional discharge) and to impose performance demands as part of the disposition (a program, community service, a fine, no arrests, and so on). In the vast majority of cases, only after a person has used up what one prosecutor described as his or her "bites at the apple" do prosecutors even attempt to seek a criminal conviction and formal punishment. By the time a defendant is in a position of being offered a plea to a criminal conviction and jail time, he or she has usually racked up an extensive record such that prosecutors and judges, even if not assured of factual guilt in this particular case, are less concerned that they are engaging the heavy machinery for someone who does not regularly violate the law. Defendants *come to be* the type of person who ought to be convicted by achieving a certain status in misdemeanorland, a status that is only to varying degrees achieved by establishing violations of specific provisions of the penal law.

Consider Frank, who was arrested for taking up two seats on the F train in July 2010. On this day during my initial summer of fieldwork, the courtroom was more packed than usual because a slew of local reporters were awaiting the arraignment of an EMT worker who had been arrested for a string of brutal rapes in public housing complexes. They seemed indifferent to the procession of typical misdemeanor cases until a four-foot-two man with a severe limp was brought out on charges of taking up two seats on the subway. His appearance caught the attention of the crowd because it stalled the rapid pace of proceedings; it took him almost one minute to walk from the defendant benches to the podium on account of his disability. Frank had been arrested and "put through the system," as opposed to being issued a summons for this violation because the arresting officer had radioed in his name after the initial encounter and found he had a number of outstanding warrants for unanswered summonses for public consumption of alcohol. The prosecutor agreed to ACD all of the unanswered summonses, but insisted that Frank plead to a "dis con" with the sentence of time served for the subway infraction.

Simone, his defense attorney, forcefully declined the offer on behalf of her client, asking the court to dismiss the current charge as facially insufficient. Addressing the judge, she stated that the arrest charge, § 1050.7 (j)(1) of the MTA rules, prohibits taking up two seats in a subway car only when doing so obstructs another passenger's seat. She noted that at the arrest time of 2:00 a.m., the F train would not have been full to capacity and, in fact, would more likely have been nearly empty. Without engaging or verifying the relevant statutory language, the judge said he would not find the summons facially insufficient. However, he called up the district attorney arraignment supervisor, who was sitting at the DA desk reviewing files as the younger assistant stood up on the misdemeanor cases, to consider granting another ACD on this matter as opposed to insisting on a violation conviction. Following a few perfunctory remarks on the importance of subway etiquette, the supervisor agreed. After a quick discussion with her client, the defense attorney accepted the disposition, and the defendant slowly made his way out of the courtroom, trailed by a piqued *New York Post* reporter. The defense attorney later explained that although she believed the summons should have been dismissed outright, she was worried her client would not show up at later court appearances necessary to fight the case, so she accepted the ACD. The next day, the *Post* ran a story titled "Short Ride Spurs Bust for Subway Seat Hog," in which Frank was quoted as saying, "I wasn't even drunk! They just needed to make an arrest."[10]

My point is not that people in misdemeanorland never violate specific provisions of the penal law; certainly they do—just as many people arrested for vagrancy-type statutes in the past probably also violated other act-specific penal law provisions. My point is that curtailing vague statutes may not do much to change the social functions to which the penal law of lesser offenses is put.[11] Frank might well have been guilty of all of the violations for which he was summoned and eventually arrested, but it was his inability to perform properly by showing up at court and paying the fine that led to his custodial arrest and the prosecutor's insistence that he plead guilty to disorderly conduct. Or Frank might have been innocent of the subway arrest charge if, as his defense attorney suggested, he was not obstructing anyone else's seat access on the F train at two o'clock in the morning. Neither the judge nor the prosecutor was particularly interested in getting to the bottom of that mystery during the packed arraignment shift. The administrative dossier of the type of person Frank appeared to be from multiple unanswered summonses drove the insistence on more social control, and his defense attorney's assessment that he would not successfully show up to fight the legal and factual issues drove the disposition decision.

Thus, even when criminal law is limited to proscribing specific acts, it can be put to the same purposes as vague or status-type criminal law under certain conditions. One set of such conditions is exemplified in New York City's lower courts in the age of Broken Windows policing. People achieve a suspect status over iterative encounters that rarely adjudicate specific allegations, and once that status is achieved, it tends to make it unbearably costly to invoke any formal mechanism to limit the state's ability to exert control or impose punishment by challenging a specific allegation. This is an unavoidable feature of implementing criminal law using a method that is both managerial *and* quasi-administrative within a system that is ostensibly adjudicative and adversarial. People come to be classified as persistent rule breakers, and are thereby at risk for transitioning to a criminal conviction, by acquiring a set of marks that are proposed to defendants as conditional dismissals. However, these marks are reinterpreted at a later time—namely, a subsequent arrest—in a different light, as at least an indication of ungovernability, and at most as a signal equivalent to a guilty plea. Prosecutors' interpretations of these marks and their resultant charging decisions and plea offers are often determinative of the outcome of the case, since managerial misdemeanor courts also are functionally administrative systems, where trials are rarely viable routes to dispute legal issues or establish factual innocence.[12] Prosecutors, judges, and the media have all criticized defense attorneys for "delay tactics" in lower courts, but the fact is that refusing a plea offer and just waiting is one of the few leverage points defendants have in misdemeanor court.[13]

Reducing statutorily authorized penalties or limiting the availability of marks are examples of policies that would give the defense some measure of power in disposition dynamics.[14] But, insofar as process costs almost always outweigh the relatively light sanctions offered by prompt dispositions in early encounters in misdemeanorland, it is hard to imagine how a system that is both managerial and quasi-administrative would not to some extent produce the same coercive leverage over people on the basis of their marked status. As Charlie Gerstein and J. J. Prescott have argued, expansive police and prosecutorial discretion on the low end of the system does not necessarily derive from broadly worded, vague statutes but rather from the opportunity costs of contesting the legality of stops or the sufficiency of evidence in individual cases.[15] This insight takes on new meaning in misdemeanorland, because people who live in highly policed spaces tend to have multiple encounters. And the most highly policed spaces in the city tend to be low-income communities of color. This brings me to some concluding thoughts from a citizen: Is there anything wrong with what I have described about misdemeanorland?

Conclusions from a Citizen

There is both an efficiency and fairness argument to be made for the managerial model in lower criminal courts. If one thinks that the proper role of criminal courts is exclusively to use the criminal process to determine factual guilt no matter what type of infractions are at issue, then the managerial model that I have described as dominant in New York City's subfelony courts is unquestionably intolerable. But it is not self-evident, at least to me, that what we *want* from misdemeanor courts is perfect adjudicative accuracy. Considered abstractly, the managerial approach of eschewing the heavy machinery of criminal law unless there is some indication the person persistently flouts legal rules is an appealing principle for responding to alleged violations of rules that—to borrow from Durkheim—do not immediately shock our *conscience collective*. Possessing small amounts of drugs, assaults that cause minor physical injuries, shoplifting, turnstile jumping—these things just do not have the same cultural status, the same moral meaning as murder, robbery at gunpoint, life-threatening assault, high-level drug sales, or other crimes classified as serious felonies.

As I have argued throughout, court actors operating under the managerial model produce *both* false positives and false negatives in individual cases. Yet I cannot say, based on any independent investigation of arrest and crime circumstances, what percentage of misdemeanor defendants plead guilty to crimes they did not commit, or what percentage were not convicted of crimes they did commit. It seems reasonable to conclude, based on the dynamics of the managerial model I have presented, that the error types are distributed unevenly among different sorts of defendants according to the marks they bear from prior encounters at the time of disposition. False negative errors are most likely among defendants with no criminal record, because the prosecution's policy is often to quickly grant conditional dismissals for many of these defendants. False positive errors are more likely higher among defendants with prior misdemeanor convictions because they face higher barriers to convince prosecutors and judges of their factual innocence and because they are less inclined to bear process costs to seek vindication, since they already have a criminal record.[16]

With respect to the false negatives (failing to convict the factually guilty), it is important to remember that managerial misdemeanor courts are *doing something* with those defendants who are granted dismissals or noncriminal dispositions. One of the defining features of the managerial model is that legal actors presume that almost anyone brought into misdemeanorland is in need of some level of social control, the precise level to be determined by how the person withstands its hassles and performs. Even when they do not attempt to convict and impose a formal punishment, court actors are using the instruments of criminal procedure to monitor and check on defendants' later behavior, building records about what type of person is involved. Thus, under the managerial model, false negative errors are not errors at all; they are part of the very logic of social control that this component of the penal system uses to deal with shallow-end offenders. Nor are false positives (convicting the factually innocent) errors, because the managerial logic is to extend a more serious mark and more extensive social control based on indications of persistent rule breaking and signs of overall ungovernability, instead of guilt in a specific case.

The policing theories that led these courts to be flooded with subfelony cases proffered an account of why the police ought to take policing of low-level offenses seriously. But it left indeterminate what courts ought to do with allegations of low-level offenses—if and in what way traditional principles of criminal law ought to guide the punishment of turnstile jumping and public urination. No philosophers or public intellectuals have, to my knowledge, offered deep rigorous thinking about what justice demands in response to these types of low-level crimes. The disposition practices in misdemeanorland evolved in reaction to the fact that legal actors demonstrated an institutional disposition to *do something* with these cases, and what they found acceptable to do reflects the cultural and moral import of the specific infraction they were called upon to process. The moral principle at work in the managerial model—that we essentially don't seek any punishment at all unless the person demonstrates a persistent disregard for social rules and otherwise seems unmoored from other institutions of social control—seems like a perfectly reasonable one for frontline legal actors to innovate and use under the practical constraints they faced.

However, even if one holds that the managerial model represents a just approach to low-level rule breaking in the abstract, this does not mean it is just in practice. One question we might ask is if the managerial system in its real-world incarnation accurately and fairly identifies persistent lawbreakers. The qualitative and quantitative data presented in chapter 2 make it clear that the current operations of lower criminal courts can be said, at best, to do so only imperfectly. The probability of conviction for a misdemeanor crime from a misdemeanor arrest increases only slightly as the number of arrests rises, but increases substantially with each subsequent criminal conviction. The transition from nonconviction dispositions to convictions is, in many misdemeanor cases, largely a factor of the temporal proximity of arrests. And the likelihood of arrest is a function not only of an individual's conduct, but also of policing practices. Those who are brought into the misdemeanor justice system, and those who stand the highest risk of being rearrested, are not a random sample of rule breakers or even persistent rule breakers. It is a sample systematically biased by certain social facts, some of which raise fundamental concerns of racial and class inequities. Descriptive statistics presented in chapters 1 and 2 show that most misdemeanor arrests are either concentrated in spaces marked by high rates of drug use, unemployment, and poverty or are of people suffering from drug addition, unemployment, or poverty as they traverse the city's busiest commercial and transportation hubs.

Thus, even if the criminal courts impartially apply the managerial model to all defendants irrespective of class, race, or immigration status, questions of fairness extend to the mechanisms that select people for misdemeanor arrests. There is substantial evidence that the underlying behaviors of some of the largest arrest categories, such as marijuana and narcotics possession or even domestic violence, are relatively evenly distributed across racial and class groups. But these groups face vastly unequal risk of arrest because of the social realities of where and how drugs are sold and used, the residential spaces where violent street crime is concentrated, and because of the density and form of policing in different spaces.[17] Some criminal conduct might be more likely to translate into an arrest because it occurs in communities where police have become an established institution of not only social control but also interpersonal and household control, or because of the conscious or unconscious biases of police officers shaping their discretion to make an arrest for low-level conduct. Other types of behaviors may be unequally distributed. For example, it is likely that turnstile jumping, one of the larger arrest categories, is more common among people in poverty. Research of a different type would be needed to apportion the relative contributions of those different factors to the clearly documented concentration of misdemeanor arrests among black, Hispanic, and low-income communities.

This brings me to what, by my lights, are the most important set of concerns that flow from this account of managerial justice. The ostensible objectives of these policing practices, much like the reforms that have led to mass incarceration, are to reduce the incidence of violence and social harm. It may well be that the people living in conditions of "social insecurity and marginality," whose life prospects have been circumscribed "in the wake of the twofold retrenchment of the labor market and the welfare state," are more likely to commit misdemeanor crimes.[18] And it may well be that we have good reason for deploying a high number of police officers to poor and minority neighborhoods because they suffer disproportionately from violent crime. And these policing techniques may indeed be effective in creating order and repressing serious crime—although that question is hotly debated among social scientists who have studied the issue.[19] Insofar as the techniques are effective, the crime-reduction benefits from these policing strategies accrue to the residents of these neighborhoods.

But the costs of these strategies fall on the same people. And the costs are tremendous. The residents inside these communities are the ones who come to have criminal records that hinder their employment and housing prospects, endure the degradation of arrest and prosecution, lose days of work and child care, and face interminable demands to go back and forth to court to deal with arrests and summonses for low-level infractions. They increasingly feel disrespected and oppressed by a police presence designated for their safety and demeaned by a legal system designed to dole out justice. As long as we, as a society, are comfortable with securing social control and order primarily with the tools of criminal law and punishment, this will be the case.

The crucial problems raised by mass misdemeanors—just as with mass incarceration—are political and social questions. This, I believe, is the primary problem identified by my analysis, not false positive or false negative errors, or even the failure of lower criminal courts to live up to a due process adjudicative ideal. It seems that we, as a political community, are comfortable relying on the instrumentalities of criminal law as the primary social control mechanisms in urban spaces of concentrated poverty and insecurity. If we hope to change that, then we must first honestly confront the human costs and moral meanings that our current approach entails.

NOTES

Introduction

1. Although the definition is somewhat contested, "mass incarceration" references a gestalt of legal and policy changes in the content and tenor of criminal law and its enforcement that together operated to produce not just a stunning increase in the number of people held in penal confinement, but also a systematic relegation of certain social groups to a permanently denigrated status bearing the mark of a felony conviction. David Garland, ed., *Mass Imprisonment: Social Causes and Consequences* (London: Sage, 2001); Mary E. Pattillo, David F. Weiman, and Bruce Western, *Imprisoning America: The Social Effects of Mass Incarceration* (New York: Russell Sage Foundation, 2004); Bruce Western, *Punishment and Inequality in America* (New York: Russell Sage Foundation, 2006); John Pfaff, *Locked In: The True Causes of Mass Incarceration—and How to Achieve Real Reform* (New York: Basic Books, 2017). Those effects and policies are now a widely cited fact. Pick up a recent publication addressing any aspect of the criminal justice system in the United States, and chances are it begins with a ceremonial nod to the numbers: 2.3 million people in prisons or jails and over 5 million people on probation or parole supervision at risk of imprisonment. Lauren Glaze, *Correctional Populations in the United States, 2011* (Washington, DC: Bureau of Justice Statistics, 2011), http://www.bjs.gov /content/pub/pdf/cpus11.pdf.

2. Amy E. Lerman and Vesla M. Weaver, *Arresting Citizenship: The Democratic Consequences of American Crime Control* (Chicago: University of Chicago Press, 2014); Andrew Gelman, Jeffrey Fagan, and Alex Kiss, "An Analysis of the New York City Police Department's 'Stop-and-Frisk' Policy in the Context of Claims of Racial Bias," *Journal of the American Statistical Association* 102, no. 479 (2007): 813–23; Amanda Geller and Jeffrey Fagan, "Pot as Pretext: Marijuana, Race, and the New Disorder in New York City Street Policing," *Journal of Empirical Legal Studies* 7, no. 4 (2010): 591–633; Victor M. Rios, *Punished: Policing the Lives of Black and Latino Boys* (New York: NYU Press, 2011); Sarah Brayne, "Surveillance and System Avoidance: Criminal Justice Contact and Institutional Attachment," *American Sociological Review* 79, no. 3 (2014): 367–91; Forrest Stuart, *Down, out, and under Arrest: Policing and Everyday Life in Skid Row* (Chicago: University of Chicago Press, 2016).

3. Eric H. Monkkonen, *Police in Urban America, 1860–1920* (Cambridge: Cambridge University Press, 2004), 103. And for most of the history of policing in American cities, low-level "public order" arrests were the most common types of arrests made by police. Eric H. Monkkonen, "A Disorderly People? Urban Order in the Nineteenth and Twentieth Centuries," *Journal of American History* 68, no. 3 (1981): 539–59.

4. Alexes Harris, *A Pound of Flesh: Monetary Sanctions as Punishment for the Poor* (New York: Russell Sage Foundation, 2016); Chris Albin-Lackey, *Profiting from Probation: America's Offender-Funded Probation Industry* (New York: Human Rights Watch, 2014); Sarahi Uribe, "Minor Offenses, Major Penalties: An Introduction to the Judicial Process in the Atlanta Mu-

nicipal Court" (ms on file with author, 2016); Theodore M. Shaw et al., *The Ferguson Report: Department of Justice Investigation of the Ferguson Police Department* (Washington, DC: US Department of Justice Civil Rights Division, 2015).

5. There is a dearth of comparable and reliable data on subfelony arrests and case filings because states have so many different statutory provisions that define subfelony offenses, entities that cite for these offenses, and administrative configurations of lower courts. One of the only reliable sources that collects data from many states, the National Center for State Courts, reported that there were about 9.5 million misdemeanor criminal cases filed in thirty-five sampled states compared with 2.4 million felony cases filed in those same states. Data available at http:// www.ncsc.org/Sitecore/Content/Microsites/PopUp/Home/CSP/CSP_Criminal. I use the term "subfelony" to include misdemeanor criminal offenses plus other unclassified misdemeanors, infractions, and violations that are not classified as criminal offenses.

6. Disposition data is even harder to find than case filing data. But, for example, data provided to Injustice Watch by the Office of the State's Attorney show that in Cook County, Illinois, over the years 2011 to 2015 no more than 56 percent of the misdemeanor dispositions resulted in a guilty plea; somewhere between 25 and 46 percent of misdemeanor dispositions were dismissals of charges as *nolle* or "stricken off leave" (SOL); and more might have been dismissed as a conditional discharge or non-suit, but consistent data was not provided. *Nolle* and SOL are almost identical, except that a *nolle* requires the prosecutors to bring new proceedings, while a case on SOL remains open. In Texas, where "justice courts" and "municipal courts" *only* have jurisdiction over misdemeanors and violations where punishment upon conviction is limited to a fine, there were 1,941,881 such subfelony criminal cases filed in the former and 5,237,007 filed in the latter in 2015. The conviction rate was less than 50 percent in both types of courts. Constitutional county courts have jurisdiction over misdemeanors punishable by jail, and Statutory County Courts have jurisdiction over A and B misdemeanors in populous counties; of the 53,361 misdemeanor cases filed in the former courts in 2015, only about 42 percent terminated in a conviction, and of the 451,290 cases filed in the latter, 49 percent terminated in a conviction. See *Annual Statistical Report for the Texas Judiciary*, http://www.txcourts.gov /media/1308021/2015-ar-statistical-print.pdf. In the state of Florida, about 30 percent of the subfelony cases processed in county criminal courts resulted in some form of a dismissal over the years 2010 to 2016. See Trial Court Statistics, http://trialstats.flcourts.org/TrialCourtStats.aspx, for disposition data by county; dismissal rates include "no file," speedy trial dismissals, and all other forms of pretrial dismissal. In Philadelphia Municipal Court (which oversees basic misdemeanors and preliminary felony hearings) in 2013, 26 percent of disposed cases were withdrawn/dismissed, 10 percent ended in guilty pleas, 13 percent ended in "accelerated rehabilitative disposition" (for first-time offenders), and 29 percent were held for court. See *2013 Caseload Statistics of the Unified Judicial System of Pennsylvania*, http://www.pacourts.us/assets/files/setting-768 /file-3597.pdf?cb=e49abc

7. Some have argued that the precise tactics used by the NYPD did not conform to the model of Broken Windows as expressed in the original article whose title gave this sort of policing its name (George L. Kelling and James Q. Wilson, "Broken Windows," *Atlantic*, March 1982, http://www.theatlantic.com/magazine/archive/1982/03/broken-windows/4465) or that the NYPD always used quality-of-life policing as a pretext to engage more serious crime and was never expressly concerned with quality of life as such. Franklin E. Zimring, *The City That Became Safe: New York's Lessons for Urban Crime and Its Control* (New York: Oxford University Press, 2011), 129–31. While it is unlikely that a massive and complicated enforcement effort will match the policy prescriptions of a short magazine article, I use the term Broken Windows or quality-of-life policing because those are the terms the designers and implementers used to signal their inspiration from the theoretical claims in Wilson and Kelling's original writing.

8. "Criminal Court" is a special designation for the courts in New York City that have trial jurisdiction over all offenses other than felonies (i.e., misdemeanors, violations, and preindictment felonies), whereas indicted felonies are handled in what is called Supreme Court. New York Criminal Procedure Law (hereafter NY CPL) § 10.10 (3)(b).

9. The term "social control" has a long and complicated history in sociology, and I do not presume to review, much less resolve, any semantic and conceptual battles here. Edward Alsworth Ross, "Social Control," *American Journal of Sociology* 1, no. 5 (1896): 513–35; Morris Janowitz, "Sociological Theory and Social Control," *American Journal of Sociology* 81, no. 1 (1975): 82–108; Robert Meier, "Perspectives on the Concept of Social Control," *Annual Review of Sociology* 8 (1982): 35–55.

10. Joel Feinberg, "The Expressive Function of Punishment," *Monist* 49, no. 3 (1965): 397–423. There are of course many philosophical accounts of what constitutes *punishment* as a distinctive social act, and I do not directly engage those debates in this book. I cite this classic account because I contend that on almost any account, misdemeanorland represents an interesting case where legal actors are using the tools of criminal law to accomplish social control, often without imposing something that looks distinctively like punishment.

11. Émile Durkheim, *The Division of Labor in Society* (1893; New York: Free Press, 1984); David Garland, *Punishment and Modern Society: A Study in Social Theory*, Studies in Crime and Justice (Chicago: University of Chicago Press, 1990).

12. Max Weber, *Economy and Society: An Outline of Interpretive Sociology* (1922; Berkeley: University of California Press, 1978), 54.

13. Georg Rusche and Otto Kirchheimer, *Punishment and Social Structure* (New York: Russell and Russell, 1968); Garland, *Punishment and Modern Society*.

14. Garland, *Mass Imprisonment*; Jonathan Simon, "Rise of the Carceral State," *Social Research: An International Quarterly* 74, no. 2 (2007): 471–508; Marie Gottschalk, "Hiding in Plain Sight: American Politics and the Carceral State," *Annual Review of Political Science* 11, no. 1 (2008): 235–60; Vesla Weaver and Amy Lerman, "Political Consequences of the Carceral State," *American Political Science Review* 104, no. 4 (2010): 817–33; Marie Gottschalk, *Caught: The Prison State and the Lockdown of American Politics* (Princeton, NJ: Princeton University Press, 2015).

15. Jennifer Schuessler, "Michelle Alexander's 'New Jim Crow' Raises Drug Law Debates," *New York Times*, March 6, 2012, http://www.nytimes.com/2012/03/07/books/michelle-alexanders-new-jim-crow-raises-drug-law-debates.html; Michelle Alexander, *The New Jim Crow: Mass Incarceration in the Age of Colorblindness* (New York: New Press 2010); Jonathan Simon, *Governing through Crime: How the War on Crime Transformed American Democracy and Created a Culture of Fear*, Studies in Crime and Public Policy (New York: Oxford University Press, 2007).

16. Michel Foucault, *Discipline and Punish: The Birth of the Prison*, 2nd ed. (New York: Vintage, 1995); Garland, *Punishment and Modern Society*.

17. Foucault famously engaged Jeremy Bentham's design of the panopticon—a circular prison with cells facing a central guard tower in the middle, subjecting the confined subjects to constant visibility and knowledge—as a physical manifestation that "makes it possible to perfect the exercise of power . . . [b]ecause it is possible to intervene at any moment and because the constant pressure acts even before the offences, mistakes or crimes have been committed . . . [b]ecause, in these conditions, its strength is that it never intervenes . . . without any physical instrument other than architecture and geometry, it acts directly on individuals; it gives 'power of mind over mind.'" Foucault, *Discipline and Punish*, 206.

18. Alessandro De Giorgi, *Re-thinking the Political Economy of Punishment: Perspectives on Post-Fordism and Penal Politics*, Advances in Criminology (Aldershot, UK: Ashgate, 2006); Loïc Wacquant, *Punishing the Poor: The Neoliberal Government of Social Insecurity* (Durham: NC: Duke University Press, 2009), xvi, 296.

19. Lauren Glaze and Thomas Boncar, *Probation and Parole in the United States, 2010* (Washington, DC: US Bureau of Justice Statistics, 2011).

20. Michelle S. Phelps, "Mass Probation: Toward a More Robust Theory of State Variation in Punishment," *Punishment and Society* 19, no. 1 (2017): 53–73; Michelle Phelps, "The Paradox of Probation: Community Supervision in the Age of Mass Incarceration," *Law and Policy* 35, no. 1 (2013): 51–80; Rios, *Punished*.

21. Alice Goffman, "On the Run: Wanted Men in a Philadelphia Ghetto," *American Sociological Review* 74, no. 3 (2009): 355.

22. Katherine Beckett and Bruce Western, "Governing Social Marginality: Welfare, Incarceration, and the Transformation of State Policy," *Punishment and Society* 3, no. 1 (2001): 43–59; Western, *Punishment and Inequality in America*; Devah Pager, *Marked: Race, Crime, and Finding Work in an Era of Mass Incarceration* (Chicago: University of Chicago Press, 2007); James B. Jacobs, *The Eternal Criminal Record* (Cambridge, MA: Harvard University Press, 2015); Devah Pager, "The Mark of a Criminal Record," *American Journal of Sociology* 108, no. 5 (2003): 937–75.

23. Marc Mauer and Meda Chesney-Lind, *Invisible Punishment: The Collateral Consequences of Mass Imprisonment* (New York: New Press, 2002); Christopher Mele and Teresa A. Miller, eds., *Civil Penalties, Social Consequences* (London: Routledge, 2004); Megan Comfort, "Punishment beyond the Legal Offender," *Annual Review of Law and Social Science* 3 (2007): 271–96; Jeannie Suk, *At Home in the Law: How the Domestic Violence Revolution Is Transforming Privacy* (New Haven, CT: Yale University Press, 2009); Becky Pettit, *Invisible Men: Mass Incarceration and the Myth of Black Progress* (New York: Russell Sage Foundation, 2012).

24. Brian C. Kalt, "The Exclusion of Felons from Jury Service," *American University Law Review* 53 (2003): http://papers.ssrn.com/sol3/papers.cfm?abstract_id=420840; Jeff Manza and Christopher Uggen, *Locked Out: Felon Disenfranchisement and American Democracy*, Studies in Crime and Public Policy (New York: Oxford University Press, 2006).

25. Manza and Uggen, *Locked Out*; Gottschalk, "Hiding in Plain Sight"; Weaver and Lerman, "Political Consequences of the Carceral State."

26. Christopher Uggen, Jeff Manza, and Melissa Thompson, "Citizenship, Democracy, and the Civic Reintegration of Criminal Offenders," *Annals of the American Academy of Political and Social Science* 605 (May 1, 2006): 281–310; Sara Wakefield and Christopher Uggen, "Incarceration and Stratification," *Annual Review of Sociology* 36 (2010): 387–406.

27. Loïc Wacquant, "Class, Race and Hyperincarceration in Revanchist America," *Daedalus* 139, no. 3 (2010): 78. One innovative project has identified "million dollar blocks," where "states are spending in excess of a million dollars a year to incarcerate the residents of single city blocks." Million Dollar Blocks, http://spatialinformationdesignlab.org/projects/million-dollar-blocks.

28. Western, *Punishment and Inequality in America*, 12; Bruce Western and Becky Pettit, "Incarceration and Social Inequality," *Daedalus* 139, no. 3 (2010): 11. The racial disparities extend to the mark of a felony conviction. According to sophisticated estimates, by 2010 about 13 percent of all adult males had a felony conviction record, compared with over 33 percent of African American adult males. Sarah K. S. Shannon et al., "The Growth, Scope, and Spatial Distribution of People with Felony Records in the United States, 1948–2010," *Demography* 54, no. 5 (2017): 1795–818.

29. Although there are significant differences in their views, the two most famous accounts that discuss the functional continuity of the succession of America's peculiar institutions are by Loïc Wacquant and Michelle Alexander. See, e.g., Wacquant, "Deadly Symbiosis," *Punishment and Society* 3, no. 1 (2001): 95–133; Alexander, *The New Jim Crow*. For a recent treatment of racial subjection in courtroom practice, see Nicole Gonzalez Van Cleve, *Crook County: Racism and Injustice in America's Largest Criminal Court* (Stanford, CA: Stanford University Press, 2016), and for how the criminal justice system can function as a mechanism for reproducing

racial inequality even in a majority black jurisdiction, see James Forman Jr., *Locking Up Our Own: Crime and Punishment in Black America* (New York: Farrar, Straus and Giroux, 2017).

30. By "model," I mean something akin to the sociological favorite of a Weberian ideal type—an analytic construct that simplifies a complex system and highlights certain features in order to reveal what the researcher claims to be the important features and mechanisms of the phenomena under study. More detail is provided in chapter 2.

31. Samantha Schmidt, "City Report Suggests Progress in Effort to Curb Violence at Rikers Island," *New York Times*, August 2, 2016, http://www.nytimes.com/2016/08/03/nyregion/rikers-island-inmates-correction-officers.html; Michael Schwirtz and Michael Winerip, "New Plan to Shrink Rikers Island Population: Tackle Court Delays," *New York Times*, April 13, 2015, http://www.nytimes.com/2015/04/14/nyregion/mayor-de-blasios-plan-to-shrink-rikers-population-tackle-court-delays.html; Winerip and Schwirtz, " 'Time in the Box': Young Rikers Inmates, Still in Isolation," *New York Times*, July 7, 2016, http://www.nytimes.com/2016/07/08/nyregion/rikers-island-solitary-confinement.html. The majority of people in New York City Department of Corrections custody are there for pretrial detention. According to a John Jay report, about 75 percent of admissions in 2015 were for pretrial detention (felony and misdemeanor cases), and about 13 percent were for city sentences (most of which are for misdemeanor convictions, but not necessarily from misdemeanor arrests). Preeti Chauhana et al., and the Misdemeanor Justice Project at John Jay College of Criminal Justice, *Trends in Custody: New York City Department of Correction, 2000–2015* ([New York]: John Jay College of Criminal Justice, 2017), 20, http://misdemeanorjustice.org/wp-content/uploads/2017/04/DOC_Custody_Trends.pdf.

32. Douglas Hay, "Property, Authority and the Criminal Law," in *Albion's Fatal Tree: Crime and Society in Eighteenth-Century England*, ed. Douglas Hay et al. (New York: Pantheon, 1976).

33. Forrest Stuart, *Policing Rock Bottom: Regulation, Rehabilitation, and Resistance in America's Skid Row* (Chicago: University of Chicago Press, 2016).

34. William J. Stuntz, "Plea Bargaining and Criminal Law's Disappearing Shadow," *Harvard Law Review* 117 (2004): 2549.

35. "Conceptualization" is shorthand here for engaging a research question with a particular operational notion of what sort of thing law is as well as how it operates and produces outcomes. Thus, to conceptualize law as an abstract rule that commands or a clear statement of values that provides ultimate ends will elicit a certain set of research questions (e.g., the classic "gap studies" between law-on-the-books versus law-in-action) and position the explanatory factors in a certain, perhaps predictable, way (i.e., as distorting influences). Malcolm M. Feeley, "Two Models of the Criminal Justice System: An Organizational Perspective," *Law and Society Review* 7, no. 3 (April 1, 1973): 407–25; David Nelken, "Gap Problem in the Sociology of Law: A Theoretical Review," *Windsor Yearbook of Access to Justice* 1 (1981): 35; Issa Kohler-Hausmann, "Jumping Bunnies and Legal Rules: The Organizational Sociologist and the Legal Scholar Should Be Friends," in *The New Criminal Justice Thinking*, ed. Sharon Dolovich and Alexandra Natapoff (New York: NYU Press, 2017), 246–70.

36. "Logic" is the best term I could devise to capture a meaningful pattern of activity organized around a recognizable set of understandings and orientated to a particular, but general, purpose. To say that actors in a particular field follow a logic of action does not imply that their regular activities are necessarily effective in achieving a set of outcomes. The activity is principled and reasoned within bounds, but the designation of an overarching "logic" is a synthetic construct of the researcher trying to capture the way elements are systematically arranged. To offer an imperfect analogy, my household habits might follow an environmental logic—minimize waste, compost food, bring reusable bags to the store, recycle—but I know this activity does little to actually stem the tide of global climate change, and it is not necessarily motivated by the desire to achieve those ends. Identifying a logic is a way of connecting disparate habits and practices.

37. Matthew Desmond, "Relational Ethnography," *Theory and Society* 43, no. 5 (2014): 547, 554 (emphasis added). "[A] relational approach incorporates fully into the ethnographic sample at least two types of actors or agencies occupying different positions within the social space and bound together in a relationship of mutual dependence or struggle."

38. Andrew Gelman, "Causality and Statistical Learning," *American Journal of Sociology* 117, no. 3 (2011): 955; Mario Luis Small, "Causal Thinking and Ethnographic Research," *American Journal of Sociology* 119, no. 3 (2013): 597–601.

39. Gabriel Abend, "Styles of Sociological Thought: Sociologies, Epistemologies, and the Mexican and U.S. Quests for Truth," *Sociological Theory* 24, no. 1 (2006): 10; Gabriel Abend, Petre Caitlin, and Michael Sauder, "Styles of Causal Thought: An Empirical Investigation," *American Journal of Sociology* 119, no. 3 (2013): 632.

40. Abend, "Styles of Sociological Thought," 632. This mode of explanation might be, as some have suggested, not only a venerable tradition in sociology, but also satisfying in a visceral sense. A. Abbott, "The Causal Devolution," *Sociological Methods and Research* 27, no. 2 (1998): 148–81; Andrew Abbott, "Of Time and Space: The Contemporary Relevance of the Chicago School," *Social Forces* 75, no. 4 (1997): 1149–82; Andreas Glaeser, *Political Epistemics: The Secret Police, the Opposition, and the End of East German Socialism* (Chicago: University of Chicago Press, 2011).

41. Forrest Stuart, *Down, out, and under Arrest: Policing and Everyday Life in Skid Row* (Chicago: University of Chicago Press, 2016). Stuart also explains his selection of Los Angeles's Skid Row to study therapeutic policing as the choice of an extreme, intense case of a phenomenon on display to a lesser degree in other locales precisely because—quoting Zussman—"extremes, unusual circumstances, and analytically clear examples . . . are important not because they are representative but because they show a process or a problem in particularly clear relief." Robert Zussman, "People in Places," *Qualitative Sociology* 27, no. 4 (2004): 362.

42. See note 5 above.

43. Members of Borough A's district attorney's office were very open and generous with their time, but as a political office, those in leadership positions exercised a fair amount of control over whom I spoke with on the lower end of the hierarchy in formal interviews.

44. Mitchell Duneier, "How Not to Lie with Ethnography," *Sociological Methodology* 41, no. 1 (2011): 1–11.

45. Data were provided by the DCJS in the form of micro-level arrest incidents and de-identified individual ID numbers. The analysis, opinions, findings, and conclusions expressed herein are mine alone and not those of the DCJS. Neither New York State nor the DCJS assumes liability for its contents or use thereof.

46. Because there are different agencies keeping records in different systems, their numbers are often not exactly comparable (for example, the NYPD's number of misdemeanor arrests will not exactly match DCJS's number because the NYPD is counting arrests logged into its online booking system, whereas the DCJS is counting arrests for printable offenses entered into the Office of Court Administration's database).

47. NY CPL §§ 160.50, 160.55.

Chapter 1: The Rise of Mass Misdemeanors

1. Kelling and Wilson argued that the historic function of urban police forces was order maintenance, not crime solving. "From the earliest days of the nation, the police function was seen primarily as that of a night watchman: to maintain order against the chief threats to order—fire, wild animals, and disreputable behavior. Solving crimes was viewed not as a police

responsibility but as a private one." They also claimed that residents of high-crime spaces were not well served by the exclusive focus on the latter by modern police forces: "Outside observers should not assume that they know how much of the anxiety now endemic in many big-city neighborhoods stems from a fear of 'real' crime and how much from a sense that the street is disorderly, a source of distasteful, worrisome encounters. . . . [People], to judge from their behavior and their remarks to interviewers, apparently assign a high value to public order, and feel relieved and reassured when the police help them maintain that order." George L. Kelling and James Q. Wilson, "Broken Windows," *Atlantic*, March 1982, http://www.theatlantic.com /magazine/archive/1982/03/broken-windows/4465.

2. William J. Bratton, Rudolph W. Giuliani, and New York (N.Y.) Police Department, *Police Strategy No. 5: Reclaiming the Public Spaces of New York*. ([New York]: Police Dept., City of New York, 1994), 5.

3. William Bratton, interview by author, July 21, 2013.

4. Kelling and Wilson, "Broken Windows."

5. Bratton, Giuliani, and NYPD, *Police Strategy No. 5*, 7.

6. Some have argued that the precise tactics used by the NYPD did not conform to the model of Broken Windows as expressed in Kelling and Wilson's original writing, or that the NYPD always saw quality-of-life policing only as a pretext to engage more serious crime and were never expressly concerned with quality of life as such. See, e.g., John A. Eterno and Eli B. Silverman, *The Crime Numbers Game: Management by Manipulation* (Boca Raton, FL: CRC Press, 2012), 195; Jeffrey Fagan and Garth Davies; "Street Stops and Broken Windows: *Terry*, Race, and Disorder in New York City," *Fordham Urban Law Journal* 28 (2000): 464–73; Franklin E. Zimring, *The City That Became Safe: New York's Lessons for Urban Crime and Its Control* (New York: Oxford University Press, 2011). Without attempting to settle those debates, I note there is evidence that the police meant what they said in numerous public comments and documents, which was to address some of these low-level offenses as public order issues in and of themselves *and* to engage low-level offenses in an effort to reduce serious street crime. Both the new mayor and the new police chief in 1994 publicly announced their commitment to addressing so-called nuisance crimes in various contexts as a means of improving the experience of living in New York and keeping residents from leaving the city. Rudolph Giuliani, "State of the City Address," January 11, 1995, http://www.nyc.gov/html/records/rwg/html/96/city95.html; Rudolph Giuliani, "Inaugural Address," January 2, 1994, http://www.nyc.gov/html/records/rwg/html/96/inaug .html; William Bratton and Peter Knobler, *The Turnaround: How America's Top Cop Reversed the Crime Epidemic* (New York: Random House Digital, 1998), 228.

7. He served from the start of the de Blasio administration, January 2014, until about September 2016.

8. William J. Bratton and George L. Kelling, "Why We Need Broken Windows Policing," *City Journal*, 2015, http://www.city-journal.org/html/why-we-need-broken-windows-policing-13696 .html; William Bratton, *Broken Windows and Quality-of-Life Policing in New York City* ([New York]: New York City Police Department, 2015); Ken Auletta, "Fixing Broken Windows," *New Yorker*, September 7, 2015, http://www.newyorker.com/magazine/2015/09/07/fixing-broken-windows; "NYPD's Bratton Releases Report on Why 'Broken Windows' Works," *NY Daily News*, updated May 1, 2015, http://www.nydailynews.com/new-york/nyc-crime/nypd-bratton-releases -report-broken-windows-works-article-1.2204978; Zolan Kanno-Youngs, "Report Challenges NYPD's 'Broken Windows' Approach to Fighting Crime," *Wall Street Journal*, June 23, 2016, sec. US, http://www.wsj.com/articles/tactics-change-didnt-affect-crime-report-1466642022; "Commissioner Bratton Says Most Concerning Violence of 2015 Was Gun-Related," *Brian Lehrer Show*, produced by WNYC, January 1, 2016, http://www.wnyc.org/story/commissioner-bratton.

9. Bratton, *Broken Windows and Quality-of-Life Policing in New York City*, 2–3.

10. Ibid. Another recent report makes a similar claim: James Austin, Michael Jacobson, and Inimai Chettiar, *How New York City Reduced Mass Incarceration: A Model for Change?* (New York: Brennan Center for Justice and Vera Institute, 2013), http://www.brennancenter.org /publication/how-new-york-city-reduced-mass-incarceration-model-change. Such causal claims are hotly consented, to put it mildly. See, e.g., David F. Greenberg, "Studying New York City's Crime Decline: Methodological Issues," *Justice Quarterly* 31, no. 1 (2014): 182; Bernard E. Harcourt and Jens Ludwig, "Broken Windows: New Evidence from New York City and a Five-City Social Experiment," *University of Chicago Law Review* 73 (2006) 314–16; Steven F. Messner et al., "Policing, Drugs, and the Homicide Decline in New York City in the 1990s," *Criminology* 45 (2007): 404–7; Richard Rosenfeld et al., "The Impact of Order-Maintenance Policing on New York City Homicide and Robbery Rates: 1988–2001," *Criminology* 45 (2007): 377–79.

11. Harcourt argues that the original Broken Windows thesis, and various versions that have proliferated around it since, posit a specific mechanism whereby low-level enforcement fundamentally reconstructs the social environment and elicits different responses from potential lawbreakers: "[T]he social meaning of order influences the disorderly to resist their inclinations to commit crime, and influences law abiders to walk more freely in the streets at night." Bernard E. Harcourt, *Illusion of Order: The False Promise of Broken Windows Policing* (Cambridge, MA: Harvard University Press, 2001), 44. As he points out, this social meaning–norms mechanism is a distinct causal pathway from, say, specific deterrence, incapacitation, or direct surveillance.

12. Kelling and Wilson, "Broken Windows."

13. Bratton and Knobler, *The Turnaround*, 235–36.

14. Bratton, interview by author, July 21, 2013.

15. There was some disagreement as to the relative focus the police should put on quality-of-life offenses and toward what end. Jack Maple, deputy police commissioner under Bratton and one of the innovators of CompStat, argued for quality-of-life *plus*. By appending "plus" to quality-of-life, he meant that the use of these tactics should be linked to data-gathering initiatives and to target police resources on those who were responsible for serious crime. Maple argued: "[W]e need to be more selective about who we are arresting on quality-of-life infractions. When a team of cops fills up a van with arrestees, the booking process can take those cops out of service for a whole day in some cities. The public can't afford to lose that much police protection for a bunch of first-time offenders, so the units enforcing quality-of-life laws must be sent where the maps show concentrations of crime or criminals, and the rules governing the stops have to be designed to catch the sharks, not the dolphins." Jack Maple and Chris Mitchell, *The Crime Fighter: How You Can Make Your Community Crime Free* (New York: Broadway Books, 1999), 155–56.

16. Harcourt has argued that insofar as this form of policing has decreased street crime, it is more likely through this mechanism—the "enhanced power of surveillance offered by a policy of aggressive misdemeanor arrests"—as opposed to the transformation of social norms. Harcourt, *Illusion of Order*, 100–103.

17. New York City Police Department, supplied to Frank Zimring, available at Oxford University Press, http://global.oup.com/us/companion.websites/9780199844425. Data post 2009 supplied by NYPD to author.

18. The patrol force has fluctuated between 15 and 26 percent above 1990 levels. Crime rates are the number of reported offenses per 100,000 population. Sources: FBI, Uniform Crime Reports, prepared by the National Archive of Criminal Justice Data.

19. The order maintenance role of police is not new. Throughout the history of American policing, there is a substantial record of using various formal and informal enforcement mechanisms and significant experimentation at the local level with rules and procedures for addressing low-level conduct with warnings, social services, tickets, citations, and different

forms of arrest. David Thacher, "Order Maintenance Reconsidered: Moving beyond Strong Causal Reasoning," *Journal of Criminal Law and Criminology* 94, no. 2 (2004): 381–414; Thacher, "Order Maintenance Policing," in *The Oxford Handbook of Police and Policing*, ed. Michael Reisig and Paul Kane (Oxford: Oxford University Press, 2014); George L. Kelling and Catherine M. Coles, *Fixing Broken Windows: Restoring Order and Reducing Crime in Our Communities* (New York: Simon and Schuster, 1997).

20. James Q. Wilson, *Varieties of Police Behavior: The Management of Law and Order in Eight Communities* (Cambridge, MA: Harvard University Press, 1978); George L. Kelling, *"Broken Windows" and Police Discretion* (Washington, DC: US Dept. of Justice, Office of Justice Programs, National Institute of Justice, n.d.); New York City Police Department, *New York City Police Department Patrol Guide Manual*. Although order-maintenance policing in theory has often been associated with "zero tolerance" or axiomatic misdemeanor arrests in practice, Kelling, Wilson, and Coles often emphasize *in their writings* the importance of informal, educational interventions, and they propose using "the least intrusive means of intervention," where possible and appropriate.

21. The arrest charges are reviewed by a representative from the district attorney's office and can be changed before arraignment, but the initial police arrest charge is determinative of what type of arrest procedures are instituted.

22. Often, studying how the police engage disorder or low-level offending tells us more about the political role of the police and reigning models of social control in a particular era than it does about underlying offending patterns. Eric Monkkonen argues that historical trends in arrests for things like public drunkenness or disorderly conduct is not an imperfect indicator of the "dark figure" of the objectively true rate of these behaviors, but rather a perfect indicator of formal penal responses to them. Monkkonen, "A Disorderly People? Urban Order in the Nineteenth and Twentieth Centuries," *Journal of American History* 68, no. 3 (1981): 539–59; 540. Risa Goluboff also explains that the enforcement of vagrancy laws tells us less about vagrancy than it does about the anxieties and concerns of social actors in a particular place and time. Goluboff, *Vagrant Nation: Police Power, Constitutional Change, and the Making of the 1960s* (New York: Oxford University Press, 2016). Stuart offers a brief history of enforcement activity in Skid Row of Los Angeles and explains how low-level enforcement activity has long been the handmaiden of paradigm shifts between forms of control or containment of extremely marginal populations. Forrest Stuart, *Down, out, and under Arrest: Policing and Everyday Life in Skid Row* (Chicago: University of Chicago Press, 2016).

23. Summons data officer, interview by author, October 12, 2010.

24. Bratton and Knobler, *The Turnaround*, 152–53, 168; Norimitsu Onishi, "A Quality-of-Life Offense? It Could End Up in Arrest," *New York Times*, June 30, 1994, http://www.nytimes.com/1994/06/30/nyregion/a-quality-of-life-offense-it-could-end-up-in-arrest.html.

25. Infractions and violations can be found in various codes, such as in the Vehicle and Traffic Law or in New York Codes, Rules, and Regulations. Non-printable offenses usually receive a summons, but the police have the authority to make an arrest. Although the NYPD issues the largest number of summonses, there are a number of different agencies that are authorized to do so—from the NYC Department of Sanitation to the Parks Service to the Department of Health.

26. NY CPL § 160.10 defines the offenses that are fingerprintable and also allows for printing in a limited number of violations, such as loitering for the purposes of prostitution, because convictions to those noncriminal violations are linked to a person's rap sheet via fingerprints. What are called "unclassified misdemeanors" are usually non-fingerprintable offenses. Most non–penal law misdemeanors are not fingerprintable and therefore not recorded in DCJS data.

27. NY CPL § 160.20–40. See also Justin A. Barry and Lisa Lindsay, *Criminal Court of the City of New York: Annual Report 2016* (New York: New York City Criminal Court, 2016), 3, 18, 27, https://www.nycourts.gov/COURTS/nyc/criminal/2016-Annual-Report-Final.pdf.

28. For example, turnstile jumping is a noncriminal violation of the New York City Transit Rules of Conduct, 21 New York Codes, Rules, and Regulations (NYCRR), Part 1050.4, for which police officers can issue a summons, and is punishable by up to a $25 fine, a civil penalty, or up to ten days in jail. Turnstile jumping is *also* a Class A misdemeanor (New York Penal Law (hereafter NY PL) §165.15). The same conduct could also support an arrest for criminal trespass (NY PL § 140.05, a violation) or criminal trespass in the third degree (NY PL § 140.10, a B misdemeanor).

29. NY PL § 70.15.

30. NY CPL § 160.10(2) allows for fingerprinting for an arrest for any offense in limited circumstances, such as if the police cannot determine the person's true identity. There are other instances when a judge might see a rap sheet on a non-printable offense. For instance, if a person is arrested for a fingerprintable offense and has an outstanding warrant for a non-printable offense, the judge would address both cases at the same appearance and obviously see the rap sheet, and sometimes courts generate non-NYSID-based criminal history reports for non-fingerprintable online arrests.

31. Article 150 governs all appearance tickets; what the police (and the public) call summonses are a subset of appearance tickets. NY CPL § 150.10. Desk appearance tickets (DAT) are another form of appearance tickets governed by this statute.

32. For more extensive information on summonses in New York City, see Preeti Chauhana et al. and the Misdemeanor Justice Project at John Jay College of Criminal Justice, *The Summons Report: Trends in the Issuance and Disposition of Summonses in New York City 2003–2013* ([New York]: John Jay College of Criminal Justice, 2015), http://misdemeanorjustice.org/wp-content/uploads/2016/08/The-Summons-Report-2003-2013.pdf; Barry and Lindsay, *Criminal Court of the City of New York: Annual Report 2016*, 3, 31–36, https://www.nycourts.gov/COURTS/nyc/criminal/2016-Annual-Report-Final.pdf.

33. NY CPL § 140.10 (1). Arrests for violations are department policy when, for example, the person lacks a government-issued ID, is subject to the "subway recidivist" program, or has an active warrant for any case or unanswered summons, but are allowed at the discretion of the police officer. The NYPD issues guidelines on the issuance of DATs and summonses through the Patrol Guide, namely, sec. 208-09, and also through various Operations Orders.

34. There is even some latitude for certain felonies classified as lower level, e.g., NY CPL §§ 140.40, 150.10, et seq.

35. In recent years there have been somewhere between 3 to 3.6 times as many online arrests as DAT arrests. Barry and Lindsay, *Criminal Court of the City of New York: Annual Report 2015*, 22.

36. NY CPL § 160.10.

37. NY CPL § 150.10. See also, Barry and Lindsay, *Criminal Court of the City of New York: Annual Report 2016*, 3, 18.

38. Section 150.20 authorizes DAT arrests for all arrestable offenses (defined under §140.10) *except* a Class A, B, C, or D felony or a violation of §§ 130.25, 130.40, 205.10, 205.17, 205.19, or 215.56 of the penal law.

39. To my knowledge, the Criminal Court does not break down DAT and online arrests for felonies versus misdemeanors, but clearly a higher percentage of misdemeanor arrests are DAT arrests, because only a limited range of felony crimes (essentially E felonies) are statutorily authorized for DAT arrests. The NYPD released a 2015 document stating that in 2006 only 14 percent of misdemeanor arrests were DATs, which rose to 34 percent in 2010 and 41 percent in 2014 after the NYPD instituted a new policy for marijuana arrests (which had been driving

the high number of online arrests for over a decade as the top arrest category). Bratton, *Broken Windows and Quality-of-Life Policing in New York City*, 22.

40. Bratton, interview by author, July 21, 2013. See also Bratton and Knobler, *The Turnaround*, 169–70.

41. Bratton, Giuliani, and NYPD, *Police Strategy No. 5*, 11; Bratton and Knobler, *The Turnaround*, xv.

42. Bratton, Giuliani, and NYPD, *Police Strategy No. 5*, 27–28; Maple and Mitchell, *The Crime Fighter*, 156.

43. Bratton, Giuliani, and NYPD, *Police Strategy No. 5*, 13, 36–38, 41, 49–50; Bratton and Knobler, *The Turnaround*, 229.

44. Bratton, Giuliani, and NYPD, *Police Strategy No. 5*, 26.

45. William J, Bratton, Rudolph W. Giuliani, and NYPD, *Police Strategy No 4: Breaking the Cycle of Domestic Violence* ([New York]: Police Dept., City of New York, 1994), 14–15.

46. Ibid., 16.

47. Patrol Guide, sec. 208-36.

48. See Clifford Krauss, "State Legislators Agree to Restore Arrests for Minor Offenses," *New York Times*, November 11, 1995, http://www.nytimes.com/1995/11/11/nyregion /state-legislators-agree-to-restore-arrests-for-minor-offenses.html. Another notable example is that until 2010, the NYPD maintained a database of every person stopped, questioned, or frisked, even if no arrest was made, and actively fought against legislation that eventually put a stop to that practice. The department also resisted destroying the contents of the database for years after the legislation went into effect. Bob Herbert, "Watching Certain People," *New York Times*, March 2, 2010, http://www.nytimes.com/2010/03/02/opinion/02herbert .html; "Lawsuit Challenges Stop-and-Frisk Database," *City Room* (blog), *New York Times*, May 19, 2010, http://cityroom.blogs.nytimes.com/2010/05/19/lawsuit-challenges-stop-and-frisk -database; Al Baker and Colin Moynihan, "Paterson Signs Bill Limiting Stop-and-Frisk Data," *City Room* (blog), *New York Times*, July 16, 2010, https://cityroom.blogs.nytimes.com/2010/07/16 /paterson-signs-bill-limiting-street-stop-data/?_r=0; Joseph Ax and Jackie Frank, "Lawsuit over NYPD's 'Stop and Frisk' Data Can Move Ahead," Reuters, December 20, 2012, http://www .reuters.com/article/us-usa-newyork-stopandfrisk/lawsuit-over-nypds-stop-and-frisk-data-can -move-ahead-idUSBRE8BJ1EV20121220.

49. "Mayor de Blasio Signs the Criminal Justice Reform Act," Official Website of the City of New York, June 13, 2016, http://www1.nyc.gov/office-of-the-mayor/news/530-16/mayor-de -blasio-signs-criminal-justice-reform-act. The NYPD forcefully argued for its ability to maintain the right to make online arrests. Stephen Davis, a department spokesman, said, "It provides us more discretion. . . . Where appropriate, the civil option is probably going to be the go-to option. But you have to have the criminal option available." J. David Goodman, "New York City Is Set to Adopt New Approach on Policing Minor Offenses," *New York Times*, January 20, 2016, http://www.nytimes.com/2016/01/21/nyregion/new-york-council-to-consider-bills-altering-how -police-handle-minor-offenses.html.

50. Patrol Guide, sec. 209-03 designates anyone who fits one of those three criteria an "OATH recidivist," which stands for Office of Administrative Trials and Hearings, the court to which the civil summonses are returnable. This, like many of the NYPD's "recidivist" criteria, include prior *arrests*, not just convictions, which could only be known accurately if the NYPD accessed sealed arrests.

51. Robert K. Merton, "The Unanticipated Consequences of Purposive Social Action," *American Sociological Review* 1, no. 6 (1936): 894–904.

52. David Remnick, "The Crime Buster," *New Yorker*, February 24, 1997, http://www .newyorker.com/archive/1997/02/24/1997_02_24_094_TNY_CARDS_000378987; Maple and Mitchell, *The Crime Fighter*.

53. Remnick, "The Crime Buster."

54. Ibid., 96; Maple and Mitchell, *The Crime Fighter.*

55. Bratton and Knobler, *The Turnaround*, 171; Auletta, "Fixing Broken Windows."

56. Eli B. Silverman, *NYPD Battles Crime: Innovative Strategies in Policing* (Boston: Northeastern University Press, 1999), 99–102.

57. Ibid., 100.

58. Many specialized policing activities were relocated out of separate citywide squads, such as drug or vice squads, into the precincts during this era. William J. Bratton, Rudolph W. Giuliani, NYPD, *Police Strategy No. 7: Rooting Out Corruption; Building Organizational Integrity in the NYPD* ([New York]: Police Dept., City of New York, 1995), 11. Bratton and Knobler, *The Turnaround*, 230–34; Bratton, Giuliani, and NYPD, *Police Strategy No. 5*, 14–16; Eli B. Silverman and Paul E. O'Connell, "Organizational Change and Decision Making in the New York City Police Department: A Case Study," *International Journal of Public Administration* 22, no. 2 (1999): 217–59.

59. Bratton and Knobler, *The Turnaround*, 231.

60. Ibid., 232–39; Paul O'Connell and Frank Straub, *Performance-Based Management for Police Organizations* (Long Grove, IL: Waveland Press, 2007), 83.

61. Interestingly, upon returning to command the NYPD under Mayor de Blasio, Bratton expressed concern about the drift occasioned by CompStat from measurement of enforcement activity to an end in itself. In a 2015 speech, he said: "[W]hen I left L.A. and moved back to New York as a private citizen, I noticed something: the crime-prevention outcome—the results—was being confused with the enforcement inputs—the means. When we designed CompStat, 'more' was never the point. 'Safer' was the point. And in New York, we've returned the system to its roots. We care about results, not numbers. It's what the numbers represent that matters." "William J. Bratton Remarks at NOBLE William R. Bracey CEO Symposium, Friday, March 13, Atlanta, GA," National Initiative for Building Community Truth and Justice, https://trustandjustice.org /resources/article/william-bratton-remarks-at-noble-friday-march-13-atlanta-ga.

62. Bratton and Kelling, "Why We Need Broken Windows Policing."

63. O'Connell and Straub, *Performance-Based Management for Police Organizations*; Silverman, *NYPD Battles Crime*, 98; Silverman and O'Connell, "Organizational Change and Decision Making in the New York City Police Department."

64. Bratton, *Broken Windows and Quality-of-Life Policing in New York City*, 3. See also, Bratton and Kelling, "Why We Need Broken Windows Policing."

65. Peter Michael Blau, *The Dynamics of Bureaucracy: A Study of Interpersonal Relations in Two Government Agencies* (Chicago: University of Chicago Press, 1955). Merton pointed out in 1940 that "[a]dherence to the rules, originally conceived as means, becomes transformed into an end-in-itself; there occurs the familiar process of *displacement of goals* whereby 'an instrumental value becomes a terminal value.'" Robert K. Merton, "Bureaucratic Structure and Personality," *Social Forces* 18, no. 4 (1940): 563.

66. Eterno and Silverman, *The Crime Numbers Game.*

67. Graham Rayman, "The NYPD Tapes: Inside Bed-Stuy's 81st Precinct," *Village Voice*, May 4, 2010, http://www.villagevoice.com/news/the-nypd-tapes-inside-bed-stuys-81st-precinct-6429434.

68. New York State Senate, Open Legislation, http://legislation.nysenate.gov/pdf/bills/2009 /S2956A. The statute defines a quota as "a specific number of (a) tickets or summonses for violations of law for which a ticket or summons is authorized by any general, special or local law, which are required to be made within a specified period of time; or (b) arrests made for violations of provisions of law for which such arrest is authorized by any general, special or local law, which are required to be made within a specified period of time; or (c) stops of individuals suspected of criminal activity within a specified period of time." N.Y. Lab. Law § 215-a.

69. Saki Knafo, "A Black Police Officer's Fight against the N.Y.P.D.," *New York Times*, February 18, 2016, http://www.nytimes.com/2016/02/21/magazine/a-black-police-officers-fight-against-the-nypd.html. Eterno and Silverman, *The Crime Numbers Game*; Ernie Naspretto, "Ex-NYPD Captain Didn't Fudge Crime Statistics in Past—He 'Delayed' in Reporting Them," *New York Daily News*, February 7, 2010, http://www.nydailynews.com/new-york/nypd-captain-didn-fudge-crime-statistics-delayed-reporting-article-1.198561; John Eterno and Eli Silverman, "The Trouble with Compstat: Pressure on NYPD Commanders Endangered the Integrity of Crime Stats," *New York Daily News*, February 14, 2010, http://www.nydailynews.com/opinion/trouble-compstat-pressure-nypd-commanders-endangered-integrity-crime-stats-article-1.197215.

70. Al Baker, "An Anti-quota Bill and a TV Officer's Arrest," *City Room* (blog), *New York Times*, July 22, 2010, http://cityroom.blogs.nytimes.com/2010/07/22/an-anti-quota-bill-and-a-tv-officers-arrest; Benjamin Weiser, "Class-Action Lawsuit, Blaming Police Quotas, Takes On Criminal Summonses," *New York Times*, May 17, 2015, http://www.nytimes.com/2015/05/18/nyregion/class-action-lawsuit-blaming-police-quotas-takes-on-criminal-summonses.html.

71. E.g., *Raymond v. City of New York*, docket no. 1:15-cv-06885 (S.D.N.Y. August 31, 2015) (class action filed by Latino and African American NYPD officers alleging that they faced retaliation for failure to meet illegal quotas for arrests, summons, and tickets, with a disparate impact on Latino and African American officers); *Matthews v. City of New York*, docket no. 1:12-cv-01354 (S.D.N.Y. February 23, 2012) (Craig Matthews, an NYPD officer in the 42nd Precinct, filed suit alleging that he faced retaliation after complaining to supervisors about illegal quotas for arrests, summonses, and stop-and frisks); *Stinson et al. v. City of New York*, docket no. 1:10-cv-04228 (S.D.N.Y. May 25, 2010) (class action filed by individuals whose summons were later dismissed for facial insufficiency alleging a pattern or practice of the NYPD to issue summons without probable cause in response to pressure to meet minimum summons quota requirements). In 2017, the city settled the *Stinson* lawsuit for a record $75 million while still insisting that quotas had never been used. Benjamin Weiser, "New York City to Pay up to $75 Million over Dismissed Summonses," *New York Times*, January 23, 2017, https://www.nytimes.com/2017/01/23/nyregion/new-york-city-agrees-to-settlement-over-summonses-that-were-dismissed.html.

72. "NYPD's Bratton Releases Report on Why 'Broken Windows' Works." Ben Fractenberg, "Bill Bratton Calls Officer's Claims about NYPD Quotas 'Bulls--t,' " DNAinfo New York, February 23, 2016, https://www.dnainfo.com/new-york/20160223/civic-center/bill-bratton-calls-officers-claims-about-nypd-quotas-bulls--t.

73. The 2015 document heralding the "peace dividend" announces that "we expect to see nearly a million fewer enforcement contacts like arrests, summonses, and reasonable-suspicion stops when compared to their respective historic highs," which was 2011. Bratton, *Broken Windows and Quality-of-Life Policing in New York City*, 5. It presents a steeply discounted cumulative bar graph contrasting 2011 and 2014 tallies of arrests, C-summonses, and "reasonable suspicion" stops, but it is clear from that figure that most of the dramatic decline in this cumulative number comes from the massive decrease in recorded stops and summonses, and there has been a much more modest decrease in misdemeanor arrests. The thirtyfold reduction in stop, question, and frisk numbers is the result of years of intense organizing and activism in the city and a successful federal lawsuit challenging the constitutionality of the way in which it was practiced by the NYPD. Misdemeanor arrests in 2015 were down 23.4 percent from the highest point in 2010, largely because of a huge cut in the number of marijuana arrests.

74. Misdemeanor arrests data from DCJS on file with author.

75. Crime counts are based on official crime reports submitted to DCJS through the Uniform Crime Reporting and Incident Based Reporting systems. Index offenses include the violent crimes of murder, forcible rape, robbery, and aggravated assault; and the property crimes of burglary, larceny, and motor vehicle theft. For more information regarding this data, see New

York State Division of Criminal Justice Services, "County Index Crime Rates," http://www .criminaljustice.ny.gov/crimnet/ojsa/countycrimestats.htm. These figures show the number of arrest events, and therefore unique individuals are overcounted to the extent that they have multiple arrests per year.

76. There are only four fingerprintable misdemeanor offenses specified under NY PL § 140. Changes in misdemeanor arrests under this article are driven entirely by changes in criminal trespass in the second or third degree (NY PL §§ 140.10 and 140.15) and not by changes in possession of burglar's tools or unlawful radio devices (NY PL §§ 140.35 and 140.40). NYPD arrest data by subsection on file with author.

77. "Transcript: Mayor de Blasio, Police Commissioner Bratton Announce Change in Marijuana Policy," Official Website of the City of New York, November 10, 2014, http://www1 .nyc.gov/office-of-the-mayor/news/511-14/transcript-mayor-de-blasio-police-commissioner -bratton-change-marijuana-policy. In 2015, the city reached a settlement in *Davis et al. v. City of New York et al.*, a class action lawsuit, "brought by individual residents and guests of New York City Housing Authority (NYCHA) residences on behalf of a plaintiff class that challenged the NYPD's unlawful policy and practice of routinely stopping and arresting NYCHA residents and guests without reasonable suspicion or probable cause of illegal conduct in a racially discriminatory manner." Legal Aid Society, http://www.legal-aid.org/en/criminal/criminalpractice /davissettlement.aspx. *Ligon v. City of New York*, a class action suit on behalf of residents and guests of privately owned buildings whose owners had authorized the NYPD to patrol hallways, was resolved with the order in the companion case, *Floyd v. City of New York.*

78. Bratton, Giuliani, and NYPD, *Police Strategy No. 5*, 37.

79. K. Babe Howell, "Broken Lives from Broken Windows: The Hidden Costs of Aggressive Order-Maintenance Policing," *New York University Review of Law and Social Change* 33 (2009): 271 (showing the substantial variation within a week of misdemeanor arrests, peaking on Wednesdays, when police patrol staffing is at its greatest, and plummeting on Sundays, when it is at its weekly low).

80. NY PL § 221.10.

81. There are innumerable accounts of facts indicative of the marijuana *violation* leading to a marijuana *misdemeanor* arrest. For a select few, see the Bronx Defender Marijuana Arrest Project, http://www.bronxdefenders.org/programs/the-marijuana-arrest-project; "Trouble with Marijuana Arrests," *New York Times*, September 26, 2011, http://www.nytimes.com/2011/09/27 /opinion/trouble-with-marijuana-arrests.html; Ray Rivera, "5 in Bronx Contend Police Distorted Marijuana Searches to Create Misdemeanors," *New York Times*, May 1, 2013, http://www.nytimes .com/2013/05/02/nyregion/5-in-bronx-contend-police-distorted-marijuana-searches-to-create -misdemeanors.html; Elizabeth A. Harris, "Minor Marijuana-Possession Charges Require Public View," *New York Times*, September 23, 2011, http://www.nytimes.com/2011/09/24/nyregion /minor-marijuana-possession-charges-require-public-view.html.

82. New York State's highest court has held that there is no "plain touch" exception to the warrant requirement for searches under the New York State constitution (*People v. Diaz*, 81 N.Y.2d 106 (1993)) in contrast to the rule adopted in the United States Supreme Court recognizing such an exception as an extension of the *Terry* stop (*Minnesota v. Dickerson*, 508 U.S. 366 (1993)). This means that if even if an officer is conducting a stop and frisk for weapons lawfully as a *Terry* stop, she is not authorized to reach into that person's pocket if she pats something that feels like contraband.

83. "No Day in Court—A New Report by the Bronx Defenders," Bronx Defenders, May 1, 2013, http://www.bronxdefenders.org/no-day-in-court-a-new-report-by-the-bronx-defenders.

84. Rivera, "5 in Bronx Contend Police Distorted Marijuana Searches to Create Misdemeanors"; "New Data Released: NYPD Made More Marijuana Possession Arrests in 2011

than in 2010; Illegal Searches and Manufactured Misdemeanors Continue despite Order by Commissioner Kelly to Halt Unlawful Arrests," Drug Policy Alliance, January 31, 2012, http://www.drugpolicy.org/news/2012/02/new-data-released-nypd-made-more-marijuana-possession-arrests-2011-2010-illegal-searche.

85. Thomas Kaplan, "Bloomberg Backs Plan to Limit Arrests for Marijuana," *New York Times*, June 4, 2012, http://www.nytimes.com/2012/06/05/nyregion/mayor-supports-plan-to-change-marijuana-arrest-policy.html; "Governor Cuomo Announces Legislation to Bring Consistency and Fairness to the States Penal Law and Save Thousands of New Yorkers from Unnecessary Misdemeanor Charges," Governor Andrew M. Cuomo, September 28, 2014, https://www.governor.ny.gov/news/governor-cuomo-announces-legislation-bring-consistency-and-fairness-states-penal-law-and-save.

86. Thomas Kaplan and John Eligon, "Cuomo Bill on Marijuana Doomed by Little Support from Senate Republicans," *New York Times*, June 19, 2012, http://www.nytimes.com/2012/06/20/nyregion/cuomo-bill-on-marijuana-doomed-by-republican-opposition.html; Thomas Kaplan, "Marijuana Plan Seems Dead as New York Legislature Winds Down Session," *New York Times*, June 18, 2012, http://www.nytimes.com/2012/06/19/nyregion/marijuana-plan-seems-dead-as-new-york-legislature-winds-down-session.html.

87. Jim Dwyer, "Despite de Blasio's Promise, Marijuana Arrests Persist in New York," *New York Times*, October 21, 2014, http://www.nytimes.com/2014/10/22/nyregion/despite-de-blasios-promise-marijuana-arrests-persist.html.

88. "Order for Summons, in Lieu of Arrest, for Possession of Marijuana," *New York Times*, November 10, 2014, http://www.nytimes.com/interactive/2014/11/11/nyregion/11marijuana-summons-policy.html.

89. Trespass is largely a proactive, officer-driven arrest resulting from dedicated enforcement initiatives in public housing or low-income private apartment buildings.

90. "Mass incarceration suggests that confinement concerns large swaths of the citizenry (as with mass media, mass culture, and mass employment), implying that the penal net has been flung far and wide across social and physical space." Wacquant, "Class, Race and Hyperincarceration in Revanchist America," 78.

91. The unit of analysis here is the arrest event, not the arrestee. It is possible that the breakdown of unique arrestees by sex would be different if, for example, men are arrested more frequently in a given year.

92. See also the statistical appendix linked to on the Princeton University Press website, http://press.princeton.edu/titles/11264.html.

93. DCJS counts the person at the time of his or her first arrest in cases of multiple arrests in the same year. The 1980 and perhaps even the 1985 figures likely undercount the percentage of misdemeanor arrestees with prior felony convictions (and perhaps also misdemeanor or violation convictions) because DCJS's disposition data were incomplete prior to 1978.

94. Bratton and Knobler, *The Turnaround*, 154. Speaking of the fare-beating crackdown in the early 1990s when he was Transit commissioner, Bratton said, "For the cops this was a bonanza. Every arrest was like opening a box of Cracker Jack. What kind of toy am I going to get? Got a gun? Got a knife? Got a warrant? Do we have a murderer here?" See also Auletta, "Fixing Broken Windows."

95. The micro-level DCJS is also in the form a "top charges" file, meaning the arrest event is coded through its cycle (arrest to disposition) by the most serious offense category, and even in the file that contains all charges it would be impossible to know which charge initiated the arrest event.

96. That is, administrative data could reveal two arrest charges for a single docket—say, criminal possession of a firearm and criminal possession of marijuana in the fifth degree—and

there is no way to know from that document alone if the police found the marijuana incident to the gun, the gun incident to the marijuana, or some other version of events.

97. There are two levels of claims: one is that misdemeanor arrests in the aggregate act as general deterrence in some spatial unit (block, census tract, precinct, borough, city), and the other is that misdemeanor arrests act as specific deterrent to individuals. See David F. Greenberg, "Studying New York City's Crime Decline: Methodological Issues," *Justice Quarterly* 31, no. 1 (2014): 154–88, for a discussion of the methodological issues involved in testing the aggregate-level claim. The individual-level claim rests on a theoretical notion that there *is* such a thing as innate propensity to commit felony crime that is being deterred by the experience of misdemeanor arrests. Methodologically it requires identifying a counterfactual control group that is identical to the treated group in all respects, including propensity to commit felony crime prior to the treatment of misdemeanor arrest.

98. The unit is misdemeanor arrest, not unique person, meaning that the number of arrests of minority residents reflects both that more black and Hispanic individuals are being arrested for misdemeanor crimes and that some of those individuals are being rearrested at a higher frequency than white individuals.

99. The proportion of the city's population classified as "white" by the census went from 42 percent in 1990 to 35 percent in 2000 to 33 percent in 2014. US Census for 1990, 2000, 2010 demographic data; ACS Surveys for 2010–2014 demographic data. Demographic arrest data from DCJS.

100. Over this time period, the proportion of the city's population classified as "Hispanic" by the census went from 21 percent in 1990 to 23 percent in 2000 to 29 percent in 2014. Over the same period, the proportion of the city's population classified as "black non-Hispanic" by the census went from 29 percent in 1990 to 27 percent in 2000 to 23 percent in 2014.

101. One of the highest misdemeanor arrest precincts that does not have high black or Latino populations, the Midtown South Precinct (the 14th), has a high population-adjusted misdemeanor arrest rate because it has a relatively low residential population but covers the city's transportation hubs and a very dense commercial sector, including Times Square. In addition, because it is a tourist center, it is highly policed. Others, such as the Lower East Village (the 7th) is only 45 percent black or Hispanic but has a high density of public housing, and the geographical unit of the precinct is too large to tell where within the precinct (such as in the NYCHA housing complexes that are primarily black and Hispanic) the misdemeanor arrests are happening.

102. Robert J. Sampson, *Great American City: Chicago and the Enduring Neighborhood Effect* (Chicago: University of Chicago Press, 2012); Patrick Sharkey, *Stuck in Place: Urban Neighborhoods and the End of Progress toward Racial Equality* (Chicago: University of Chicago Press, 2013); Lisa Miller, "Violence and the Racialized Failure of the American State [Guest Post by Lisa L. Miller]," Lawyers, Guns and Money, December 8, 2014, http://www.lawyersgunsmoneyblog .com/2014/12/violence-racialized-failure-american-state-guest-post-lisa-m-miller.

103. New York City Criminal Justice Agency, *Annual Report 2015* (New York: New York City Criminal Justice Agency, 2015), 9, http://www.nycja.org. The proportion of full-time employed or in-school defendants are fairly stable over the past few years of CJA's annual reports.

104. This was the argument of the city in opposition to the Equal Protection challenge in *Floyd*, which the plaintiff's experts argued against by submitting extensive statistical evidence showing that the racial composition of spaces predicted stops even after including a barrage of other theoretically relevant predictor variables including violent crime rates. *Floyd v. City of New York*, 959 F. Supp. 2d 540, 589 (S.D.N.Y. 2013), *appeal dismissed* (September 25, 2013). For what it's worth, I think asking if race "explains" the concentration of, for example, misdemeanor arrests or SQFs by looking to see if a racial composition variable survives inclusion of all other

conceivably related variables is deeply mistaken, which is not a critique of the expert methods in this case but of the reigning conceptions of discrimination. Issa Kohler-Hausmann, "The Dangers of Counterfactual Causal Thinking about Detecting Racial Discrimination" (October 10, 2017); available at SSRN, https://papers.ssrn.com/sol3/papers.cfm?abstract_id=3050650.

105. Bratton, *Broken Windows and Quality-of-Life Policing in New York City*, 7.

106. This issue has been studied and debated in the extensive literature on the war on drugs. See, e.g., Alexander, *The New Jim Crow*, 98–100; Katherine Beckett, Kris Nyrop, and Lori Pfingst, "Race, Drugs, and Policing: Understanding Disparities in Drug Delivery Arrests," *Criminology* 44, no. 1 (2006): 105–37; Robin S. Engel, Michael R. Smith, and Francis T. Cullen, "Race, Place, and Drug Enforcement," *Criminology and Public Policy* 11, no. 4 (2012): 603–35.

107. See, e.g., Alice Goffman, "On the Run: Wanted Men in a Philadelphia Ghetto," *American Sociological Review* 74, no. 3 (2009): 339–57; Victor M. Rios, *Punished: Policing the Lives of Black and Latino Boys* (New York: NYU Press, 2011); and Jeannie Suk, "Criminal Law Comes Home," *Yale Law Journal* 116 (2006): 2.

108. For example, it is likely that turnstile jumping, one of the larger arrests categories, is more common among people in poverty.

Chapter 2: Managerial Justice

1. Quoted in William K. Rashbaum, "In New Focus on Quality of Life, City Goes after Petty Criminals," *New York Times*, May 22, 2002, http://www.nytimes.com/2002/05/22/nyregion/in-new-focus-on-quality-of-life-city-goes-after-petty-criminals.html.

2. These models are poles on a continuum, not mutually exclusive modalities. Although others have used the term "managerial" in different contexts, I stake out a new meaning here. For example, Judith Resnik's famous article uses the term to indicate a style of judging—an overly administrative mindset held by federal judges centered on docket control and case supervision that she argues grew at the cost of impartial deliberation. In sociological scholarship, scholars such as Cohen, Feeley, and Simon, have used the term to identify a trend in regulating deviance more focused on control of outward behavior than inner rehabilitation of offenders. See Judith Resnik, "Managerial Judges," *Harvard Law Review* 96, no. 2 (1982): 374; Stanley Cohen, *Visions of Social Control: Crime, Punishment, and Classification* (New York: Polity Press, 1985); Malcolm Feeley and Jonathan Simon, "The New Penology: Notes on the Emerging Strategy of Corrections and Its Implications," *Criminology* 30, no. 4 (1992): 449–74; Jonathan Simon, *Poor Discipline: Parole and the Social Control of the Underclass, 1890–1990*, Studies in Crime and Justice (Chicago: University of Chicago Press, 1993), 109.

3. Debra Livingston, "Police Discretion and the Quality of Life in Public Places: Courts, Communities, and the New Policing," *Columbia Law Review* 97 (1997): 596.

4. Roscoe Pound, *Criminal Justice in America* (New York: H. Holt, 1930), 190–91.

5. Samuel Dash, "Cracks in the Foundation of Criminal Justice," *Illinois Law Review* 46 (1951): 388.

6. Caleb Foote, "Vagrancy-Type Law and Its Administration," *University of Pennsylvania Law Review* 104 (1956): 604–5.

7. At the time, many of these provisions were intentionally drafted with maximum vagueness in order to extend the discretionary powers of law enforcement and court officials. As Foote points out, the laws were "of use" to police as a weapon precisely because of such vagueness. Ibid., 609, 630. See, generally, Risa Goluboff, *Vagrant Nation: Police Power, Constitutional Change, and the Making of the 1960s* (New York: Oxford University Press, 2016).

8. Norval Morris, *The Honest Politician's Guide to Crime Control* (Chicago: University of Chicago Press, 1972); Sanford H. Kadish, "The Crisis of Overcriminalization," *American Criminal Law Quarterly* 7 (1968): 30; Katherine Beckett and Steven Kelly Herbert, *Banished: The New Social Control in Urban America* (New York: Oxford University Press, 2010); Joseph Goldstein, "Police Discretion Not to Invoke the Criminal Process: Low-Visibility Decisions in the Administration of Justice," *Yale Law Journal* 69 (1960): 543.

9. Herbert L. Packer, *The Limits of the Criminal Sanction* (Stanford, CA: Stanford University Press, 1968), 292; Task Force on the Administration of Justice of the President's Commission on Law Enforcement and Administration of Justice, *Task Force Report: The Courts* (Washington, DC: Government Printing Office, 1967), 29–36, National Criminal Justice Reference Service, https://www.ncjrs.gov/App/publications/Abstract.aspx?id=147397; Foote, "Vagrancy-Type Law and Its Administration."

10. Livingston, "Police Discretion and the Quality of Life in Public Places," 586.

11. The Supreme Court struck down some "status" crimes between 1962—in *Robinson v. California*, 370 U.S. 660, 666–67 (1962) (finding that a law that "makes the 'status' of narcotic addiction a criminal offense, for which the offender may be prosecuted 'at any time before he reforms,'" under which "a person can be continuously guilty of this offense, whether or not he has ever used or possessed any narcotics within the State, and whether or not he has been guilty of any antisocial behavior there," constituted cruel and unusual punishment in violation of the Eighth and Fourteenth Amendments)—and 1972 in *Papachristou v. City of Jacksonville*, 405 U.S. 156 (1972) (striking down Florida's vagrancy statute on the grounds that it was unconstitutionally vague because it "'fails to give a person of ordinary intelligence fair notice that his contemplated conduct is forbidden by the statute,' and because it encourages arbitrary and erratic arrests and convictions") but upheld others such as in *Powell v. Texas*, 392 U.S. 514 (1968) (holding that a Texas law making it a crime to be drunk in public did not impose criminal liability for a status but for a class of voluntary, public behavior). See also Goluboff, *Vagrant Nation*, for an account of how this battle to challenge vagrancy laws emerged simultaneously in many locations and settings across the country during this period.

12. E.g., John M. Junker, "The Right to Counsel in Misdemeanor Cases," *Washington Law Review* 43 (1968): 685, arguing that in the absence of the Supreme Court's recognition of the "indigent misdemeanant's right to appointed counsel," millions are left to "face the bewildering, stigmatizing and (especially at this level) assembly-line criminal justice system" alone; Ralph H. Nutter, "The Quality of Justice in Misdemeanor Arraignment Courts," *Journal of Criminal Law, Criminology and Police Science* 53 (1962): 216 (noting that lower court officials are like "assembly line workers in a factory . . . which makes it appear that nothing may be permitted to interfere with the smooth operation of the line"). The 1967 Task Force on the Administration of Justice Report has an entire chapter titled "The Lower Courts," which starts with the following sentence: "No findings of this Commissioner are more disquieting than those relating to the conditions of the lower criminal courts." The chapter goes on to rehearse fifty years of admonishments from lawyers, bar associations, and public commentators to take notice of the injustices in lower courts; reports that "[s]hort jail sentences of one, two, or three months are commonly imposed on an assembly line basis"; and imparts the "inescapable conclusion is that the conditions of inequity, indignity, and ineffectiveness previously deplored continue to be widespread." Task Force on the Administration of Justice, *Task Force Report: The Courts*, 29, 31.

13. *Argersinger v. Hamlin*, 407 U.S. 25 (1972).

14. Ibid., 407:36.

15. Malcolm Feeley, *The Process Is the Punishment: Handling Cases in a Lower Criminal Court* (New York: Russell Sage Foundation, 1979), xxiv, 31.

16. *Mapp v. Ohio*, 367 U.S. 643 (1961); *Argersinger v. Hamlin*, 407 U.S. 25 (1972).

17. Feeley, *The Process Is the Punishment*, 127, 138, 249, 255. Feeley reported that prosecutors decided to *nolle prosequi* in over one-third of the cases and that jail was imposed in only about 5 percent of the cases.

18. Ibid., 30, 31, 192, 241–42.

19. Ibid., 13, 160, 69, 150–67.

20. Ibid., 4.

21. David Garland, *The Culture of Control: Crime and Social Order in Contemporary Society* (Chicago: University of Chicago Press, 2002); Mitchell Duneier, *Sidewalk* (New York: Macmillan, 2001).

22. James B. Jacobs, *The Eternal Criminal Record* (Cambridge, MA: Harvard University Press, 2015); Alec C. Ewald and Marnie Smith, "Collateral Consequences of Criminal Convictions in the American Courts: The View from the State Bench," *Justice System Journal* 29 (2008): 145–65; Jason A. Cade, "The Plea Bargain Crisis for Noncitizens in Misdemeanor Court," *Cardozo Law Review* 34 (2013): 1751–820; American Bar Association, *Standards for Criminal Justice: Collateral Sanctions and Discretionary Disqualification of Convicted Persons*, 3rd ed. (Washington, DC: American Bar Association, 2004), 7, 9. Reentry Net presents local collateral consequences issues for each state for various levels of conviction: http://www.reentry .net/library/folder.137076-General_Tools_Resources_on_Collateral_Consequences.

23. While not all scholars have invoked that precise metaphor, many present misdemeanor courts as processing cases without distinguishing between defendants, mechanically convicting them all, and imposing undifferentiated punishment. See, for example, Alexandra Natapoff, "Misdemeanors," *Southern California Law Review* 85 (2012): 1343, 1374; Alexandra Natapoff, "Misdemeanor Decriminalization," *Vanderbilt Law Review* 68 (2015): 1064, 1115; Alexandra Natapoff, "Misdemeanors," *Annual Review of Law and Social Science* 11 (2015): 256, 258–60; Stephanos Bibas, "Bulk Misdemeanor Justice," *Southern California Law Review Postscript* 85 (2012): 73; Josh Bowers, "Legal Guilt, Normative Innocence, and the Equitable Decision Not to Prosecute," *Columbia Law Review* 110 (2010): 1655–725; M. Chris Fabricant, "War Crimes and Misdemeanors: Understanding Zero-Tolerance Policing as a Form of Collective Punishment and Human Rights Violation," *Drexel Law Review* 3 (2011): 373, 403; K. Babe Howell, "Broken Lives from Broken Windows: The Hidden Costs of Aggressive Order-Maintenance Policing," *New York University Review of Law and Social Change* 33 (2009): 271–330; J. D. King, "Procedural Justice, Collateral Consequences, and the Adjudication of Misdemeanors," *SSRN ELibrary*, November 15, 2011, http://papers.ssrn.com/sol3/papers.cfm?abstract_id=1953880.

24. Various authors have combined both forms of the critique. My aim is merely to show that the assembly-line understanding of misdemeanor justice is prevalent and that it can encompass two conceptually distinct notions, which in turn generate very different hypotheses about the actual empirical regularities of the courts.

25. All tables and figures of misdemeanor dispositions are limited to cases where the top charge was a misdemeanor at arrest; they do not include cases where the top charge at arrest was a felony but the final disposition involved a conviction to a misdemeanor crime.

26. NY PL §§ 70.15, 70.30; N.Y. Correction Law § 804.

27. Max Weber, *The Methodology of the Social Sciences*, trans. and ed. Edward A. Shils and Henry A. Finch (New York: Free Press, 1949), 90. "The ideal typical concept will help to develop our skill in imputation in research: it is no 'hypothesis' but it offers guidance to the construction of hypotheses. (It is not a description of reality but it aims to give unambiguous means of expression to such a description.)"

28. Lon L. Fuller, "The Forms and Limits of Adjudication," *Harvard Law Review* 92 (1978): 363.

29. See Issa Kohler-Hausmann, "Jumping Bunnies and Legal Rules: The Organizational Sociologist and the Legal Scholar Should Be Friends," in *The New Criminal Justice Thinking*, ed.

Sharon Dolovich and Alexandra Natapoff (New York: NYU Press, 2017), 246–70, and works cited therein.

30. Martin Shapiro, *Courts: A Comparative and Political Analysis* (Chicago: University of Chicago Press, 1981), 1.

31. Feeley and Simon, "The New Penology," 452, 457.

32. For another example of risk-based logic using folk "intuition and personal investigative" approaches in the context of parole, see Mona Lynch, "Waste Managers? The New Penology, Crime Fighting, and Parole Agent Identity," *Law and Society Review* 32, no. 4 (1998): 839–70.

33. Gerard E. Lynch, "Our Administrative System of Criminal Justice," *Fordham Law Review* 66 (1998): 2121. See also Rachel E. Barkow, "Institutional Design and the Policing of Prosecutors: Lessons from Administrative Law," *Stanford Law Review* 61 (2009): 869; Stephanos Bibas, "Plea Bargaining outside the Shadow of Trial," *Harvard Law Review* 117 (2004): 2464; David E. Patton, "Federal Public Defense in an Age of Inquisition," *Yale Law Journal* 122 (2013): 2578; William J. Stuntz, "Plea Bargaining and Criminal Law's Disappearing Shadow," *Harvard Law Review* 117 (2003): 2549.

34. Lynch, "Our Administrative System of Criminal Justice," 2122–23.

35. Barkow, "Institutional Design and the Policing of Prosecutors," 873–74.

36. Ibid., 882–83, 887; Lynch, "Our Administrative System of Criminal Justice," 2120.

37. Herbert L. Packer, "Two Models of the Criminal Process," *University of Pennsylvania Law Review* 113, no. 1 (1964): 4–6, 9, 13–14.

38. Ibid., 11, 13–14.

39. Ibid., 4. Working on this factual presumption of guilt to minimize process, it tolerates false positives in the interest of efficiency up until the point where "general awareness of the unreliability of the process leads to a decrease in the deterrent efficacy of the criminal law." Ibid., 15.

40. I thank Gerard Lynch for pushing me on this point in an e-mail exchange over an early draft of this work, even though he may disagree with my ultimate conclusions.

41. My account does not attempt to settle subjective motivations or individual psychological states that produce a set of behaviors. Instead, it aims to describe the pattern of use of the tools of criminal law and the logic of legal action and how these relate to the larger function of criminal law. Furthermore, I do not have data to settle whether criminal justice actors are assuming guilt, or if they are choosing a course of action under significant uncertainty. I do have data to show that even in cases with minimal evidence of guilt, and sometimes with affirmative evidence of innocence, they insist on some ability to mark and track, and that they take this same course of action even in cases with strong evidence of guilt. That is, variation in apparent guilt does not explain a significant amount of the variation in the dispositions offered.

42. Bernard E. Harcourt, *Illusion of Order: The False Promise of Broken Windows Policing* (Cambridge, MA: Harvard University Press, 2001). Dan M. Kahan, "Social Influence, Social Meaning, and Deterrence," *Virginia Law Review* 83, no. 2 (1997): 349–95; Tracey L. Meares and Dan M. Kahan, "Law and (Norms of) Order in the Inner City," *Law and Society Review* 32, no. 4 (1998): 805–38; Tracey Meares, "Broken Windows, Neighborhoods, and the Legitimacy of Law Enforcement or Why I Fell in and out of Love with Zimbardo," *Journal of Research in Crime and Delinquency* 52, no. 4 (2015): 609–25.

43. The term "technique" is intended to capture the overarching method or mode of knowing, tracking, and regulating penal subjects. Technique also locates a site and manner by which costly effects are experienced and identifies a means of sanctioning and control.

44. Some media reporting on lower courts seems to suggest that if legal actors just understood the inefficiency, it could be rationally avoided, e.g., William Glaberson, "Justice Denied: Bronx Court System Mired in Delays," *New York Times*, April 13, 2013, http://www.nytimes .com/2013/04/14/nyregion/justice-denied-bronx-court-system-mired-in-delays.html.

45. Commensuration is the practice of transforming qualitatively distinct things—in misdemeanorland, modes of tracking, testing, or punishing such as coming back to court, having a criminal record, going to jail—into some common metric of penal control in order to trade off and achieve a consistent quantum of penal experience from various combinations of these techniques. Wendy Espeland and Mitchell L. Stevens, "Commensuration as a Social Process," *Annual Review of Sociology* 24 (1998): 313–43.

46. *Hollender v. Trump Vill. Co-op., Inc.*, 58 N.Y.2d 420, 424 (1983) (emphasis added).

47. "Theft of services" is turnstile jumping or fare beating.

48. N.Y. Veh. and Traf. Law § 510(2)(b) (license suspended for six months or more for drug offenses).

49. Between 1980 and 2010, New York City's total population grew from 7,071,639 to 8,175,133, an increase of about 15.6 percent in thirty years. The size of the MJACD cohort grew by about 2,167 percent during the same period.

50. So, for example, if a person entered the 1980 cohort with an initiating MJACD and was arrested and convicted of a felony the next year, I would count the disposition from that felony arrest because it happened when he had no prior criminal convictions and it was within five years of the initiating disposition. However, if he was arrested for a misdemeanor the year after the felony conviction, I would not count that arrest in these tallies, because the point is to see if we can detect a shift in the pattern of misdemeanor and felony dispositions for people without prior criminal convictions in two different eras. I chose just those four cohorts because it gives me five years of observations for two cohort pairs fully within the pre-Broken Windows era (1994) and two cohort pairs fully after the rise of the Broken Windows era.

51. Because these are 100 percent stacked bars, they do not reflect the different number of arrests that each cohort pair experienced that met the criteria for inclusion in this analysis, which was arrest within five years after the initiating MJACD and if the disposition happened at a time when the person had no prior criminal conviction. The 1980–81 and 1985–86 cohorts were much smaller and had fewer misdemeanor and felony arrests (for a total of 4,791 misdemeanor arrests and 2,951 felony arrests) than the 2000–2001 and 2005–6 cohorts (for a total of 61,210 misdemeanor arrests and 22,585 felony arrests).

52. I use multinomial logit models that estimate the likelihood of various discrete case dispositions—dismissal, violation/infraction conviction, misdemeanor conviction, felony conviction. There are four models: separate models for misdemeanor and felony arrests in each of the two time periods (pre-1991 and post-2000). The models pool all arrests from both the MJACD and first-time misdemeanor conviction groups separately by type and time period to estimate various disposition outcomes using predictors available in the data. The figures presented use these models to generate the predicted probability of one outcome—conviction to a misdemeanor crime from a misdemeanor arrest or conviction to a felony crime from a felony arrest—at specific levels of the predictor variables. For detailed discussion, see the statistical appendix linked to the Princeton University Press website, http://press.princeton.edu/titles/11264.html.

53. Naive comparison of coefficients between logit models estimated for different groups can be misleading because the residual variation between groups can vary, but predicted probabilities are accurate even if the residual variation differs between the two groups. Scott Long, "Group Comparisons in Logit and Probit Using Predicted Probabilities," working paper, 2009, http://www.indiana.edu/~jslsoc/files_research/groupdif/groupwithprobabilities /groups-with-prob-2009-06-25.pdf.

54. Since the underlying models are nonlinear, the predicted probabilities vary by the values at which they are estimated. This chapter shows the predicted probability only where all other independent variables have been set to their means. The substantive story is unchanged by predicting the probabilities at different values of the independent variables.

55. This analysis does not exploit the cohort structure of the data but rather pools all observations of any cohort that fits the selection criteria for the model. Therefore, for example, the post-2000 models will include observations from the 1980 through 2010 cohorts if the arrest occurred after the start of 2000.

56. Criminal courts have limited jurisdiction to take pleas to felony crimes, even if the defendant waives his right to indictment by grand jury. They can take pleas if reduced to a misdemeanor, but rarely would do so at the first court appearance.

Chapter 3: Working in Misdemeanorland

1. Norbert Elias, *The Civilizing Process*, vol. 2, *State Formation and Civilization* (1939; Oxford: Basil Blackwell, 2000), 366.

2. The term "practical circumstances" is drawn from the ethnomethodology tradition. See, e.g., Harold Garfinkel, *Studies in Ethnomethodology* (New York: Wiley, 1991); Don Zimmerman, "Tasks and Troubles: The Practical Bases of Work Activities in a Public Assistance Agency," in *Explorations in Sociology and Counseling*, ed. Donald A. Hansen and Jessie Bernard (New York: Houghton Mifflin, 1969), 237–66.

3. Zimmerman, "Tasks and Troubles," 239.

4. Certainly the dominance of plea bargaining is not a recent development. Most historical accounts estimate it was the primary mode of case disposition in urban and federal jurisdictions in the United States at least by the beginning of the twentieth century—by some estimates accounting for somewhere between 50 and 90 percent of dispositions. Albert W. Alschuler, "Plea Bargaining and Its History," *Columbia Law Review* 79 (1979): 6, 26–30. Some put the rise of plea bargaining even earlier, e.g., George Fisher, *Plea Bargaining's Triumph: A History of Plea Bargaining in America* (Stanford, CA: Stanford University Press, 2003), 36. Trials were nearly extinct as a means of securing guilt in felony cases in New York by the late 1970s. DCJS data on felony dispositions on file with author.

5. Martin Shapiro, *Courts: A Comparative and Political Analysis* (Chicago: University of Chicago Press, 1981), 1. Shapiro argues this idealization is almost never found in reality, but the triad is the idealization of adversarial dispute resolution.

6. Organizational decoupling is a concept developed originally by John Meyer and his students; see John W. Meyer and Brian Rowan, "Institutionalized Organizations: Formal Structure as Myth and Ceremony," *American Journal of Sociology* 83, no. 2 (1977): 340–63. See also Abraham S. Blumberg, *Criminal Justice* (New York: New Viewpoints, 1974); John Hagan, John D. Hewitt, and Duane F. Alwin, "Ceremonial Justice: Crime and Punishment in a Loosely Coupled System," *Social Forces* 58, no. 2 (1979): 506–27; Jerome H. Skolnick, "Social Control in the Adversary System," *Journal of Conflict Resolution* 11, no. 1 (March 1, 1967): 52–70; Milton Heumann, *Plea Bargaining: The Experiences of Prosecutors, Judges, and Defense Attorneys* (Chicago: University of Chicago Press, 1977).

7. By "ill suited," I mean the approach is not likely to generate illuminating new insights. Organizational sociologists have been arguing for decades that, after a generation of studies consistently finding the existence of elements and practices inside organizations that were not established or anticipated by formal organizational plans, this insight should no longer be offered as a satisfying conclusion to the research program. Rather, it ought to be the premise of the research program. See, e.g., Amitai Etzioni, "Two Approaches to Organizational Analysis: A Critique and a Suggestion," *Administrative Science Quarterly* 5, no. 2 (1960): 257–78; and Robert Peabody and Francis Rouke, "Public Bureaucracies," in *Handbook of Organizations*, ed. James G. March (New York: Rand McNally, 1965), 802–37. See also Issa Kohler-Hausmann, "Jumping

Bunnies and Legal Rules: The Organizational Sociologist and the Legal Scholar Should Be Friends," in *The New Criminal Justice Thinking*, ed. Sharon Dolovich and Alexandra Natapoff (New York: NYU Press, 2017), 246–70.

8. Max Weber, *Economy and Society: An Outline of Interpretive Sociology* (1922; Berkeley: University of California Press, 1978), 220–21, 956–57.

9. There are many formulations of the concept of a legal field. For Bourdieu, a field is a semiautonomous social universe constructed "on the one hand, by the specific power relations which give it its structure and which order the competitive struggles . . . that occur within it; and on the other hand, by the internal logic of juridical functioning which constantly constrains the range of possible actions and, thereby, limits the realm of specifically juridical solutions." Pierre Bourdieu, "The Force of Law: Toward a Sociology of the Juridical Field," *Hastings Law Journal* 38 (1987): 816. As Bourdieu argues, it is less important to specify a perfect definition than to "put [it] to work empirically in a systematic fashion," which in this case means looking at how the actors in the system are interacting because "[t]o think in terms of a field is to *think relationally*." Pierre Bourdieu and Loïc J. D. Wacquant, *An Invitation to Reflexive Sociology* (Chicago: University of Chicago Press, 1992), 96. See also Lauren B. Edelman, Gwendolyn Leachman, and Doug McAdam, "On Law, Organizations, and Social Movements," *Annual Review of Law and Social Science* 6, no. 1 (2010): 656; and Neil Fligstein and Doug McAdam, *A Theory of Fields* (Oxford: Oxford University Press, 2012), 9–11.

10. "It is crucially important not to conflate rules that define valid exercises of power with rules that impose obligations to exercise those powers only in certain ways." Scott J. Shapiro, *Legality* (Cambridge, MA: Harvard University Press, 2011), 61.

11. H.L.A. Hart, *The Concept of Law* (Oxford: Oxford University Press, 2012), 28.

12. A case must be dismissed if the prosecutor is not "ready" for trial within these time periods, but as discussed below, many periods are "excludable" from these calculations.

13. *Baldwin v. New York*, 399 U.S. 66 (1970).

14. That is, although criminal laws are the paradigmatic duty-imposing legal rules (commands back by sanctions), that is true only with respect to how they direct us to conform our conduct vis-à-vis the standards set forth, but not with respect to how they direct agents of the state to select and shape enforcement of those laws. Criminal law does not "impose duties or obligations," on prosecutors to undertake a particular law enforcement action; instead [it] "provide[s] [them] with *facilities* for realizing their wishes, by conferring legal powers upon [them] to create, by certain specified procedures and subject to certain conditions, structures of rights and duties with the coercive framework of the law." Hart, *The Concept of Law*, 27–28.

15. NY PL § 70.10; § 65 authorizes, for example, probation and conditional discharge sentences; § 80 authorizes fines as sentences; NY CPL §§ 170.55 and 170.56 authorize conditional dismissals as a disposition.

16. John Dewey, *The Human Nature and Conduct: An Introduction to Social Psychology* (New York: Henry Holt, 1922), 223.

17. "Ends are, in fact, literally endless, forever coming into existence as new activities occasion new consequences." Ibid., 232.

18. "Ends are foreseen consequences which arise in the course of activity and which are employed to give activity added meaning and to direct its further course. They are in no sense ends of action." Ibid., 225.

19. Emirbayer and Maynard argue that ethnomethodology picked up on this pragmatist "idea of obstacles in experience giving rise to efforts at creative problem-solving, that is, to concrete practices aimed at resolving difficulties and accomplishing, in real time, a revised or reconstructed social order." Mustafa Emirbayer and Douglas W. Maynard, "Pragmatism and Ethnomethodology," *Qualitative Sociology* 34, no. 1 (2010): 223.

20. NY PL § 10.10: "'Misdemeanor' means an offense, other than a 'traffic infraction,' for which a sentence to a term of imprisonment in excess of fifteen days may be imposed, but for which a sentence to a term of imprisonment in excess of one year cannot be imposed."

21. NY PL §§ 60, 70, 80, 85.

22. NY PL § 70.15.

23. They are not technically criminal offenses, even though a jail sentence of up to fifteen days is an authorized penalty (for most, but not all, violations).

24. Émile Durkheim, *The Division of Labor in Society* (1893; New York: Free Press, 1984), 40, 39, 63, 81–82.

25. David Garland, *Punishment and Modern Society: A Study in Social Theory*, Studies in Crime and Justice (Chicago: University of Chicago Press, 1990), 56.

26. See also Philip Smith, *Punishment and Culture* (Chicago: University of Chicago Press, 2008).

27. See figure 1.5. Under a recent initiative of Mayor de Blasio, there has been a sharp decrease in marijuana arrests.

28. Assault in the third requires "impairment of physical condition or substantial pain," NY PL § 10.00(9). Starting in 1996, the NYPD adopted a "must arrest" policy in certain instances where the allegation involved what was classified as a "family offense." Most of the city's DA's offices have specific policies once a complaint is classified as a family or domestic offense.

29. Michael Lipsky, *Street-Level Bureaucracy: Dilemmas of the Individual in Public Services* (New York: Russell Sage Foundation, 1980), 30.

30. See, e.g., Blumberg, *Criminal Justice*; Skolnick, "Social Control in the Adversary System"; Stephanos Bibas, "Plea Bargaining outside the Shadow of Trial," *Harvard Law Review* 117 (2004): 2464; Wolf V. Heydebrand and Carroll Seron, *Rationalizing Justice: The Political Economy of Federal District Courts* (Albany: State University of New York Press, 1990).

31. Malcolm M. Feeley, "Two Models of the Criminal Justice System: An Organizational Perspective," *Law and Society Review* 7, no. 3 (1973): 418.

32. Although he does not formulate his work in this way, I see Feeley's *The Process Is the Punishment* as a classic not because of the famous findings—defendants experience most burdens in the process of adjudication—but because of *how* he explains those findings: the new rules and burdens of the due process revolution provided legal actors an occasion to consider if they needed to engage in formal sentencing and punishment in order to satisfy their desire to achieve substantive justice.

33. Data in this chapter are supplied by the New York City Chief Clerk's office and Office of Court Administration. Where noted, Bronx data are not included in the citywide averages reported here until 2012 because an administrative experiment merging Criminal and Supreme Court made it impossible to see the activity of misdemeanor court independent of felony court in the borough. The nonfelony arraignment number in figure 3.1 is higher than the misdemeanor arrest numbers reported in figure 1.3 because it includes arraignments on cases where the top charge was below a misdemeanor, such as an infraction or violation.

34. In many proactive arrest cases, the arresting officer witnessed the charged crime firsthand and, therefore, her or his supporting deposition can verify the complaint, and it can be deemed converted to an information at arraignment. NY PL §§ 100.05, 100.10, 100.15–30.

35. The first two years of this policing model seems to have produced a significant jump in the number of pretrial hearings, which dropped off quickly.

36. David Feige, "Waiting and Waiting for Justice," *New York Times*, May 1, 2013, http://www .nytimes.com/2013/05/02/opinion/waiting-and-waiting-for-justice.html; William Glaberson, "Justice Denied: For Misdemeanor Cases, Trials Are Elusive," *New York Times*, April 30, 2013, http://www.nytimes.com/2013/05/01/nyregion/justice-denied-for-misdemeanor-cases

-trials-are-elusive.html; Michael Schwirtz and Michael Winerip, "New Plan to Shrink Rikers Island Population: Tackle Court Delays," *New York Times*, April 13, 2015, http://www.nytimes .com/2015/04/14/nyregion/mayor-de-blasios-plan-to-shrink-rikers-population-tackle-court -delays.html.

37. Defendants with three or more arrests (two for nonfelony offenses) within the previous twelve months and two or more misdemeanor convictions (at least one within the past twelve months) would have their rap sheets marked by the clerk's office before arraignment as "Operation Spotlight."

38. Justin A. Barry and Lisa Lindsay, *Criminal Court of the City of New York: Annual Report 2016* (New York: New York City Criminal Court, 2016), 25, 51, https://www.nycourts.gov /COURTS/nyc/criminal/2016-Annual-Report-Final.pdf.

39. Arnold Kriss, Esq., "A Report to (Former) Mayor Ed Koch concerning an Allegation by the *New York Times* regarding the New York City Police Department's Practice of Arresting Individuals for 'Out of Your Pocket' Marijuana Possession," (on file with author), August 20, 2012, p. 23.

40. "No Day in Court—A New Report by the Bronx Defenders," Bronx Defenders, May 1, 2013, http://www.bronxdefenders.org/no-day-in-court-a-new-report-by-the-bronx-defenders.

41. "Giuliani Wins It All in Legal Aid Battle," *New York Times*, January 29, 1995, http://www .nytimes.com/1995/01/29/nyregion/giuliani-wins-it-all-in-legal-aid-battle.html.

42. "Topics of the Times; Aid for Legal Aid," *New York Times*, June 2, 2000, http://www .nytimes.com/2000/06/02/opinion/topics-of-the-times-aid-for-legal-aid.html; "Avoid Overkill on Legal Aid," *New York Times*, May 19, 1997, http://www.nytimes.com/1997/05/19/opinion /avoid-overkill-on-legal-aid.html; Jane Fritsch and David Rohde, "Legal Aid's Last Challenge from an Old Adversary, Giuliani," *New York Times*, September 9, 2001, http://www.nytimes .com/2001/09/09/nyregion/legal-aid-s-last-challenge-from-an-old-adversary-giuliani.html.

43. Testimony of the Legal Aid Society on the Mayor's Fiscal Year 2011 Preliminary Budget, Steven Banks, Attorney-in-Chief, https://www1.nyc.gov/assets/hra/downloads/pdf/news /testimonies/2016/sept/OCJ_Hearing092616_FINAL.pdf.

44. John Eligon, "State Law to Cap Public Defenders' Caseloads, but Only in the City," *New York Times*, April 6, 2009, http://www.nytimes.com/2009/04/06/nyregion/06defenders.html.

45. Defense organizations have investigators on staff, but they are often stretched very thin and focused on felony matters. Many assigned attorneys undertake misdemeanor investigations themselves. Clients who are "in" on bail are at a disadvantage because they have a much harder time participating in the collection of evidence and witnesses and because it is logistically more difficult for attorneys to keep in touch with their incarcerated clients.

46. Adam Gershowitz and Laura Killinger, "The State (Never) Rests: How Excessive Prosecutor Caseloads Harm Criminal Defendants," *Northwestern University Law Review* 105 (2010): http://papers.ssrn.com/abstract=1583462.

47. NY CPL §§ 30.30, 170.30.

48. There is voluminous case law on readiness for purposes of 30.30, and it is probably one of the most contentious issues in lower court. See, for example, *People v. Urrea*, 214 A.D.2d 378, 378 (1st Dep't 1995) (holding that "when the People request a particular adjourned date, but the earliest date open to the court is some time thereafter . . . the People are chargeable with only the actual period they requested"); or *People v. Cain*, 291 A.D.2d 326, 327 (1st Dep't 2002) (excluding adjournments caused by "the People's need for a reasonable time to prepare for trial after the rendering of decisions on motions" under NY CPL § 30.30(4)(a)). A recent Court of Appeals case, *People v. Sibblies*, 22 N.Y.3d 1174 (2014), holding that the time between a court appearance when the prosecution declared "not ready" and declared "ready" off-calendar by mailing a certificate of readiness could be chargeable to the prosecution against the 30.30

clock has not revolutionized lower court practice, to put it mildly. First, although the reversal of the Appellate Division was unanimous, the reasoning behind it was splintered, so lower courts have interpreted the holding differently: the majority opinion held that after declaring "ready" off-calendar "a period of prosecutorial unreadiness may not be excluded from the speedy trial period unless . . . [it] is occasioned by an exceptional fact or circumstance," whereas the concurrence reasoned on more narrow grounds, that the unreadiness can be excluded only if the initial declaration of "ready" was illusory or untruthful. Second, many judges find a wide range of issues that regularly present in misdemeanorland to meet the "exceptional fact or circumstance" standard.

49. NY CPL § 170.70 (stating that misdemeanor defendants in custody pending disposition for more than five days, excluding Sunday, without the prosecution having converted the *complaint* to an *information* must be released unless good cause is shown for delay).

50. NY CPL § 30.30(4).

51. Armando Lara-Millán, "Public Emergency Room Overcrowding in the Era of Mass Imprisonment," *American Sociological Review* 79, no. 5 (2014): 866–87; Peter Michael Blau, *The Dynamics of Bureaucracy: A Study of Interpersonal Relations in Two Government Agencies* (Chicago: University of Chicago Press, 1955); Lipsky, *Street-Level Bureaucracy*, 152.

52. Each morning, the files for that day's calendared cases are transported from the DA's office to the appropriate courtrooms. The assigned assistant district attorney for each of those cases is supposed to include a "note" or "status sheet" in the file before it is moved. That note should contain the specific information on the posture of the cases and what is supposed to happen at the court appearance—for example, if there is a new offer or recommendation, if there is a motion to be filed, some new evidence to be turned over to the defense, or if the assigned is "ready" for trial.

53. Joshua Wakeham, "Managing in the Face of Ambiguity and Uncertainty: The Problems of Interpretation and Coordination in Juvenile Justice Organizations" (PhD diss., Harvard University, 2012), 29; Karl E. Weick, *Sensemaking in Organizations* (Thousand Oaks, CA: Sage Publications, 2001), 7.

54. NY CPL § 100.10. There are additional pieces of paperwork also.

55. NY CPL § 510.30 lists the criteria controlling determination of bail.

56. New York City Criminal Justice Agency, *Annual Reports*, http://www.nycja.org/library.php#.

57. Prosecutors almost invariably reduce the arrest charge to a B misdemeanor before trial to assure a bench and not a jury trial. There were only one hundred jury trials and over four hundred bench trials in 2011.

58. Justin A. Barry and Lisa Lindsay, *Criminal Court of the City of New York: Annual Report 2012* (New York: New York City Criminal Court, 2012), 53.

59. See, e.g., New York City Criminal Justice Agency, *Annual Report 2013, Annual Report 2014, Annual Report 2015* (New York: New York City Criminal Justice Agency, 2013–15), p. 17 (in each report), reporting that in 2013, 2014, and 2015 about 54, 53, and 52 percent, respectively, of the cases disposed at arraignments were guilty pleas.

60. Estimations come from exhibits 10 and 11 reported in New York City Criminal Justice Agency, *Annual Reports*.

61. New York City Criminal Justice Agency, *Annual Report 2014* (New York: New York City Criminal Justice Agency, 2014), 23, 30, http://www.nycja.org; Jamie Fellner, *The Price of Freedom: Bail and Pretrial Detention of Low Income Nonfelony Defendants in New York City* (New York: Human Rights Watch, 2010), 13, 22.

62. Fellner, *The Price of Freedom*, 31–33; Mary Phillips, *Bail, Detention, and Nonfelony Case Outcomes* (New York: New York City Criminal Justice Agency, 2007), https://www.ncjrs.gov/App/publications/Abstract.aspx?id=240693.

63. Barry and Lindsay, *Criminal Court of the City of New York: Annual Report 2012*, 16. In the busiest boroughs, the open misdemeanor/violation dockets in each criminal courthouse can be as large as 11,500 to 13,500 at a time.

64. Establishing paternity can be a lengthy affair for nonmarried parents if the biological father is not present at the birth to sign the birth certificate and the Voluntary Acknowledgment of Paternity form. See Office of Child Support Enforcement, Paternity Establishment.

65. *Hollender v. Trump Vill. Co-op., Inc.*, 58 N.Y.2d 420, 424 (1983).

Chapter 4: Marking

1. Émile Durkheim, *The Division of Labor in Society* (1893; New York: Free Press, 1984).

2. David Garland, *Punishment and Modern Society: A Study in Social Theory*, Studies in Crime and Justice (Chicago: University of Chicago Press, 1990). Philip Smith, working in Durkheim's tradition, has argued that marking and punishing offenders is not just about rationally achieving instrumental values such as "regulating the politically dangerous or economically costly nor even maintain[ing] the 'social order,'" but about meaning-making, "eliminating the disgusting and unruly, effecting the decontamination of the spiritually and morally offensive, banishing evil, and enforcing cultural classifications and boundaries by shutting down liminal possibilities." Smith, *Punishment and Culture* (Chicago: University of Chicago Press, 2008), 170–71.

3. Harold Garfinkel, "Conditions of Successful Degradation Ceremonies," *American Journal of Sociology* 61, no. 5 (March 1, 1956): 420.

4. Erving Goffman, *Stigma: Notes on the Management of Spoiled Identity* (New York: Simon and Schuster, 1963); Howard S. Becker, *Outsiders* (New York: Simon and Schuster, 1963); Richard D. Schwartz and Jerome H. Skolnick, "Two Studies of Legal Stigma," *Social Problems* 10, no. 2 (1962): 133–42.

5. Becker, *Outsiders*, 33.

6. Devah Pager, *Marked: Race, Crime, and Finding Work in an Era of Mass Incarceration* (Chicago: University of Chicago Press, 2007), 5, 4. See also James B. Jacobs, *The Eternal Criminal Record* (Cambridge, MA: Harvard University Press, 2015).

7. I primarily focus on their use and meaning inside the judicial apparatus instead of in the larger social and economic realm, but sometimes address the latter issue when it is relevant to the types of incentives defendants face in misdemeanor court.

8. My discussion of case dispositions concerns the universe of arrests after the point of transfer to Central Booking and fingerprint transmission to the DCJS. Some arrests are discarded at the precinct, which means the DCJS would not have a record of the event.

9. New York case law holds that a person should be arraigned within twenty-four hours of arrest and provides that a defendant held in excess of twenty-four hours prior to arraignment should be released unless the state can provide an adequate explanation for the delay. *People ex rel. Maxian v. Brown*, 77 N.Y.2d 422 (1991) (interpreting NY CPL § 140.20(1).

10. NY CPL §§ 170.55 and 170.56. A judge can authorize a marijuana ACD even without the prosecutor's consent if the defendant has never been convicted of any crime; if the defendant has a prior criminal conviction, the prosecutor must consent to the MJACD.

11. Cases are only adjourned for shorter periods before sealing if the defense counsel makes a compelling argument as to why immediate sealing is necessary, such as to avoid severe immigration ramifications.

12. The court could issue a "do not seal" order upon the motion of the prosecution or its own motion, but the defense is entitled to be heard on such motions. NY CPL § 160.50(1).

13. DCJS disposition data for top arrest charge, NY PL § 221.10, on file with author.

14. In November 2014, Mayor de Blasio, recently elected, and his reappointed police commissioner, Bill Bratton, announced a new policy that "allows for the issuance of a Criminal Court summons, in lieu of arrest, to people found in possession of a small amount of marijuana—defined as twenty-five grams or less—in a public place and open to public view." Operations Order 43, dated November 11, 2014. Marijuana arrests since then have plummeted, and marijuana summonses have not significantly increased. J. David Goodman and Matt Flegenheimer, "Bratton and de Blasio Offering Mixed Signals over Marijuana," *New York Times*, March 9, 2015, http://www.nytimes.com/2015/03/10/nyregion/on-marijuana-bratton-and-de-blasio-back-policy-but-still-show-divide.html.

15. See discussion in chapter 3 and notes 47–50 to that chapter.

16. *Consequences of Criminal Proceedings in New York State* (New York: Bronx Defenders, 2015), 78–80.

17. New York City is one of the few jurisdictions with a recently enacted local statutory framework directing the city not to honor ICE detainers in certain cases (see N.Y. Admin. Code § 9–131, recently amended by Local Law 21), such as those in which the defendant's case is resolved without a criminal conviction and there are no other pending criminal cases or felony convictions). However, the law is riddled with exceptions, and in many cases, contact for misdemeanor offenses can still lead to deportation or other serious immigration consequences. Jason A. Cade, "The Plea Bargain Crisis for Noncitizens in Misdemeanor Court," *Cardozo Law Review* 34 (2012): 1751–820. This statute was passed under the Obama administration, and it is not clear how well this and related practices will succeed in shielding misdemeanor arrestees from serious immigration consequences under the Trump administration's aggressive anti-immigrant policies.

18. DCJS data on file with author; see figure 2.2.

19. See figure 2.2.

20. DCJS could only provide a sample of this data once every five years; thus I do not have continuous values.

21. See NY PL § 240.20. For example, defendants regularly plead to disorderly conduct if the sole arrest charge was misdemeanor possession of a controlled substance.

22. See NY PL § 65.05(3)(b) and NY CPL § 160.55, which also directs the New York State Division of Criminal Justice Services to destroy the fingerprints and de-link the NYSID upon sealing of these convictions, provided the person has no prior criminal convictions.

23. Prosecutors can, and in some boroughs often do, demand a permanent waiver of sealing as a condition of violation pleas. The DA can also make a motion to block sealing in "the interests of justice" to the court within a specified time period after disposition. NY CPL § 160.55(1). In addition, section 160.55 exempts certain violation and infraction convictions from eventual sealing. Since dispositions are still manually entered by data clerks, whether or not dispositions effect sealing on rap sheets is a function of the data entry practices at the individual Criminal Court in each borough.

24. Prosecutors, and some judges, regularly search for sealed cases in their own internal files or in court files. This practice still continues despite a Court of Appeals holding In re *Katherine B. v. Cataldo*, 833 N.E.2d 698 (N.Y. 2005), that "law enforcement agency" as used in § 160.50(1)(d)(ii) of the New York Criminal Procedure Law does not include a prosecutor—and that therefore judges may not issue *ex parte* unsealing orders to prosecutors seeking information about sealed cases. Ibid., 702–3. Whether or not using information about cases sealed under §160.55 to form plea and sentence offers violates the sealing law has never been litigated, but this practice is even more common, because prosecutors and judges have easy access to that information in the Office of Court Administration database.

25. In certain instances, a misdemeanor arrest can result in a felony conviction because the prosecutor charges a higher-order offense after reviewing the facts alleged by the police or—more

likely—the arrest charge is eligible for a "felony bump up" because of prior convictions, such as in the case of weapons possession. NY PL § 265.02(1). A felony conviction from a misdemeanor arrest is rare in practice: only about 450 dispositions were convictions for felony offenses when the top arrest charge was a misdemeanor (out of over 226,000 dispositions) in 2012. Data from DCJS, "New York City: Adult Arrest Disposed" (unpublished report on file with author).

26. The state has long provided for a "Certificate of Relief from Disabilities," subject to various qualifying restrictions, that ostensibly mitigates some of the collateral consequences, but in practice the effects of such certificates are limited. See N.Y. Corrections Law §§ 701, 703-a. Also, as of April 2014, the Office of Court Administration announced it would no longer report *a single* misdemeanor conviction that was more than ten years old, excluding a list of certain misdemeanor convictions (https://www.nycourts.gov/apps/chrs/Misdredempollink .pdf). NY CPL § 160.59.

27. Data from Chief Clerk of Criminal Court New York City, on file with author.

28. If a person is held in custody on a misdemeanor arrest, the case is adjourned to what is colloquially called the "170.70 day," after the NY CPL provision that states that the defendant must be released if the prosecution has not converted the *complaint* to an *information*, unless good cause can be shown for delay. However, if five days after arraignment would hit on a Saturday (i.e., because arraignment happened on Tuesday), then the case should be adjourned to Friday, because a Monday adjournment would put the person in custody longer than five days, even excluding Sunday.

29. There is no constitutional right once the case is reduced to a B misdemeanor, because the maximum jail time authorized as a sentence is three months. See *Baldwin v. New York*, 399 U.S. 66, 69 (1970); NY PL § 70.15 (2).

30. NY CPL § 340.40(2) (McKinney 2013); see also NY PL § 70.15 (McKinney 2013).

31. *People v. Molineux*, 168 N.Y. 264, 293 (1901), holding that evidence of other crimes is not admissible to show a general criminal propensity, but is admissible for other purposes, such as "to prove the specific crime charged when it tends to establish (1) motive; (2) intent; (3) the absence of mistake or accident; (4) a common scheme or plan embracing the commission of two or more crimes so related to each other that proof of one tends to establish the others; (5) the identity of the person charged with the commission of the crime on trial."

32. "[T]he proponent of the evidence must identify some material issue, other than the defendant's criminal propensity, to which the evidence is directly relevant; once the requisite showing is made, the trial court must weigh the evidence's probative value against its potential for undue prejudice to the defendant." *People v. Cass*, 18 N.Y.3d 553, 560 (2012).

33. "NY Judiciary Launches Nation's First Statewide Human Trafficking Intervention Initiative," press release, New York Unified Court System, September 25, 2013, https://www .nycourts.gov/press/PR13_11.pdf.

34. If a person is found unfit after a psychiatric exam, the misdemeanor is dismissed, but the person is automatically transferred to the custody of a state civil psychiatric center for evaluation and admission under the provisions of the Mental Hygiene Law. NY CPL § 730.40.

35. NY PL § 215.50–55. The misdemeanor charge can be bumped up to a felony if the defendant has a prior contempt conviction within five years or damages to property worth more than $250.

36. Home insecurity can be the cause and effect of criminal justice entanglements; see Matthew Desmond, *Evicted: Poverty and Profit in the American City* (New York: Crown Publishing, 2016). Many young men I met were not officially homeless but lacked a stable residence. As one man put it, "Homelessness is not having your name on a lease."

Chapter 5: Procedural Hassle

1. Harold Garfinkel, "Conditions of Successful Degradation Ceremonies," *American Journal of Sociology* 61, no. 5 (1956): 420–24.

2. Erving Goffman, *Asylums: Essays on the Social Situation of Mental Patients and Other Inmates* (Chicago: Aldine/Transaction, 1961), 4–6. Goffman describes total institutions as those that "breakdown ... the barriers ordinarily" separating the different spheres of life such that "all aspects of life are carried out under the same single authority ... in the immediate company of a large batch of others, all of whom are treated alike and required to do the same thing together," and "all phases of the day's activities are tightly scheduled ... with whole sequences of activities being imposed from above by a system of formal ruling and a body of officials."

3. Ibid., 14.

4. Jannelle is a gender-nonconforming woman who, when I met her after arraignments, had on jeans and a hooded sweatshirt. Although she never explained specifically what she meant by "look the part," she used the phrase a number of times and mentioned that she felt she had been targeted for stops by the police because of the way she looks and dresses. She also said that she felt she was roughed up by the police during the arrest because of her gender identity. She explained: "[O]ther officers that came proceeded upon me like a man. I'm like—I'm not a man. I know my attire is that, you know. But at the end of the day I'm still female, and I know that. I'm not acting any way to make you say that hey, I'm a guy. You don't call me out my name. I'm not being disrespectful. Please, you know? And I was like—who are you talking to? 'I'm talking to you, man; turn around, man, before I throw you on the floor.' . . . I can't even do anything because if I do something, I'm going to still be wrong."

5. Goffman, *Asylums*, 23.

6. Tom R. Tyler, *Why People Obey the Law* (Princeton, NJ: Princeton University Press, 2006).

7. Amy E. Lerman and Vesla M. Weaver, *Arresting Citizenship: The Democratic Consequences of American Crime Control* (Chicago: University of Chicago Press, 2014), 2.

8. Sarah Brayne, "Surveillance and System Avoidance: Criminal Justice Contact and Institutional Attachment," *American Sociological Review* 79, no. 3 (2014): 2.

9. NY Veh. and Traf. Law § 510(2)(b)(v).

10. Frances Fox Piven and Richard A. Cloward, *Poor People's Movements: Why They Succeed, How They Fail* (New York: Vintage Books, 1979), 20.

11. Ibid.

12. NY CPL § 530.12–13.

13. Jeannie Suk, "Criminal Law Comes Home," *Yale Law Journal* 116 (2006): 42.

14. Jeannie Suk, *At Home in the Law: How the Domestic Violence Revolution Is Transforming Privacy* (New Haven, CT: Yale University Press, 2009).

15. Michael Lipsky, *Street-Level Bureaucracy: Dilemmas of the Individual in Public Services* (New York: Russell Sage Foundation, 1980), 89.

16. Megan Comfort, *Doing Time Together: Love and Family in the Shadow of the Prison* (Chicago: University of Chicago Press, 2008), 27.

17. See chapter 3, note 60.

18. Goffman, *Asylums*, 9.

19. Comfort, *Doing Time Together*, 43–44; Barry Schwartz, *Queuing and Waiting: Studies in the Social Organization of Access and Delay* (Chicago: University of Chicago Press, 1975); Schwartz, "Waiting, Exchange, and Power: The Distribution of Time in Social Systems," *American Journal of Sociology* 79, no. 4 (1974): 841–70.

20. Schwartz, "Waiting, Exchange, and Power," 844.

21. Gresham M. Sykes, *The Society of Captives: A Study of a Maximum Security Prison* (Princeton, NJ: Princeton University Press, 1958), 74.

22. Comfort, *Doing Time Together*, 27.

Chapter 6: Performance

1. Michel Foucault, *Discipline and Punish: The Birth of the Prison*, 2nd ed. (New York: Vintage, 1995), 189.

2. Yeheskel Hasenfeld, "People Processing Organizations: An Exchange Approach," *American Sociological Review* 37, no. 3 (1972): 256, 257; Yeheskel Hasenfeld and Paul P. L. Cheung, "The Juvenile Court as a People-Processing Organization: A Political Economy Perspective," *American Journal of Sociology* 90, no. 4 (1985): 804.

3. Hasenfeld, "People Processing Organizations," 257.

4. Megan Comfort, *Doing Time Together: Love and Family in the Shadow of the Prison* (Chicago: University of Chicago Press, 2008), 28.

5. John Gilliom, *Overseers of the Poor: Surveillance, Resistance, and the Limits of Privacy* (Chicago: University of Chicago Press, 2001); David A. Super, "Offering an Invisible Hand: The Rise of the Personal Choice Model for Rationing Public Benefits," *Yale Law Journal* 113 (2004): 815; Vicki Lens, "Confronting Government after Welfare Reform: Moralists, Reformers, and Narratives of (Ir)Responsibility at Administrative Fair Hearings," *Law and Society Review* 43, no. 3 (2009): 563–92; Frances Fox Piven and Richard Andrew Cloward, *Regulating the Poor: The Functions of Public Relief* (New York: Vintage Books, 1993).

6. Jeffrey Manditch Prottas, "The Cost of Free Services: Organizational Impediments to Access to Public Services," *Public Administration Review* 41, no. 5 (1981): 526–34; Super, "Offering an Invisible Hand"; Michael Lipsky, *Street-Level Bureaucracy: Dilemmas of the Individual in Public Services* (New York: Russell Sage Foundation, 1980).

7. Piven and Cloward, *Regulating the Poor*; Michele Landis Dauber, *The Sympathetic State: Disaster Relief and the Origins of the American Welfare State* (Chicago: University of Chicago Press, 2013); Julilly Kohler-Hausmann, "'The Crime of Survival': Fraud Prosecutions, Community Surveillance, and the Original 'Welfare Queen,'" *Journal of Social History* 41, no. 2 (2007): 329–54.

8. NY PL § 265.00(5). Police officers receive significant training in how to flick open common folding knifes that have a bias toward closure (i.e., with mechanism holding the knife closed until overcome with force) in a manner that allows them to be charged as "gravity knives." New York courts have interpreted the statute to apply to any knife that can be opened by anyone at any time with the flick of the wrist, irrespective of whether the knife was designed to be easily opened in that way, the carrier of the knife could do so, or knew it was possible to do so. *People v. Parrilla*, 27 NY3d 400, 404 (2016), holding that NY PL § 265.01(1) imposes "strict liability to the extent that defendants need only be aware of their physical possession of the knife," not that the knife "met the statutory definition of a gravity knife." The "wrist flick test" is the subject of ongoing (at the time of publication) litigation challenging it as unconstitutionally vague as applied to common folding knives sold widely in New York State, because a reasonable consumer could never know if someone, at some time, could possibly with some amount of force from the flick of a wrist open a knife that is designed to have a bias toward closure. *Copeland v. Vance*, 230 F Supp 3d 232 (SDNY 2017).

9. Trials constitute less than 0.005 percent of all case dispositions; about 500 out of 250,000 misdemeanor case filings end in a trial in New York City.

10. New York City Administrative Code, chap. 1, § 10-133.

11. Indeed, the average age of a case at trial in this borough is over four hundred days, so his case is not an anomaly.

12. Elijah Anderson, "The Iconic Ghetto," *Annals of the American Academy of Political and Social Science* 642, no. 1 (2012): 9.

13. Javier Auyero, *Patients of the State: The Politics of Waiting in Argentina* (Durham, NC: Duke University Press, 2012), 154–57.

14. Foucault, *Discipline and Punish*; Gresham M. Sykes, *The Society of Captives: A Study of a Maximum Security Prison* (Princeton, NJ: Princeton University Press, 1958); Erving Goffman, *Asylums: Essays on the Social Situation of Mental Patients and Other Inmates* (Chicago: Aldine/Transaction, 1961).

15. Goffman, *Asylums*, 1961, 16–17; Sykes, *The Society of Captives*, 23, 40–43.

16. Jeannie Suk, "Criminal Law Comes Home," *Yale Law Journal* 116 (2006): 2–71. As Suk notes, the criminal law seeks to reorder intimate lives with the order of protection. Yet, it is only sporadically successful in doing so. In my interviews with domestic violence defendants, the preponderance openly admitted to regular contact with the person named on the order, and a significant number continued to live together with an active temporary full order of protection.

17. If a defendant is in custody, the state has five days to convert the complaint (excluding Sunday). If the state fails to do so, the charges are not dismissed, but the defendant must be released on his or her own recognizance, and the prosecution has the remainder of the 30.30 time to convert and be trial ready. NY CPL § 170.70.

18. New York City Criminal Justice Agency, *Annual Report 2015* (New York: New York City Criminal Justice Agency, 2015), 33–36.

19. Alice Goffman, "On the Run: Wanted Men in a Philadelphia Ghetto," *American Sociological Review* 74, no. 3 (2009): 339–57. However, unlike most of the men described in Goffman's book, the great majority of summons or misdemeanor warrants are not for cases that would likely terminate in jail time, much less prison time.

20. Fellner, "The Price of Freedom Bail and Pretrial Detention of Low Income Nonfelony Defendants in New York City," 42.

21. NY CPL § 510.30(2)(a)(vi).

22. Piven and Cloward, *Regulating the Poor*; Super, "Offering an Invisible Hand."

23. Armando Lara-Millán, "Public Emergency Room Overcrowding in the Era of Mass Imprisonment," *American Sociological Review* 79, no. 5 (2014): 871.

24. Jonathan Simon, *Poor Discipline: Parole and the Social Control of the Underclass, 1890–1990*, Studies in Crime and Justice (Chicago: University of Chicago Press, 1993), 203, 166, 168, 198.

25. For an excellent comprehensive treatment of the use of fines and fees and its role in reproducing inequality, see Alexes Harris, *A Pound of Flesh: Monetary Sanctions as Punishment for the Poor* (New York: Russell Sage Foundation, 2016).

26. See, e.g., Michael Willrich, *City of Courts: Socializing Justice in Progressive Era Chicago* (Cambridge: Cambridge University Press, 2003); Foucault, *Discipline and Punish*; David Garland, *Punishment and Welfare: A History of Penal Strategies* (Aldershot, UK: Gower, 1985); David J. Rothman, *The Discovery of the Asylum: Social Order and Disorder in the New Republic* (1971; New York: Routledge, 2017).

27. David Garland, ed., *Mass Imprisonment: Social Causes and Consequences* (London: Sage, 2001); Katherine Beckett, *Making Crime Pay: Law and Order in Contemporary American Politics*, Studies in Crime and Public Policy (New York: Oxford University Press, 1997).

28. Loïc Wacquant, *Prisons of Poverty* (Minneapolis: University of Minnesota Press, 2009); Mary E. Pattillo, David F. Weiman, and Bruce Western, *Imprisoning America: The Social Effects of Mass Incarceration* (New York: Russell Sage Foundation, 2004); Bruce Western, *Punishment and Inequality in America* (New York: Russell Sage Foundation, 2006); Jonathan Simon and

Malcolm Feeley, "The Form and Limits of the New Penology," in *Punishment and Social Control*, ed. Thomas G. Blomberg and Stanley Cohen (Piscataway, NJ: Transaction Publishers, 2003), 75–115; David Garland, *The Culture of Control: Crime and Social Order in Contemporary Society* (Chicago: University of Chicago Press, 2002).

29. David Garland, " 'Governmentality' and the Problem of Crime: Foucault, Criminology, Sociology," *Theoretical Criminology* 1, no. 2 (May 1, 1997): 184; Aya Gruber, Amy J. Cohen, and Kate Mogulescu, "Penal Welfare and the New Human Trafficking Intervention Courts," *Florida Law Review* 68, no. 5 (2016): 1333–402.

30. This program, like many others, was actually designed and run by the DA's office in-house. It has since been transformed by the statewide Human Trafficking Intervention Courts program.

31. See Gruber, Cohen, and Mogulescu, "Penal Welfare and the New Human Trafficking Intervention Courts," for a cogent discussion of how mandated services in the absence of radical supports in housing and employment can lead to reliance on traditional penal tools despite transformative rhetoric.

32. Welfarist and risk management techniques are often intertwined into a single enterprise in various penal sites. Philip Goodman, " 'Another Second Chance': Rethinking Rehabilitation through the Lens of California's Prison Fire Camps," *Social Problems* 59, no. 4 (2012): 437–58; Mona Lynch, "Rehabilitation as Rhetoric The Ideal of Reformation in Contemporary Parole Discourse and Practices," *Punishment and Society* 2, no. 1 (2000): 40–65; Michelle S. Phelps, "Rehabilitation in the Punitive Era: The Gap between Rhetoric and Reality in U.S. Prison Programs," *Law and Society Review* 45, no. 1 (2011): 33–68; Allison McKim, " 'Getting Gut-Level': Punishment, Gender, and Therapeutic Governance," *Gender and Society* 22, no. 3 (2008): 303–23; Nikolas S. Rose, *Powers of Freedom: Reframing Political Thought* (Cambridge: Cambridge University Press, 1999).

33. Cohen, for example, argues that community corrections movements have moved away from the "extraordinarily difficult" goal of remaking the inner life of the offender toward the more limited goal of asking him "to show an ability to maintain the overt demands of a conforming life." Stanley Cohen, *Visions of Social Control: Crime, Punishment, and Classification* (New York: Polity Press, 1985), 145.

34. Garland argues that in our late-modern, control-centered society "that object is now offense behavior and the habits most closely associated with it." Garland, *The Culture of Control*, 176. Feeley and Simon identify the emergence of a "new penology" that is "agnostic about the causes of crime; it is preoccupied, not with an explanation of crime as a prelude to diagnosis and response, but with the identification of high-risk offenders in order to incapacitate and manage," and with "establishing managerial control over disorderly populations." Simon and Feeley, "The Form and Limits of the New Penology," 94, 96.

35. Wendy Espeland and Mitchell L. Stevens, "Commensuration as a Social Process," *Annual Review of Sociology* 24 (1998): 313–43.

36. Andrew T. Scull, *Decarceration: Community Treatment and the Deviant; A Radical View*, 2nd ed. (New Brunswick, NJ: Rutgers University Press, 1984); Cohen, *Visions of Social Control*.

37. Maeve McMahon, "Net-Widening-Vagaries in the Use of a Concept," *British Journal of Criminology* 30, no. 2 (1990): 123.

38. William K. Rashbaum, "With Special Courts, State Aims to Steer Women away from Sex Trade," *New York Times*, September 25, 2013, http://www.nytimes.com/2013/09/26/nyregion /special-courts-for-human-trafficking-and-prostitution-cases-are-planned-in-new-york.html.

39. Sykes, *The Society of Captives*.

Conclusion

1. Although, as James Forman has argued, because "mass incarceration . . . was *constructed* incrementally," it is fair to conclude that "it may have to be dismantled the same way," I believe that the motivating force behind disparate political efforts must be a critique of our collective morality evidenced by the way our criminal justice system operates, much like the moving moral critique offered in Forman's book. James Forman Jr., *Locking Up Our Own: Crime and Punishment in Black America* (New York: Farrar, Straus and Giroux, 2017), 238.

2. Julilly Kohler-Hausmann, "Guns and Butter: The Welfare State, the Carceral State, and the Politics of Exclusion in the Postwar United States," *Journal of American History* 102, no. 1 (2015): 99 (quoting E. Clay Shaw Jr., congressional representative from Florida and coauthor of the Personal Responsibility and Work Opportunity Act, on the day the House passed this welfare reform bill in 1996); *see also* Michele Landis Dauber, *The Sympathetic State: Disaster Relief and the Origins of the American Welfare State* (Chicago: University of Chicago Press, 2013), 16.

3. This form of plea bargaining—threatening much higher sanctions if defendants invoke any procedural rights or challenge police work or evidence—is even more ruthlessly practiced in the federal felony system. Mona Lynch, *Hard Bargains: The Coercive Power of Drug Laws in Federal Court* (New York: Russell Sage Foundation, 2016); David E. Patton, "Federal Public Defense in an Age of Inquisition," *Yale Law Journal* 122 (2013): 2578–602.

4. Feeley, *The Process Is the Punishment: Handling Cases in a Lower Criminal Court* (New York: Russell Sage Foundation, 1979), 241.

5. *People v. Parrilla*, 2016 NY Slip Op 03417 (2016). The statute is not only unevenly enforced by race and ethnicity but also by borough. The New York County District Attorney's office (Manhattan) is one of the only offices to regularly "bump up" misdemeanor so-called gravity knife possession charges to felonies, a charge that carries up to seven years in prison. According to the Legal Aid Society, that office brought sixty-five felony bump up cases for mere possession of a so-called gravity knife in the period between July and December 2015, whereas every other county district attorney's office in the city brought somewhere between five and zero. Press release from Legal Aid Society, "The Legal Aid Society Calls on Governor Cuomo to Sign A9042A/S6483A and Bring an End to One of New York State's Most Discriminatory Criminal Justice Practices," on file with author.

6. Jon Campbell, "Cyrus Vance's War on Knife Law Reform," *Village Voice*, June 8, 2016, http://www.villagevoice.com/news/cyrus-vances-war-on-knife-law-reform-8708105; Cyrus Vance, "Keep the Ban on Gravity Knives," *New York Times*, June 6, 2016, http://www.nytimes.com/2016/06/06/opinion/keep-the-ban-on-gravity-knives.html. Jon Campbell, "New York Saved a Law Used to Jail Thousands of Minorities," *Daily Beast*, October 24, 2017, https://amp.thedailybeast.com/new-york-just-saved-a-law-used-to-jail-thousands-of-minorities.

7. NY PL § 240.37. Melissa Grant Gira, "The NYPD Arrests Women for Who They Are and Where They Go—Now They're Fighting Back," *Village Voice*, November 22, 2016, http://www.villagevoice.com/news/the-nypd-arrests-women-for-who-they-are-and-where-they-go-now-theyre-fighting-back-9372920.

8. Risa Goluboff, *Vagrant Nation:* Police Power, Constitutional Change, and the Making of the 1960s (New York: Oxford University Press, 2016).

9. NY PL § 240.20 includes the catchall proscription on creating "a hazardous or physically offensive condition by any act which serves no legitimate purpose."

10. Edmund Demarche, "Short Ride Spurs Bust for Subway Seat Hog," *New York Post*, July 22, 2010, http://nypost.com/2010/07/22/short-ride-spurs-bust-for-subway-seat-hog.

11. Forrest Stuart's careful ethnography of the policing of Skid Row in Los Angeles illustrates this dynamic: the police have at their disposal a wide range of specific offenses to arrest people

(sitting on the sidewalk, obstructing pedestrian traffic, public drunkenness), and they often only need to threaten enforcement in order to get the sort of compliance they are after, which in this site is engagement with a local "service" provider or mega-shelter. The police are able to regulate the Skid Row population in functionally the same way they were able to regulate them when they has access to vagrancy-type statutes. Stuart, *Down, out, and under Arrest: Policing and Everyday Life in Skid Row* (Chicago: University of Chicago Press, 2016).

12. For some reform proposals to address these issues in federal prosecutors' offices, see Rachel E. Barkow, "Institutional Design and the Policing of Prosecutors: Lessons from Administrative Law," *Stanford Law Review* 61 (2009): 895–922; and Forman, *Locking Up Our Own*.

13. William Glaberson, "Justice Denied: For Misdemeanor Cases, Trials Are Elusive," *New York Times*, April 30, 2013, http://www.nytimes.com/2013/05/01/nyregion/justice-denied-for -misdemeanor-cases-trials-are-elusive.html.

14. One of the most important policies other states could adopt from New York is robust sealing statutes that assure arrests that do not terminate in a conviction are not available to courts, prosecutors, or the public. In most states, all arrests, even those that result in a dismissal or acquittal, print on rap sheets and are available to be searched by the public. There is some evidence that even a low-level misdemeanor *arrest* record decreases the callback rate for entry-level jobs. Christopher Uggen et al., "The Edge of Stigma: An Experimental Audit of the Effects of Low-Level Criminal Records on Employment," *Criminology* 52, no. 4 (2014): 627–54.

15. Charlie Gerstein and J. J. Prescott, "Process Costs and Police Discretion," *Harvard Law Review Forum* 128 (2015): 268.

16. See Josh Bowers, "Punishing the Innocent," *University of Pennsylvania Law Review* 156 (2008): 1117 for a discussion of this topic.

17. An extensive criminology literature debates the extent to which racial disparities in drug arrests can be accounted for by relevant legal variables or police deployment decisions guided by citizen complaints or crime incidents. Compare, e.g., Katherine Beckett et al., "Race, Drugs, and Policing: Understanding Disparities in Drug Delivery Arrests," *Criminology* 44 (2006): 105, with Stephen D. Mastrofski, "Race, Policing, and Equity," *Criminology and Public Policy* 11 (2012): 594–95. However, it should be apparent that even if police deployment is perfectly functionally rational (according to some metric such as crime rates or calls from citizens), that does not answer the moral or political questions about the acceptability of specific forms of police action, much less the decision to use penal as opposed to other forms of social control.

18. Loïc Wacquant, *Punishing the Poor: The Neoliberal Government of Social Insecurity* (Durham: NC: Duke University Press, 2009), 58, 61.

19. See, e.g., David F. Greenberg, "Studying New York City's Crime Decline: Methodological Issues," *Justice Quarterly* 31 (2014): 182; Bernard E. Harcourt and Jens Ludwig, "Broken Windows: New Evidence from New York City and a Five-City Social Experiment," *University of Chicago Law Review* 73 (2006): 314–16; Steven F. Messner et al., "Policing, Drugs, and the Homicide Decline in New York City in the 1990s," *Criminology* 45 (2007): 404–7; Richard Rosenfeld et al., "The Impact of Order-Maintenance Policing on New York City Homicide and Robbery Rates: 1988–2001," *Criminology* 45 (2007): 377–79.

INDEX

Abend, Gabriel, et al., 15
additive imperative, 82–85, 97, 98, 159, 162–64, 171
adjournment in contemplation of dismissal (ACD), 80, 83–84, 96–97, 126–30, 147–50, 163, 176
adjournments, 134–40
adjudicative and managerial models of criminal law administration, 4–5, 10, 20–21, 61, 67, 71–98, 100–101, 223, 256, 263–66, 285n2
"all-purpose" (AP) courtrooms, 110–14
Anderson, Elijah, 228
Argersinger v. Hamlin, 64–65
arraignment pressures (on court actors), 110–11, 114, 124–33, 149
arraignment procedures, 187–95, 295n9
arrest procedures, 32–37, 184–87, 190, 192–93, 277n21
"assembly-line justice," 4, 20, 62–67, 76, 286n12, 287nn23–24
authority: rational vs. tradition forms of, 6
Auyero, Javier, 230

bail, 108, 125, 135, 164–65, 177
Banks, Steven, 118
Barkow, Rachel, 75
Becker, Howard, 144
bench trials, 114, 169–170
bench warrants, 29, 74, 163, 164–65, 177, 235–37
Bloomberg, Michael, 45, 60
Bourdieu, Pierre, 291n9
Bratton, William, 25, 26–27, 28–29, 30, 33, 37–42, 45–46, 275nn6–7, 280n61, 283n94, 296n14
Brayne, Sarah, 192
Broken Windows policing, 1, 18, 25–59, 60, 85, 106, 257; enforcement of, 30–38, 42, 44, 58, 79, 276n19; Los Angeles variant on, 12, 274n41, 277n22, 302n11; NYPD's

adoption of, 2, 4, 15–16, 25, 27, 270n7, 275n6; theory of, 26–30, 58, 267, 276n11; unintended consequences of, 40–42, 58, 67, 118. See also *Police Strategy No. 5*
Brown, Lee, 30

caseload pressures, 110–24, 166, 229
child-care complications, 139, 184, 193–94, 220, 232–33
Cohen, Stanley, 243, 244, 301n33
Coles, Catherine M., 277n20
Cloward, Richard A., 197
Comfort, Megan, 214, 223
commensuration, 83, 176, 230, 244, 289n45
community service, 70, 83–85, 90, 121, 148, 176, 218, 239–40, 301n33
CompStat practices, 38–42, 280n61
conditional discharges, 69–70, 84–85, 158, 161, 219
convictions for misdemeanors, 153–59, 266; criminal vs. noncriminal, 153, 159, 161; decline in, 2, 4, 18, 60, 67–69, 85–89, 92, 100, 172, 175
criminal courts: characteristics of New York City Criminal Courts, 15–19, 271n8; older critiques of, 62–66, 257–58; role and function of, 3–5, 6, 11, 61; treatment of defendants in, 214–20; transformative goal of, 223–24; workload in, 99–106, 109–40, 166, 196, 219. *See also* social control and criminal justice system
Cuomo, Andrew, 260
custodial vs. noncustodial sentences, 3–4, 11, 65

Dash, Simon, 62
Davis et al. v. City of New York et al., 282n77
de Blasio, Bill, 27, 43, 45, 260, 296n14
decline to prosecute (DP) dismissals, 146–47
Department of Criminal Justice Services (DCJS), New York State, 19

A NOTE ON THE TYPE

This book has been composed in Adobe Text and Gotham.
Adobe Text, designed by Robert Slimbach for Adobe,
bridges the gap between fifteenth- and sixteenth-century
calligraphic and eighteenth-century Modern styles.
Gotham, inspired by New York street signs, was designed
by Tobias Frere-Jones for Hoefler & Co.